Conflict and Peace
IN THE MODERN INTERNATIONAL SYSTEM

Conflict and Peace

IN THE MODERN
INTERNATIONAL SYSTEM

EVAN LUARD
St. Antony's College, Oxford

Little, Brown and Company · Boston

LIBRARY OF CONGRESS CATALOG CARD NO. 68-13116

FIRST PRINTING

*Published simultaneously in Canada
by Little, Brown & Company (Canada) Limited*

PRINTED IN THE UNITED STATES OF AMERICA

For my Parents

PREFACE

This book attempts to provide a general introduction to international relations, based on a purely empirical approach to the subject. Each chapter seeks first to survey the evidence in the particular field examined — international systems, the motives of states, aggression, etc. — and to consider what conclusions can be drawn, both in the theory and the practice of international relations, on this evidence. Some of the main general conclusions are summarized at the end of the book.

International relations can never perhaps be in the strictest sense a science, since even less than in the other social sciences is it possible to apply experimental methods. But it is arguable that, if it is ever to approach even that condition, there must be a greater attempt than hitherto to arrive at some systematic conclusions about the motives and behavior of states, derived from a comparative examination of their actions.

Nobody is more aware than the author that this book represents only a first, very inadequate, and quite tentative contribution to developing such a science. It reaches only a fairly limited number of conclusions, and not even all these will perhaps appear to every reader to have been adequately proved.

A study of this type is inevitably directed primarily toward the problems of war and peace, since this is the aspect of the relations of states that is of principal importance to their inhabitants, as well as the aspect that has mainly preoccupied writers in this field in the past. The first half of the book, after briefly considering the nature of international systems and the motivations of states, seeks to examine the principal forms of conflict in the modern world. The second half considers the various methods that have been mainly used to try to create a more peaceful community and analyzes their effectiveness.

The book includes some material based on an earlier work, *Peace and Opinion*, published by the Oxford University Press in 1962, which is now out of print.

The author would like to thank the editorial department, especially Mr. David W. Lynch, of Little, Brown and Company for their invaluable assistance in preparing this book for publication.

Evan Luard

TABLE OF CONTENTS

TABLES

CHAPTER ONE

Systems

Types of System

In studying conflict among states, the first thing to consider is the system in which relations take place. Just as relations among individuals are influenced above all by the conventions and customs of the society within which they live, so the relations of states themselves are influenced by the conventions and customs of their system. The principal factors to be considered in each system are the types of units involved, the number and nature of their contacts, their goals toward each other, their means of achieving these goals, and the common institutions they establish.

The earliest such system of which we have much knowledge existed in China from about 720 to 220 B.C., the period known as the Eastern Chou. In Chinese history books this is divided into roughly equal parts, the "Spring and Autumn" and the "Warring States" periods.[1] Altogether nearly two hundred separate states belonged to the system at the beginning of the period (fifty years earlier there are said to have been seventeen hundred). But in practice there was something like a two-tier system. There were about fifteen major states, declining to thirteen by 480 B.C., and to seven during the last two hundred years of the period; and a large number of smaller states, often in a dependent position, many of which were annexed by the larger states during the period. This absorption of small states by larger is one of the principal causes of conflict in the system (which may therefore be termed a system of *expansive competition*). Some of the major states absorbed up to forty of the smaller states during this period. At the perimeter were a number

---

[1] The earliest document describing this period in Chinese is the so-called *Spring and Autumn Annals*, attributed to Confucius, though certainly by another author. For a good account of the period in English, see R. L. Walker, *The Multi-State System in Ancient China* (New Haven, 1953).

1

of states originally regarded as barbarian, probably different in language and race from the others, but which gradually became integral members (Ch'u, Wu, Ch'in). These were particularly expansive, perhaps because, originally, there was free territory around their borders. Two or three of them ultimately became the dominant powers in the system. The states established leagues and counterleagues. Through these something like a balance of power was sought. Treaties, for alliance or nonaggression, were many and were frequently appealed to. The leagues sometimes allied the main states of the north, based on the Yellow River, against those of the south, based on the Yangtze. Some of the middle powers, such as Sung and Ch'en, acted as balancers, either neutral or in alliance with one or other major league. Many smaller combinations were formed as well. The major states had areas as large as France and could put 100,000 men into the field. In the battlefield, the chariot drawn by mailed horses, with spearmen inside and surrounded by foot soldiers, was the dominant arm. The other arms were the sword, lance, spear, axe, and bow and arrow. Because of the huge distances covered, the horse became vital: a state's power was calculated partly according to the number of horses it could boast.

The system evolved its own rules about the conduct of one state toward another. The rules were somewhat different from those known in more recent systems. There was a rule that the ruler of one state should not attack the ruler of another state who had the same surname; that a state should not be invaded in the year in which its ruler had died; or in which an insurrection had occurred. Rules also governed relations within the individual leagues. It was generally felt that a state was more likely to survive if it obeyed the rules. Some of the more important rules governed the ceremonies surrounding missions from one state to another: these included the presentation of credentials, proposing and replying to toasts, the way officials were to be housed, and even the number of dishes to be served at the banquet given by the ruler of the host state. Official visits had to be paid for state funerals, the marriage of a ruler's daughter, the accession of a new ruler, and similar occasions. As the period progressed, these purely formal visits came to be outnumbered by diplomatic visits for political purposes, for forming or strengthening alliances, trade agreements, and other purposes. Lu, one of the smaller states, is calculated to have undertaken fifteen missions, covering six thousand miles, during twenty years in the sixth century, including three by the duke and twelve by his officials. The main forms of diplomatic contact were the Ch'ao, a court visit by one ruler to another; the Hui, meetings of officials or nobles of different states; the P'in, missions of friendly enquiry sent by one ruler to another; the Chou, hunting parties where representatives of different states met to combine business with pleasure; and the Shih, ambassadors dispatched from one state to another. The last became the most important, and though permanent ambassadors never seem to have been appointed, visits became so frequent that the situation was little different.

During the system's life more elaborate and powerful state structures were developed, first by Ch'i in the seventh century, and finally by Ch'in, the ultimate conqueror of the whole system. Patriotism also grew more powerful, both reflected and intensified by the development of official state annals. As time went on, states became more unscrupulous in their dealings with others and many conventions that had been built up began to be forgotten. Because of the frequent territorial aggressions, the sense of insecurity increased, and alliances and counter-alliances were constantly formed and reformed. The hunger for territory became more devouring, often reflecting the hunger for security.[2] As the period progressed, the group of officials who were concerned with foreign relations became larger and more important within each state. The control of foreign affairs increasingly moved out of the ruler's own hands into those of the *hsiang* or prime minister, and other officials. By the end of the sixth century, a number of prime ministers together repudiated an agreement reached among the rulers of their respective states, because it threatened traditional alliances. These statesmen, like the class of scholar advisers that arose at the same time, were less prepared to respect the old courtesies and conventions than the rulers themselves had been (this may be compared with the transition from the eighteenth-century system of international relations, mainly controlled by monarchs, exercising mutual restraint, to that of Palmerston and Bismarck).

This system was unlike almost any other that had been known in that most of the states shared a common language, religion, and traditions.

---

[2] By the middle of the period "security and power were the concern of the day. Such actions as rounding out frontiers, joining leagues, transferring alliances, treaty arrangements, fermenting civil war elsewhere, can all be interpreted in terms of the quest for security. Each of the great powers suspected the other great powers of ambition to rule all of their world and this was prevented . . . only by a strategy of balance of power which accounts for the many diplomatic revolutions recorded." R. L. Walker, *op. cit.*, p. 100.

Many acknowledged that they had once belonged to a single kingdom, and continued to acknowledge a purely theoretical allegiance to the ruler of one of the states as the current "king." Only about a century before the end of the period did the rulers of other states assume the title "king" for themselves. Around the middle of the period a number of individual states in turn acquired dominant, and even an acknowledged hegemony over much of the system. This was exercised in turn by Ch'i, Chin, Ch'in, in the north, and by Ch'u and Wu in the south (the last three all originally barbarian states). Although the larger states had little compunction in annexing a smaller one (often after having first declared it a "protectorate"), they at first practiced restraint in dealing with the other large states, usually preserving their identity even when they had been totally defeated. But during the second half of the period, warfare became more frequent and more unrestrained, until finally one of the barbarian states from the western edge of the system, Ch'in, over fifty years gradually annexed each of its neighbors in turn, destroyed the royal house, and proclaimed its ruler the first emperor of China, so bringing the whole system to a close.

Thus the principal characteristics of this system are the very large distances (measured in time) between each state, and the expansive motives of the units, leading to their progressive decline in number.

The next developed international system of which we know was that among the city-states of Greece during the latter part of the same period, from about 480 to 350 B.C. (between the defeat of the Persians and the rise of the Macedonians).[3] This was a system of two or three hundred separate units. Most of these were so small that they were unable to maintain their independence in isolation. As a result, more than in any other known system, relations were undertaken within large-scale alliances of federations. For most of the period the system was bipolar, being dominated by the two rival leagues led by Athens and Sparta. Before the period began, during the Persian invasion, Sparta had linked most of the states of the Peloponnesian peninsula, as well as some from the north, in a loose federal league to fight the Persians. Shortly afterward Athens established the Delian League, joining many of the mainland states: this was even more closely integrated, with periodic meetings of

---

[3] The best-known original account of this period is in Thucydides' *Peloponnesian War*. For an account of the period in English see N. G. L. Hammond, *A History of Greece to 322 B.C.*, London, 1959, and the *Cambridge Ancient History*, Vols. 1–8.

the council, a permanent executive, and regular revenues levied from the states by the center. But each alliance was inevitably almost totally dominated by the leading power. In the Delian League, the command of the fleet, disciplinary power over the forces, and above all the assessment of the contributions, were entirely in Athenian hands. Some states were forced to join a league against their will.

Besides the two leading powers, there were the middle-sized states, such as Argos, Thebes, Corinth, and Aegina, which were at once the prizes for which the great powers struggled, and balancing powers, turning against the dominant power of the moment (Corinth and Thebes were against Athens during the Peloponnesian War, when Athens seemed most powerful, but against Sparta when it became the dominant power; Argos moved from neutrality, first toward Athens, then against her, while Athens herself later held the balance between Sparta and Thebes). By these means they were able to win for themselves some autonomy — Thebes even gained eventual dominance. In addition, there were external powers such as Persia and Egypt, not themselves part of the system, which occasionally intervened or were called in at crucial moments: Persia was allied with Sparta during part of the Peloponnesian War but later was against her.

The basic, and almost unique feature here was the stability of the alliances in which many of the states were linked almost throughout, with only a few marginal states shifting from one to another (it may therefore be named a system of *bipolar alliance competition*). Allegiances were partly geographic: most of the Peloponnesian states were with Sparta throughout most of the period, and most of the northern states with Athens. They were also partly tribal: a rough division separated Doric (on the Spartan side) and Ionian (on the Athenian), though this was never exact. The alignment was also partly ideological: as the Peloponnesian War continued, the democracies generally joined with Athens and the oligarchies with Sparta. But there was also a secular trend toward democracy even though (or because) Sparta became more successful militarily. Moreover, there were links between the factions in different states, so the bipolar contest was (as in the modern system) conducted by internal war as well as external. Alliances were also partly imposed by agreement between the great powers: such settlements as the Thirty Years' Truce (446) and the peace of Nicias (421) apportioned the cities between the two alliances largely regardless of their own wishes. Finally, the system was further complicated by local rivalries between the lesser states — such as Corinth and Corcyra, Thebes and Plataea — which therefore allied themselves with the great powers primarily to be able to destroy their own rivals.

Thus conflict in this system was largely between large-scale alliances, often for control of particular cities, or for ideological reasons. The system led, more perhaps than any other, to a perpetual search for allies, whether willing or unwilling. Because almost every state was too weak to survive alone, the dominant problem was how some autonomy could be reconciled with a stable and assured alliance. In practice, alliance was often imposed: Sparta imposed its will on other states in the name of "autonomy," just as Athens had done earlier in the name of "democracy." Sparta founded puppet oligarchies, just as Athens had founded pseudo-democracies (another feature that has echoes in the modern system). There was a general tendency for the weak to combine against the strong and for the most powerful state eventually to overreach itself, usually by excessively dominating its allies: Athens, Sparta, Thebes, and Syracuse in turn won dominance for themselves, only to be finally destroyed by large combinations that usually included some of their ex-allies. As in China, ambitions became more nakedly brutal as time progressed: in the final stages such powers as Syracuse, Thessaly, and finally Macedonia pursued blatantly aggressive designs against their neighbors. The main institutions of the system were those of the two alliances, in which representatives of the smaller powers had genuine opportunities to put forward their views in the council, though the leaders always had the last word.

As in China, diplomatic contacts through the dispatch of missions were frequent, but there were no permanent embassies. More universal institutions were occasionally attempted. In one or two universal treaties, such as the King's Peace (386), all states pledged themselves to maintain a particular system of alliances or nonalliances. In 371, a general conference even agreed on general and complete disarmament (just as a similar conference did in the Chinese system in 546 B.C.). But in practice, order in the system depended primarily on the stability and the balance between the separate alliances.

Here the distinguishing features of the system are the strongly bipolar character, the small size and large number of the units, and their partly ideological motives.

During the Hellenistic period and the Roman Empire, relations were so dominated by one or two main powers that there cannot be said to have been any defined state system. The same seems to have frequently

TABLE I·1

Types of International Community, 500 B.C.–A.D. 1965

	Size of community	Time scale and distance between capitals	Forms of contact, official	Forms of contact, unofficial	Main types of agreement	Main types of organization	Main types of information
Ancient	Close neighbors	Months	Ad hoc envoys	Some traders	Ad hoc bilateral (peace or trade)	None	Tales of traders and envoys
Medieval	Continents (a dozen or so states)	Weeks	Mainly ad hoc envoys (permanent embassies begin about 16th century)	Traders	Bilateral (alliance, peace, or trade)	Alliances	Accounts of envoys, traders, and travelers
Nineteenth century	Comity of Nations (20 to 40 states)	Days	Permanent embassies or legations in chief capitals, rare visits by statesmen	Traders and travelers	Bilateral or multilateral treaty (alliance, trade, or peace)	Alliance, Congress System, first functional organizations	Books of travelers, newspaper reports, general knowledge
Interwar	All sovereign states (excluding dependent territories: 50 to 60 states)	Less than a day	Permanent embassies or legations in most capitals, visits by statesmen	Tourists and traders	Multilateral or bilateral treaty (international organization, defense, or trade)	League of Nations, some functional organizations	Newspaper and radio reports, films, books, education
Postwar	All sovereign states (60 states in 1945 rising to more than 120 by 1965)	Hours	Permanent embassies in all capitals, frequent visits by statesmen	Tourists, businessmen, delegations, sportsmen, etc.	Multilateral charter and multilateral treaty (international organizations, defense, or trade)	United Nations and its specialized agencies, regional organizations	Newspaper reports, TV, films, books, education, travel, personal contacts

7

been true in India, and our knowledge in any case is scanty. Thus the next organized system of states of which we know arose at the end of the Middle Ages in Europe. Here contacts between states again became sufficiently continuous for a discernible system, with its own customs and institutions, to emerge.[4]

The system that came into being in the sixteenth and early seventeenth centuries is characterized by the number and heterogeneity of the units, ranging in size from the Hapsburg Empire, for a time controlling almost half of Europe, to the ministates of Germany and Italy. It is also characterized by the still unformed state of the atlas, with large areas controlled by foreign rulers or petty local princes (the Netherlands and parts of Italy by Spain, the Baltic by Sweden, the Balkans by Turkey) and often (in north Italy, Flanders, and the Baltic coast) disputed by two or more monarchs. Finally, it is characterized by the great internal instability of most of the members, mainly as a result of religious wars: many disputes of the period arose out of internal conflicts, often religious, leading to external intervention. The system is thus one of *dispersed territorial competition* among emergent state structures.

Throughout the period state power is gradually strengthened and centralized in almost every member. The dominant type of state structure was absolute monarchy, so that foreign relations were conducted mostly by the sovereigns, with some advice from ministers. Personal rivalries between sovereigns are an important factor. Much of the period is dominated by recurrent conflicts between the royal houses of Spain and France, the two most powerful states. Others are fought for unassimilated territory: Russia, Sweden, and Poland fight for the Baltic lands, Sweden and Denmark fight for Lapland, just as Spain and France fight for Milan, Naples, Flanders, and Burgundy. The period was marked by a continuing decline in Spain's power. While still seeking to maintain a huge overseas empire, she was involved in almost every European struggle, and confronted not only by powerful foreign armies, but by revolts in the Netherlands, Catalonia, Andalusia, and Portugal. The two sea powers, Britain and Holland, enjoyed a corresponding rise in power.

Ideological factors, as in Greece, play a considerable role. They range Protestant against Catholic, and the Christian states as a whole (with one or two notable exceptions) against the infidel Turk. It was as shocking to Catholics that France proclaimed herself "protector of the Ger-

[4] For a general account of this system, see Sir C. Petrie, *Earlier Diplomatic History, 1492–1713*, London, 1949.

manic liberties" and pledged herself to intervene if necessary on their behalf, as it was to all Christians that she allied herself with Turks. As in more recent ideological systems, internal conflicts are often exploited by external powers: Philip of Spain assisted Irish Catholics against Britain, as Elizabeth of England assisted Flemish Protestants against Spain. In military technology, firearms acted as an equalizer not only among individuals within states, but between states, helping Holland and the Swiss Cantons to win independence against overwhelming odds. There were no truly international institutions, and the only regulating factor in the system was the resistance of other states to the dominance of the most powerful, first Spain and later France. Some embryonic international norms begin to be devised in theoretical writings on international law, but they are little heeded. Through them, however, the rules of chivalry governing individuals in relations to other individuals came to be replaced by the rules governing states and sovereigns in relation to other states.

The main features of this system are the highly disparate units with variable frontiers and growing nationalism replacing ideology as the main motive.

During the late seventeenth and eighteenth centuries (from the Treaty of Westphalia in 1648 to the Congress of Vienna of 1815) a different system began to appear.[5] Eight or ten major units, reasonably equally matched, now dominate the system: France, Britain, Prussia, Austria, Russia, Sweden, Spain, Portugal, Poland, and Turkey. These units had become more highly organized and contacts beetween them more firmly established. Foreign affairs were normally in the hands of ministers, more or less closely controlled by sovereigns. Armies were often mercenary, professionally skilled, but not motivated by nationalist sentiments, and indeed often of foreign nationality. They depended principally on firearms and cannon, and the ability to sustain long wars of maneuver, and to mount long baggage trains to supply the armies, became essential to military success.

States themselves still do not closely correspond with linguistic boundaries or ethnic consciousness, so that conflict is still among royal houses rather than nation-states (it might be called a system of *dynastic competition*). Even the dynasties were not national. More than half the major dynasties were of foreign origin: England had German rulers; Spain,

---

[5] For a general account of this system, see E. V. Gulick, *Europe's Classical Balance of Power*, New York, 1955, R. N. Rosecrance, *Action and Reaction in World Politics*, Boston, 1953, pp. 17–30.

French; Russia, German; Tuscany, French; and so on. Intellectual life too was European rather than national: Voltaire, Locke, Hume, Rousseau, and Goethe were known and appreciated as much in other lands as in their own. This non-national contest has the advantage that certain conventions and understandings emerge between the monarchs and their advisers about the system functioning (the phrase "the European system" becomes current at this time). The states accepted a conscious commitment to preserve the "balance of power" (though there is widespread disagreement about what this consists of). Many conflicts are fought out by limited means for essentially limited aims — almost never for the total destruction of an enemy state. Prussia and Austria fight for limited objectives in Silesia, Russia and Sweden on the Baltic coast, Britain and France in Canada and India: none of them part of the heartlands of any power, which are almost never occupied. None of the wars cost anywhere near as much in human life as the religious wars of the previous age or the national wars of the next.

There is no major change in the structure of the system till the end of the period. France, the most powerful state at the beginning, declined in power after successive defeats by Britain, while Prussia gained in power in relation to Austria. Russia finally overcame Sweden for control of the Baltic and began the series of encroachments on Turkey, which was to continue throughout the succeeding century. Only at the end of the period, in the Napoleonic Wars, did the scale of conflict enormously increase, and then it began to be injected with an ideological and a nationalistic flavor.

After 1815, yet a different type of system arose. This is characterized by a recognized two-tier structure. There are five, later six, great powers, "the Powers;" now generally acknowledged to occupy a dominant position in determining the affairs of the continent. They meet regularly to settle many issues, not all affecting their own territories. Many of the most important changes in the system are *imposed* by the great powers, sometimes by force, through multilateral action: Greek independence is imposed by joint action on Turkey, Belgian independence on Holland. The autonomy of Egypt, Serbia, Romania, and Bulgaria and to some extent the partition of Africa are internationally decided. This system works well enough when only interests of lesser powers are at stake, (Turkey, Holland); or only marginal areas (Egypt, the Congo, China); or where the two great powers concerned were prepared to compromise (Luxemburg, Bosnia and Herzegovina). But when there arose direct and vital clashes of interest between the great powers themselves — as between Prussia and Austria in 1866, Prussia and France in 1870, Austria and France in Italy, or Austria and Russia in the Balkans — the system could no longer function effectively.

This was above all a system of *nationalist rivalry*. The most basic development within the system was the rise of nationalist sentiment, and the perpetual increase in the power and territorial possessions of Germany and Russia, mainly at the expense of the decaying Austrian and Turkish empires. Developments within these decaying empires and in their successor states often provided the sparks of international conflict: at least three-quarters of the wars arose from this cause. The development of overseas empires provoked numerous tensions among the European powers, but never led to war between them. Sometimes pressures within Europe are relieved by expansion elsewhere. But in the final stages, even overseas territory was exhausted. The major powers became linked in more and more firmly defined alliances, roughly equally matched. Britain, having long stood aloof from all continental entanglements, finally ranges herself with her traditional enemies, France and Russia, against Germany, Austria, and Italy. But even these well-matched combinations could not prevent major conflict. The combination of Austria, its power declining but determined to reassert its traditional rights, and Germany, its power rising, and determined to establish its power against its major rivals, together was sufficient to bring the whole system to destruction.

In a military sense the system is characterized by a marked rise in the absolute military power available to nations: heavy artillery and high explosives and far greater mobility are developed, large conscript armies replace professional mercenaries, nationalist sentiment is mobilized on an unprecedented scale, and military expenditure increases greatly, especially toward the end of the period. Prussia's use of conscript armies and their ultra-rapid mobilization revolutionized the scale and speed with which power could be mobilized against another state. In World War I the trench, the tank, the torpedo, heavy artillery, and aircraft inflicted casualties in unheard of numbers.

The transition to the modern system began after 1918 (though it is not yet complete). Distances became shorter and mobility increased many times over. Especially after 1945 a totally new type of system became evident. Power becomes concentrated among two or three superpowers, with many nations of medium size and smaller grouped around them, more or less closely dependent. The world has been reduced in size so much that both great and small are far more vulnerable and far more interdependent. Geographic remoteness, which previously isolated China, the United States, and even Russia, no longer counts significantly. This is reflected in military technology. The most significant change is not the increased destructive power in high explosives, gas, and nuclear weapons, devastating though it is, but the new capacity to deliver that power, and men as well if necessary, to the opposite side of the world, or to the very heart of one's enemy, within hours. The other major change is the widening military gap corresponding to the growing economic distance between nations: between the superpowers and the medium powers, as much as between the developed and less developed. Smaller and newer powers are not alone in depending almost entirely on advanced nations for their military equipment and capacities: even advanced powers have become dependent, as in no previous age, on two or three superpowers for the most sophisticated and advanced weapons. As a result, far more than ever before, the very great powers are in a class of their own as regards power.

The shrinking of distance has other effects. The political complexion of other governments more directly interests those elsewhere both morally and strategically. The typical wars are civil wars between rival ideological factions, with or without external support. Nations come to be grouped as much by political allegiance as by strategic interest: so that such nations as Cuba, or Formosa, or Albania may have to look to distant powers for support through ideological sympathies rather than strategic interest. Ideological arguments are in part a rationalization to justify national interests and the political allegiance of nations is sometimes the *effect* of the interests of great powers (as in Eastern Europe or in parts of Central America and the Caribbean). But they also genuinely reflect the fact that nations no longer demand territory so much as influence and allies. Thus, over the competition of nations is superimposed a competition of ideologies.

Within continents too, integration is increasing, fostered above all by economic interdependence. There may be acute friction between individual nations within continents: often the important ideological divisions are *within* a continent or region (as between traditional monarchies and nationalist republics in the Middle East, or between Conservative-militarist, Castroite, and Christian-Democrat forces in Latin America). Yet the overall trend is toward increasingly close association within the same continent, an association often implemented in continental institutions. And though integration *between* continents takes place in certain fields — communications, trade, development assistance, personal intercourse — it is accompanied by increasing friction in others: sometimes friction *results* from increasing integration (as over trade and investments). Because the division between continents often corresponds with the economic gap, which becomes increasingly conspicuous and unacceptable, continental integration is accentuated by class rivalry. Such conflicts are sometimes deliberately exploited and fomented by a power or an ideology (as by China and her political philosophy). So a system of interacting continents and regions becomes superimposed on one of interacting ideologies and nations.

In a system of this kind the more severe conflicts arise in the marginal areas falling between the gravitational fields of the superpowers or those of ideologies and continents: Berlin and Germany between the West and the East, Southeast Asia on the watershed between the United States and China; Yemen and South Arabia between Egypt and Saudi Arabia; Rhodesia between black and white Africa (just as in the nineteenth century they often came on the margins between the European powers and their empires: the Balkans, North Italy, Alsace, Persia, or Tibet). Conflicts of this sort occur not so much because each contestant wishes to ensure the area concerned for himself, as because he needs to deny it to others. The reduction of distance also brings far greater consciousness of economic disparities between nations and of human rights questions, though such conflicts do not normally lead to war. The rise of many new nations makes the international community far larger, with extreme disparities of size, power, culture, and political development between units. For the first time permanent international institutions arise, which both reflect these divisions and begin marginally to bridge them. These are without the power to affect relations crucially, but they bring disputes under constant multilateral as well as bilateral discussion.

Thus different systems bring different types of conflict arising from different causes. It is necessary next to consider the factors that determine the nature of each system.

Communication

International systems, like other systems, are partly determined by the communications that link them.

The first factor here is the *distance* separating members.

There is, first, the *traveling distance*, measured in the time of a journey. This determines the *frequency* of contacts: of travelers, merchants, diplomatic representatives, or military forces. It thus affects familiarity, the capacity to judge the intentions of foreign governments, concern for the interests of foreign states, awareness of underlying trends within foreign states, and other factors influencing decisions. In the first systems we considered, knowledge of other nations, among both governments and peoples, was so scanty that highly fanciful and distorted images resulted. These created a far greater sense of strangeness of other lands (and differences in such circumstances, where there is less cultural interchange, are in reality greater), together with the fear that often accompanies this. It also brought stereotyped images, the branding of particular peoples as "barbarians" or "foreign devils," "wogs" or "Froggies," "enemies" or "friends." Distance of this kind also affects the importance attached to events elsewhere. In the early nineteenth century, events in China, then four or five months distance away, appeared about as important as events on the moon to Europe: today, only hours away, they are of immediate concern to it.

Next, there is *diplomatic distance*, affecting the type of contact between governments and the whole way in which relations are conducted. This depends partly on traveling distance, but also on the kind of contacts established, and on technology (for example, wireless telegraphy). In the ancient world, contacts could take place only through special missions, sent to undertake particular negotiations. The decision-making authority ("full powers") then had to be accorded to the "plenipotentiary" on the spot, who thus exerted a great personal influence on relations. Even in the early nineteenth century, distances to the Far East were so great that the government in Britain could have no knowledge of negotiations undertaken on its behalf until three or even six months after they were concluded. As a result, in 1841, British and Chinese governments had to accept the final result of negotiations that both heartily disliked. In the modern system an ambassador has no power or authority at all, since wherever he may be, very many messages a day may be sent to him from his capital, giving precise instructions on every detail. On the one hand, decision making in foreign relations becomes highly concentrated, controlled by the Foreign Office in the capital; on the other, far more questions may be discussed in more detail with foreign governments than ever before.

Military distance affects the system just as crucially, and especially the forms of conflict. In the eighteenth century the maximum threat that any nation feared from another was that within months a foreign army from a neighboring country might be marching against its territory; today it is the threat of an instant air attack from any country anywhere in the world. This has transformed the ability to bring coercion to bear, and therefore the nature of military pressure, defense, and the balance of power among states. A country such as Russia was then given relative security by the vast distances that protected it, as Napoleon discovered to his cost; by the time of the Crimean War, this was reduced; today it is destroyed altogether. Distance, for the same reason, transforms the meaning of an *alliance*, one of the basic means available within the international system. In the eighteenth century, an alliance represented a promise to assemble and bring an army, within months or even years, to help a threatened ally. Today it implies assistance within days, if not hours. Even within the past twenty years this meaning has changed beyond recognition. In the thirties an alliance between France and Poland or Czechoslovakia represented only a promise by France to fight to recover their territory after they had already been defeated; today the United States can give guarantees even to the most distant nations, which may offer genuine prospect of security to the recipient country.

International systems also vary according to the *variation* in distances separating their members. The eighteenth-century system in Europe was characterized by the fact that of ten or a dozen major countries, some were several times more distant from each other than others; while powers such as China might have been in another universe. Nations protected by a sea, such as Britain, enjoyed distance that land powers could never hope for. Today distances are so shrunk that all nations are neighbors, and distances vary only marginally between the nearest and the farthest.

But an international system is characterized not only by the distances within the system, but by the type of communication established between governments. The main form of communication between governments has been through diplomatic contacts. Even among early societies, heralds, messengers, and accredited envoys who were inviolate, and could pass through enemy lines unharmed, brought spasmodic communication. After the first great empires were established in the third millennium, B.C., there were more extensive contacts and official embassies from one court to another: the first known treaty between states is that between Egypt and the Hittites in about the fifteenth century B.C., which was probably negotiated among representatives of this sort. Among the Greek city-states, from the sixth century it was customary to choose the finest orators as ambassadors, so that they might plead the cause of their state effectively before the assemblies of foreign cities, and members of diplomatic missions were accorded certain immunities and special consideration.[6] The emperors of the Byzantine Empire appointed ambassadors who had the function, like modern ambassadors, not only of giving or receiving messages, but of reporting generally to their government on conditions in the countries to which they were sent. At least by 1455, ambassadors were being appointed not merely to undertake particular negotiations or missions, but as permanent representatives of their own state at another court, so bringing regular communication. By the end of the sixteenth century permanent posts were normal, though ambassadors were frequently regarded as much as spies and deceivers as normal representatives: in the words of Sir Henry Wooton, an ambassador of the day, they were "honest men sent abroad to lie for the good of their country." A class of officials and archivists, "diplomatists" in the strict sense, also developed, whose function it was to administer, interpret, seal, and preserve the official documents and treaties affecting relations with foreign states.

The full evolution into modern diplomatic practice did not take place until the Congress of Vienna in 1815. Four categories of representatives were then established: Ambassadors, envoys extraordinary and ministers plenipotentiary (originally appointed for a special mission, though later most ministers were given this name), ministers resident, and chargés d'affaires (in charge during the absence of an ambassador or minister). Precedence, previously hotly disputed, came to be accorded strictly according to these ranks and the date of the appointment to the post. Ambassadors reported to Foreign Ministers, not monarchs. At about the same time there began a gradual development and expansion of foreign offices, many of which were established only in the eighteenth century (as the British Foreign Office in 1782) and in career diplomatic services. Many governments followed the French in establishing a career consular service.

In the nineteenth-century system, the volume of diplomatic work rapidly expanded. This expansion accelerated greatly during the twentieth century. Even in 1914, there were still only 150 career diplomats in the British Foreign Service, and only 446 altogether, including consular as well as diplomatic services; fifty years later the number had risen to more than 10,000. In 1916 there were only 176 people in the Foreign Office, including doorkeepers and cleaners; fifty years later, more than 1,000. The cost of running the services had risen from less than £1 million to nearly £20 million in the same period. By this time foreign em-

[6] See H. Nicholson, *Diplomacy* (Oxford, 1963), for a general history.

bassies contained, along with diplomatic and consular staff, commercial, labor, cultural, and information sections, as well as military attachés of all services. Thus there was not only greater volume but greater variety of official contacts. Diplomatic wireless facilities enormously increased communication between capitals and embassies. Sixty or seventy years ago only a limited number of communications could be sent by a diplomatic bag, leaving perhaps once a week, and taking ten days or so to arrive; today several hundred telegrams may pass between Washington and London each week, many more letters will be sent by air bag within a day, and on urgent matters there may be telephone contacts as well (the United States Department of State exchanges more than 5,000 messages a day with its overseas posts).

Improved communications have brought other radical alterations in international relationships. Today statesmen themselves frequently travel abroad and thus meet their opposite numbers in person, instead of having to rely on intermediaries. Lord Palmerston, as Foreign Secretary, though in constant contact with many governments, rarely traveled abroad, except for an important international conference, perhaps once in two years. Mr. Dulles, when United States Secretary of State, is said to have traveled 130,000 miles in two years. This makes for greater personal solidarity, familiarity, and sometimes mutual trust among statesmen than a century ago, when they often communicated with personalities totally unknown and unvisualized.

Perhaps the communication system's most important effect is in determining the *size* of the international community at any one time. In much of the ancient world, each organized state usually experienced contact with only one or two other such states, together with occasional incursions from more primitive people. In medieval Europe, a community of about a dozen principal states was in fairly regular contact. In the nineteenth century the community had increased to twenty or so major European states, dominated by five or six great powers. But extra-European states, even large and organized, such as the United States, were not accepted as members of the system, and did not usually take part in conferences and congresses. In the League period the community became global, having a membership of about fifty states, including the Latin American countries, the independent Commonwealth nations, and a handful of independent Asian and African states. Only after World War II did there emerge a genuine world community, no longer dominated by the European powers, with a widely distributed representation of every continent and more than 120 members.

Goals

The most fundamental factor determining the character of an international system is the goals that are mainly pursued by its members. A system in which the main goal of every member is territorial expansion, and in which all available territory is already occupied, for example, will clearly be characterized by frequent wars. This may also be true in systems in which the desire to attain dominance over other states is a main objective, or the desire to attain security, perceived mainly as territorial control, is dominant. Though each of these is a simplified model, they have a relevance to the Chinese Warring States period, nineteenth-century Europe, and twentieth-century Europe respectively. On the other hand, if the desire to maximize standards of living, or to secure peace at any price, are the most influential goals, war will be less likely to result. In such a system the balance of military power may be of little importance. Though each of these is only a model, none of which corresponds exactly to any actual system, it explains clearly enough how the system is shaped by the goals dominant among its members. These will be quite as important as the power relations between states. Indeed, the effect of power relationships depends entirely on the motivations prevailing among the system's units. It is thus useless to analyze systems without considering dominant motives.[7]

In practice, of course, no system is dominated by a single motivation among its members. It is therefore the balance between the goals that are held by many within the system, or by key members, which is vital in characterizing it: whether desire for territory prevails over desire for influence or for good name, whether military security outweighs security conceived as political detente, whether the desire for political control

---

[7] Models, system theory, and games theory, recently much used in the study of international relations, for this reason can have significance only if they pay as much attention to the varying possible motivations among the actors as to the number and power of the participants. They need to take account of variations not only in basic goals, but in *attitudes* toward others within the system. Models and theories of this type generally oversimplify even the power relations of real systems (e.g., in considering "bipolar," "balance of power," or "collective security" systems that have never in fact operated). By omitting motivations, they leave out even more essential variables, and so distort still further the nature of real systems, removing themselves from the realm of science to that of art. Starting from only theoretical premises, they reach only theoretical conclusions. For conclusions relating to the real world, it is necessary to study reality itself: the international systems that have actually existed.

through a sympathetic government outweighs the desire for direct control through military power. A system in which one balance of goals prevails will have very different characteristics from one in which others do. Where the desire for political control begins to take precedence over the desire for territorial expansion (as in the last fifty years), a wholly new kind of system will emerge, as we shall see in later chapters.

Clearly, goals will not be equally shared among all members, any more than individuals within society share common motivations. But in both cases certain goals may predominate sufficiently to characterize the system or society as a whole.

Within the international system of the sixteenth century and the first half of the seventeenth century in Europe that we examined earlier, a dominant motive and cause of war was *religious evangelism*. In the civil conflicts of Germany, France, England, Switzerland, Bohemia, Ireland, and other countries, in the wars against the Turks, in the Thirty Years' War and other conflicts of the period, a main objective was not so much territorial as spiritual control. It is true that, as in the ideological disputes of the present day, these aims became entangled with national rivalries and the one used as a rationalization for the other, but the dominant consideration in determining many of the actions of states was religious fervor. In the international system of the late seventeenth and the eighteenth centuries, a dominant objective was *dynastic power*, including overseas empire. Many wars of the period, those of Louis XIV, of the Spanish and Austrian succession, the Seven Years' War, even the American Revolutionary War, as well as the struggles for overseas possessions, concerned succession, or the rival power of princes, as much as, or more than, the rival aspirations of nations. In the nineteenth-century system, on the other hand, a more powerful motive was *nationalism*, the urge for national power, and unity, as felt by peoples rather than by rulers or governments, and this dictated the form of the system. In the independence struggles of Greece, Bulgaria, and Serbia, in the revolutions of 1848, in the Italian wars, in the three Prussian wars, in the Balkan wars, and to a large extent in World War I, the dominant motive was national independence, national power, and national identity. In the system from 1917 onward, though national rivalry remained important, *ideological evangelism* became even more powerful. In the civil wars in Russia, Spain, and China, in the struggles against German and Italian totalitarianism, in the cold war in Europe and the Far East, and in the internal struggles of Latin America and the Middle East, the dominant aim has been to secure power for an ideological creed or faction, rather than to win territory for the nation-state; and this too has radically affected the type of war and the total system.

That particular motivations were characteristic of particular systems does not of course mean that they were exclusive to that system. Religious evangelism affected national motives at periods other than the sixteenth and seventeenth centuries: for example in the Crusades, or the Crimean War. Dynastic rivalries were important before the eighteenth century and, to some extent, after it. Nationalism can be traced back before the nineteenth century and persists, in some areas virulently, until today. But each has been at its peak, and has been an especially dominant motive at these times.

Similarly, the dominant motive has not been manifested equally by every member of each system. Countries like Russia, whose traditional religious faith was not threatened, were less affected by religious evangelism than those, such as Sweden, which had recently acquired a new religion, or Spain, which felt its religion threatened by others at home and abroad. Nationalism was felt less violently in countries such as England, Russia, Switzerland, and the Scandinavian countries, whose national identities were not seriously threatened for a comparatively long time, than those among which national identity had been suppressed (Greece, Serbia, or the Balkan countries), or those in which it had been retarded by internal divisions (Germany and Italy). Thus the motives of nations, like those of individuals, are partly influenced by past experience, and partly by immediate situations. Each of these is peculiar to each nation. But they are also influenced by the environment as a whole: the religious enthusiasm of one state arouses the religious sentiments of another, national competition by one state stimulates national assertion by another, ideological expansion by one power or group of powers will bring about expansion by another, if only in self-defense. In all these ways the system reaffirms and reinforces itself.

The type of motive that dominates determines many features of each system. Dynastic power or nationalist systems are basically systems of all against all, in which each unit competes with every other: therefore the units are more likely to be independent in action or to undertake temporary and politic alliances, each working for its own advantages. But systems of religious or ideological evangelism are basically systems of some against others. Here the groupings are mostly predetermined by basic convictions. Therefore large-scale and relatively consistent alliances (such as the Protestant Union and the Catholic League, or NATO and the Warsaw Pact) are more likely here than in the dynastic or nationalist systems, in which rapid and drastic changes of alliance (as between 1748 and 1756, or in the first seven years of the twentieth century) may take place.

Differences in goals will also determine the importance of relative power and size within the system. Differences of this kind are more important in systems of the second and third types, where relatively self-contained units are competing against other roughly comparable units. In the first and fourth types, where each unit is usually joined with others sharing similar beliefs, it is the strength of the total alliance, rather than of individual powers, which counts for most. Similarly, where conflicts are mainly small and internal, as in the modern world, the size of each nation counts for less than in systems in which the maximum power of each nation is deployed in major wars. Again, written treaties, alliances, pacts of nonaggression, and other formal obligations have inevitably affected more directly systems of the second and third type, where the units are governments dealing with other governments than in the first and fourth, where the authority of governments counts for less in relation to the will of individuals and groups.

Means for Attaining Goals

Systems are also characterized by the means mainly chosen to attain ends, or the combination among them that is favored.

What are the principal means available?

The first, and most elementary, is *negotiation*. This may be designed to attain goals in full by persuasion alone, or it may seek to threaten as well as to persuade. Very often it will use a combination of these: it may offer a compromise settlement, yet leave in the background a veiled hint of force if this is not accepted.

Another means available to states for attaining their ends is the *mobilization of support* from elsewhere. If a state is already allied with one or more other states, it may induce them to join in diplomatic representations, or in economic or military pressures. If all belong to an appropriate international organization, it may raise the matter there to gain the advantage of third-party support. A government may seek support within the other state, or even within the government with which it is dealing.

Another available instrument of policy is *economic pressure*. Trading and other contacts may be developed, and budgetary assistance offered (like German economic relations with Turkey, or French with Russia, before World War I). Contracts may be offered or sought (as the Italians did in the Arab and African world between the wars and after). Economic aid or technical assistance may be given or withheld (the aid given by the United States to Formosa, or the Soviet assistance withdrawn from China in 1960). An embargo covering some or all goods may be imposed (the sanctions imposed on Italy in 1935–36, embargoes on the Soviet Union in the fifties, or on China and Cuba in the sixties). All these may be used for political as well as economic ends.

The ultimate sanction available to states is *force*. Naval vessels may be dispatched as a warning or threat (the gunboats used by Britain in the Far East in the nineteenth and early twentieth centuries, or the United States Sixth and Seventh fleets kept in the Mediterranean and China seas since 1945). Troops may be mobilized or advanced to a frontier to indicate firm resolve (the Russian mobilization in 1914, or the dispatch of tanks by both sides to East and West Berlin in 1961). Threats of large-scale military action may be aired (like the threats made by Palmerston against China and other countries, or Hitler's against Austria and Poland, or Soviet threats of nuclear strikes after the war). Force may be actually exerted but in a limited way (the United States blockade of Cuba in 1962). Invasion may take place without permanent occupation (the British invasion of Tibet in 1904). Invasion and occupation may take place without change of sovereignty (as in the Austrian invasion of Bosnia and Herzegovina in 1908). Guerilla activity can be initiated or supported (like the support from both sides for factions in Laos and Vietnam). Finally, full-scale war, whether limited or total, may be launched.

These various means are not usually alternatives. Negotiation, the mobilizing of support, economic pressure, and threats of force may take place simultaneously. The first two are taking place, explicitly or implicitly, among states all the time. Even while war is proceeding, all the other means may be employed as well. In judging a system, or a state's policy, it is not the individual choices that count, but the balance maintained between the various means employed.

The degree to which any of these means has been used has depended partly on the issue; partly on the motives of those involved and the lengths to which they may go to achieve satisfaction. But it has depended also on the system: on what is *expected* within the system as a whole. In a system in which force is rarely used, or very risky, or highly disapproved, a veiled threat of force will be less effective (as well as less likely) than it is in one in which force is commonly used. The choice will depend partly on the communication system, and how far this facilitates or impedes the use of any particular means. In a system in which there is little diplomatic contact (say in Europe in the early Middle Ages), negotiation has been less likely to be adopted than where contacts are frequent and close. In a system where contacts exist but are defective, or are ineffectively used (as in Europe in 1914), negotiation may fail to secure its objectives. Where there are multilateral organizations, within which contacts take place and pressure for a settlement from outside can be brought to bear, negotiation is more likely to be adopted in relation to other means.

But the choice of means has also depended on the motives dominant within each system. In the sixteenth and early seventeenth centuries, when religious evangelism was a dominant motive, assistance to religious leaders in foreign lands (Philip II's assistance to Irish Catholics or that given by Charles I to French Huguenots), royal marriages for religious as much as for dynastic reasons (Phillip of Spain's to Mary of England, or Henry VIIIth's to Anne of Cleves), the dispatch of agents from one country to another to convert particular rulers, or to murder rulers persecuting a particular faith (the attempts made by Spain in Elizabethan England) became common instruments of foreign policy. In an age of dynastic rivalry, such as the late seventeenth and eighteenth centuries, dynastic marriages, agreements on disputed successions (such as those concerning Louis XIV and Maria Theresa), exchanges or purchases of foreign territory (those in the Treaty of Utrecht and the Treaty of Paris) become the favored instruments of policy. In an age of nationalism, nationalist economic policies, mercantilism and protectionism, preferences for colonial territories, support for nationalist movements elsewhere (British support for the South American and Greek independence movements, French for the American and Italian movements, or Russian for the Slav territories in the Turkish and Austrian empires), and the deliberate encouragement of nationalist sentiment and nationalist fervor through national anthems, emblems, and uniforms, become dominant means. In an age of ideological competition, support for political movements elsewhere, the engineering of revolutions and *coups d'état by* sympathetic factions, the organizing of ideological alliances and the use of high-powered propaganda techniques directed at foreign populations, become some of the principal means used by governments in their international relations.

Changes in technology also affect the choice of means. A change in military technology may increase the amount of power that can be brought to bear by a particular state (the invention of the tank in 1916 or the atomic bomb in 1945), or by any state (the invention of high explosive). It may also change the *relative power* of states (as when the airplane and the submarine reduced the invulnerability of a sea power such as Britain). Finally, it may transform the whole nature of military relations, by increasing the total *risk* that a nation may incur through military action (as germs, gas, and nuclear weapons have done). In the modern system, as a result, large-scale war is a less favored means. A change in industrial technology may affect relative power among states, or may increase or reduce their interdependence. The growing industrial strength of superpowers has increased their military predominance in the modern system. Changes in communication technology affect the knowledge within one state of another, and the degree of sympathy one feels for another's interests.

Possibly more important than the choice of means is the choice between total strategies. International relations systems have been characterized by deterrence and threat policies (in which economic or military pressures are most important), or by conciliation and appeasement policies (in which negotiation and bargaining count for more). Since World War II the former policy has been favored by Western nations, whereas during the years between the wars the latter was prevalent. The choice between the two will depend on a number of factors. Probably most important is the mood prevailing at the time.

But the choice depends also on technical factors. A deterrent policy will be possible only if military power can be brought to bear rapidly: in the postwar world nuclear weapons, long-range bombers, and missiles made this more easily attainable than before 1959. Similarly, a deterrent policy is rational only in a system in which it is possible to rely on the opposing decision makers' rationality, and their capacity to perceive the risks of taking particular steps: it may be rational against calculating Russian chess players, or prudent Chinese mandarins, in a way it could not be against a paranoid fanatic such as Hitler, who might only have been provoked into war by threats.

Usually, neither conciliation nor deterrence will succeed when pursued in isolation. Excessive conciliation without an adequate backing of strength may both encourage the appetite to grow with what it feeds on, and ensure disaster if war nonetheless finally materializes. On the other hand, uncompromising deterrence without any willingness to make concessions may only encourage rigidity and hostility in the opponent and nonetheless finally fail in its ultimate objective, since, as we shall see, there is no evidence that nations are overwhelmingly influenced by balances of strength in decisions favoring war. The interwar and postwar periods illustrate the danger of either in isolation.

Institutions

Finally, international systems, and the wars that occur within them, are characterized by the institutions for resolving conflicts among states established in them. These are the stabilizers that preserve the system from destruction.

The first, and most elementary, of the instruments that have been adopted for this purpose are bilateral agreements between the states involved. These may be in the form of a *treaty*, a formal document binding on both parties to undertake certain actions in certain circumstances: the subject will vary according to the type of system, and in different periods has primarily dealt with territorial arrangements (seventeenth and eighteenth centuries), spheres of influence and guarantees (nineteenth century), nonaggression, commercial relations, and arbitration arrangements (early twentieth century), international institutions and cultural exchanges (mid-twentieth century), or other matters. It may be a less formal agreement, such as a *memorandum of understanding*, setting down an understanding between states that does not require formal ratification. It may be an *exchange of letters*, setting out understandings that have been incorporated in correspondence between the states. It may be merely a *declaration*, setting out the views of two governments on a particular matter between them. It may be an *informal agreement*, never published to the world. It may be an *understanding* communicated orally, but never written down. It may even be a *tacit understanding*, not made explicit either in speech or in writing, but nonetheless mutually understood. Whatever the agreement, the nation's freedom to act, insofar as it is prepared to honor the undertaking, is henceforth restricted. A formal treaty normally will need to be ratified by the legislature of the country, or by whatever procedure is laid down for this purpose. Since 1918, it has also required to be registered and published by the Secretariat of the League of Nations or United Nations — it might otherwise be unenforceable. Possibly for these reasons, informal agreements have become more common than formal treaties since 1918.

Next, a number of third-party procedures have been developed to help in resolving differences among states. From at least the eighteenth century, governments have occasionally been willing to offer their "good offices" to help in settling disputes between two other states. In time offers of "mediation" over disputes came to be more formal: a third government would not merely explore the issue, but suggest a settlement. In 1825, Britain successfully mediated between Portugal and Brazil over Brazilian independence and in 1830 between the United States and France over the interpretation of the Treaty of Paris; France used her good offices to bring settlement between Britain and Greece in 1849–50. In the nineteenth century mediation was quite frequently exercised by several powers or by "the Powers" as a whole: the Powers successfully mediated between Greece and Turkey, first in 1868–69 over Crete, and again in 1879–80 over their frontiers; Britain, France, Austria, and Prussia attempted to mediate between Russia and Turkey before the Crimean War in 1853. In several cases (the Austro–Prussian War, the war between Greece and Turkey in 1897, and the Russo–Japanese War), mediation was instrumental in bringing to an end a war already begun. In the Declaration of Paris of 1856, it was stated that "states between which any misunderstanding might arise should, before appealing to arms, have recourse so far as circumstances might allow to the good offices of a friendly power." At the Hague Conferences of 1899 and 1907, it was provided that any power should be entitled to offer good offices or mediation to powers who are in dispute, and that this should not be regarded by either party as an unfriendly act.

Another procedure, also developed at the Hague Conferences, was that of "Enquiry" for use in certain types of disputes (this was used in the dispute between Russia and Britain over the Dogger Bank in 1905). There emerged, especially during the 1920's, a procedure of "Conciliation," by which a third power, or a conciliation commission, established under a number of treaties, could be asked to examine a dispute and suggest a settlement that would not, however, be binding on the parties. Finally, in some cases, a procedure for "arbitration," in which the third party not merely proposed a settlement, but the two disputants undertook in advance to accept it, was used successfully over a number of nineteenth-century frontier disputes in which a foreign sovereign was asked to arbitrate. At the end of the century a large number of arbitration treaties were signed among states undertaking to use this procedure in appropriate cases, and setting up the machinery for that purpose. Such arbitration is usually based on existing treaties and international law, but the parties may agree to accept arbitration *ex aequo et bono*, that is, on the basis of equity. When arbitration is undertaken by an international court, without the right of the parties to choose the judges, it is known as *judicial settlement*. All these procedures also represented, insofar as they were used and respected, a type of restraint on the initial freedom to act of the nations concerned. The nature, and degree of use, of international procedures of this sort have a vital bearing on the system.

A third means of resolving the disputes among states was provided by the development of international organizations. The system of diplomatic links, though it provided some form of contact between states, in practice served for a long time as a substitute for meetings among rulers or statesmen themselves. Only in 1815 was a system of regular consultation among the principal powers formed. It was designed to consider all the more important events within the continent, whether or not they directly affected any of the powers themselves. Though the arrangement for regular meetings established by the Quadripartite Treaty did not last more than five or six years, the system of holding congresses to discuss matters of common interest remained in force throughout the nineteenth century. During the hundred years between 1815 and 1914, there were only thirty-six in which a congress or conference of some kind was not held, and only four times did more than two years elapse between meetings.[8] But only after World War I was a permanent organization of states formed, relatively comprehensive in its membership. The League of Nations provided an opportunity for comparatively rapid discussion of most of the major issues of the time, and for pronouncing collective judgments on them. The organization failed in its main purpose, for reasons that will be considered later (see Chapter Nine, below). But this does not diminish its importance in establishing the principle of rapid consultation among all, or nearly all, the main states of the period over any event of international importance. This system was developed in a more elaborate form in the UN structure after the war. Multilateral discussion and third-party influence were now built even more firmly into the system. Under the League, discussion of disputes had been likely and a recommendation possible; under the UN, discussion was almost certain and a recommendation probable. A forum for perpetual negotiation, and continuous third-party influence, were thus provided.

[8] For a fuller account, see P. Reuter, *International Institutions* (London, 1958), pp. 55–56.

As regulatory instruments such institutions cannot enforce a settlement on unwilling parties, but they can provide, on the one hand, a ready-made channel for discussion and negotiation; second, a focus for outside influence to make itself felt; third, a delaying mechanism, which may allow passions to subside while discussions continue; and fourth, an autonomous organization, whose officials, traditions, or principles may exert an influence of their own on the actions of states.

The fourth development that serves to modify relations between states is the formulating of principles of conduct to influence their behavior. These emerged first in the field of diplomatic relations: conventions arose covering the envoys having a protected status. Next, conventions began to form about commercial relations: the Greek states began to develop a common code of commercial law among themselves, and in the Middle Ages fairly well developed rules relating to piracy, navigation, contracts, and other matters took shape. By the eighteenth and nineteenth centuries such norms began to cover the ways of conducting wars, neutrality, treatment of prisoners, and similar matters. During the nineteenth century, rules on the validity of treaties, their ratification, state succession, and other matters vital to the state system began to evolve. Finally, slowly and imprecisely, laws and conventions concerning not merely the conduct of war, but its initiation and the circumstances in which it was "just" or "unjust," began to develop: though, as we shall see, the rules in this respect have been, and are even today, vague, disputed, and often disregarded.

Each of these means for resolving differences of ends — bilateral agreements, third-party procedures, international institutions, and norms of conduct — provides different kinds of restraint on the uninhibited freedom of nations. International systems vary, not only according to the influence of all these on the actions of states, but on the relative importance among them. They may affect choices by governments not only of the means they adopt, but even of ends. They all serve, in different ways, to reduce the conflicts of ends that might otherwise ensue.

Thus earlier international systems have been conditioned by the prevailing communication system; the goals mainly held among states; the means mainly adopted to pursue them; and the institutions for reconciling them. But communications, means, and institutions can only be influential insofar as they affect goals. It is thus motives that are the finally dominant factor in any system. And in examining the modern system, it is to motives among states that we must first turn.

Bibliography

Cambon, Jules, *The Diplomatist*, London, 1931.

Fox, W. T. R. (ed.), *Theoretical Aspects of International Relations*, Notre Dame, 1959.

Horn, D. B., *The British Diplomatic Service*, Oxford, 1961.

Iklé, F., *How Nations Negotiate*, New York, 1964.

Kaplan, M., *Systems and Process in International Politics*, New York, 1957.

Knorr, K. and Verba, S., *The International System*, Princeton, 1961.

Nicholson, H., *Diplomacy*, London, 1963.

Reuter, P., *International Institutions*, London, 1958.

Rosecrance, R., *Action and Reaction in World Politics*, Boston, 1963.

Satow, Sir E. M., *A Guide to Diplomatic Practice*, London, 1922.

Strang, Lord, *The Diplomatic Career*, London, 1962.

CHAPTER TWO

Motives

The Motives of States

What evidence have we for the motives of states?

The evidence consists partly of the *actions* of states. Where behavior is sufficiently consistent, it may be legitimate, among nations as among individuals, to attribute consistent intentions, conscious or unconscious, to its authors. Evidence of this kind may be obtained from records of state actions as in any history of modern international relations.

It also consists of evidence of the *purposes* of decision makers. These may be assessed from their own expressions of intention and policy. Here greater weight will be given to private expressions of intention (for example, within the cabinet room) than to those designed for the ears of the public, which may express desirable, rather than actual, motives. And we may also have to allow for subconscious motives that policy makers themselves are not aware of. Evidence of this kind may be obtained from the speeches of statesmen and other public pronouncements of government policies. More reliable will be their subsequent recollections of motives, or records of private statements at the time.[1]

Finally it consists of the *deliberations* of states, as revealed, for example, by records of discussions; or recollections of those who play a large part in decision making without themselves bearing ultimate authority, such as professional diplomats and foreign office officials. These

---

[1] For example, such books as Sir Winston Churchill, *History of the Second World War*; Sir Anthony Eden, *Facing the Dictators, The Reckoning, Full Circle*; Harry Hopkins, *The White House Papers*; Herbert Feis, *Churchill, Roosevelt, Stalin*, give evidence of national motives during the war years — an especially important period since nations have greater opportunities for realizing their motives in wartime.

may be in a position to judge fairly accurately and objectively the principal aims governments have sought to attain in reaching decisions.[2]

In general, such evidence suggests that national policies are governed by widely ranging motivations, some comparatively stable and unvarying, and others more short-term. There does not appear to be any consistent hierarchy by which all short-term goals are related to long-term ends; still less by which all goals are subordinated to one overriding, long-term objective. The dominant goal at one time will depend, as for individuals, on the type of situation then experienced. Goals that at one point are thought of as a means may become ends in their own right: wealth, demanded first as a means, may become an end in itself. And goals that are sometimes ends may become means to other ends: armed power may be desired as a way of winning influence, or influence as a means to power. The goals will be pursued in different proportions at different moments, in different spheres of activity, and in different actions.

Among the various ends that appear often to serve governments as *general and long-term goals* of their state, in approximate order of importance, are: survival; security; independence; status; influence; prosperity; popularity; good name; peace; protecting the interests, commercial and personal, of individual citizens; promoting a particular ideology or political creed and frustrating others; and achieving a stable, harmonious, or otherwise desirable international community.

The most important of the basic ends are certainly those listed here first: survival and security. Their weight can be measured somewhat by the dominant and consistent place that policies designed to secure them have assumed in the foreign policies of major states: the neutrality and protection of the Low Countries for Britain, the Rhine frontier for France, the Monroe Doctrine and supremacy in Central America for the United States, dominance in Poland and Eastern Europe for Russia. Sometimes the unit whose survival and security is demanded is extended: to the empire, so that control of the Suez Canal and the ap-

---

[2] Evidence of this kind may be obtained from cabinet records and memoirs of ministers and officials (Lord Strang, *Britain in World Affairs*; Lord Vansittart, *The Mist Procession*; Sir Isaac Kirkpatrick, *The Inner Circle*; Harold Nicholson, *Diplomacy*; Neville Henderson, *Failure of a Mission*; A. François-Poncet, *Souvenir d'une Ambassade à Berlin*; R. Coulandre, *De Staline à Hitler*; E. von Weizsäcker, *Erinnerungen*, etc.); this type of source is discussed in academic works such as J. Frankel, *The Making of Foreign Policy* (London, 1963) and R. E. Snyder, et al., *Decision-making as an Approach to the Study of International Politics* (Princeton, 1954).

proaches to India becomes as weighty for Britain in the late nineteenth century as security in Europe; or to the alliance, so that the power of Austria becomes of prime interest for Germany in the thirty years before 1914; or to the ideological group, so that the security of Europe or the Middle East become deeply important to the United States today, irrespective of their importance for her own security.

Concern for these two ends does not necessarily induce military preparedness or strong alliances: it may induce a policy of neutrality, as for Switzerland and Sweden; or nonalignment, as among many new nations today. This may win slightly less of the first two values, survival and security, but more of the third, independence. On the other hand, other nations — such as Britain after 1900, West European countries after 1945, or India after 1960 — may decide to assure themselves more of the first two at the expense of the third. Though the ends of survival and security normally are synonymous, they may diverge: a policy of conciliation or neutrality sometimes may give a higher chance of security and a lower one of survival. This is only one example of the choices between values that have to be made by nations, consciously or unconsciously, all the time. Every decision about defense expenditure involves a choice between security and prosperity; about an alliance, between security and independence; about a trade agreement, between prosperity and promoting ideological principles; about a particular intervention, between security and good name; about a UN vote, between solidarity and independence. Normally survival and security seem to be chosen as higher ends in any such choice — because they involve the nation's very existence, and therefore the raison d'être of the national decision makers. Only when they are assured can the others be more freely pursued.

That independence is a predominant objective of nations is made evident by the many wars of independence among emerging national states in the last century and this; by the frequency with which smaller countries will combine to prevent excessive dominance by a single power, as we noticed in the last chapter; and by the intense resentment that smaller powers feel toward excessive interference by larger nations in their affairs, or toward the attempt to use economic assistance to influence their policies. That status is significant is suggested by the importance attached to "sovereign" equality by smaller powers at all times; by the efforts to acquire great power status by Italy and Japan before World War I; by the bitter struggle for permanent seats in the League Council between the wars, and the efforts to acquire nuclear status at huge economic cost afterward. That influence as a goal is important is suggested by the diplomatic activities of governments traditionally devoted to this end, by the efforts to acquire "spheres of influence," close alliances, and "special relationships" for this purpose, and by the attempts in recent years to use economic aid or military assistance agreements as a means of acquiring influence. The importance of prosperity, popularity, good name, and peace is self-evident, though the relative importance attached to them will vary among different nations at different times.

That these objectives might be accepted as long-term goals by decision makers if specifically questioned on the subject is no indication of how influential such motives are in individual decisions. The evidence suggests that very many decisions are made without any regard, certainly without conscious regard, to long-term objectives. Probably many governments will rarely formulate explicitly ultimate goals of this type: for this reason alone their influence on officials or statesmen is reduced. Even where there are occasional attempts to formulate such goals, it is unlikely that they have any direct influence, though they may be strengthened as unconscious motives. The decision on how to respond to a particular diplomatic note, how to vote on a particular resolution, whether to ratify a particular convention, and still more the far larger number of smaller decisions that are arrived at within foreign offices every day will be influenced far more by other, and *short-term objectives*.

These more immediate objectives might include the need to retain the friendship of a particular ally; the need to promote relations with a particular country or type of country; the desire not to exacerbate relations with another; the need to promote the interests or cohesion of a particular alliance and to frustrate the interests of another; the need to promote *particular*, rather than general interests, economic and political, of the nation and its nationals; the need not to offend a particular interest group or governing party at home. Perhaps the most important and common of all such aims is simply the need to respond to the existing situation, to find a way forward from, or a solution to, the particular problem or state of affairs immediately faced. Though some of these goals may originally have been related, more or less closely, to the attainment of the long-term objectives, they may increasingly become ends in their own right, pursued without regard to their original instrumental purpose. For this reason the division between the first-order and second-order goals is never clear or consistent.

Other factors will influence national conduct. The traditions of policies undertaken in the past may continue to exert influence, even though consciously they are no longer regarded as goals. The political sympathies and personal characteristics of governing groups and officials will exert an influence. Policies influence each other. Sometimes one objective will eliminate another: the desire for national security or status may temporarily override the desire for peace. Sometimes goals that are contradictory, or at least conflicting, will be pursued simultaneously. It is the sum total of the actions of a state that may be taken as evidence of its collective motives.

Generalized theories attributing all the actions of states to a single dominant motivation or objective — such as the extension of national power, aggressive impulses, or economic self-interest — are as misleading as corresponding attempts in the field of individual motivations. We have no more evidence to show that the actions of nations are all, or even mainly, directed by a single goal, than that the actions of individuals are directed by single motives, such as sexual desire, or economic interest, or the will to power. It can be shown without difficulty that all national actions seek to maximize the "national interest," if that term is in turn defined as "what nations seek to maximize"; just as individuals can be shown to pursue only "pleasure" or "desire" by using equally tautological definitions. But this is not a very useful conclusion.

Generalizations seeking to show that nations attempt always to maximize "power" are particularly misleading. If power is defined merely as interest, or "what states want," such statements are as tenable, and as meaningless, as those relating to "national interest." But in many cases the term is not defined at all. It may be used to cover a very wide range of meaning, including armed strength, status, influence, capacity to coerce, or even control over territory or resources. These are so varying in effect and significance that they cannot conveniently or meaningfully be covered by a single term. Moreover, the term is used frequently without discrimination between the *object* of policy and the *instrument* by which other objectives may be secured. In fact, it seems likely that armed strength, or the capacity to coerce (perhaps the only two satisfactory possible definitions of "power") are both normally desired by governments as the means toward other ends, such as security, influence, and status, rather than as ends in themselves. And this fact alone shows it is unlikely that they represent the dominant, or the only, object of national policies. Power may be a particularly important means because it is the means to very important ends, including survival, security, independence, and others. But it is not usually an end in itself.

The motives of states will be influenced not only by the long-term and short-term goals but by the *life history* of each nation, especially more recent experiences. Some of the types of national life history that condition national mentality and behavior are comparable to those exerting a similar effect on individuals. A national existence totally isolated from the international community may lead to a wholly unsocialized mentality (comparable to that of the isolated individual or feral child). To this category, early hunting communities and some of the marauding peoples of history, such as the Huns, the Norsemen, and the Mongols, almost entirely untamed by other contacts, might be said to belong. More common in recent times are nations, comparable to psychopathic individuals, which are isolated, feel themselves unloved, and develop in consequence antisocial and aggressive tendencies. To this category, Germany between the wars, Japan in the same period, and perhaps South Africa and China in recent years, could be held to belong. Or nations may possess, like individuals, a permanent feeling of insecurity, and, like insecure individuals, exhibit aggressive traits. To this type Serbia before 1914, pathologically insecure in relation to Austria, China in its relation to the United States in recent years, or Israel and Syria in relation to each other, might be held to belong: there is undoubtedly a very great difference between the foreign policy mood of those whose borders have not been violated in recent years (such as Switzerland, Norway, and Canada) and those which have suffered such violations relatively often (such as Albania, Korea, or China), which adopt not more cautious but more extreme positions. Or there may be, especially among small, newly arrived, or recently humiliated states, a kind of group inferiority complex, an exaggerated demand for respect, status, and the letter of their rights: here Nationalist China, de Gaulle's France, or Sukarno's Indonesia might be taken as examples. Even commoner are the aggressive drives that derive from a perpetual competition for status. These are shared to some extent by all, through the influence of a highly competitive system, but they are encountered especially among those experiencing a sudden accretion of power; Germany and Russia in the second half of the nineteenth century, and a number of newly independent nations today provide examples (though in the contemporary world urges for status and dominance are often expressed as much in aspirations to scientific achievement, sports victories, a high standard of living, or competitive economic beneficence as to military supremacy). Finally nations may acquire the type of mentality, corresponding to that encountered among individuals, which has become obsessed with crusading zeal or moral aspiration, frequently, among nations as among individuals, having a partly aggressive tinge; here the classic examples are perhaps those of ancient Israel, the Arabs, or the Christian Crusaders, whereas modern prototypes may be found in Communist China and the United States of the Dulles era.

Thus it is evident that the motives of states are highly complex. They vary not only from state to state but from generation to generation. Even for the same state at the same time they will be inconsistent and confused. It is thus no more meaningful of nations than of men to declare that they are "by nature" competitive or cooperative, power-seeking or sociable. Nations may, like men, be capable of different natures. These will vary (like those of individuals) both according to their own experience and history, and to their own immediate situations. But they will be influenced, above all (again like individuals'), by the social environment within which they exist: the community of nations and its institutions. The significant problem, therefore, in both cases, is not to discover the "essential" nature of men or of communities; but to know the *potential* natures which the society they inhabit may induce in them.

Motives of Individuals Within States

Clearly, to speak of the motivations or objectives of "states" is a simplification. For general description, purposes or policies may legitimately be attributed to a collective body on the basis of the sum total of its actions. But motives will not be consistent, or equally shared, among the population of a nation. They may not even be among those reaching decisions within it. Individuals, interest groups, departments of the government, ministers, or politicians normally become more concerned over certain goals than others. In decisions of defense departments, security will be more influential than popularity, but the reverse holds of foreign offices. Individual personalities may be more or less aggressive, cooperative, concerned with the peace, wealth, or status of their nation. And in consequence policies of states vary to some extent, both from time to time and between nations, according to the relative influence of particular statesmen, political parties, interest groups, government departments, or sections or individuals within a foreign office.

But foreign policy decisions are made in a national framework, in interaction with other nations, and it is national aspirations and interests that are dominant, not those of individuals or parties. Although *assessments* of national interests and desires may vary marginally, experience suggests that such assessments do not radically differ among individuals of the same nation. There is usually some variation along the progressive-conservative and liberal-authoritarian axes.[3] But the consistency of foreign policies pursued by successive governments of different parties, the homogeneity of national mood and emotion within particular national situations, the predictability of policy for particular states, all provide evidence that these are marginal.

There may be variations among reactions within *different* states in comparable situations. Responses may vary according to the personalities of those involved in making decisions. They may vary according to the institutional machinery in each state: especially the number of individuals whose opinions influence decisions. And they may vary according to national temperament and political traditions. Systematic analysis of the responses of states needs therefore to consider differences within states: new or old, democratic or authoritarian, rich or poor, under military government or civilian.[4]

Even variations between types of states do not, however, seem to be decisive. So many people are involved in most decisions that variations in individual temperament or aggressiveness are evened out. The differences between the structures of governments in the modern world probably become less and less, even between governments of totally different ideologies and traditions. The basic pattern of diplomatic intercourse, bureaucratic techniques, foreign office and parliamentary procedures, the number of people involved in decisions, do not vary decisively between states. There is little evidence that differences in decision-making procedure influence the kind of decision reached. Above all, the traditions and norms of the international community as a whole are common to all states. For these reasons there appears to be in general, as will be seen later, a remarkable homogeneity between the responses of different states in similar situations at any one time.[5]

The main factor influencing the motives of individuals within nations is undoubtedly the stimulus situation in which their nations are placed. Beyond this is the effect of the international environment as a whole, which is roughly constant for all states at any one time. Internal factors

[3] Cf. H. J. Eysenck, *The Psychology of Politics* (London, 1954); T. W. Adorno et al., *The Authoritarian Personality* (New York, 1950).
[4] For studies of these factors see J. Frankel, *The Making of Foreign Policy* (London, 1963); R. C. Synder, et al., *Decision-making as an Approach to the Study of International Politics* (Princeton, 1954); R. C. Snyder and James Robinson, *National and International Decision-Making* (New York, 1961).
[5] See below, pp. 54–59, 65–71, 94–97, 124–126, 144–146, and *passim*.

count for little against these. Just as, among individuals, even the most varied personalities, having the most divergent backgrounds, will react in generally similar ways to corresponding situations, nations very often behave similarly, as we shall see, in similar national situations. Study of international relations today thus needs to be directed increasingly toward the study of the behavior of nations in particular types of situations.

The general conceptions of the situation and role of one nation, though normally fairly consistent among its own population, may vary widely from the expectations prevailing in another. Between nations therefore there may often emerge a *conflict of expectations*. It is from such conflicts, above all, that violence in the behavior of states arises. The situation that provokes violence is always to some extent the effect of a clash of expectations. Among individuals this may be seen in many of the situations that most commonly provoke violent responses. It is the radical disturbance of deeply held expectations that results from the jilting of a fiancé by his bride-to-be, the suddenly discovered adultery of a wife presumed faithful, which may, by upsetting legitimate expectations, provoke an uncontrollable reaction. Similarly, among nations it may be the sudden access to power by a rival, the appearance of a threat never anticipated — such as, in the last twenty years, the unexpected nationalization of installations regarded as inviolate (at Suez), the sudden defection of a previously submissive satellite (Hungary) or the installation of secret missiles in a nearby hostile state (Cuba) — which most often brings about violent responses. At root, the point in dispute in such situations is what may be expected in relations between states. In the pages that follow we shall examine many other examples of the way in which conflicting expectations underlie most instances of violence between states.

Such conflicts arise partly as a result of contradictions in the *goals* pursued by two or more states. In certain spheres of activity states have cooperative values and common interests; in others both interests and values may conflict. Although activity designed to increase equilibrium, international trade, or peace for one state will automatically produce a similar increment in them for others (at least some others), an attempt by any state to increase its relative status, influence, popularity, or power must bring a corresponding reduction in the same value for some or all other states. The degree of conflict between states thus depends partly on the goals. It depends also on the *means* chosen by states to pursue their goals. Whatever goals are chosen, states may adopt either *coercive* means for attaining them (that is, means designed to assure that their own goals are attained without modification), or *concessive* means (that is, means that recognize that some sacrifice may have to be made to others in order to attain the desired ends). How often concessive rather than coercive means are chosen will depend partly on *realism*, or understanding the difficulty of securing goals, and partly on *recognition* of the rights and interests of others. (For a fuller analysis of conflicts between goals and means, see Appendix I.) In the modern system, though goals often remain exclusive, means are more often concessive than before.

The Learning of National Motivations

The first of the sources from which national motivations are derived are the innate drives of individuals within states. These include aggressive drives, fear, demands for security, and perhaps some gregarious instincts. Individual drives are channeled by the culture into specific directions. Some (the aggressive drives) may find expression mainly in collective forms; others (the sexual drive) can be satisfied only in personal forms. Acquired characteristics also affect international attitudes. Those who have had an authoritarian upbringing are often especially nationalistic in outlook. The collective drives that result, such as aggression, may be relatively stable in disposition (against all foreigners or all Russians), as an individual's might be habitually directed against wife or employer. But they will usually, like personal drives, be aroused especially by particular situations (such as those causing frustration or anger).

Second, desires (as the desire for national status) and activities (say, collective aggression or national philanthropy), which are not necessarily related to innate drives, may be learned from the international culture. They may be acquired principally by imitation and suggestion, as are the corresponding individual desires and activities. And they are reinforced by the rewards and punishments that are experienced in gains or losses in national power, prestige, popularity, and good name. By this procedure nations learn, just as individuals do, the most effective means of securing objectives and values within the limitations set by the environment and the range of choice available. Something like what psychologists call "operant conditioning" and the "law of effect" may take place, so that by trial and error relatively stable attitudes and tendencies to action result.

Conversely, certain activities are inhibited or redirected by social taboos, the different types of communal norm discussed in the next section. Sometimes the assessment of rewards and punishments will depend on the direction of attention. Action that brings punishment in the form of disapproval from the international community may bring rewards in approval of the home electorate (just as, for the individual, action that brings punishment in the form of social censure may bring rewards in personal drive-satisfaction). Which is most valued will depend on education and the degree of socialization in each case.

The cultural environment will channel and direct individual drives and desires in different ways at different times. For example, it may in one age direct individual aggression against other nations, while in another it directs it against other classes, and in a third, against opposing ideologies and political creeds. The actors involved will vary at different times. Besides nations there are such groups as regional organizations (such as the Arab League or the Organization of American States), economic unions and free trade areas, international organizations, international political parties, ideological groupings, and others. But because nations exercise a command over loyalties and over armed force far more direct than do these groupings, and become engaged in armed conflict in a way that the others do not, it is with nations and their motives that any study of international relations must be mainly concerned. And even if, in time, they come to be replaced by continents, exercising a corresponding command over loyalties and armed power, similar considerations are likely to apply to these as to nations today.

The communal drives that result are clearly not strictly analogous to individual drives. Because the innate element is small and divided among numerous individuals, the cultural influence on them is more important. The drives are thus less constant in their effect on national conduct. But the common national situations which individuals often share, and the powerful conditioning established by traditional responses to particular situations, may mean that, unless new conditioning and expectations are set up, nations will respond in similar and to some extent predictable ways to similar stimuli.

The stimulus involved may be, as for individuals, either internal or external. Just as the drives of individuals may be set in motion either by purely internal changes (such as hunger or thirst) or by external perceptions (such as the aggressive response of a robin to a bunch of red feathers, or the maternal activity aroused in a mother by any threat to her own offspring), so communal drives may be stimulated by purely internal changes (such as the rise of a nationalist government or widespread unemployment) or by external ones (such as threats from a neighbor or humiliations from a rival).

Similarly, just as their drives will lead individuals to a restless and variable activity until the drive is satisfied, so among nations the drive, for example for security, may lead to a variable and restless national activity that is not satisfied until the threat, such as a hostile regime coming to power in a border state, is removed (consider the actions undertaken by the Soviet Union, the United States, and China in their border areas). In each case the movement is appetitive, designed to bring about a particular end-situation, rather than a mechanical response to a particular stimulus.

Cultural influences will determine not only the type of response chosen for particular situations, but the entire range of situations demanding a response. The situations calling for armed retaliation bear little relation to their intrinsic importance to the nation. Nations today, for example, continue to respond with great violence to the occupation of small and totally valueless strips of border territory, or to insults to national prestige. But even the most bitter dispute about trade terms, tariff regulations, immigration laws, investment and aid, the functioning of the UN system or the powers of the Secretary General will not lead to warlike responses, though they may be of much greater long-term importance to the state concerned. The culture pattern does not tolerate war on these grounds. And it is this which finally determines national behavior and motivations.

Norms and Motives

Expectations therefore are vital in relations between states. Every social order is based ultimately on expectations — the expectations of members toward the relationships that should prevail within it. In narrower societies most of this assumed structure of relationships is inherited. The expectations required are inculcated among all members from a very early age. They will be disputed, at any time, only in marginal degrees or by marginal groups. And they will be altered only by gradual adjustments. The socializing agencies of the community — parental upbringing, education, communication media, and public opinion — are able to sustain a consistent pattern of expectations throughout the community.

Over relationships *between* communities there is as yet no such consistent pattern of expectations. Yet relationships between communities — large and small, national and subnational, economic or social — may be as important to their members as are those within them. With extended communications, increased contacts, and the more and more complex organization of modern societies, individuals today increasingly belong to a large number of disparate groups, entering into complicated relationships with each other. Individuals may undertake personal relationships with individuals in other communities elsewhere. But those relationships themselves are more than ever conditioned politically, economically, even socially, by the relations of the larger communities to which they belong. *Communal relationships* become as important to man's welfare as individual relationships. *Communal drives*, the desires and aspirations of the group, become as powerful in influence, and more dangerous in effect, than the drives of individuals and may equally lead them into violent conflict. And *communal expectations*, the assumptions shared within each group on relations between them, become the main factor influencing relationships and drives alike.

The type of communal relationship that is by far the most important to individuals today is that between nation states. For these alone are not themselves subject to other, sovereign authorities that may, in the ultimate resort, regulate their interaction. And these alone dispose of the type of power which may make their relations fatal to their members.

Between communities, as within them, the absence of any commonly expected structure of relationships will give rise to an interaction regulated by vagary and violence. Here too, relationships may come to be ruled by a system of competition and conflict, providing insecurity for the weak, and instability for all. Here, too, aggressive drives and self-seeking instincts will set up a mode of existence governed by brute force alone. Here, too, therefore, only socializing agencies to inculcate a commonly expected pattern of relations, comparable to those which already govern relationships within communities, could create the basis for a harmonious interaction.

Within societies there is a wide spectrum of such agencies. These vary in their working from unconscious conditioning through explicit persuasion to physical coercion. Their effect is to bring individualistic drives and impulses into sufficient reconciliation to make possible a stable and harmonious existence for all. The most satisfactory forms of control will seek to create the basis for a mutually compatible intercourse without destroying the capacity for individual spontaneity; to instill a modicum of restraint with the minimum of constraint.

For this purpose, societies employ, first, *practices*, ad hoc procedures and habits of interaction, adopted among two or more parties, which set up firm expectations concerning behavior in specific situations. Here the object is only mutual convenience; and the sanctions against violation are those of reciprocity, the disapproval and retaliation of other parties, together with less immediate disadvantages arising from disrupting established procedures. Next there are *conventions*, forms of behavior that are approved by a wider society, and which thus come to enjoy an authority independent of the immediate advantages derived by the parties. Here the expectations are those of society as a whole, and the sanctions are the disapproval of society as a whole. Third, there is *morality*, including custom among primitive societies and ethical codes today, where the expectations aroused are more powerful and surrounded by a more emotional, often religious, sentiment of awe, fervor, and dread, than in the other cases. Here the sanctions are usually conceived as religious in form, imposed by supernatural beings, mana, karma, God, or other spiritual forces, though immediately imposed through the self-punishment of the conscience; and, because exhortations to conformity, and warnings against violation, are more intense and deeply instilled, they create a more inescapable personal imperative than surrounds any of the other codes. Finally, there is *law*, a code more explicit and detailed than the others, covering more variegated fields of existence than practices and conventions, but less colored by religious emotion than moral codes. Here the sanction is the coercive power wielded by enforcement agencies.

Each of these codes creates *norms* of conduct, of varying degrees of precision and persuasiveness. The effect of these is to set up expectations in the minds of the members of the group that, in given types of situations, a particular type of response is demanded. They thus come to modify the motives deriving from other sources, innate drives, experience from the past, and others. They establish *rules*, to *regulate* conduct, by setting up *regularities* of behavior. Such rules provide the main instrument of government among all societies. By reducing insecurity and unpredictability, they provide the stability essential to a harmonious and well-balanced existence for each individual member. They contain the essential element of impartiality and objectivity which personal rule in its arbitrary and subjective character may lack. And even apparently coercive authorities depend in practice largely on principles of this type to maintain their power. It is rules, rather than rulers, that everywhere exert ultimate authority.

But the *type* of norm predominantly employed determines more than anything else the social structure and social character of each community. Each type of norm possesses its own typical form of sanction. The function of the various sanctions is to create a self-regulating mechanism, which provides the subject with a *self-interest* against violation: the interest in avoiding the sanction creates an interest in conforming with the norm. But the sanction characteristic of each norm is not exclusive of others. Law may be sustained by the moral conscience, social convention, and mutual convenience, as well as by policemen. Practices whose original purpose is immediate convenience may come to be reinforced by social conventions, moral sentiment, even the forces of the law as well. The specific element of each code consists in the particular emotional aura that surrounds it, as much as in the sanction typical for each.

The conformity achieved with each code is not necessarily directly determined by the sanctions imposed, either individually or collectively. The effectiveness of each code is perhaps more crucially governed by the process of conditioning through which each is instilled.

The conditioning consists of a number of elements. These include the initial *inculcation*, and the source, type, and period of life of this will be crucial to the type and degree of conformity secured. Next, there is the process of *reinforcement*: the unceasing reminders not only from the original sources, but from new reference groups, peer groups, cultural media, religious, or other influences, and the new rewards and punishments these may impose. Finally, the effect will depend on *habituation*, the degree to which the original inculcation succeeds in creating a set pattern of behavior that becomes partly automatic, and unrelated either to the specific content of the rule or to the currently available inducements to conformity.

But the effectiveness of each code will be influenced not only by sanctions and conditioning, but by more conscious processes. These consist partly of attitudes toward individual rules or systems (though even these will be affected by earlier conditioning) and partly of more general conceptions of rule obedience. In some cases men perform an action, not because of conviction of its correctness in the particular circumstances, but out of recognition of the advantage of preserving a general rule concerning such actions. Not only may they perform a particular act they dislike to avoid violating a general rule they approve. They may consistently obey a *rule* of which they disapprove, in order to avoid disturbing the total system of rules; or obey a whole system of rules to avoid destroying the basis of society of which it is an element. This last source of conformity may be regarded as an application of the rational faculty; that is, of mentally universalizing from particular cases.

Different kinds of community are ordered by different kinds of code, sanctions, and conditioning. There have been many in which almost the only code governing the members' actions was that surrounded by religious emotion and enforced by religious sanctions. Among a few, conduct has been controlled almost entirely through a secular code enforced by public opinion. In some, conditioning has been instilled primarily within the small family; in others, through the peer group. In others again, it takes place mainly through the community as a whole. In considering, therefore, the means of providing a system of order between communities, it may be necessary to consider what types of norm are most likely to have an application within the society of states.

Norms Among States

The problem of establishing norms among a society of sovereign and conflicting national states clearly differs significantly from that which arises within other societies. The first and fundamental difference lies in the fact that, although within national societies ultimate power, in the shape of armed force, is concentrated at the center, so that principles of interaction may be partly *imposed* on its members, in the international community both power and loyalties remain dispersed. One of the most important agents of social order within states is here, therefore, lacking. Attempts to secure a more stable international order have often taken the form of efforts to bring about in the international community a concentration of power at the center similar to that which exists in individual states. Such efforts are unlikely, for reasons that are discussed more fully later,[6] to prove effective within the foreseeable future. And the problem of creating order within such a community, therefore, remains different in kind from that which arises within national societies.

This does not, however, as it is often suggested, mean that there can be no basis of order. The absence of coercive power may exclude the possibility of *law* (in the sense defined above). But law is not the condition of order. It is, in fact, only among the most modern and advanced communities that coercive force at the center has ever been the main basis of order. Even within those societies force is not the only, nor necessarily the most important, sanction on which order is based. And among the vast majority of less developed societies, including many of the most ordered and well-disciplined, no such coercive power has existed.[7] Such

---

[6] See below, pp. 250–257.

[7] See L. T. Hobhouse, G. C. Wheeler, and M. Ginsberg, *The Material Culture and Social Institutions of the Simpler Peoples* (London, undated), pp. 53–61.

societies have been able to sustain a stable order because they were able to make use of alternative socializing agencies. The condition of good order is not the *submission* of members to the coercive demands of authority; but their *conformity* to the approved canons of conduct. It is regularities of behavior, not its regulation, that are required. And so long as these are secured, by one means or another, the lack of a system of compulsory law enforcement may not be crucial in its effect.

The international community today appears to have more in common with a primitive community than with any more developed society. Its individual members exist, more perhaps than in any other society, in that state of mutual suspicion and fear sometimes held to be the natural condition of man himself. But the *voluntary* submission to a central authority that might provide security for all, such as has been imagined taking place within human societies,[8] is as improbable in this case as in the other. For in each case mutual suspicion, and the consequent difficulty of agreeing on the ways in which authority may be used, is likely to mean that greater security will be found in known methods of private defense than in imaginary systems of public enforcement. As in other primitive communities in which the individualistic urges of their members have not yet been strongly restrained by social pressures, *coercive* power therefore remains unavailable within the foreseeable future. But this does not exclude the other possible agencies of social control. Each of these has been employed effectively in many societies in which centralized force was not available (including some national states, until relatively recent times). And each may have its application within the international community today.

In the international community there may exist *communal practices*: agreed forms of interaction between two or more communities to serve their mutual interests as similar practices serve those of individuals. In the relations of states, as in those of individuals, there is often a need merely for standardized forms, set procedures on which each party is able to rely. A common interest in these may be held where little else is held in common. To some extent such communal practices already exist in the international field in elementary form, in bilateral or multilateral agreements or understandings on trade and navigation, customs procedures, diplomatic practice, or even more crucial aspects of their mutual relations, such as respect for frontiers, notification of troop movements, and other usages.

---

[8] As in Hobbes' *Leviathan*.

The international community also makes use of *communal conventions*, to establish more general and more formal understandings concerning national conduct. These may create common expectations more dependable, permanent, and universal in application than those which exist between individual nations. They enjoy the more effective sanctions exerted by common international opinion, instead of remaining dependent on that of individual aggrieved parties. These are to be seen in international conventions that have received widespread ratification, in those international customs which have come to have the force of international law, and in some other provisions of current international law which are generally recognized.

Finally, communities may be restrained by *communal morality*, the provisions of which are more compulsive and inward than other principles governing their behavior. Certain antisocial activities of communities, it can be argued, are as fundamental in their effect on common order and individual welfare, and may be as much an affront to deeply rooted convictions, as the actions that have become subject to individual moral codes. They may equally be made the subject of the most binding and fervently revered proscriptions and injunctions. The sentiments that have grown up within the international community concerning acts of aggression, genocide, threats and bullying, war crimes, and certain other forms of national conduct, already have something of the quality that colors moral revulsion in other spheres. Any other provision of international law that was as universally and profoundly revered by the members of the international community could equally come to perform the function of communal morality. So far such a code

TABLE II · 1

Norms: Personal and National

Personal norms	Typical sanctions	Typical incentives	National norms
Practices	Personal inconvenience	Personal convenience	Bilateral agreements or understandings
	Private disapproval	Private good will	
Conventions	Public disapproval	Public approval	International custom and law
Morality	Cosmic retribution	Cosmic reward	International morality
	Self-punishment by conscience	Self-satisfaction	
Law	Coercive force	Liberty	

is only embryonic, both in the scope of its provisions, and in the degree
of respect accorded it. And even the provisions generally accepted are,
as will be seen later, so ill-defined that it is, even more than in cases of
individual morality, made easy to find convincing rationalizations to
justify exceptions.

In certain respects norms between communities differ in their functioning from those within them. Both the form and sources of the socialization that takes place in a community of nations must clearly be
different from that which takes place in a smaller society.

First, the process of internalization, by which individuals make social
codes into personal convictions, does not take place in the larger grouping in any such direct sense as in other communities. At first sight codes
within the larger community differ in acting only on governing authorities, which *mediate* between their own group and the wider society. Yet
this difference is partly illusory. For the government that seems to stand
between code and individual is itself composed of individuals little different from other citizens, and themselves directly influenced by that
code. It is in fact the *sources*, rather than the subjects, of socialization
that are here different.

The role played in smaller societies by parents, peer groups, and other
reference groups in inculcating the code in the international field is
largely eliminated. Their part is taken by impersonal agencies, international authorities, national governments, international lawyers, politicians, editorial writers, television commentators, and others; and it takes
place by indirect means, resolutions, judgments, speeches, subsequently
reported at second hand, rather than by direct, face-to-face do's and
don'ts. Second, the period of inculcation is usually far *later* in time, so
that the code may be less internalized. No one is told in childhood:
"Do not commit aggression." We learn much later, when we are less
impressionable, that it has been said of our own state or another, in a
UN resolution. Next, because it applies to the actions of the group as a
whole, it will not evoke the sense of immediate, *personal* responsibility,
nor the personal liability to sanctions, that occurs for individual codes.
Finally, international codes have to be *superimposed* on pre-existing,
and sometimes conflicting, codes inculcated by the smaller group (including those glorifying the nation state, and those instilled by particular political or religious creeds) that may themselves be conceived as
partly moral in kind. The fact that despite all these inhibiting factors,
individuals may, even now, feel a sense of guilt over their own nation's
actions is sufficient proof that communal norms can, nonetheless, exert

some effect on individuals, whether key decision makers or the legendary man in the street.

TABLE II · 2

Typical Sources of Socialization: Personal and National

Types of socialization	Sources, personal	Sources, national
Inculcation	Parental teaching of rules and morality	Press and other accounts of international laws and norms
Reinforcement	Peer groups, general culture, religious authorities	Resolutions of international organizations, international law courts, etc.
Sanctions	Personal rewards and punishments for conformity and deviation (e.g., good name and ill repute)	National rewards and punishments for conformity and deviation (e.g., good name and ill repute)
Habituation	Personal behavior patterns and social precedents	National behavior patterns and international precedents
Rationality	Concepts of social relationships and personal rights	Concepts of international relationships and national rights

Second, the functioning of such codes differs within the international society in that there do not at present exist there the emotional attachments, the loyalties, the myths and symbols, that, through the working of innumerable cultural pressures, have been built up to sustain rule observance within more limited and cohesive communities. The importance of this difference should not be exaggerated. Undeniably there is today no deep sense of loyalty to the international community; nor have there yet been created an international cultural mythology, flags and anthems and rhetoric, that help to unite other societies. But this fact does not prove whether a situation of stable coexistence is possible there or not. For the influence of those factors in creating or maintaining a peaceful order is itself doubtful, as the innumerable civil wars of the past two centuries demonstrate. National societies often command today an intense and deeply rooted sense of *loyalty;* but this, though it may secure cohesion against threats without, will not always secure peace within. A genuine sense of *community* is almost as much lacking within states as between them. Such states are often artificial creations, built up usually within the last few hundred years only out of culturally disparate, or even hostile, peoples. But social norms remain effective influences there. A comparable process may in time take place within the international field.[9]

There is, finally, a difference in the international community in the fact that the tradition of independence and autonomy among nations is such that it may seem impossible, in default of powerful sanctions, that they will ever be bound by a commonly accepted code. The diversity of values and preconceptions among their leaders is such as to make it seem unlikely that any common code could emerge as within narrower communities, where other members appear of like kind and hold similar values. But in fact even the premise here cannot be fully sustained. Among many communities, obligations will be acknowledged to those who are by no means regarded as like, and whose views on most topics are wholly divergent. Codes of interaction may themselves create common values. And it is arguable that, with modern communication of persons and ideas, the sense of essential likeness — even the community of values — among members of different nations today is at least as great as existed between the disparate elements and classes of many well-ordered societies until the most recent times.

For different types and levels of authority different degrees of consensus are required. Within the international community there is no necessity, nor desire, for any all-comprehensive authority or law to regulate detailed aspects of its members' conduct as do legal codes within states. All that is required are principles of interaction sufficient to create the conditions for a peaceful coexistence between them. These need not condition the way of life *within* the communities to which they are applied. Nor do they demand common attitudes on those questions which most give rise to diverging valuations within states: political principles and moral codes. The only element of community required is the common interest in security among states.

It is in some ways the similarity, rather than the difference, between the community of nations and that of individuals which is impressive. The fact that the behavior of states (as we shall see) resembles that of individuals need not surprise us. For when we talk about "Britain" and "France" taking a certain action, we use a shorthand to represent the collected individuals, whether many or few, determining the actions of those countries. And because the communities to which they belong become in a sense extensions of their own personalities, which may

9 For an examination of some of the factors influencing this, see K. Deutsch, *Political Community at the International Level* (Princeton, 1954). See also pp. 259–267, below.

provide satisfactions and experiences, sources of pride, shame, or anger, almost as immediate as those they enjoy as individuals, it is inevitable that the various situations and experiences through which the nation passes create emotional situations and experiences which possess considerable similarity for all their individual members. But it is still the emotions, desires, and aspirations of individuals that are ultimately in question. A threat to the nation's security, an insult to its pride, a blow to its honor, a gratification of its vanity, all these may provoke reactions for its members that reflect with great accuracy the reaction that similar situations will evoke in their personal lives. And we shall observe in the pages that follow detailed examples of the way in which, in consequence, the psychology of nations mirrors that of individuals.

Whatever rules of interaction are established clearly need to be closely related to the behavior of states in the contemporary world. It is a study of the behavior of states that is attempted below. The study of peace must inevitably consist mostly of the study of the wars that negate it. In the following chapters, therefore, the main types of conflicts that occur in the modern world will be examined and their causes analyzed.

Bibliography

Boasson, C., *Approaches to the Study of International Relations*, Assen, 1963.

Burton, J. W., *International Relations*, London, 1965.

Claude, I. L., *Power and International Relations*, New York, 1962.

Frankel, J., *International Relations*, London, 1964.

———, *The Making of Foreign Policy*, London, 1963.

Haas, E. B. and A. S. Whiting, *The Dynamics of International Relations*, New York, 1956.

Halle, L. J., *Men and Nations*, Princeton, 1962.

Hinsley, F. H., *Power and the Pursuit of Peace*, Cambridge, 1963.

Hoffmann, S. (ed.), *Contemporary Theory in International Relations*, Englewood Cliffs, N.J., 1960.

Morgenthau, H., *Politics Among Nations*, New York, 1963.

Padeford, N. J. and G. A. Lincoln, *International Politics*, New York, 1954.

Rosenau, J. N. (ed.), *International Politics and Foreign Policy*, Princeton, 1961.

Schwarzenberger, G., *Power Politics*, London, 1964.

Snyder, R. C., H. W. Bruck, and B. Sapin, *Decision-making as an Approach to the Study of International Politics*, Princeton, 1954.

CHAPTER THREE

Aggression

The Causes of External Wars

The most elementary type of national behavior incompatible with international order is a direct assault by the forces of one state against the territory of another.

What, first, are the causes of this type of behavior?

The concept of "cause" in this context requires careful definition. The factors involved in an outbreak of war may include the immediate occasion of dispute; other sources of conflict between the two parties; long-term rivalries and resentments; the believed chance of success in the conflict (as determined by the existing balance of power, the strength of alliances, the possibility of outside intervention, and other factors); the believed costs of war, military, economic, and psychological; the possible gains, whether consciously or unconsciously conceived (including political, military, and economic gains, or purely psychological benefits such as the release of anger, frustration, or uncertainty, and the satisfaction of aspirations to dominance or of unconscious aggressive urges). Each of these factors — issues, conflicts, rivalry, chances of success, believed costs, and believed gains — may be present in entirely different proportions in different disputes, in different types of dispute, among different countries, in different regions, and in different ages of history. Attempts to attribute the causes of "war" and "aggressiveness" to any one factor (the will to power) or class of factors (economic causes) are thus unlikely to prove well founded.

It is possible to distinguish the *objectives* war has procured. Objects have changed radically in different ages. In early times conflict was probably as often accidental as designed, arising from chance contacts

52

between isolated, precarious, and suspicious groups, habituated already to conflict with other animal species. As populations became denser, war perhaps began to appear attractive as a deliberately chosen activity. It could provide then a means of securing cheap food, vengeance, satisfaction for wrongs, sexual gratification, or mere exhilaration. With the invention, some ten thousand years ago, of systems of settled food production, victory could procure food supplies for those whose traditional sources had failed. It could provide the permanent occupation of a favorable living space. And it could bring, not merely immediate conquest, but a more lasting subjugation.

When, five thousand years later, the earliest empires began to appear, the conquest of foreign peoples could become the instrument for increasing the glory of the state and the power of its ruler. The annexation of lands not previously controlled began to be culturally established as the natural object of national ambitions. Though not necessarily desired for its own sake, war might still be attractive as a means to security, trading advantage, and above all, prestige. This cultural influence continued to determine decisions to resort to war. Even within the modern community of nations, conquest and the acquisition of territory remained a symbol of status. When the young nation-states of Europe began, at regular intervals, to make war against each other, it was still assumed that when the proceedings came to a close, the less successful would be obliged to pay forfeits to the victorious in the form of real estate. Peace treaties provided above all for transfers of territory, especially those having strategic or commercial value, for acknowledgments of dynastic rights, and similar gains. With the final partition of the globe in the late nineteenth century new annexations became less attractive and more expensive. With the growth of nationalist movements, the development of the principle of self-determination, the spread of modern armaments all over the world, and the firmer delineation of the atlas everywhere, the acquisition of territory became not only less and less easy to justify, but more and more difficult to achieve. During the twentieth century, moreover, the desires and demands of nationality came to be increasingly replaced by those of ideology. Territory was no longer the main objective. The motives for particular wars are examined in the next section. But in general it can be said that the recruitment of other nations for favored creeds, their integration within specific alliances, their salvation for the forces of "socialism," "democracy," or "revolution," rather than their conquest for national purposes, now come to be the dominant motives, and the main consequence of wars.

It is more instructive, perhaps, to examine the kind of *situations* most liable to provoke external war. For the effects of a war are not necessarily good indications of its *causes*. And in many cases wars might not have occurred without the immediate occasions that sparked them off.

Analysis of the wars of the past two hundred years suggests that certain types of situations have most commonly served to signal a warlike response. One such class has been those in which the "honor" of the nation was held to have been insulted: questions of national *pride*, comparable to situations between individuals requiring a challenge to "satisfaction." Such situations might result from humiliation or injury to national subjects (as in the War of Jenkin's Ear of 1739); the boarding of national ships (as in the Anglo-American war of 1812); insult to the national flag (as in the Anglo-Chinese war of 1859); the murder of a national (as in the Franco-Chinese war of the same year); above all, any act held to involve disrespect to the sovereign power, the "crown," the "majesty," the "imperial dignity" of the nation affronted (as when at the outbreak of the Anglo-Chinese war of 1839, Lord Palmerston declared that his government "demanded satisfaction" for Chinese action toward a British official in "utter disregard of the respect due to an officer of the British crown," and dispatched the armed force "necessary in order to vindicate the honour and dignity of the British crown . . ."). The fact that in some cases, as over the humiliation to France manufactured by Bismarck in 1870, it was necessary to invent an incident belonging to this category to justify war is itself clear proof of the effectiveness of insult in evoking the required warlike reflex. These may be regarded as signals for a certain type of response. Although in this century such signals have become perhaps less powerful in their effect, they have remained important factors (as in the insult rendered to Austrian national pride in 1914). And even within the last few years, the lowering or tearing of national flags (as in Panama in 1963), the burning of effigies of national leaders (as between Indonesia and Malaysia), the violation of a national frontier (as in the Sino-Indian dispute), the insulting or ill-treatment of national subjects (as between the United States and Cuba) may still serve to inflame emotions surrounding "national honor," and so provoke or intensify warlike sentiments.

A more important class of situation arousing a warlike response is that in which it is felt that a violation of national *rights* has occurred.

Perhaps the most common form of action to arouse emotions of this kind is the violation, however inadvertent, of a national frontier (as by Turkey against Russia in 1735 and by Russia against Turkey in 1769). A somewhat similar response may be evoked by the denial of the "right" to trade (as before the Anglo-Chinese war of 1839), or of the "right" to diplomatic intercourse (as before the Anglo-Chinese war of 1859), of the "right" to financial repayment (as before the action by Britain and France against Egypt in 1876), or of "rights" of residence (as by China before 1839 and 1860). A similar sentiment of infringed rights may be aroused by the sudden incursion of one power into an area traditionally regarded as its own sphere of influence by another (as by France at Fashoda in 1898, by Germany in Morocco in 1906 and 1911, or by the Soviet Union in Cuba in 1962). All these have the effect of inflaming the emotions of the power believing its rights infringed, and so create the *psychological* (though not necessarily all the other) preconditions of war.

Next, aggressive responses may be intensely aroused, among nations as among individuals, by any situation involving *frustration*. Frustration may be seen in its simplest form where a nation is suddenly deprived of some intensely desired national objective (as when Bulgaria, thwarted of the gains she expected from the First Balkan War of 1912, turned in fury against her allies in the succeeding year). It may result from the deprivation of some asset previously possessed, encouraging resentment and a desire for restitution (such as the loss of Alsace-Lorraine for France after 1870 and for Germany after 1918, or the deprivation of Kashmir for Pakistan, Formosa and the offshore islands for China, or West Irian and the Borneo territories for Indonesia since 1945). It may result from more general restrictions and disabilities, frustrating desires for status and self-respect (as felt by Germany between the wars). For a rising power, even situations that represent no loss may create frustration (like the lack of colonies for Germany and Italy in the late nineteenth and early twentieth century, or the obstruction by the Western powers of Japan's expansionist designs between the wars). Finally, among declining powers, the failure to secure the respect once everywhere accorded may stimulate a form of frustration (as felt by Turkey and Austria in East Europe in the early twentieth century, and by some colonial powers today). In the contemporary world, the failure of Portugal to return to India her colonies there and the defiance by Egypt of Britain and France in 1956 are examples of other frustrating situations arousing aggressive responses. Reactions will be particularly fierce where irritations or impediments are placed in the way of a large and powerful power by a small one. The ferocity of Spanish action against Holland, or British against Ireland, can only be interpreted in this light. More recently the attitude of Russia to Poland, or Austria to Serbia in the late nineteenth and early twentieth century, of Italy to Ethiopia and Germany to Czechoslovakia between the wars, or of Britain to Egypt and the United States to Cuba after, are perhaps all examples of the same type.

But situations that in recent years have signaled the most powerful national emotions have been those where a threat to national *security* has been felt to exist. Traditional United States interference in Central and South America, British intervention to protect the Low Countries, French apprehensions about the Rhineland, as we saw, represent examples of such a factor at work. Even when, as in recent times, the more flagrant aggressions have become less common, situations of this kind have continued to evoke a violent response. As we shall see in the next section, many of the recent examples of direct aggression come within this category. Soviet actions in East Europe, United States actions in the Caribbean, and Chinese actions in Korea and Indo-China are examples of apprehensions about vital border areas inspiring aggressive responses. The emotions that such situations arouse may be compared to the access of panic and pugnacity stimulated among individuals when a sense of insecurity is suddenly aroused. And, as among individuals, their intensity will, once more, be conditioned partly by past experience and partly by immediate occasion.

Such situations most closely correspond to the "occasions" of our initial analysis. As already seen, the number of factors affecting the likelihood of a situation developing into war are many and complex. In some cases the immediate occasion may be among the least important. Few would suggest that Bismarck's three wars, between 1864 and 1870, were directly "caused" by the particular issues which finally triggered them. But this is not the most normal situation, especially today. In very many cases all the other causes might never have served to precipitate conflict, had the immediate occasion not arisen to serve as a signal. The situation that existed before World War I might have persisted for a long time, and might in time have been quite transformed, had it not been for the stimulus created by the Sarajevo assassination.

The effect immediate stimuli exert is influenced by other, more lasting conditions.

They may be magnified by an old *rivalry* between two powers. This is seen in its simplest form in traditional antagonisms, comparable to those between two tribes, as between certain of the North American Indian tribes. In this situation an incident may be regarded rather as an opportunity than as a provocation for warlike response. Among nations, the situations between France and Germany or Russia and Turkey, during the second half of the nineteenth century, may be regarded as falling within this category. If two powers share some common objective (such as Alsace-Lorraine), it may serve as a perpetual source of resentment to one side or the other. In the contemporary world the traditional enmity between Israel and the Arab States, Cambodia and Thailand, Germany and Poland, or India and Pakistan are examples of this type. In this situation the antagonist may be already categorized as "enemy" even before specific incidents arise. The effect may be that each move by either side is interpreted by the other only in relation to the conflict, so that every situation which could serve as a signal is enormously magnified.

Sometimes the influence of the stimulus situations is strengthened by *internal* factors. The culture of individual nations may itself serve to glorify war, heroism, and military valor, so that each stimulus is intensified. Thus although the degree of war-permissiveness within the international community as a whole may vary from age to age, the same factors may also diverge from nation to nation: between the warlike state of Ch'in and the pacific state of Yen at the end of the Warring States period in China, or between Bismarck's Prussia and the United States in the nineteenth century. Within modern times the character of the internal culture in Germany, Italy, and Japan between the wars served to intensify national reactions to specific stimuli. The influence of military classes, the rule of military dictators or juntas, though not necessarily directly related, may exert indirectly a comparable effect.

There is also some evidence that disposition to war is influenced by the *age of nationhood*. The recurrent conflicts between the Latin American states in the nineteenth century, the record of Germany from 1866 onward and Italy from 1870, the aggressive conduct of Serbia and other newly created Balkan states in the late nineteenth and early twentieth centuries, and the nationalistic policies of the new East European states between the wars all suggest that newly created states may be more unstable in their external relations than older nations. Of the armed conflicts of all kinds since 1945, none have taken place among the older established nations of Europe and North America despite the intense ideological divisions among them. There are a number of fairly simple reasons for this. The greater cost of war among the more developed states, the susceptibility of new nations to disputes through the very fact of independence (for example, over frontiers), the greater internal stability of the older states, their membership in defense alliances are perhaps the most important among them.

Finally, reactions to particular situations may be magnified by the influence of *past experience*, whether humiliations or successes. The humiliations heaped on France in 1870, Germany in 1918, and China between 1839 and 1949 served to intensify nationalist sentiments there. The easy successes available to Russia during the nineteenth century on her eastern and southern borders, or by Prussia in the middle of that century, or by colonial powers in Asia and Africa, served to stimulate the appetite for further exploits. Reactions to past history may serve, therefore, among nations as among individuals, to supplement those to immediate situations. Reward learning takes place for communities as much as for persons. Favorable *opportunities* too may serve to stimulate the desire for rewards that can be easily attained. The fact that, in the interwar years, Germany and Japan were able to win a series of successes with little exertion or opposition only served to whet their appetites for more.

Clearly there is no immediate causal relationship between the emergence of a particular type of *situation*, or the long-term *conditions* we have just examined, and the outbreak of war. The nexus between the former and the latter depends on states of mind: the expectations of populations and leaders concerning the appropriate responses to particular situations and the possible rewards for particular conduct. Within certain cultures (among the North American Indians) particular kinds of situation (insults to the name of the tribe or totem) will automatically, according to the rules of the culture, lead to a state of mind, and thence to a decision, in favor of war. Similarly in Europe, in the golden age of the nation state, certain insults to the ruling monarch, or other offenses to national honor, became, as we have seen, culturally stamped as normal, or possible, occasions for war.

This cultural influence may determine the effect of each of the different contributory factors mentioned above.[1] Whether or not external causes of dispute, or a state of continuing tension, lead to the sentiment (conscious or unconscious) that war must follow is culturally determined. Whether or not the believed *physical* costs of war, in lives or treasure lost, are thought to be worth the prizes gained is equally the result of the prevailing culture and the relative values placed there on national glory or power, national "honor" or "security" on the one hand, and human life on the other. Whether or not, finally, the *psychological* and *moral* costs of initiating a war are regarded as too high in relation to the psychological satisfactions in winning it, is, more clearly than in any other case, culturally determined, depending largely on the form and influence of the communal morality current within that culture and the types of self-justification the culture makes available.

To speak of assessments of costs in such a situation is not to suggest that such assessments are usually, or even often, conscious and calculated. The emotional factors influencing a decision may be such that any calculation is largely unconscious. This does not, however, mean that it does not take place at all. Governments, like individuals, are not *wholly* emotional in their decisions, any more than they are wholly rational. And whether or not they are explicitly formulated, conceptions of the respective rewards and punishments, psychological and material, that may be expected to result from particular decisions will always play a major part in influencing those decisions. It is these rewards and punishments, or the way they are assessed, which cultural factors will, above all, determine. Cultural influences serve to uphold the value of war not as an end, but as a means (except perhaps by some primitive people, war has rarely been desired for its own sake). War has come to appear a lesser evil in certain circumstances; a recourse in particular types of impasse; one way of resolving particular disputes.

There is thus nearly always some element of intention in the outbreak of war. Nations will usually prefer to attain the objectives they desire, or to protect the interests they treasure, without resort to war. But, where those desires or interests are powerful, they may feel impelled to take action which they know involves the *risk* of war. The degree of risk such action involves will range in a wide spectrum from the likelihood of war resulting when a nation undertakes an unprovoked invasion of its neighbor's territory (where the likelihood

[1] See above, p. 52.

of war is almost total) to the risk involved in the mobilization of troops or the stationing of new types of weapon on the borders of another state (where the likelihood may be relatively remote). In cases where the latter type of action does result in war despite the low degree of intention on the part of the initiating nation, that of the other must have been correspondingly high to account for the unbalanced nature of its response.

Whenever war occurs, therefore, there is nearly always, at the very least, a high degree of *readiness* for war on one side or the other — sometimes on both. It is very difficult to find examples in history of wars that have been entirely "unintended" by both sides. Though either may have hoped that certain actions would not evoke a warlike response, this has always been accepted as a *possible* outcome by one and often by both. World War I, sometimes cited as an unintended conflict, seems rather a case wherein the readiness was not highly positive, but was at the same time far from negative among a number of the parties. Given the required stimulus this was intensified into positive intention: neither the Austrian Government in presenting its ultimatum to Serbia and rejecting Serbia's reply, nor the German Government in encouraging them, nor the Russian Government in mobilizing troops in retaliation were under any illusions about the probable eventual outcome — all expected war, though they may not have expected the exact lineup that finally occurred.

The proportion of deliberation to emotional response in decisions to make war may vary. Among primitive people, a mass decision to retaliate with warlike action may perhaps be classified as mainly "emotional" while decisions reached by a cabinet after long deliberation may be regarded as more "rational." Decisions by individual autocrats may be found less rational than those reached within democratic governments (where a number of minds must give consent at once). But all have usually been undertaken by sane and normal individuals. They have resulted often from a considered balancing of the ends to be attained against the costs to be incurred in the process. Such decisions have therefore probably usually been no more and no less rational than most other elements of human behavior. And they have been, like human behavior generally, conditioned principally by the cultural mores current in the community: what provocation is felt a "reasonable" ground for war. This influence of the culture, though universal, will not be *uniform*: provocations may be acceptable to weak nations that would spur a more powerful one to war.

Basically, provocations, whether short-term situations or long-term conditions, lead to war if they cause severe conflict between the expectations, justifiable or otherwise, of the government concerned. Here is the *conflict of expectations* that, as we have seen, is so often the cause of war.[2] The expectations of one nation may lead it to regard the assassination of its archduke as an unacceptable threat to traditional power and influence while those of another may regard the reparation demanded for this as an unacceptable threat to independence. Or again, one nation may regard the nationalization of an important, internationally used waterway as an illegitimate breach of obligations; but the other may regard it as a legitimate act of sovereignty. One may regard the stationing of missiles near its borders by a foreign power as an unacceptable threat to expectations of security, and action to prevent this as wholly justifiable; but the other may regard the first move as a justifiable complement to similar action by the other and the retaliation, involving forcible blockade, an unacceptable violation of its own expectations. Wherever no acknowledged norms exist, or so long as acknowledged norms diverge, such clashes of expectations will continue to lead to warlike conflict.

External Wars in the Modern World

A list of the external wars in the century from 1865–1965 appears below, divided into twenty-five-year periods,[3] with the assumed main

---

[2] See above, p. 38.

[3] For comparison, during the years 1650–1850, it has been calculated there were fifty external wars involving fully sovereign states belonging to the recognized international system. Under this reckoning (and counting the Napoleonic wars as a single war), there was a steadily declining number of wars of this category in each fifty-year period, from 18 in the first period, 13 in the second, 10 in the third, to 9 in the last. Among the motives involved, a very large proportion of the conflicts can be regarded as having mainly territorial objectives, though some were essentially dynastic disputes (like the Wars of Spanish and Austrian Succession) or ideological in aim (like the French revolutionary wars). The average period of participation by states in wars was about two and one-half years, though the average length of the wars themselves was nearer four years. The size of armies, battles, and casualties increased throughout the period, and afterward until World War I (though the proportion of casualties and deaths in each *battle* declined). The number of participants in each war fluctuated from an average of 3.5 in the seventeenth century to 4.8 in the eighteenth century and 3.1 in the nineteenth (these figures include wars of the colonial type, which usually had only two participants and became more common later). These figures, adapted from Q. C. Wright, *A Study of War* (Chicago, 1942), include only wars among states of

motivation of the initiating power. The list includes only wars involving sovereign states or relatively organized communities. It does not include limited frontier conflicts, colonial wars (that is, wars within territories already established as colonies) or civil wars.

This table reveals certain facts. First, the number of wars in this category has declined constantly, from 22 in the first period through 16 in

TABLE III · 1

External Wars, 1865–1965

1865–1890	Countries involved	Motivation
1864–65	Spain–Peru, Chile	coercive
1865–70	Paraguay–Brazil, Uruguay, Argentina	expansive
1866	Prussia–Austria, Bavaria, Saxony, Hanover	irredentist
1867–68	Britain–Ethiopia	colonizing, irredentist
1870	Prussia–France	irredentist
1873–74	Britain–Ashanti	colonizing
1875	Abyssinia–Egypt	expansive
1876–77	Serbia–Turkey	anticolonial, expansive
1877–78	Russia–Turkey	coercive
1878	Austria–Bosnia, Herzegovina	expansive
1878–80	Britain–Afghanistan	colonizing
1879	Britain–Zululand	colonizing
1879–83	Chile–Peru, Bolivia	expansive, coercive
1881	France–Tunisia	colonizing
1881–85	Sudan–Britain, Egypt	expansive
1882	Britain–Egypt	coercive
1882–85	France–Tongking	colonizing
1883–88	France–Madagascar	colonizing
1885	Serbia–Bulgaria	coercive
1886–97	Britain–Nyasaland	colonizing
1887	Italy–Abyssinia	colonizing, expansive
1887	Britain–Burma	colonizing
	Total 22	colonizing 10
		coercive 5
		expansive 7
		irredentist 2
		anticolonial 1

"modern civilization" and therefore exclude wars of "Hindu, Chinese, Iranian" or civilizations other than the "Christian civilization of Europe." The list is therefore not complete and is not strictly comparable to the figures here given for subsequent periods.

TABLE III · 1 *(Cont.)*

1890–1915	Countries involved	Motivation
1889, 1892–94	France–Dahomey	colonizing
1890	France–Senegal	colonizing
1894–95	Japan–China	expansive, colonizing
1894–95	France–Madagascar	colonizing
1894–96	Italy–Abyssinia	colonizing
1897	Greece–Turkey	expansive
1898	US, Cuba–Spain	anticolonial, expansive
1899–1902	Britain–Boers	coercive, colonizing
1900	Britain–Ashanti	colonizing
1903	Britain–North Nigeria	colonizing
1904–05	Japan–Russia	expansive
1909–10	Spain–Morocco	colonizing
1911	Italy–Turkey, Libya	colonizing
1912–13	Greece, Bulgaria, Montenegro, Serbia–Turkey	anticolonial, expansive
1913	Bulgaria–Greece, Serbia, Romania, Turkey	expansive
1914–18	Austria-Hungary, Germany, Turkey, etc.–Serbia, Russia, France, Britain, etc.	coercive, expansive

Total	16		
		colonizing	10
		coercive	2
		expansive	7
		anticolonial	2

1915–1940	Countries involved	Motivation
1918–20	Poland–Soviet Union	expansive
1919	Afghanistan–Britain	coercive
1919–20	Romania–Hungary	coercive
1919–22	Greece–Turkey	expansive
1920	Poland–Lithuania	expansive
1930–35	Paraguay–Bolivia	expansive
1931, 1933, 1935, 1937–45	Japan–China	expansive
1932–34	Peru–Colombia	expansive
1935–37	Italy–Ethiopia	colonizing
1938	Germany–Austria	irredentist
1939	Germany–Czechoslovakia	expansive
1939	Italy–Albania	expansive
1939–45	Germany, etc.–Poland, Britain, France, Soviet Union, United States, etc.	expansive

TABLE III · 1 (*Cont.*)

1915–1940	Countries involved	Motivation	
-----------	--------------------	-----------	
1939	Soviet Union–Finland	expansive	
1940	Soviet Union–Baltic States	expansive	
	Total 15	colonizing	1
		coercive	2
		expansive	11
		irredentist	1

1940–1965	Countries involved	Motivation	
-----------	--------------------	-----------	
1941	Peru–Ecuador	expansive	
1947, 1965	Pakistan–Kashmir[a]	coercive, expansive	
1947	India–Hyderabad[a]	irredentist	
1948–49	Arab States–Israel[a]	coercive, irredentist	
1950–53	North Korea–South Korea and UN forces	irredentist	
1954	Nicaragua–Guatemala[b]	coercive	
1956	Soviet Union–Hungary	coercive	
1956	Israel, Britain, France–Egypt	coercive	
1962	India–Goa	irredentist	
	Total 9	colonizing	0
		coercive	5
		expansive	2
		irredentist	4

[a] These three wars are classified under "New Frontiers" in Chart VII.2 on pp. 183–184, but are included here for the sake of comparability with other periods.

[b] Nicaragua is named since it was from Nicaraguan territory that the invasion took place. There is some evidence of United States instigation.

the next, 15 in the following, to 9 in the last (the total for each period in the analysis by types does not necessarily correspond to these because some wars are included under two categories). This does not, however, necessarily indicate a similar progression for wars in general, since external wars in recent times have been a minority of total wars (see Table VII.2, pp. 183–185).

Second, the scale and the length of the average war have declined. At all times there have been brief wars, but more recently the majority have lasted no more than a few weeks (this again, does not refer to wars in other categories, such as civil wars, some of which have lasted many years). This change probably results primarily from modern military techniques and means of communication, though it also reflects the smaller scale and limited aims of a number of recent wars of this kind.

Third, the objectives of wars have changed. Colonizing wars, those aimed at conquering nonadjacent, relatively underdeveloped territories for permanent occupation, which in the first two periods were the most common, are now almost extinct; there have been none over the last twenty-five years. Colonial wars, or wars of independence, began only in the third period and became more common in the fourth: these, which are not classed as external wars, are considered in Chapter Five. Perhaps it is more significant that wars of expansion, aimed at conquering substantial adjacent territory (instead of limited frontier areas), the most common motive even in the interwar period, have become far less dominant. In recent years, external wars have been conducted entirely either for coercion on some specific issue or for national reunification.

Fourth, it is worth comparing the geographical incidence of these wars. All except three of the wars in the first period involved at least one European power, although less than a quarter actually took place in Europe. The rest were divided among Africa, Latin America, and Asia, in that order. In the second period, all except one war involved European powers; the proportion taking place in Africa rises to over half; and the proportion in Europe remains about a fifth. In the third period, the number involving only non-European powers rises slightly to three; there is one war in Africa and two each in Asia and Latin America, but the number in Europe rises sharply to more than half the total. In the final period, the number not involving European powers rises to nearly three-quarters; only one takes place in Europe; and the rest are divided between Asia, Latin America, and Africa in that order. This is the most radical change in the incidence of external wars throughout the century.

Fifth, this evidence provides some important conclusions about national behavior and motivations. It is worth considering first how many of the wars that have occurred can be said to have been planned in advance, and how many emerged directly out of the incidents that sparked them off. Here it is necessary to distinguish conscious planning of war, often with deliberate engineering of incidents to provoke conflict; a general willingness for war, with the exploitation of any favorable opportunity that might occur; and a general unwillingness for war that is overcome only by the exigencies of an immediate crisis. In the whole of this list there appear to be very few wars of the first type, that is, that have been deliberately planned and engineered in advance: possibly the Japanese war against Russia in 1904–1905, the Italian war against Ethiopia in 1935, and Hitler's wars of 1938–39 (though even of these last the idea that they fall into the second category has been persuasively argued).[4] This suggests that the contention that nations are (or were) inherently aggressive requires at least qualification and definition. It could be said of approximately a third of these wars that they came in the second category: that there was a high degree of readiness for war, so that a relatively small incident could be seized on as a justification. But it would seem that in nearly two-thirds of the cases the wars genuinely resulted from the specific issues over which they were fought, in the sense that if these incidents had not occurred, war between those states probably would not have occurred either.

Next, examination of this list does not support some of the general theories about the motivations of war that have been suggested in the past. Except, possibly, in the Japanese attack on Southeast Asia, economic factors do not seem to have been an important cause of conflict. This applies to underlying economic difficulties as much as to immediate economic aims. Equally, there is little evidence here to show that any particular *kind* of government, liberal or authoritarian, communist or democratic, even military or civilian, is more likely to undertake armed attack than other kinds. Examples of all kinds appear in all periods. Areas of many military governments, Latin America and the Middle East, do not have larger numbers of wars. Finally, though ideological conflict may contribute to the intensity of international hostility, there is little evidence that in itself it leads to external war (this does not, of course, apply to civil wars). The only possible exceptions, those of Korea and Guatemala, can better be regarded as being caused by urges for national reunification and strategic interest respectively.

Last, it is striking that action of this kind over the past century has occurred primarily in areas where sovereignty, or allegiance, was for some reason tenuous or ambiguous. This was true of many of the colonial conflicts of the first two periods which occurred in areas where there were no recognized frontiers and where no sovereignty in the full sense was recognized by the European powers. In the late nineteenth century it was true of the semisovereign "autonomous"

[4] A. J. P. Taylor, *The Origins of the Second World War* (London, 1963).

units — such as the Principalities, Bulgaria, Bosnia-Herzegovina, Crete, Tibet, and others — which, though created to ease the decolonization of Turkey, in effect served through their ambivalent status to promote subsequent conflict. Between the wars it was true of a number of the issues stimulating conflict, including Vilna, Memel, Manchuria, Danzig, Austria, even, in a sense, in the Sudetenland and Slovakia. Finally, since the last war it has been true of a considerable proportion of conflicts, including the situations in Berlin, Korea, Suez, the off-shore islands and Formosa, as well as in all the divided countries of the world.

Conditions over the last fifty years are so different from the period of European expansion and pre-eminence before 1914 that it is worth analyzing the conflicts of this time separately from the rest. A list of these wars, using different categories to take account of the changed conditions, appears in Table III.2.[5]

TABLE III · 2

Wars of Aggression: Motivations, 1914–1964

Type	Interwar	Postwar
Expansive	Poland–Soviet Union (1918) Japan–Manchuria (1931) Japan–China (1933, 1935, 1937) Italy–Ethiopia (1935) Germany–Czechoslovakia (1939) Italy–Albania (1939) Germany–Poland, Norway, Low Countries, etc. (1939, 1940, etc.)	
Irredentist	Germany–Austria (1938) Germany–Czechoslovakia (1938) Soviet Union–Poland (1939)	North Korea–South Korea (1950) India–Goa (1961)
Strategic	Soviet Union–Finland (1939) Soviet Union–Baltic States (1940)	Nicaragua–Guatemala (1954) Israel–Egypt (1956)

Coercive	Austria–Serbia (1914)
	Romania–Hungary (1919)
	Greece–Turkey (1919)
	Italy–Greece (1923)
		Britain, France–Egypt
		   (1956)
		Soviet Union–Hungary
		   (1956)

[5] This examination again excludes actions related primarily to frontiers, which are considered separately (see below, 92 ff). It also in this case excludes actions deriving from the creation of new states, such as the Arab–Israel and India–Pakistan wars, which are considered in Chapter Four (pp. 92–116).

Expansive wars, whose main aim was the conquest of foreign territories not previously controlled, in the interwar period were still
common. There were the successive Japanese actions against Manchuria,
North China, and China itself, the Italian invasions of Ethiopia
and Albania, and the German invasion of non-German Czechoslovakia,
Poland, Norway, Denmark, the Low Countries, the Balkans, and the
Soviet Union. The Soviet absorption of the Baltic States was partly of
this type. In the postwar world there were no actions that fell fully
within this category. *Irredentist* wars, directed against territories inhabited mainly by people of the same race as the conquerors, to
bring about the reunification of a nation, whether conceived in ethnic,
linguistic, or historical terms, declined. Between the wars there were
the German occupation of Austria and German-speaking Czechoslovakia, Hungarian and Polish participation in the dismemberment
of Czechoslovakia, the Soviet occupation of Poland east of the Curzon
line, and the Italian occupation of part of Savoy. After 1945, the
North Korean attack on South Korea[6] and the Indian attack on Goa
might be placed in this category. Third, there are attacks of which
the basic motivation is *strategic* interest, induced by a threat, real
or imagined, from third powers. In the interwar period, the Soviet
invasions of Finland and the Baltic States were partly of this type. In
the postwar period, the United States and other involvement in the
invasion of Guatemala,[7] the Israeli part in the Suez campaign, and
the Soviet reconquest of Hungary should probably be placed in
the same class. Finally, there were some actions that may be termed
coercive in purpose. In the interwar period, the Italian occupation of
Corfu, and in the postwar world, the Anglo-French attack on Egypt
came within this category.

More conclusions can be drawn from this list. Among the recent
situations which most often provoke violent action are those where
movements for national unity or reunification among peoples of a
single ethnic or linguistic group meet persistent frustration. The disturbances in the Austrian and Turkish empires before World War I,
German and Hungarian ambitions between the wars, and the dan-

---

[6] This is distinguished here from a "civil war" by the fact that action involved the
crossing of a firmly established frontier-line, and that there existed on both sides
widely acknowledged governments.

[7] United States Government participation in the Cuban invasion of 1961 is here
regarded as sufficiently marginal to place this conflict within the category of "civil
war" rather than "aggression." The Vietnam war and Chinese action against the
Offshore Islands are also regarded as essentially civil wars.

gerous tensions of the four divided countries of the world after World War II, besides the actual coups of Germany against Austria and Czechoslovakia and the armed actions in Korea, Vietnam, and Goa, all provide evidence of the continued danger of irredentist war. Second, there is evidence that the danger of sudden loss, especially of strategically important and traditionally subservient states, often gives rise to an aggressive response, comparable to that arising in individuals from the sudden removal of support. The violent responses of China, the Soviet Union, and the United States respectively to the sudden loss, or threat of loss, of Korea, Hungary, and Cuba in the postwar world provide clear examples of this reaction at work. Third, a great power, especially a declining one, that finds its authority threatened by a much smaller power, especially one once subject to it, will even in modern times react in a violent fashion. Austrian determination to crush Serbia in 1914, United States action in Mexico and Nicaragua between the wars, Soviet action in Hungary, and British and French in Egypt after the war, were all certainly influenced by this factor.

Fourth, besides national reunification, strategic interest and coercion become the dominant motives. Of the external wars after 1945, besides the two undertaken for purposes of national reunification (one or two considered later as "civil wars" could also be regarded as in this category), two, or perhaps three, were cases where strategic interests were felt paramount (Guatemala, Israel–Egypt, and perhaps Hungary — this also applies to some cases of intervention in civil wars), and two were in part to procure the political submission or overthrow of another government (Britain–Egypt, France–Egypt, and Hungary).

About the five cases that occurred after 1945, a number of common features are apparent (the two wars against Suez may be reckoned as one). In this period each attack was launched in the expectation that it would be possible to confine the conflict within the borders of a single country (which was in every case accomplished). Each was launched on the assumption that the nation attacked would remain without assistance from elsewhere (an object three times attained). Each was launched by superior forces in the confident expectation that victory would be swift and sure (in three cases this was achieved). Finally, each was launched in the certainty that the party attacked was not in a position to retaliate with nuclear weapons.

The hope of limiting the conflict, except in a purely geographical sense, and of the victim remaining without assistance, proved mistaken in two of the five cases. Successful brigandage requires some degree of privacy. But the continual shrinking of distance, and the increasing area and self-confidence of UN authority, make the world less and less a private place. In the interwar period, most of the victims of aggression, China, Ethiopia, Poland, received no effective help from elsewhere. In the postwar world, even where there was no alliance, the shrinkage of distance has made assistance a more practical possibility that has had to be reckoned with. The communist world discovered in Korea that even in the utmost extremities of Asia, attempts to assert its will by force could provoke retaliation from the farthest corners of the world. Colonial powers learned, as in Indonesia and Egypt, that neither the United States nor the Soviet Union would always stand by in polite indifference when they sought to take the law into their own hands. The United States was told in the clearest of language that the Monroe Doctrine is now dead, so that even within the confines of the Americas she may face intervention from without. The extension of multilateral economic and defensive commitments across the globe, though often condemned, has thus probably reinforced, rather than endangered, world security. The supply of Soviet and Chinese military aid to Cuba, United States involvement in the defense of Formosa, British commitment to Malaysia — these are easily condemned as "mischievous" interventions. But they may in fact have served to extend the military balance into areas where otherwise uncertainty might persist. Sometimes a threat in one area (such as Cuba) is balanced by a threat in another (such as Berlin). Small and weak nations, of perverse political convictions, standing alone, can easily become tempting objects of ideological imperialism. So long as collective security cannot be adequately insured by a universal international authority, it may be maintained by more limited associations better than by none at all.

There are some further conclusions about external wars since 1945. Though engagements have been fought often for essentially political objectives — to support a particular government or to win political concessions, rather than to win territory — *control* of foreign territory, even without sovereignty over it, is still coveted. In four of the five cases of this type listed, the immediate object of attack was to acquire physical control over the territory involved. And even in the fifth, the attack on Egypt, the desire for temporary possession of a part of that country's territory was a primary motive, equally for Israel and for Britain and France. Sometimes, it is true, dominion is required not for the nation state, but for the ideology: it is spiritual, not national, dominion that is required. And sometimes it may be only temporary control, sufficient to make over the area to "democratic," "progressive," or "anticolonial" native forces, that is desired. But military conquest may be necessary for this purpose.

Second, it is particularly when strategic interests are involved that this desire for physical control has proved overwhelming. This is especially true of the strategic interests of the larger powers. For perhaps the most striking conclusion from this survey is that the strategic motivation has manifested itself primarily in one form: the demand of very large powers for security in smaller, immediately neighboring or otherwise strategically important, areas. In four out of the five post-1945 cases listed, this factor can be accounted an important, perhaps the essential, factor in inducing aggressive action by one or another of the powers involved. Even in the attack on Goa it may have been a contributory, though not the principal, motivation. In Korea, Guatemala, Suez, and Hungary it was a vital one (in the Korean case it is possible that Chinese apprehensions contributed not only to China's own participation but to the original outbreak as well). Similar motives have played a large part in other cases not classified here under "aggression," such as the actions concerning Cuba, Laos, Indo-China, Algeria, and elsewhere. It would seem that one could postulate here something like a general law: the danger of aggressive action arises most often in the contemporary world in situations where nations, especially large nations, feel anxiety concerning immediately neighboring areas believed essential to their security.

Finally, it is necessary to recognize that assaults of this kind may still assure tangible and undeniable benefits to those who undertake them. The belief that the fruits of war are a great illusion is difficult to substantiate, especially in the case of smaller engagements. The invaders of Guatemala secured a victory in that country for their own side and security for the outside power involved, as the Soviet troops in Hungary did for theirs. In Korea, China won increased security, though the other parties settled for a draw. India assured to herself permanently the booty she acquired in Goa. Only after the attack on Egypt was the vacating of aggressively acquired territory successfully secured. Thus there are still sometimes advantages to be gained, even by the more flagrant assaults, if the physical benefits are felt to outweigh the moral costs.

Legal Restraints on External War

What have been the methods applied by the international community in meeting this type of activity?

Efforts to create acknowledged principles of interaction among nations have so far principally taken the form of attempts to establish a code of law, comparable in scope and effect to that applied within states.[8] Most important in this attempt has been the effort to define certain actions between states as acts of "aggression," contrary to the terms of that code, and so to be outlawed from the practice of states.

Clearly, if a system of law could have been evolved under which every *initiation* of armed force by one state against another could have been defined, if those acts had been proscribed, and if that proscription had been effectively observed, the basis of a system of order between states would have been achieved. Unfortunately, under the system of international law practiced until today, none of these three conditions has been fulfilled. No widely accepted system has proscribed every initiation of armed force. No definitions of "aggression" have been generally accepted either among international lawyers or among states. And at no time have even the agreed provisions of the law been widely respected by states themselves.

Important exceptions to the principle that every initiation of armed force represents aggression have been acknowledged from the earliest beginnings of international law.

The first class of exceptions concerns acts of war designed to prevent other acts. Grotius, the main founder of that system in modern Europe, included among the defenses of "just wars" "an injury not yet inflicted which menaces either person or property"[9] or action by states "to forestall an act of violence which is not immediate, but which is seen to be threatening from a distance."[10] Vattel declared that the natural right to security enjoyed by nations included the right to "use force where necessary," not only for immediate defense but to "anticipate the other's design" or "to prevent a recurrence of . . . attacks."[11] This right of "anticipatory self-defense" has been

---

[8] A general description of this system's growth will be found in Chapter Eight.
[9] Grotius, *De Jure Belli ac Pacis*, Book II, Chapter I, ii.
[10] *Ibid.*, II, 1, xvi.
[11] Vattel, *Le Droit des Gens*, Book II, Chapter IV.

maintained by nearly all international lawyers from that time to the present. The Permanent Advisory Committee on the definition of aggression, set up by the League of Nations, listed among acts which, being potentially aggressive, might justify a military response "industrial and military mobilization, or even the attitude of the press of the potential aggressor." The plea of "self-preservation," permitting the use of force in case of imminent danger from another state, first laid down as justification for the use of force in 1837, is upheld by most international lawyers still today. It was implicitly reaffirmed by the Nuremberg Tribunal in 1946: that tribunal defined crimes against peace to include the "planning" and "preparation" of war, equally with its "initiation or waging," so presumably justifying action to counter that crime. And the most recent edition of the best-known authority on international law in the English language declares that "it is of the essence of self-defence that recourse to it must, in the first instance, be left to the unfettered judgment of the party which deems itself to be in danger." [12]

Second, writers on international law have accepted that that law, whether conceived of as a law of nature or as a positive law dependent on explicit acceptance by nations, did not exclude the right of nations to resort to war to preserve their "rights" or interests. Grotius accepted among the just causes of war "wrongs not yet committed or wrongs already done," [13] "reparation for injury," [13] the need to secure guarantee "against a threatened wrong or security against an anticipated injury," [14] the need for "recovery of property," [14] and the "right to exact punishment." [15] Vattel upheld the right of nations to use force where necessary "for the preservation of their rights" [16] or for "the maintenance of the balance of power." [16] This exception too has been sustained by most writers on international law, as well as by governments themselves, to the present day. Oppenheim's *International Law*, perhaps the most authoritative English-language textbook, lists seven cases in which forcible intervention is legal and by right, including intervention where another state violates provisions of the law of nations recognized by custom or laid down in treaties, intervention where the form of government is guaranteed by treaty, and

[12] Oppenheim, *International Law* (8th ed.; London, 1955), II, 187.
[13] Grotius, *De Jure Belli ac Pacis*, II, 1, iii.
[14] *Ibid.*, II, 1, ii.
[15] *Ibid.*, II, 1, xvi.
[16] Vattel, *op. cit.*, III, Chapter I.

action taken to protect the nation's citizens abroad.[17] In addition, there are interventions not by right but nonetheless in the interests of the balance of power.[18] Many nations, in undertaking in the Pact of Paris the renunciation of war, or accepting an obligation to compulsory arbitration, have made explicit exceptions of actions initiated to protect "vital" or "essential" national interests. In most cases they reserved the right themselves to determine which such cases were. Once again, therefore, the interpretation of the law's scope depended largely on private judgments.

A third form of intervention excepted by international law from the general prohibition of the initiation of armed force was that which took the form of a "reprisal" "for the purpose of compelling [a state] to consent to a satisfactory settlement of a difference created by its own international delinquency." [19] This justification could be claimed, for example, when action was taken for the protection of property or to exact legal or financial redress. Exemption was also claimed for action in hot pursuit of the vessel of another state on the high seas pursuant to an offense, though this has been circumscribed by a judgment of the International Court of Justice. But once again Oppenheim's *International Law* declares that, despite this judgment, "the admissibility of intervention in clearly specified cases, and in a manner not inconsistent with the Charter of the United Nations, must still be regarded as a rule of international law." [20] Finally, there have been other traditional exceptions justifying the use of force such as that of "humanitarian intervention" to "punish injustice or those guilty of crimes," chronic disorder in a neighboring state, to enforce the provisions of a peace treaty, and others.[21]

In the modern world, besides these older forms of justification, new exceptions which might make legitimate the use of armed force have been claimed, by states if not by lawyers. The ancient right of a state to intervene to protect its own subjects has been revived (as in Suez and the Dominican Republic). The right to "liberate" certain areas held to be under tyrannical or unrepresentative governments has been claimed (as in Goa, Hungary, and other cases). Certain acts, even those commonly engaged in by states, such as subversion,

---

[17] Oppenheim, *International Law* (London, 1955), I, 306–310.
[18] *Ibid.*, I, 310–312.
[19] *Ibid.*, I, 136.
[20] Oppenheim, *op. cit.*, I, 311.
[21] *Ibid.*, 313.

espionage, propaganda, and others, have been classed as "indirect aggression," giving the right to a forcible response (as in the Middle East). Proposals for "preventive war," comparable to the old justification of anticipatory self-defense, have occasionally been aired. Certain types of war, such as "wars of liberation" or "anticolonial wars" have been declared in some countries to be "just wars," and so again exceptions to the general prohibition of aggression.

The possibility that war might be, even theoretically, proscribed through the prohibition of all forms of "aggression" has thus been excluded. Justifications have existed which could always be called on if necessary where armed action was required. Sometimes such rationalizations have been explicitly used for that purpose. When, for example, Germany invaded neutralized Luxembourg on August 1, 1914, even before general war in West Europe, she declared this act was justified by the acknowledged right of "self-preservation," which the preparatory moves of France gave her title to. When Japan manufactured an incident in Manchuria and proceeded to invade the whole of that region, she claimed this to be based on the recognized right of "self-defense" against China. Even the most direct and blatant onslaughts of Hitler's Germany were defended at the Nuremberg Trial on the grounds of the established legal doctrines of "anticipatory self-defense" and "self-preservation."

The second condition for creating a peaceful international order through the proscription of aggression has also not been met. Attempts to arrive at more exact definitions of the word "aggression" have failed. Such attempts were begun under the auspices of the League and renewed at intervals during the interwar period. They have been continued almost without a break since World War II. But they have failed to find an agreed definition.[22] Certain exceptions to the general prohibition of initiations of armed force have continued to be claimed. Proposed definitions of the "rights and duties of states" have not been accepted by most states. Legal disputes have continued on the meaning of "intervention" and other vital terms.

Such a situation was indeed inevitable. For the main purpose of the term "aggression" has never been its descriptive value. It was its pejorative flavor. Nations, like individuals, have no difficulty in uniting in abstract opposition to sin. All were ready to express, with

---

[22] For an account of these discussions, see *Everyman's United Nations* (New York, 1964), pp. 433 ff. For an analysis, see Ian Brownlie, *International Law and the Use of Force* (London, 1963).

the utmost vigor and conviction, their denunciation of the general iniquity "aggression." Difficulty only arose when it became necessary to decide which particular deeds were sinful. Though it is easy to see that the assaults of one's enemies are wrongful, and thus "aggressive," it is usually equally clear that the warlike activity engaged in by one's own nation, or even by its friends, can never come within this category.

As a result, the third condition of order on this basis, effective obedience to the rules devised, could also not be met. When the need for the use of force arose, suitable justifications, within or without the legally recognized exceptions, could always be found. If warlike action must be taken at all, this was for "self-defense" or other legally recognized purposes; or "to restore law and order," "to protect minorities," "to insure international justice," "to resist aggression, or intended aggression," "to liberate an oppressed people," or any other generally applauded motive. Even in earlier times wars had usually been fought for commendable objectives. Few, in resorting to force, had declared their object to "commit aggression." And since there existed neither policeman to apprehend, jury to convict, nor judge to pronounce sentence, it was easy to be confident that such self-justification would not be overruled.

During the twentieth century, it began to be necessary to find slightly more persuasive justifications for the resort to force. But this in itself presented little difficulty. An "incident" could be manufactured (as when Japan annexed Manchuria in 1931 and attacked China in 1937). A frontier dispute could be adduced (as when Italy attacked Abyssinia in 1935). The support of the local population could be claimed (as when Germany invaded Austria in 1938). Some minority could be found in need of protection (as when Germany invaded Czechoslovakia and Poland in 1939). The need to protect the nation's interests against hostile demonstrations could be asserted (as when Italy annexed Albania). Since, in any case, no government felt ready to enforce the law, many governments and peoples found such casuistries convenient pretexts for inactivity. New doctrines of "nonrecognition" (as applied in Manchuria) or of "nonintervention" (as used in the Spanish Civil War) provided the ideological justification for following — in the most literal sense — the line of least resistance. And it was only when essential national interests coincided with the principle proclaimed, that two among the nations of Europe were ready to intervene to resist the transgression they had so virtuously denounced.

After World War II "aggression" became more than ever the object of universal opprobrium, and more than ever, therefore, attributed only to antagonists. Though aggression in its crudest forms had become less attractive to governments, when vital interests caused such a course to be adopted nonetheless, the capacity to find justifications was little less than before. When North Korea attacked her southern neighbor, she felt it sufficient to resort to the schoolboy plea, "He started it," asserting that she was merely retaliating against an attack launched from the other side of the frontier; a contention which, even if it could have served to excuse retaliation, could not convincingly justify an attempt at total conquest. When armed invasion of Guatemala was carried out from the territory of neighboring states, it was claimed the whole affair was nothing but a civil war which did not warrant collective counteraction. When the Soviet Government employed its troops to suppress a national uprising in Hungary, it first declared it was acting at the request of the Hungarian prime minister; and when this prime minister himself demanded withdrawal, claimed that his government had been displaced by another requesting assistance; finally, protested that war was for the protection of the Hungarian state against reactionary counterrevolutionaries. When Britain and France dispatched troops and aircraft against Egypt in October, 1956, this was said to be to put a stop to fighting between Egypt and Israel; or, alternatively, to protect an international waterway; or to secure respect for international obligations; or to save the Middle East from communism; or to rescue Egypt from dictatorship. When India invaded Goa, it was because law and order within that territory had broken down; because she herself had been attacked; or because efforts at negotiation had been exhausted.

Even within the traditional law plentiful pretexts could still be discovered. When Britain and France attacked Egypt in 1956, Britain's highest legal authority explicitly declared that such action was justified under the established doctrine of intervention to protect national citizens, as well as by the more general right to preserve vital interests. When the Belgian Government sent troops to the Belgian Congo in 1960, it justified its action by referring to the legal right of "intervention" to protect its nationals. Finally, when the United States Government declared its intention to search Soviet ships and blockade Cuban ports in 1962, it claimed these actions could be justified on the basis of the right of "peaceful blockade" acknowledged in international law textbooks.

Thus legal doctrines of "aggression," neither universally agreed nor generally respected, have no more been able to prevent armed action in the modern world than in former times. Subjective assessments have always remained able to claim that specific situations fell within the categories where armed action was justifiable. Such a result was foreseeable so long as the main concern was with the determination of how far particular actions represented "aggression" — with the degrees, that is, of guilt or of justification — rather than with the more fundamental objective, the preservation, or the restoration, of the peace.

International Organizations and External Wars

What has been the contribution of international organizations in containing external wars?

At first sight a direct assault appears the easiest type of issue for an international organization to counter. At least the offense is unambiguous and the crisis immediate. Even the Concert of Europe was able to confront effectively a number of international wars while they were still in progress and determine a settlement. The war of independence of Naples against Austria was considered and settled at the Congresses of Troppau (1820) and Laibach (1821). The London Conference in 1827 considered the Greek war of independence while it still continued: the battle of Navarino, and the action of French troops in the Morea, might be regarded as the first cases of collective enforcement action by great powers to impose a settlement, as envisaged in the UN Charter. Mohammed Ali's attack on the Ottoman Empire's eastern provinces was debated at the London Conference in 1838, the Vienna Conference of the next year, and again in London in 1840. Once again joint action by the forces of great powers, though opposed by France, was put into effect and a settlement imposed by great powers not themselves immediately concerned. In 1849, after the Austro-Sardinian war, a general conference was demanded, but this was frustrated by Austria's refusal to attend. In 1850, after armed action by Denmark to settle the Schleswig-Holstein question, a conference of the powers was called to resolve the issue. In 1853, after the crisis over the Holy Places, and the Russian occupation of the Principalities, a great-power conference called at Vienna suggested terms for a settlement, though it did not succeed in securing peace. In 1860, disorder in Syria and the subsequent French intervention there led to a congress and the legitimation of the settlement by great-power agreement. In 1878 the Congress of Berlin resolved the war between Russia and Turkey of the previous two years, on terms dictated by powers other than those who had participated. And the powers intervened in a number of other conflicts, including Crete (1897), Morocco (1906), and the Balkan Wars (1912–13) in the period before World War I. But the system was not fully institutionalized: a number of outbreaks of conflict were not even considered, especially if they involved two of the great powers. The Concert made no attempt to consider the three Prussian wars, the Russo-Japanese war, or any of the colonial conflicts of the period. The meetings were designed to insure that the outcome of a particular outbreak was generally acceptable and would not damage the "balance of power," rather than to maintain international peace and security. But the system did often serve to bring a mutually acceptable resolution of these external conflicts. Sometimes it even managed to combine this with some element of peaceful change, as in the progressive dismantling of the Ottoman Empire.

The League, animated by a totally different principle, adopted totally different procedures. Here the assumption was that every "aggression" would be considered as soon as it was initiated. Discussion would be the means of halting the attack, rather than determining the settlement. In practice the procedure was not so dissimilar. Italian unofficial occupation of Fiume in 1919 was not reversed but settled by the Treaty of Rapallo a year and a half later. Italian official occupation of Corfu in 1919, though ultimately renounced, was in effect bought off by a demand by the League for Greek reparations for another incident. Polish seizure of Vilna in 1920 was ultimately rewarded by official League recognition. Lithuanian seizure of Memel from League authority in 1923 was equally accepted by the League without serious remonstrance. The Greek invasion of Bulgaria in 1925 was confronted more effectively with the dispatch of a League Commission of Inquiry, and the recommendation of another reparations payment by Greece. Both the Japanese invasion of Manchuria and the Italian invasion of Ethiopia were met in effect by diplomatic initiatives, comparable to those of the Concert, rather than any military confrontation. The main difference in the League's attempts over issues of this sort was that they were not only unsuccessful in securing reversal of the aggression in most cases, but, because some of the

major powers were not members of the League, and others brought
no effective pressure to bear, they less often produced effective
negotiation and compromise over the settlement than the procedures
initiated by the Concert of Europe.

Under the UN, the record has been variable. Certainly the major
acts of aggression have been fully discussed and denounced. For,
though powers with aggressive intentions can still find reasons to
justify their actions to themselves, such justifications rarely sound
equally convincing to others. Even the League condemned the actions
against Manchuria, Ethiopia, and Finland, though little effective assistance was provided for the victims. In three out of the five postwar cases outlined here — Korea, Egypt, and Hungary — overwhelming
majorities in the UN condemned, implicitly or explicitly, the action
of the attacking power. In two of these, action was taken by the
organization which was largely instrumental in assuring that the attack
was successfully repelled: forces were established, for fighting or for
patrolling, to restore the status quo. These episodes, in Korea and
Egypt, represent perhaps the two principal triumphs of the organization's history, the occasions on which it most unquestionably proved
its superiority to its predecessor.

Here the UN had little difficulty in identifying, condemning, and
even repelling illegitimate uses of force. This was not, however, the
case in Guatemala and Goa. Over Hungary, despite condemnation,
no effective action could be taken. Thus the procedures so far adopted
by the organization in situations of this kind have varied over the
widest possible spectrum, from total inactivity to the mobilization
of large-scale military counteraction (see Table III.3 on p. 82). This
variability, even in the most flagrant cases, clearly limits UN effectiveness.

There are a number of difficulties which an international organization
faces in seeking to meet a case of this type. First, where a substantial
measure of violence has already been called into play, it will not
be easy to mobilize countervailing forces of sufficient strength to
overcome it. In many cases the task is not to resist aggression but to
reverse it. Where the UN has successfully created "peace forces" to
meet a threat to international security, it was to deal with situations
in which little actual fighting was to be expected. When in the Congo
the Security Council passed a resolution calling on such troops to
resort to force if necessary, some of those contributing immediately
expressed reservations; one, as soon as its forces became involved in

an expensive engagement, immediately withdrew from the operation altogether, and the resolution finally proved impossible to put into practice effectively. In most situations which can only be restored by the exercise of considerable strength, states will be reluctant to contribute forces, unless (as in Korea) they consider that this is essential to their own national or ideological interests. It could indeed be argued that the Korean case is the *only* one in which an international action to resist aggression has taken place at any time. Even here, only sixteen member states participated, and the response was more in the nature of action by a defensive alliance to defend its interests than an effective application of the principles of collective security or international enforcement. Thus, it could be maintained, these two systems, the two methods of preserving peace most widely discussed and championed over the last fifty years, have each still to be put into practice.

Second, the fact that today military operations for direct aggression normally take the form of limited actions confined within the borders of a state makes the initiation of an international response far harder. Aggression may be denied or disguised. Attacks will be dressed up in some more respectable garb. They will be undertaken, like that on Guatemala, in the guise of civil conflict; like that on Egypt, to stamp out the flames of conflict; like that on Hungary, to restore law and order. Some forces may be sent in the form of "volunteers" (as in Korea and Malaysia). Revolutionaries of one state may be sent from the borders of another (as in Vietnam or Cuba). Action may be undertaken by special operations forces that do not form part of the regular armed forces (such as communist guerillas, the CIA, and corresponding organizations). There will rarely be an assault so flagrant that no alternative interpretation can be put upon it. In these circumstances the reaction of the UN will often be hesitant and divided. Rival resolutions may be hawked around, each making a different assessment of the rights and wrongs, each proposing some slightly different solution. And the organization will be inhibited from any effective action.

The third difficulty in dealing with such emergencies is that, in the existing state of ideological rivalry, many of the issues that are brought to the UN will be interpreted and handled only in relation to that rivalry. An attack which seems to favor one side or faction may be regarded by its adherents with indulgence (as a majority of the UN regarded the attacks on Guatemala and Goa) whereas any such action favorable to other parties will be resisted with the utmost tenacity (as the same states regarded those against Hungary and Egypt). There has not been sufficient impartiality to maintain clear-cut categories of behavior to be condemned or resisted. When the dispute is among the newly emerging states themselves, divided sympathies, between continents or groups, progressives or reactionaries, may prove equally inhibiting. Unless the rights and wrongs of the case are very clear, no clear consensus or action emerges.

Fourth, as a result, the UN has been unable to maintain the *consistency* in its judgments that is essential to their effectiveness. This influences responses on future occasions. If exceptions are sometimes made in favor of those politically congenial or influential or if certain cases of violence, as today, are not brought before that body at all (like Berlin, Laos, Vietnam, and others), transgressors will be tempted to believe, at

TABLE III · 3

Acts of Aggression: UN Counteraction, 1945–1965

War	UN action
North Korea–South Korea	Dispatch of UN enforcement forces to defend South Korea
Nicaragua, etc.–Guatemala	None
Israel, Britain, France–Egypt	Resolutions. Dispatch of UN peace force to Sinai
Soviet Union–Hungary	Resolutions. Establishment of commission of inquiry
India–Goa	None

moments of crisis, that they may be able to escape condemnation or to persuade opinion in their favor. For the same reason members confronting a new crisis are tempted to repeat previous inactivity. It is unlikely that international bodies will be able to exercise influence on the actions of governments, comparable to that exercised by social pressures on individuals, until governments and their publics are as accurately aware in advance of the reactions their actions will evoke elsewhere.

Finally, as long as attention is mainly directed to attributing responsibility rather than to seeking methods of restoration, international responses will continue to be paralyzed by the difficulty of knowing exactly where responsibility lies. Overwhelming majorities in favor of UN action in Korea were made easier because, at the moment the hostilities began there, a UN commission was operating near the threatened border and was therefore able to provide a widely accepted verdict on the circumstances. But in many cases when the circumstances are confused or disputed, it has proved difficult to be certain which of two sides is more responsible (as in incidents between Cambodia and South Vietnam, Israel and Egypt, or India and China). Conflicting accounts may inspire conflicting votes which, in the absence of evidence, may be conditioned rather by ideological or other loyalties than by the facts themselves. Not only international organizations but international opinion is uncertain and immobilized. And all effective international responses are made impossible.

What international organizations can do in cases of this kind is to bring the influence of those powers not directly involved to bear. These will usually have a sufficient common interest in stability, especially if the superpowers are not involved, to be able to reach some kind of common position (as over the India–Pakistan war in 1965). Almost unanimous calls for a cease-fire were passed over Indonesia (1948), the first Arab–Israeli war (1949), Suez (1956) and the India–Pakistan war (1965), and each was succeeded quickly by a truce. If the superpowers can reach agreement, pressure of this kind is especially likely to be successful. A kind of multilateral diplomacy takes place which, sometimes at least, may arrive at a settlement acceptable to all. Since 1945, the crises over Berlin (1948), Korea (1951), Suez (1956), Lebanon and Jordan (1958), and several others were resolved partly through negotiation in the UN. In a number of cases, mediators or special representatives of the Secretary-General have played a significant part both in bringing the position of two sides nearer to each other, and in providing more objective information on the facts to UN members (as over the Muscat–Saudi Arabia dispute, Cambodia–Thailand, and Cyprus). The relative success of these various procedures is analyzed in Appendix IV.

Conclusions

What conclusions may be reached from this survey?

Over the last century external wars appear to be a declining proportion of all wars; to be declining also in absolute numbers; and perhaps to be on a somewhat declining scale (at least in the last twenty years). They are less often now for purely territorial purposes, and since 1945 are often associated with the strategic preoccupations of great powers or with attempts at national reunification. Yet they remain an important class of the conflicts that arise and include a few of the most serious of all. Until now, purely legal restraints, though often quoted, seem to have had little influence on the outbreak of such conflicts, though they are perhaps a more serious consideration in the motives of governments than in any earlier time. International organizations too, though also certainly a significant influence, have not been able to exercise much restraint on those which have occurred.

This suggests that, if, as just noted, armed action today is often justified on the basis of some special exception to the general rule against force, a peaceful order could exist only if *all* such exceptions were abandoned. The exceptions traditionally sustained by international law, and the new exceptions sometimes allowed today, must inevitably destroy the basis of any effective order, for they remain as legalizations to be called into use whenever required. If international bodies themselves sometimes accept justifications of first use of force — because of political sympathies (as over Goa), or ideological partiality (as over Guatemala), because the conflicts are on a small scale (Hyderabad), or complex (Malaysia), or remote (Ruanda),[23] or impossible to deal with (the Sino-Indian border) — the effect of any rule is destroyed. The UN Charter itself, under some interpretations at least, prohibits all first uses of force. Possibly the very generality and baldness of this prohibition "of the use or threat of force" serves to reduce its influence. A more explicit categorization of prohibited actions, as has sometimes been proposed, might help to exclude ambiguities. Whatever the difficulties in formulating in legal terms explicit and comprehensive definitions of aggression, it should not be difficult to outlaw in practice every *first* use of force by the forces, regular or irregular, of one state against the territory of another.

This principle alone, however, would not outlaw the resort to force in certain situations: where there were differences over legitimate sovereignty (since two states might here claim a legitimate use of force in the same area). It is no coincidence that, as we have seen, over the last fifty years conflict has occurred mainly where there were, or it was possible to claim, ambiguities or uncertainties over sovereignty or national rights in particular areas: in Manchuria, the Rhineland, and Danzig between the wars; in Korea, Berlin, Formosa, and the Suez and Panama Canals since. Such doubts about sovereignty not only lead to conflicts of expectations among protagonists but in international bodies and international opinion as well. Second, therefore,

---

[23] Hyderabad, Malaysia, and Ruanda are all considered in the next chapter under new frontiers, but the principle involved here is the same.

to reduce the risk arising from such divergent expectations, more accurate definition of sovereignty and rights in time of peace is often required. If left until conflict has already broken out, it is usually too late.

Means of achieving this in purely territorial disputes are discussed below (Chapter Five, pp. 113–116). But similar differences occur over other aspects of coexistence between states. Over rights of communication (access to Berlin or in the Suez Canal), over the conditions of foreign investment (the nationalization of the Anglo-Iranian Oil Company and other assets), over the economic rights of acknowledged governments (blockades and embargoes imposed against the Soviet Union, China, Cuba, and others), over the use of water resources (disputes on the waters of the Indus and the Jordan), and on many other matters, differences concerning legitimate rights may provoke bitter conflicts. Sometimes such "rights" are felt to involve national honor. Any concession will then be regarded on both sides as a sign of weakness or disgrace (as in the Berlin Corridor or the nationalization of the Suez Canal). The establishment of generalized rights and duties in times of peace will not only act as a guide to outside opinion at times of tensions, but will inhibit the freedom of action of disputants themselves.

Sometimes in such situations all that is required (as over the Berlin Corridor) is an accurately defined *modus vivendi*. This may serve as a regulator of expectations on both sides, as a guide to outside opinion in judging rights and wrongs in case of violation, and above all as a definition of the situation to be restored once it is disturbed. In other cases (rights of nationalization or legitimate trading rights) generalized principles governing such rights may be formulated. These again serve to influence prevailing assumptions of respective "rights" in all comparable situations. More accurate definition serves to reduce differences concerning what is to be expected, and is therefore acceptable, in particular situations among the parties themselves. It may lessen the temptation to exploit ambiguous situations precisely because they are ambiguous. Above all, by establishing the existing situation unmistakably for outside opinion, it increases the political cost of attempts to change it. In some cases general international opinion can be among the most important deterrents to warlike action. Because foreign as well as home opinion is prized, the gains to be acquired by direct aggression may often seem not worth the cost incurred in international good will. Even over the limited assaults of

the present age (Suez, Hungary, the Bay of Pigs), opinion can sometimes exert a significant effect, at least on future actions. It is already
a significant deterrent, or influence, against blatant violations of frontiers.

But opinion cannot exert influence if it is not clear whether the
acts involved represent a transgression. Where it is uncertain whether
particular kinds of action — support for native forces from outside the
frontiers, the engineering of coups d'état, the training or dispatch of
volunteers or special forces — are permissible or otherwise, its effect is
neutralized.

Thus the third, and perhaps most fundamental principle which
the present state of international relations seems to require is that
international organs, when such international breaches of the peace
occur, should seek first, not to assess relative guilt for acts of aggression, but to *preserve* or *restore* the previously existing status quo.
This is not, as sometimes suggested, to deny the possibility of change
within the international order, but to deny the legitimacy of attempts to bring about changes through armed force. The UN unfortunately has never consistently applied such a principle. It was adopted
to some effect in the assault on Egypt: all the powers involved were
then required to yield up what they had acquired before any further
steps were taken. But in other cases the UN has itself flouted it.
By determining to use its apparently commanding position in Korea
to bring about the forcible unification of the country, it transformed
a war to resist aggression into an attempt at annexation. In other
cases where territory has been acquired by force — in Palestine, Kashmir
(when first acquired), Guatemala, and elsewhere — little attempt has
been made by the organization to insure that conquest was reversed.
And each time might is permitted to become the arbiter of right, it
is made more attractive as an object of policy.

This involves the abandonment of the primitive and meaningless
concept of "aggression." International opinion remains at present bemused by that catchword. Although it demands that international
councils should take effective counteraction against the offense, it remains wholly uncertain when it has occurred. The ambiguity of many
situations, and the small descriptive content of the word, rob it of
effectiveness.[24] The result is that, though the Charter does not confine

---

[24] The use of such concepts as "indirect aggression" to cover ambiguous activities is
not helpful in meeting this problem. These extend rather than define the meaning. Because "aggression" is universally acknowledged as a vice, it constitutes a

international counteraction to acts of "aggression" (Chapter VII can be invoked for "threats to the peace"), nor even demand it be taken only against the wrongdoer, in practice the response of international bodies and the sanction of opinion are powerful only where it can be shown there has been an act of "aggression."[25]

This suggests that what international action needs is not a better definition of aggression, but the total abandonment of that concept: replacement of the empty tautology that wrongdoing is evil by concentration on the principles that should be observed in remedying the situation. Action designed to contain "aggression" involves an act of judgment directed to the apportionment of guilt. This, in the existing state of ideological and racial strife, international authority will usually find impossible to achieve (the UN will not often possess the ideological homogeneity it possessed at the time of Korea). Where judgments are divided, all may declare themselves justified. On the other hand, if international action and resolutions were directed not to the assigning of responsibility but to the restoration of the situation disturbed, that action would be more readily predictable in advance. There is less scope here for subjective judgment. If governments tempted toward aggression knew, through consistent UN principle and practice, that the organization would compel them ultimately to relinquish any territory or advantages they had acquired by force, they might regard the enterprise as less worth undertaking.

Thus international bodies would need to ensure that, *irrespective of where guilt lies*, neither party should be enabled to acquire an ad-

---

valid occasion for recourse to a forcible rejoinder. And since many of the activities comprehended by the new term — espionage, propaganda, sedition, and support for revolution — have been engaged in by almost every power on earth at one time or another, its general adoption could provide a ready-made excuse for armed attack by any nation which chose to issue a vague accusation of "indirect aggression" against another.

25 This difficulty affects national as well as international responses. Defense pacts, just as much as the constitutions of international bodies, are normally directed against "aggression": those types of assault which are most unlikely to take place in naked form, but most difficult to identify in any other. In such cases a pact can only function effectively when there is general agreement that a particular action does constitute "aggression." This may not always be easy to achieve in ambiguous cases (as was demonstrated by differences among the members of SEATO concerning their obligation to respond to events in Laos in the autumn of 1960; similar differences might arise in NATO in the case of confused incidents on the border of East and West Germany, or unilateral action by the East German authorities in Berlin). Military pacts as much as international authority, therefore, and a collective security system as a whole, may be made ineffectual by the use of such subjective terms.

vantage over the other at the conclusion of proceedings. All would combine to underwrite the status quo. This would sometimes need to include the political status quo; otherwise assaults for political ends may still be attractive. If such a principle were agreed and consistently enforced, armed interventions would be deterred more effectively than by any other means. And the age-old justification, "He started it," would be robbed of all relevance or force.

Where hostilities have already broken out, a universal consensus that the previously existing situation should be exactly restored becomes even more important. Only this could remove the main motivation to carry the struggle through to a successful conclusion. Only this provides a politically neutral basis for a settlement. It is in crisis situations, where there is a danger of move and countermove building up to the point of large-scale war, that the existence of an accepted convention in favor of restoration may be most important. It is these (as over Cuba in 1962) that perhaps present the greatest danger of large-scale war today (in Cuba this principle was in fact applied effectively). Here even rational decisions may sometimes produce shows of strength on either side, each one provoking a new response from the other. Escalation becomes continuous. The effect of this principle is to strengthen crisis management. Apprehensions and suspicions would be reduced, move and countermove restrained, by enhancing the probability that the status quo would be restored. It provides an immediately available compromise solution representing little loss of face to either side. If the principle of restoration were firmly established by international bodies, and powerfully reiterated at time of crisis (as was done during the India-Pakistan war of 1965), the continuation of competitive build-ups might seem less worth while. Change would remain possible·but only by peaceful means.

Certain conclusions for national policy, too, follow from the facts of contemporary conflicts that have been noted. If, as we have seen, a very large proportion of cases of direct aggression today occur as a result of the anxieties of great powers concerning the areas in their immediate neighborhood, there would clearly be advantage in restraint by other great powers in stationing troops or offensive weapons in such areas. Much as a Monroe Doctrine banning the stationing of missiles or bombers in Cuba may be useful, so could similar doctrines banning them in the China Seas or on the borders of the Soviet Union. International organizations could establish accepted conventions to encourage this. In the areas that lie on the borders of two spheres of influence, such as Southeast Asia between China and the United States, the Middle East between the United States and the Soviet Union, Yemen between Egypt and Saudi Arabia, there may be value in attempts at full-scale neutralization, whether in formal agreements (as in Laos and Austria) or in tacit conventions (as in Finland and Afghanistan). What powers are often most concerned about in such circumstances is not that they should hold these areas, but that they should not be held by their opponents.

International principles would be insufficient without international *procedures* to supplement them. The main procedures which international organizations may bring into play in situations of this kind are *discussion*, to bring international pressures to bear in any situation as early as possible; *communication*, to keep disputants in close touch with each other both in open UN meetings and through private contacts; *conciliation*, by which compromise proposals may be made available from an uncommitted party, whether a special commission, an officially appointed mediator, or the Secretary General and his staff; *verification* by an appropriate body or individual, to establish the facts on the spot, whether of violations of a border, the degree of foreign involvement and other disputed points; *inquiry* on wider issues, the general background of a dispute, with recommendations for its resolution; *stabilization* of the situation on the spot, by the dispatch of observers or a peace force; or, finally, *adjudication* by a legal body, whether ad hoc arbitrators or the International Court of Justice for disputes of a primarily legal character. These various procedures are described and analyzed at greater length in Appendix II. By a judicious choice among them with careful regard for suitability, and empirical study of their effectiveness in a particular situation, international bodies may be able to bring a more effective influence to bear on situations of tension.

Eventually an additional procedure, directed at the settlement of the issues underlying certain disputes, might be needed. For though international order depends on the proscription of forcible change, it may be attainable only if change by other processes remains available. A totally rigid order will be as precarious between states as within them. Here it is necessary to distinguish between the political status quo and the territorial status quo. Although there will always be anti-status quo forces within the international, as within a national, community, the adjustments these demand will not always be territorial. Often today, the anti-status quo forces within the international com-

TABLE III · 4

Aggression: Available International Principles and Procedures

Principles	Procedures (in time-sequence)
Existing justifications of first use of force abandoned.	*Discussion* (in UN to bring international opinion to bear)
	Communication (with and between parties)
	Conciliation (by Secretary General, mediator, or ad hoc committee)
Status quo, territorial and political, formally defined in time of peace.	*Verification* (to determine disputed facts on the spot)
	Inquiry (to determine general background)
Restoration of status quo in time of conflict.	*Stabilization* (through UN presence, observers, or peace force)
	Adjudication (of legal questions by ICJ or arbitrator)

munity demand change in the sense of new social structures, new methods of economic development, new distributions of power within international organizations, new distribution of control over the world's wealth, or new distribution of status, rather than territorial change, as demanded by comparable powers thirty years ago. In these circumstances, the necessity for "peaceful change" does not automatically require territorial change any more than stability of territorial borders need presuppose rigidity in political, economic, or other conditions.

But a peaceful order sometimes requires adjustments of other sorts. Where other elements of the status quo are challenged — the rights of minorities, rights over communications facilities, the use of water resources and other matters — political machinery for determining the disputed issues may be the condition of restraining attempts to do so by armed force. This machinery may take a variety of forms. Sometimes some procedure already considered — mediation, or adjudication by arbitrators, the International Court, or other legal bodies (as occurred under the League in minority disputes) — may be used to secure adjustments. In others ad hoc committees may be set up to make recommendations (as was attempted for Indonesia). In others determination by the Assembly itself would be more effective (as was done in Palestine, West Irian, and other matters). To determine questions of rights or sovereignty in particular areas, the UN may recommend, or even undertake, the organization of plebiscites or referenda (as occurred in Malaysia). Certainly unless international bodies seek more commonly some means of resolving disputes of this sort, they will not deter attempts to determine the issue by *force majeure*. The establishment of regular and recognized procedures can create alternative opportunities for securing desired objectives and establish new expectations concerning available recourses.

The basic object of such measures is to provide the foundation for that expected pattern of relationships which, as already seen, is the condition of peaceful order in any community. Acknowledged procedures of settlement and acknowledged principles of behavior, if sufficiently firmly established, serve gradually to mold prevailing expectations among governments and publics alike and so affect their disposition to conflict. Even where the order is temporarily overthrown, the form of its re-establishment may be accepted in advance. Attempts to overturn it by armed force would become less and less worth while; perhaps ultimately, even, less and less desired.

Bibliography

Aron, R., *Paix et Guerre entre les Nations*, Paris, 1962.

Bowett, D. W., *Self-Defence in International Law*, London, 1954.

Brownlie, I., *International Law and the Use of Force by States*, Manchester, 1958.

Buchan, A., *War in Modern Society*, London, 1966.

Hoffman, S., *The State of War*, London, 1965.

Howard, Michael (ed.), *The Theory and Practice of War*, London, 1965.

Stone, J., *Aggression and World Order*, London, 1958.

Tucker, R. W., *The Just War*, Baltimore, 1960.

Waltz, Kenneth, *Man, the State and War*, New York, 1959.

Wolfers, A., *Discord and Collaboration among States*, Baltimore, 1962.

Wright, Q. C., *A Study of War*, Chicago, 1964.

CHAPTER FOUR

Frontiers

Frontiers in International Relations

Even if major aggressions against the territory of other states were eliminated, disturbances of the international order might still arise in disputes over the frontiers between them.

The frontiers that divide states are among the most fundamental elements serving to regulate their relationships. For the frontier limits and defines the authority each wields.

The frontiers that perform this function vary widely. They have differed both from place to place and from age to age. They range from imaginary and indeterminate lines along a wild and unmarked border to unmistakable barbed-wire emplacements measuring every inch of the line; from clearly defined natural landmarks to lines that are wholly arbitrary in their situation; from those which may be crossed at will by the inhabitants on either side, and therefore exert little impact on their minds, to those which are traversable only with the utmost difficulty and the maximum formalities. Above all, they vary in the extent that they are conceived as permanent and unchanging national barriers or as temporary compromises that may quickly be overturned when circumstances are favorable. As a result, the form in which frontiers regulate the relations of states also varies widely.

The situation of frontiers has usually derived primarily from the hazards of history, conquest, or compromise. They do not necessarily reflect any clearly detectable divisions of race or language, religion or culture. And any cultural and other links that join the peoples bounded by them are normally the effect, rather than the cause, of their common nationhood. The international order in this sense has never been a rational order which could easily be explained or justified according to other principles. It has rested, in this as in other matters, largely on convention.

At various points in history there have been attempts to re-create nations on some more rational basis, particularly language or national consciousness. Greek and Roman rulers, though their own homelands became with foreign contacts increasingly polyglot and ill-defined, dealt with the various peoples and tribes they conquered abroad on the basis of their tribes or language, marked their maps in this sense, and often established proconsuls and ambassadors accordingly. Later, when the nation state emerged as the basic unit of international organization in Europe at the end of the Middle Ages, sovereignty began to rest increasingly on the chance limits of the power exerted by individual sovereigns. During the early nineteenth century, when the rule of absolute monarchs, speaking foreign languages, became increasingly unacceptable, there were new attempts to create nations on the basis of "nationality" or "culture." From the end of that century, and increasingly during the twentieth century, such principles even began to be put into practice in the process of nation-making. Both during World War I, and during the dissolution of the colonial empires thirty years later, the ideal of "self-determination" was invoked to speed the process of change. In the first case the principle became the basis for the actual foundation of new states. In the second, almost every state that emerged was conditioned not by race, language, culture, nor even by self-determination itself, but by the pre-existing frontier lines of the colonial system.

Nations cannot normally be made or remade at will. Even if they could have been, no wholly rational criterion for determining frontiers could have been found. For the various bases used, ethnic, religious, or linguistic, those of historical claim, economic viability, or geographical homogeneity, never coincide in such a way as to create unmistakably logical, or universally acceptable, national entities. Conflicts could arise according to the criterion used. Because particular criteria have become enshrined in popular psychology and ideology, each has served sometimes, and still serves, to stimulate, or to justify, claims for revision. France could challenge German occupation of Alsace-Lorraine on the basis of culture, whereas Germany could challenge that of the French on the basis of language. Claims could be based on ethnic grounds (like German claims on the Sudetenland in the interwar period); or on strategic grounds (French claims for a frontier on the Rhine); on natural geographical boundaries (Spanish claims to Gibraltar); or on self-determination (British claims to the same place). Thus, so long as a rational basis for the situation of frontiers is demanded, the number of challenges to their authority is as unlimited as the number of criteria available. Their essentially conventional character is more than ever obscured. And their role within the international community is transformed.

Challenges to existing boundaries will inevitably be especially stimulated in an international environment where frontiers are subject to frequent change. The effect of the international environment in this respect has varied widely at different periods of history. When, during the Roman empire, certain boundaries were well known and stable over a considerable period of time, such as the Rhine frontier, they could come to represent a relatively permanent influence on expectations. But when boundaries everywhere become subject to frequent alteration, as during the nineteenth and early twentieth centuries, all are encouraged to believe that they may, with sufficient skill or strength, secure revisions in their own favor. The successive manufacture at frequent intervals during the nineteenth century of totally new states, such as Greece, Serbia, Belgium, Romania, Bulgaria, Albania, and Norway at the whim of the powerful; the cumulative dismemberment of Poland, Austria, and Turkey; the making or unmaking within a few years of such indeterminate, "autonomous," half-sovereign entities as Moldavia, Wallachia, Rumelia, Montenegro, Crete, Tibet, Bosnia and Herzegovina — all these naturally encouraged the sense that frontiers were purely temporary arrangements that could quickly be adjusted in one's own favor when the right conditions prevailed. Each change of one frontier weakened all others. The revisionist claims of Germany and Hungary between the wars were directly encouraged by the example of the perpetual rewriting of frontiers over the previous seventy years. And they could be justified as merely the more efficient accomplishment of the ideals of national self-determination sanctified in the settlement of Versailles. Similarly, a great many of the "autonomous" or semi-sovereign areas were precisely those which later led to conflict: the Principalities, Rumelia, Crete, Tibet before World War I, Memel and Danzig afterward. The effect of frequent readjustments of boundaries and the ambiguities that result may thus be used to convert frontiers from a stabilizing to a destabilizing factor in international relations.

Over the last century, as administration has penetrated more deeply into remote areas, and as populations of diverse culture have become more firmly assimilated within existing political entities, the outlines of the atlas have become more clearly delimited. "Autonomous" areas, protectorates, spheres of influence, and other destabilizing fractions of sovereignty have been almost eliminated. The atlas is thus probably less subject to challenge than in most earlier periods. The periodic exchanges of large border areas, such as Alsace-Lorraine, Silesia, Bessarabia, Moldavia, and other areas, which have been common over the past century, are less likely to occur today in most parts of the world. Even now, however, a large number of frontiers remain, at least in their details, open to challenge (see p. 183). And in areas where new nations have come into being the artificial nature of the boundaries created sometimes provokes a challenge to their entire existence. A significant proportion of the warlike confrontations of the past twenty years have in fact concerned the situation of frontiers (see Chart VII.2 on pp. 183–185 below). And conflicts of this kind could still represent the *casus belli* of struggles on a far larger scale.

In some disputes of this type, there is no clearly demarcated boundary at all; and dissension centers on *where this line should lie.* More often there is already some de facto line; and the dispute concerns *whether or not this should be changed.*

A list of the frontier disputes since 1918 that have led to armed conflict, arranged by type, is contained in Table IV.1. This is worth analyzing in some detail. First, these cases may be compared with those disputes which have not led to conflict (see Table VII.2 on p. 183). Analysis of all claims of both kinds shows that disputes have been based on one, or several, or a number of grounds. Sometimes they have been based on the assertion that the area in question was occupied by the aggrieved state at some period more or less distant in the past (the Moroccan claim to Mauretania); sometimes that it had once been subject to the overlordship of the claimant power or of one of its constituent parts (the Indonesian claim to Sarawak); or that Western imperialism has robbed the claimant of its rightful property (the Guatemalan claim against British Honduras); or that traditional boundaries have become obscured or subverted by the intervening period of imperialism (the Chinese claim to parts of Kashmir and Northeast India); on the principle of self-determination (like the Afghan claim against Pakistan); on ethnic grounds (the Somali claim against Kenya); on cultural grounds (the Thai claim against Cambodia); on geographical grounds (the Spanish on Gibraltar); or on historical grounds (like the Arab against Israel).

TABLE IV · 1

Principal Frontier Conflicts: by Cause, 1918–1965[a]

Uncertainly defined or uncertainly demarcated frontier	Peru–Colombia, 1932 Saudi Arabia–Abu Dhabi, Muscat, 1952
	Cambodia–Thailand, 1953– China–Burma, 1956–60 Egypt–Sudan, 1958 India–Pakistan, 1965
Rival definitions	Paraguay–Bolivia, 1930 Afghanistan–Pakistan, 1950–62 China–India, 1954–62 Chile–Argentina, 1965 Somalia–Ethiopia, sporadic
New frontiers (on decolonization)	India–Pakistan (including Kashmir), 1947–49, 1965 India–Hyderabad, 1947 Arab States–Israel, 1948–49 Indonesia–Malaysia, 1963– Dahomey–Niger, 1963–64 Ruanda–Burundi, 1963–64
Demands for new frontiers (after decolonization) —	Lithuania–Poland, 1920 Eire–N. Ireland, 1921–60 Arab States–Israel, 1949–56, 1967 Iraq–Kuwait, 1962 Algeria–Morocco, 1962 Somalia–Kenya, 1963– Yemen–Aden, sporadic

[a] This list includes only cases in which some type of armed action has taken place. For a list of frontier *disputes* in recent years see Chart VII.2 on p. 183.

Whether those *claims* are converted into frontier *conflicts* seems to depend on a number of factors. It is likely to depend on the degree of passion which the claim arouses among the populations of the claimant state; the susceptibility of the government concerned toward such pressures; the support which the claimant anticipates from countries outside; the readiness of either party to attempt a settlement by armed force; and on the relationship between the power that is available to sustain a claim and that at hand to resist it. These may vary in quite different proportions. The Spanish claim on Gibraltar is not today a serious danger to peace because, though the first factor is perhaps positive, all the others are negative. The Guatemalan claim to British Honduras is not serious because only the first two factors are positive. The Moroccan claim to Mauretania though serious, is not immediately acute, because, though the first three factors are probably positive, the last two are the reverse. The Indonesian claim against Malaysia was more dangerous, because here the fourth as well as the first three factors were positive. But the claims that seem to be most likely to erupt in conflict are those in which, irrespective of the first three, the last two factors are simultaneously fulfilled. The Chinese claims on Hong Kong and Macao are not a serious danger at the moment because, although the last factor is positive, the fourth is not. The Chinese claims against India, on the other hand, have represented a grave threat to peace, because here, whether or not the first three factors were positive, the last two undoubtedly were.

Next, we may examine other differences between the cases in which frontier claims over the last fifty years have led to armed conflict and those in which they have not. First, it will be seen that it is above all on remote, bare, largely uninhabited frontiers — the tropical forests between Paraguay and Bolivia, the hill country between Pakistan and Afghanistan, the mountains of Ladakh and the northeast border of India, the rough grassland between Ethiopia and Somalia, the Sahara Desert between Algeria and Morocco, or the wild jungles between Indonesia and Malaysia — that armed clashes have mainly occurred. Second, conflict has been most likely where (as in all the cases mentioned above) there was no physical demarcation of the border. It has not broken out in serious form, despite intense emotional conflicts, where the border has been unmistakably established (as between Spain and Gibraltar, or on the east and western borders of Germany). Of the two categories of possible frontier differences mentioned earlier, therefore, conflict seems to result more often from the uncertainties concerning the border than from differences about its proper situation. At the same time, as one would expect, recent frontiers are more subject to challenge than old. New states (as in Afro-Asia) are more likely to challenge frontiers by force than are old states (as in Europe). And about half these cases result directly or indirectly from the process of decolonization.

Such engagements may also be analyzed according to the objectives of one or both sides. Where there is no defined or no demarcated boundary, the object is sometimes *pre-emptive*, that is, to stake out a claim for one's own nation and to prevent the other side from doing so. This was partly the object of action by Poland at Vilna, in the Bolivia–Paraguay war, on the Algerian-Moroccan border, and by China against India. Sometimes there may be a conventional line, acknowledged, for example, in all or most maps, with or without physical demarcation. Here armed action may be *demonstrative* in effect, that is designed to demonstrate a presence, and so a claim, in defiance of the conventional line. Of this kind have been activities by Irish nationalists against Northern Ireland, by Somalia against Ethiopia, or by Chile and Argentina in the Antarctic. Finally, where the frontier is both defined and clearly demarcated (though not accepted), military action may be *revisionist* in purpose, that is, it may be designed to revise an already established status quo. As we have seen, there have been very few examples of this, though deliberate infiltration of the Israel border or sporadic sorties from Guatemala to Honduras perhaps come somewhere between this category and the demonstrative.

In some cases such disputes arise over the particular *period* in the past to be regarded as validating claims. The Permanent Court's judgment on Norwegian claims in Greenland in 1931 traced the history back to the tenth century. The Bolivia–Paraguay war of 1932–34, was concerned with the situation of frontiers first laid down in the sixteenth century. The Iranian claim to Bahrein is based on a period of occupation in the seventeenth and eighteenth centuries. Chinese claims on the Indian borderlands were based on a period of acknowledged Chinese sovereignty over a century before. Moroccan claims to Mauretania are founded on a period of rule terminated almost as long ago. Difficulties of this sort are especially acute over the frontiers established during the period of imperialism. Since that period is discredited in many parts of the world, frontiers established then may be challenged on grounds of the unjust effects of imperialist conquest. A considerable number of recent frontier claims derive from this cause. In a few cases, however, claims have been based on the demand to *perpetuate* imperialist boundaries where these are challenged or changed. Indonesia's claims to West Irian were intended to maintain colonial boundaries, despite racial and geographic considerations, whereas her opposition to Malaysia was based on opposite grounds. Somalia wishes to overturn imperialist frontiers; Kenya and Ethiopia to maintain them.

Other cases are complicated by economic factors. The disputed area may be thought to contain valuable resources (as in the Paraguay–Bolivia case). Sometimes there exist nomadic peoples whose grazing areas fall on either side of a disputed line (the Somali frontier with Ethiopia, or the Sino-Indian border in the northeast). Sometimes peasants need to cross the border to cultivate or market (the Israel or the Hong Kong border).

Because national frontiers come to have a high symbolic and psychological importance for nations, especially those where nationalist sentiment is intense (and nations may vary over a wide scale in this respect), even small violations or demands arouse very intense passions. A clash of expectations arises here in its sharpest form, so that such situations are among those which most often serve as signals for war. Appropriate concepts and slogans, "territorial integrity," "inviolability of frontiers," or "violation of sovereignty," stimulate the necessary emotional overtones. Small and intrinsically insignificant incidents on a frontier are thus sufficient to mobilize the entire warmaking potential of either party, in a way that differences over far more vital interests — tariff policies, immigration, and investment — never will.

New Frontiers

International frictions may arise not only over existing frontiers, but over *new frontiers* resulting from the creation of new states.

Wars have long been common where newly established frontiers have come into existence. The series of conflicts that rapidly broke out between the new states which emerged in Latin America in the early nineteenth century, leading sometimes to large revisions or wholly new states; the perpetual conflicts in the Balkans after the emergence of new states there during the late nineteenth century, both among those states and between them and their former rulers, these are examples of the inflammatory effect of new frontiers. Many of the instabilities of the interwar period can be attributed to this cause. However carefully drawn the frontiers established at Versailles, they could never have satisfied all. Being so recent, they had none of the authority of history and were, therefore, especially subject to challenge. Hungary's resentments against her neighbors and her ultimate readiness to find alliance with Germany were a direct result of her territorial grievances. Germany herself could demonstrate that the newly created borders of Germany, the ambiguities of Danzig and the Saar, and the perpetual provocation of the Polish corridor were recent and artificial creations which could as easily be remade again.

In the postwar world, the dissolution of the previously existing order and the creation of innumerable new boundaries everywhere have made such disputes inevitably more serious than ever. Among the wars that have occurred in this time none aroused fiercer passions, or left more intense bitterness behind them, than those which have resulted from the creation of new states (Israel, Pakistan). However distasteful to its victims, imperialism often had the effect of concealing or suppressing the racial, religious, cultural, and other divisions it embraced. It succeeded sometimes in uniting disparate peoples in a common struggle for liberation. Emancipation from the bondage that united them and the growth of ethnic and cultural self-consciousness have sometimes exposed divisions that had been long overlaid. Examples of this are the disputes between Cambodia and Vietnam, between Mauretania and Morocco, between Algeria and her neighbors, and Guatemala and British Honduras. These are all the result of the establishment of new states which have given rise to conflicts that had previously been concealed or unpursued.

In some cases imperialism had created the frontiers and thereby the nations established within them. Often these were wholly artificial, bearing no relation to ethnic, cultural, or historical boundaries. The destruction of the imperial order has thus sometimes invited another type of challenge arising not from long-standing disputes reawakened but from attempts to establish national boundaries more closely related to ethnic or cultural factors than those the colonial powers had established. The frontier conflicts of Latin America were in part the effect of the fact that the lines established within the Spanish empire had no clear geographical, ethnic, or other basis. In Africa and elsewhere divisions between and within states have been manufactured because the new frontiers imperialism drew there were often based only on the comparative length of arm of the respective imperial powers (of this type are the disputes between Somalia and her neighbors, or between Indonesia and Malaysia). But once new nations have been established they begin to acquire a momentum of their own, however artificial their walls may appear. Innumerable vested interests in the status quo are created — among civil servants as well as politicians, soldiers as well as statesmen. New loyalties, political or economic, may arise to struggle with the already conflicting loyalties of tribe and race. Claims for revision to conform with purely ethnic boundaries thus encounter even more stubborn resistance than the attempt to sustain the existing polyglot societies.

In some cases new frontiers have been created by an act of partition. The two major conflicts that have erupted from the creation of new frontiers since 1945 — between India and Pakistan, and the Arab States and Israel — were both the effect of such solutions. In both cases, probably, no one would have wished for such a solution had another seemed attainable. In each, partition seemed perhaps the least of all the possible evils that might have been the outcome. Partition, however chosen, is always a form of compromise. It is a judgment, unlike Solomon's, designed to give some satisfaction to both parties. But, like Solomon's, it may still outrage one party — as were India and Southern Ireland. Whether it is an effective compromise, whether it is one that secures a smaller loss of life in the immediate future or a more stable basis for coexistence ultimately, only omniscience could determine. To many human problems there can be no perfect answers. To some there are no good answers at all. And it is possible that in certain situations partition may be the least bad.

But partition has nearly always left some dissatisfied. Clashes may occur (as in India) as a result of the mutual fears, suspicions, and incomprehensions between two communities already worked to a pitch of fervent nationalism. They may be the expression (as in Palestine) of a life and death struggle for *Lebensraum* between alien peoples, each believing themselves to have an incontestable historic claim. They may take the form of attacks undertaken (as in Ireland) as much for the expression of a sense of grievance as for any practical purpose that may be achieved. Even after the passage of time, the slightest conflict, arising over some small incident or insignificant patch of territory may be quickly enlarged into a national crusade.

A comparison of cases concerning new frontiers suggests that the basic motivations at work among the aggrieved parties are of various kinds. Sometimes, especially in the early stages, activity may be designed deliberately to bring about a reversal of the settlement reached (like Pakistani activity in Kashmir or Somali activity among neighboring states). Sometimes there is merely a desire to harass the opposing state with no clear political purpose (like the activities of the Southern Irish in Northern Ireland, or of Egyptian Fellaheen in Israel). Sometimes activity occurs only in consequence of specific incidents inflaming conflict (like intercommunal friction between India and Pakistan). Sometimes activity may be a response to agitation among refugees at home or minorities abroad rather than to purely national pressures (like Austrian action in the South Tyrol or West German initiatives concerning East Germany). Sometimes it may seem designed to sustain national sentiment at home as much as for purely external purposes (like the Indonesian confrontation of Malaysia). There may be particular territories (such as Kashmir) or other subjects of dispute (the disposition of waters in both Palestine and India) to preserve resentment. Minorities and refugees, on either side or both, may create new frictions. Even time will only marginally adjust such asymmetries between geography and history. And disputes over new frontiers may remain, like some in South America, a source of dissension for a century or more.

Another problem arises where *demands* for new frontiers are put forward within an existing state. Political boundaries can never exactly coincide with ethnic divisions. All over the world today there exist communities of ethnic, linguistic, or religious minorities. In some cases these groups demand some form of autonomy within the state. In some they seek complete independence from their existing rulers.

Demands by minorities for self-determination and autonomy will usually be met by governments with claims for national "unity" and strong central authority to overcome the dangers of a diffusion of power among small, weak units. Such rational assessments of administrative efficiency will, however, be irrelevant to the claims of minority groups, which are rooted in an emotional sense of solidarity and ethnic identity. Here again divergent expectations will stimulate armed conflict. And here again, opposing criteria sometimes lead to clashes of force of arms.

The main disputes of this kind since 1918 are shown in Table IV.2. Though apparently internal, these often have international repercussions. Sympathies are aroused among external powers, especially if ethnically related to the minority. These are expressed in more or less active form. The national revolutionary movements within the Austrian, Turkish, and other empires in the nineteenth century were examples of such movements which had international consequences. These were continued between the Wars by the Kurds and Tibetans, the Moslems of India, the Laotians and Cambodians of Indo-China. Many such situations have recurred in the years since 1945. These have varied in the demands put forward, the group which has sought to enforce them, and the responses met from the government to which the demands were directed.

Such a movement may call for total independence for the minority community (as among the Nagas of India). The demand may concern

TABLE IV · 2

Principal Minority Disputes, 1918–1966[a]

Dispute	International procedures
Interwar	
Germans–Poland	Committees of Three of League
Ukrainians–Poland	applying minorities provisions
	of Peace Treaties
Germans–Lithuania	None
Germans–Czechoslovakia	Committees of Three
Hungarians–Rumania	Committees of Three
Bulgarians–Greece	Committees of Three
Austrians–Italy	Committees of Three
Greeks–Turkey	Procedures laid down in Treaty of Lausanne (not effectively used)
Jews–Germany	None
Kurds–Turkey	None
Postwar	
Karens, Kachens, Shans–Burma	None
Kurds–Iraq, Iran, Turkey	None
Tibetans–China	Appeal to UN, UN discussion
Uzbeks–China	None
Chinese–Indonesia	None
Nagas–India	None
Mizos–India	None
Tamils–Ceylon	Bilateral negotiations
Somalis–Kenya	OAU consideration
Tutsis–Ruanda	Appeal by UN Secretary General
South Sudanese–Sudan	None
Buganda–Uganda	None
Austrians–Italy	Bilateral negotiations, UN discussion
Turks–Cyprus	UN peace forces, UN political representative, and UN conciliator

[a] There were also numerous cases of internal conflict between two or more races or tribes more evenly balanced in numbers: Nigeria, Guiana, Belgium, Canada, etc.

the area within which autonomy is to be enjoyed (as in the case of the German-speaking minority in Italy). The area affected may transcend existing national boundaries (as among the Kurds). Sometimes the claim is waged from outside rather than within the state in question (as with the Greek minority in Albania or the Albanian in Yugoslavia). Other demands have been for greater provincial independence (Indonesia in 1958); for greater rights for linguistic minorities (India and Ceylon); for entrenched rights for an ancient tribal dynasty and government (in Buganda); for religious as well as political rights (in the Sudan); for cultural independence (as among the French Canadians); or for a vaguely conceived "autonomy" arising from different interpretations of historical rights of sovereignty (as in Tibet).

No state can be immune from these claims. In many of the largest states of the world, the Soviet Union, China, India, the United States, and Brazil, a substantial proportion of the population consists of minorities in one sense or another. Ethnic differences may be accentuated by sharp distinctions of culture and religion. There is no clear or rational criterion for determining the issues. Feelings among the population concerned may vary widely, and there is no way of assessing average feelings toward greater independence. There are few nations of the world which would not disintegrate if all the demands for independence by national minorities, or their most vociferous protagonists, were everywhere accorded. In their extreme form such demands may continue to represent one of the most important sources of violence in the modern world. And only the development of widely recognized principles and procedures for their resolution may prevent international repercussions.

International Organizations and Frontier Conflicts

Some international procedures for dealing with frontier disputes were evolved long before World War I. For centuries such issues were occasionally resolved by a mutually agreed arbitration, often by a foreign sovereign. Under the Jay Treaty of 1794, Britain and the United States agreed to accept arbitration by mixed commissions of disputed sections of the Canadian-United States border. Subsequently there were a number of other treaties of arbitration of such disputes, usually by similar mixed commissions. In 1897, Britain and Venezuela agreed to the arbitration of the frontier between Venezuela and British Guiana by neutral arbitration, in this case by the United States. Frontier issues were also frequently resolved by international conference, since they inevitably formed the subject of the congresses and conferences called to consider major conflicts and disputes of the period. For example, the Congress of Berlin was able to make a number of territorial settlements, including some which in no way directly derived from the immediately preceding conflict.

Between the Wars, arbitration continued to be used sometimes to settle frontier disputes. Disputes between Colombia and Venezuela (1922), Chile and Peru (1925), Mexico and France (1933), and Guatemala and Honduras (1933) were settled by these means. In other cases judicial settlement by the International Court or similar body (Norway and Denmark, 1931; Finland and Sweden, 1920) took place.[1] Some were solved by the League Council but this mainly involved itself in cases arising directly out of World War I.

A table setting out the action taken by the UN in frontier conflicts (where armed action took place) is contained on p. 106. It will be seen that the action taken has varied widely from none at all over some to the dispatch of an emergency force to patrol the border between Israel and the Gaza Strip for the Arab–Israel dispute. In some cases mediators have been appointed (Kashmir and Palestine); and in later cases, a Secretary General's Special Representative (Muscat and Cambodia–Thailand). In some cases the matter has been dealt with by the UN; in others, by regional organizations (Morocco–Algeria, Somalia–Kenya, and Somalia–Ethiopia).

As can be seen from Table IV.3, the proportion of cases the UN has considered has been small. Even in those it has discussed, it has sought to avoid deciding on the merits of the claims. It discussed the claim by Morocco to Mauretania (before the latter had achieved independence) but was unable to reach any agreement on it. The Security Council considered an appeal by the Sudan over the massing of Egyptian troops in connection with a frontier dispute in 1958 but made no attempt to consider the substantive question of the claim. The claim by Cambodia about the alleged annexation of a small piece of Cambodian territory of Thailand was discussed; though eventually the governments themselves agreed to submit the dispute to the International Court, the Council itself never attempted a settlement. The General Assembly for long passed resolutions expressing the hope

---

[1] See below, p. 107.

Table IV · 3

International Action Over Frontier Conflicts, 1945–1965

Frontier conflict	*United Nations action*
Eire–North Ireland, 1945–60	None
India–Pakistan, 1947–49, 1965	Appointment of mediator. Many resolutions on Kashmir. Cease-fire resolution in 1965.
India–Hyderabad, 1947	Discussion but no action.
Arab States–Israel, 1948–49, 1949–56, 1967	Appointment of mediator (1949). Dispatch of UN emergency force to patrol frontiers (1956).
Afghanistan–Pakistan, 1950–62	None
Saudi Arabia–Abu Dhabi, Muscat, 1952	Appointment of Secretary General's personal representative to conciliate and report.
Cambodia–Thailand, 1953–	Appointment of Secretary General's personal representative to conciliate and report.
China–India, 1954–62	None, but attempts at mediation by five nonaligned Colombo powers.
China–Burma, 1956–60	None
Egypt–Sudan, 1958	Discussion but no action.
Indonesia–Netherland, 1961–62	Appointment of mediator by Secretary General.
Iraq–Kuwait, 1962	Discussion but no action.
Morocco–Algeria, 1962	None but mediation by OAU.
Indonesia–Malaysia, 1962–66	Confirmation of popular wishes in disputed area by UN commission.
Somalia–Kenya, 1963–	None but discussion by OAU.
Chile–Argentina, 1965	None but both powers ask for arbitration by British sovereign.
Somalia–Ethiopia, sporadic, esp. 1964	Appeal by Secretary General, discussion by OAU.
Yemen–Aden, sporadic	Discussion but no action.

that Indonesia and the Netherlands would negotiate on the question of West Irian; the Secretary General appointed a mediator, but there was no attempt to determine the rights and wrongs of the issue, and the Netherlands proposals for a plebiscite were not accepted.[2]

In the majority of cases frontier disputes have not even been brought to the attention of the UN. The disputes between Pakistan and Afghanistan, Yemen and the Aden Federation, Ethiopia and Somalia, Algeria and Morocco, and many others were not discussed, even on the grounds of threats to the peace when conflict arose. India never attempted to bring the Chinese encroachments on her borders before the UN. Most of these cases in fact represented "a dispute the continuation of which is likely to endanger the maintenance of international peace and security," and as such proper subjects for UN consideration under Chapter VI of the Charter. Some could properly be considered "threats to the peace," and so call for more drastic action under Chapter VII, or the recommendation of "terms of settlement" under Article 37. Most of the claims have no doubt never been considered merely because they have never been brought before the UN by the parties concerned. But, under the Charter, this need not have prevented their being raised by others.

The success of the responses which have been made has varied considerably. The most effective international action among those here listed is certainly some kind of *judicial settlement,* if this can be agreed upon. This proved successful in several cases between the Wars: Finland–Sweden (Aaland Island) 1920, Turkey–Iraq (Mosul) 1924, Norway–Denmark (Greenland) 1931. In the first of these cases adjudication was by the Permanent International Court and in the other two by the League Council, but in all the judgment was accepted. In the postwar period arbitration by the British queen (in practice British arbitrators appointed by her) was agreed on in the dispute between Argentina and Chile in 1964 and a settlement attained. Adjudication by the International Court took place unsuccessfully in the Cambodia–Thailand issue in 1962. But the Security Council never attempted final adjudications as the League Council had done.

Also quite successful in the postwar period was *mediation* by Special Representatives of the Secretary General. This occurred in the Muscat–Saudi Arabia and Cambodia–Thailand disputes. Though neither of these issues can be considered to have been totally solved, there has at least been no recurrence of fighting over them. Mediation by a third party took place on the dispute between Guatemala and

---

[2] The Venezuela claim against Guiana was inscribed on the agenda of the General Assembly in 1962 and was discussed in the Special Political Committee, but no action was taken.

British Honduras. United Nations *validation* of a settlement already reached through assessing popular wishes took place in Malaysia; and a UN referendum might be a useful procedure in other cases.

Finally a number of different kinds of *bilateral* procedure have been used. During the fifties and early sixties China entered into agreements with most of her neighbors, providing for delimitation, demarcation, and mutual acceptance of frontiers. Austria and Hungary entered into an agreement in 1964 for the joint demarcation of the frontier, and for a commission to examine claims of infringements. Britain and Venezuela entered into an agreement in 1966 by which each party agreed to accept the status quo while talks continued. The United States and Mexico, and West Germany and the Netherlands entered into agreements finally liquidating small frontier disputes which might otherwise have remained a source of grievance.

For pacifying a frontier where violence has already occurred, probably no procedure has been so effective as the UN emergency force on the border between Israel and Egypt. This was for a long time successful in ensuring almost total peace along borders that had been previously plagued by violence, and war broke out only when it left.

It is significant that a number of these cases have been considered by regional organizations. The Iraq–Kuwait dispute was considered by the Arab League, and the dispatching of an Arab force to Kuwait was an important factor in resolving the matter. In the Morocco–Algeria dispute, both the Arab League and the OAU attempted conciliation. Arab League efforts failed, but a cease-fire was arranged at a meeting with the King of Ethiopia and the President of Mali. The OAU set up a special arbitration commission with representatives of seven states to allocate responsibility for the outbreak of the fighting, study the frontier question, and propose a settlement. A demilitarized zone was established and delimited by the Ethiopian and Mali members of the commission. The commission continued to consider the matter for two years and, though no final settlement of the frontier was arrived at, was sufficiently successful in its conciliation to bring about a marked improvement in relations between the two countries. The dispute between Somalia and Ethiopia was discussed at a meeting of the OAU in February 1964, which demanded an immediate cease-fire and set up a commission to consider both this dispute and that between Somalia and Kenya. The dispute between Somalia and Kenya was discussed at the OAU meeting of July 1964, which decided that it should be remitted to a bilateral meeting. The matter was discussed again at a conference of East and Central African governments and a later summit meeting produced a detente. In both cases, though the organization was not able to produce agreement, it may have acted as a restraining influence.

This uneven record suggests that the international community has yet to develop the appropriate procedures for satisfactorily resolving disputes concerning frontiers.

Self-determination

It is tempting to suppose that all the problems of disputed sovereignty that arise, either between states or within them, could be simply disposed of by reference to some magic formula of "self-determination." A solution by which all such disputes were settled by "letting the people determine who they wish to rule" is attractive, but in most cases impracticable.

Even if there were no other difficulties involved, self-determination is a principle that can never be applied except in an arbitrary and inconsistent fashion. However sincere and passionately held a demand for nationhood by the people of Pimlico or Rhode Island, on practical grounds alone such ambitions would be almost impossible to fulfill. On political grounds, which include the feelings of those neighbors who would be affected and the tendency for majorities to override minorities, the demand would be even more certain of frustration. Yet it would be hard to say at what point a minority people, geographically concentrated and nationally self-conscious, loses the right to demand nationhood for itself. If Papua and Burundi are large and populous enough to survive as independent nations, why should not Nagaland or Katanga? If the Italian-speaking inhabitants of San Marino can retain an independent sovereignty, why should not the German-speaking people of the Alto Adige? If the Six Counties of Northern Ireland enjoy the right of self-determination, why should not the Two?

No logic could ever persuade the inhabitants of the largely Catholic Two Counties that their own claim to self-determination was ill-founded, but that that of the mostly Protestant Six was just. In practice the creation of new nations — for example when imperialism recedes — can never be anything but a compromise. Always there will be some who, though freed from foreign rule in one form, may find it reimposed in another, perhaps even more distasteful. All attempts to rewrite the atlas, however logically undertaken, may create as many conflicts as they abolish. For the answer given in the plebiscites they presuppose will depend on who the question is addressed to.

For this reason in meeting the problem of minorities *within* the state, international bodies inevitably must normally acknowledge existing sovereignty, unless overwhelming reason for a new one arises. Dismemberment cannot be imposed from outside. The conflict can be assuaged effectively only through policies undertaken by the existing governments. Given sufficient consideration, some minorities, now furiously hostile, may come to identify themselves more fully with the enclosing state, as the Scottish and Welsh have with "Britain." International organizations may encourage policies likely to achieve this. For example, standards of toleration, of linguistic and cultural autonomy, or of political devolution, may be established. Specific machinery may be set up to hear the grievances of minority peoples, like the League Committees of Three (though this carries the danger of stimulating rather than damping friction). International mediators may be sent (as in Cyprus). Artificial means of preserving a sense of regional identity through cultural rather than political autonomy (as in the Soviet Union) may be promoted. Finally, if violence nevertheless arises over such issues, the UN may encourage not only peaceful settlement (as over the Germans in Italy) but even constitutional developments likely to relieve the problem (as they have already over essentially similar problems in colonial, or white-dominated, states). Where limited outlets of this kind are provided for the aspirations of minority peoples, they may forego more extreme demands (as the Karens and the Kurds have now done). And international opinion may prove to be less sympathetic to demands for more far-reaching, and perhaps less practicable, forms of independence.

In extreme cases international bodies already consider the substance of demands for autonomy by minorities. The problem of Tibet was raised in the UN by another member. The question of the German-speaking minority in Italy, though presented in an international guise, was discussed there. Sometimes constructive outside influence can be brought to bear by this means. International action sometimes calls for negotiations (as with the Germans in Italy). It may demand a commission to study the situation (as in Southwest Africa). Human rights clauses of the Charter may be invoked to maintain a general concern for the rights of minorities (as over Tibet and the white-dominated states of Africa).

Since only "recommendations" having no binding force can be passed, affected members cannot be finally committed to obeying them. The main object is to bring to bear the pressure of outside opinion, not to coerce. Discussion need not always be damaging to governments. The UN, being a club of nation states, will not view with undue sympathy demands for the disintegration of such entities. The substance of pleas for self-determination can be judged only on practical, rather than sentimental, grounds. To champion the rights of independence for the Nagas or the Kurds is a seditious, not a philanthropic, undertaking if they can never establish a viable state.

Over *new* frontiers, too, self-determination cannot be a complete answer. Occasionally it may be used to make marginal readjustments (as occurred after World War I in Silesia). But totally new frontiers or partition are perhaps only likely to be established now in certain multiracial communities, such as Cyprus or South Africa, where a minority is unwilling to submit to rule by the majority race. Though partition avoids the worst problems of biracial societies if populations can be effectively separated and resources justly shared, often new sources of resentment will be created. A federal system, like that employed in India and Nigeria, may prevent the worst tragedies of partition (though both examples show this provides no perfect answer). Economic cooperation (such as the Indus River project or joint development in the Saar) does something to reconcile aggrieved peoples. But a rewriting of the frontier itself will very rarely be possible.

Such solutions may meet some of the basic aspirations without the expense of disrupting existing sovereignties. The more cooperation between neighbors is encouraged — the greater the freedom of movement and trade across boundaries for example — the less significance frontiers themselves may ultimately possess. Self-determination may then no longer seem the only possible objective.

Conclusions

Conflicts over external frontiers clearly remain one of the most important types of war in the modern world. They have become four or five times as common since 1945 as before (see Table IV.1 on p.

96). And though most have been on a limited scale they may develop into something much larger (India–Pakistan) and have large-scale international consequences (India–China). An effective international order clearly needs appropriate principles and procedures for the settlement of such conflicts.

The first essential is that all such disputes are accepted as of international concern. Until today few disputes that have arisen over boundary questions have been referred to the UN. And even where they have, no attempt to settle the substance has usually been made. If such resolutions could be binding on both parties, the reluctance of members to bring disputes to the UN might be attributed to a fear of prejudicing their rights, or, in the case of third parties, to a realistic desire not to place members' loyalties under too great a strain. In fact, however, no decision of the Security Council under Chapter VI, nor any decision at all of the Assembly, can be more than a "recommendation," which can have no binding force on the members.

The importance of such resolutions would be in their political, not their legal, force. A call by UN bodies for an impartial opinion from the International Court or an ad hoc subcommittee or a mediator, can be a powerful deterrent against self-help designed to redress the grievance. Thus, once the UN had reached a decision on the question of Mauretanian sovereignty, its reaction to a subsequent attempt by Morocco to seize the country could be clearly anticipated. But where the UN has failed even to consider such questions, it is made easy for the attacking party to find justification for its own activities. General opinion will be uncertain as to where the rights and wrongs lie. And it is partly because outside opinion, as well as international organizations, has difficulty in making judgments on such matters that an effort at determining the issue by force can have its attractions. The political costs of armed action are far higher where international bodies have already taken the matter under their attention. International intervention may also provide a face-saving escape for the parties involved. This is especially so where resort to force has been designed to anticipate action by the opponent. United Nations action may offer an acceptable alternative recourse involving little sacrifice of national pride for either party.

The second conclusion is that if existing frontiers are not to be perpetually subject to dispute, the frontier lines generally acknowledged now or in the recent past have priority over those of earlier periods. As we have seen, such conflicts often concern what period is held to possess validity. But if claims based on earlier periods of history remained legitimate, every frontier line in the world would be subject to challenge. Turkey could claim most of the Middle East and Austria half of Europe. This applies even to the boundaries inherited from imperialism. For here again, if claims based on the unsatisfactory nature of colonialist borders were generally upheld, most of the frontiers of Africa, Latin America, the Middle East, and many in Asia would become subject to challenge. Only a general acknowledgment of the more recent lines, therefore, by the international community, if not by the claimants themselves, could preserve stability. In the case of Africa, this principle has been explicitly acknowledged by the Organization of African Unity.

The third and most important principle required is the establishment of a *norm to be restored* in case of disturbance. It is perhaps unrealistic to hope that within the near future the UN will take it upon itself to pass recommendations on the merits of frontier or minority claims, still less that these will be voluntarily submitted to arbitration. But even without this, international action and opinion could, as over more far-reaching aggressions, lend interim support to the status quo.

To underwrite the status quo, the status quo itself needs definition. Chinese incursions against India are shocking to India and Europe because they violate Indian and European maps. They are natural and proper to China because they reassert Chinese maps. It is for this reason important that there should always exist, irrespective of claim and counterclaim some record of the existing de facto boundary. This could serve for outsiders as the norm to be re-established when the dispute breaks into open conflict. Only deliberate international efforts to establish the facts, if not the rights, before dispute arises could achieve this object.

Ideally what is required is a permanent and definitive UN atlas, whose violation would always constitute an attempt at annexation. Although this may be impossible at present, it should be possible to compile a record of existing borders of administration, the violation of which would invariably represent a breach of the peace. By this none would be asked to renounce their claims. All they need do is to reaffirm that they will pursue them only by peaceful means.

Some no doubt will be reluctant to do even this, declaring the entire undertaking a breach of sovereignty. But this need not necessarily prevent the UN from proceeding with the task. The atlas would retain its value as a record of the then existing realities, however much its legal validity was challenged. A map which is accepted by the majority makes it easier for all other members, and for the general public, to be sure who it is who wishes to subvert the status quo. It would be made increasingly difficult for any member, without grave affront to international opinion, to appeal to private atlases in justification of armed force.[3]

Once again certain procedures would be necessary to implement these principles. Sometimes the main difficulties arise, as we have seen, over the uncertainties concerning the boundary on the spot rather than over any important differences over map lines. On a number of occasions over the past twenty years, frontier incidents have arisen from misunderstandings concerning a particular boundary, or from wholly inadvertent crossings when its location is not clearly marked. Sometimes there may, therefore, be need for *physical demarcation* of boundaries.[4] In this, as in other cases, it is often important to confront the problem at a time when conditions are relatively stable. If left until one of the parties seeks to resolve it on a unilateral basis, it may be too late to reach accommodation.

In other cases international bodies, or outside mediators, can suggest the establishment of a *buffer zone* of indeterminate sovereignty (as was once achieved in the Gaza Strip between Israel and Egypt). They may demand arbitration by some mutually acceptable body (as the OAU demanded for Algeria and Morocco). They may sometimes propose as a temporary measure *alternative boundaries*, pending a final resolution of the problem (this is in effect the basis of the solution proposed by the Colombo powers for the Sino-Indian border). Finally, they may propose reference of disputes for *legal settlement* to the International Court of Justice (as occurred in the Cambodia–Thailand dispute).

The establishment of a permanent UN commission on frontiers, or of regional commissions for each continental group, could be

---

[3] The UN Economic and Social Council is at present engaged in the preparation of a world map, on the scale of 1:1,000,000. Although this is designed mainly to mark vegetation and other natural features, political boundaries will be marked on it where possible. These will be accompanied by the reservation that this marking does not imply official endorsement." But if it contains a full record of existing administrative boundaries, it could fulfill the purpose here proposed.

[4] The Truce Supervisory Organization in Palestine frequently stressed the importance of providing a clear physical barrier to mark the political boundary in the Gaza Strip.

valuable in cases of this kind. Such commissions could establish the de facto international atlas. They could examine and pronounce on the merits of legal and historical claims and recommend solutions. Above all, they could be called in to propose a settlement in time of conflict. The existence of external and impartial judgments on the merits of such disputes can exert a considerable impact on the private and subjective assessments of the parties. During the interwar period the settlement by the League by such means — often a commission of inquiry — of a number of frontier conflicts (between Bulgaria and Yugoslavia, Hungary and Romania, Albania and Yugoslavia, Poland and Germany, Turkey and Iraq, and Poland and Czechoslovakia) was one of its most notable achievements. With the proper machinery, the UN might prove as effective.

TABLE IV · 4

Frontiers: Available International Principles and Procedures

Principles	Procedures
Existing administrative boundaries internationally accepted as status quo.	UN to undertake demarcation where necessary.
Existing administrative boundaries physically demarcated where possible.	UN commissions or mediators to settle points in dispute.
UN atlas recording administrative boundaries held as evidence of status quo.	Reference of legal questions to ICJ.
	Restoration of the status quo recorded in UN atlas in case of conflict.
	UN observers or peace force for disputed frontiers.

Only in the most extreme cases, where the UN has become convinced that there were imperative reasons for reconsidering existing areas of authority — for example, where the situation became wholly incompatible with a peaceful international order, whether because of the claims of a disgruntled minority within or of an aggrieved neighbor without — might it occasionally be necessary to resort to the Wilsonian principle of self-determination. The UN has already in some cases undertaken to determine questions of sovereignty on the basis of UN-supervised elections. Attempts were made to organize a UN referendum in Kashmir. A referendum under UN supervision was the basis of the solution adopted in the Trust territories of the British Cameroons, by which each half opted to join a different nation. International plebiscites have twice been conducted in the Saar. A UN mission verified the desire of the people of Sarawak and North Borneo to enter Malaysia. Similar procedures could occasionally be useful in other conflicts over boundaries. They could today prove the only way of solving the vexed problems of Greater Somalia, Formosa, and Southwest Africa. In an age when popular sovereignty is generally acknowledged as a political principle, it is perhaps logical that the UN should sometimes be bold enough to implement that principle. This indeed provides the only method of peaceful change whose validity is widely accepted.

Some of the dangers and uncertainties that disputed frontiers create could be allayed by a combination of such means. As the importance of frontiers begins to fade, they will perhaps less and less seem worth fighting for. Until that time, established principles and procedures could at least diminish the most serious clashes that they now sometimes stimulate.

Colonies

Colonies in International Relations

Even if no attempts at external attack took place, nor any conflicts over the borders between states, the international order might still be threatened by disputes involving the rights of governments claiming authority over overseas territories and peoples of foreign race.

Colonies have existed almost as long as nations themselves. Since nations have always been disposed to conquest, they have necessarily often become rulers of distant peoples of distinct race. The empires of Amorite and Chaldean, Macedonian, and Roman, Gupta and Chin, Inca and Aztec, Arab and Turk, as much as those of Europe which followed, took possession of lands of diffuse populations and diverse cultures. All had to devise means, more or less direct, for controlling and administering the territories they acquired.

Thus colonies have over many years exercised a significant, and usually a disturbing influence on international relations. To understand this influence, it is necessary to know first what colonies are.

The meaning commonly attributed to the word is an area in which rule is imposed by one nation over another people, geographically remote and of separate race. There are, however, a number of difficulties about this definition.

First, how far is the *imposition* of rule essential to the meaning? The fact that most of the inhabitants of Hong Kong appear to have no strong wish for any alternative form of government does not make that place any less a colony. Even self-government may not prevent the territory from remaining a colony (as in Gibraltar or Rhodesia today). Equal political rights for members of all races may be enjoyed in these territories without their being regarded any less as colonies. Only complete amalgamation with the home country (as achieved by Hawaii and once proposed for Malta) could abolish the colonial state.

Similarly, the fact that the people governed are of separate race, though relevant, is not a decisive factor. New England, Canada, Australia, and New Zealand were all regarded as colonies, even though their peoples were scarcely distinguishable ethnically from those of the mother country. The same applies to the Latin American colonies of Spain. The real criterion is not the level of self-government, nor the race of the people ruled, but the lack of total independence on the one hand, or freely chosen absorption on the other, for the populations ruled.

Third, there are difficulties about the geographical relationship of colonies to the mother country. Distance alone is clearly not the important factor. Algeria was far closer in miles to Paris than are most of the outlying Soviet republics to Moscow, yet it was regarded as a colony in a way that the Soviet republics for the most part are not. But rule over the peoples of different race beyond the seas is also not a sufficient condition of a colony. There are a number of nations formed out of a collection of islands, such as Indonesia or Japan, whose overseas territories cannot be regarded as colonies, even when the race is different (as in Hokkaido or West Irian). Only where the island or territory concerned is clearly outside the natural geographical boundaries of the governing state can it be classified as a colony. In this case, even if its peoples were given identical political rights with those of the home country (as some in the Portuguese overseas territories have been), they would not cease to be regarded as colonies unless they had explicitly opted, by majority choice, for absorption in the home state.

Sometimes, however, geographical separateness is not present even in what are essentially colonial situations. Where a small white section of the population effectively rules a much larger population of different race, enjoying highly restricted political rights, the situation is that of an internal colony. And the same term might properly be used where any section of the population, such as the aborigines of Australia or some Indians in the United States, is treated, even for its own benefit, as a separate category from the majority of the population. A better definition therefore would seem to be that a colony is a territory, usually beyond the seas, in which there exists a substantial population which either enjoys lesser political rights than the ruling race or is not fully absorbed into its political structure.

In the earliest colonies (settlements in foreign lands of traders or of cultivators) such as the Greek colonies of the ancient world, the settlers lived existences largely independent both of home government and native peoples. Even the first colonists from Europe, in North America, Australasia, and other sparsely populated areas, enjoyed little contact with the indigenous people. But later European settlers found themselves in areas already densely inhabited by peoples of another stock and culture, whose existence was not to be ignored. Usually such peoples did not come under European rule as the result of deliberate acts of decision. Often European governments became embroiled in spite of themselves. Dominion was usually established through commercial zeal, rather than aggressive intention. Often (as in North America, the East Indies, and India) private trading companies undertook the initial colonization at the seaboard, the more thoroughgoing conquest subsequently found necessary, even the administration. Occasionally (as in South America) the settlers themselves, though claiming the authority of state (and Church) at home, in practice ruled according to their own whims; while the efforts of state (and Church) were often directed at restraining rather than encouraging such subjugation. Sometimes (as in Canada, the West Indies, and India) control from Europe was as much the effect of intra-European struggle as of a conscious desire to conquer strange lands.

By the early nineteenth century, whether by choice or necessity, administration as well as settlement was increasingly undertaken. Home governments became more and more involved. By now empires became a source of pride, as well as of trading opportunities and security. Only then, as cutthroat competition became an incentive in East Asia, in East Russia, in the Pacific and, above all, in Africa, did conquest become an end in itself and governments seek to outdo each other in their efforts to acquire responsibility for ruling huge areas of territory and innumerable subject peoples.

Even now, justifications had to be found. Some among the European conquerors believed themselves to have a "civilizing mission" among peoples who sometimes possessed cultures far older and richer than those of Europe. Others claimed that, by his capacity to administer, the white man inherited a unique burden of responsibility to rule those less fortunately endowed peoples who had come under his care, a burden he agreed to shoulder, not because he enjoyed it, but because those he governed were "not fit" yet to rule themselves.

Such rationalizations were perhaps less appealing to the peoples who had been overcome. But the impact of the superior technological and military prowess which Europe brought to her expansion left them for long dazed and bemused. Some perhaps regarded yet one more conquest merely as the recurrence of an eternal law of nature. As a result expectations were not for a long time such as to challenge the basis of the existing order.

In time, some began to be conscious that the rule of distant conquerors need not be eternal. New attitudes were encouraged by the political doctrines which the governing races themselves brought with them. British conceptions, first of "responsible government," later of "democracy," French ideals of "liberty, equality and fraternity," the principles of popular sovereignty for which the Dutch had themselves once battled and bled in their own anticolonial struggle — all these nourished a wholly new set of assumptions among the conquered peoples. Those of the rulers, however, remained unchanged. To them such principles were admirable when practiced at home. They appeared less cogent when appealed to by colonial peoples.

Colonies also created divergencies of expectation between the colonial powers themselves. These could result from competition for the same colonies (as between Britain and France in Canada, India, the West Indies, and elsewhere in the eighteenth century). They could be the effect of deprivation and the desire to achieve equivalent status to others in colonial possessions (Germany, Italy, and other countries at the end of the nineteenth century). Finally, they could result from efforts to eliminate the colonies of others.

This last factor was significant in transforming expectations among the colonial peoples. Already in the early nineteenth century, Britain cheerfully championed the anticolonial movements of South America and East Europe and did much to lend them impetus. By the end of the century, the European powers were even readier to decry the colonial aspirations of their rivals. Britain denounced the imperialism of Russia in Asia, just as Russia denounced that of Austria-Hungary and Turkey in Europe. France challenged British imperialism in Southeast Asia, just as Britain challenged French in Africa. And, in World War I, Britain assisted Arab nationalists against Turkey in the Middle East, while Germany rallied Africans against Britain in East Africa.

The rise of revolutionary movements in Europe and the development there of the concept of "nationalism" brought even sharper contradictions between the political principles proclaimed in Europe and those applied elsewhere. The sanctification of the principle of "self-determination" at the end of World War I intensified these strains. New justifications for empire became necessary. When, in the Middle East, European rule was further extended, colonialism was obliged to take on a more respectable garb. Colonies could now be acquired only as a "mandate" from an international authority to which the colonizing power became answerable.

During the Second World War the efforts of the imperialist nations to bring imperialism to an end became more strenuous than ever. Britain helped displace Italian power from Abyssinia, Eritrea, and Libya, and French from Syria and Lebanon. Japan served to overcome British rule in Malaya and Burma, American in the Philippines, and Dutch in Indonesia. Sometimes governments of indigenous peoples were established to take over from the former colonial power. Above all the colonial peoples themselves became increasingly self-conscious and vocal in their demands. Revolutionary claims first became articulate in countries with old cultures and large populations of educated people (as in India). They were no doubt especially intense when such people (as in the British and Dutch dependencies) were subject to racial discrimination or intolerance. The degree of education was perhaps the most vital factor. But even this was not a consistent rule. In Hong Kong, where there was a substantial body of highly educated people of an old culture, subject often to humiliating racial prejudice, demand for self-rule was insignificant. In South Africa, where the standards of education were the highest in the continent and the discrimination most glaring, the independence movement was for long less developed than in most other parts of the continent.

But once the movement started, it inevitably became universal. World War II unloosed a log jam that could not be halted. The will of the ruling power ceased to be a significant factor in the process. The rising standard of education, the universal standardization of culture, improved communications, the pressures of world opinion — all these served to transform prevailing assumptions on both sides. The humiliations which an Asian power inflicted on the mightiest of Europe had revealed that European dominance was not a law of destiny. Peoples who, under the impact of that power, had tasted the sweets of government in however debased a form, could not easily be reduced once more to servitude. The new attitudes received increasing encouragement from elsewhere. On the iniquity of colonialism, Washington and Moscow, Catholic dictators of Latin America and Moslem demagogues of the Middle East, all, however diverse their opinions on other matters, could reach agreement. Such an assumption was the one common currency of postwar political exchanges.

Thus a wholly new set of attitudes was gradually established among those colonized. But among the colonists attitudes had not always been transformed. That basic clash of expectations inevitably provoked numerous conflicts.

Causes of Colonial Disputes

The principal colonial wars of the interwar and postwar years are set out in Table V.1.

The most obvious difference between the two periods is that in the former period revolts and rebellions were very rarely successful. The only exceptions were the rebellion in Ireland and perhaps the revolt in Iraq, which was followed not long afterward by agreement for independence. But in both these cases there was no strong will for continued rule. Even in the postwar period, a number of the struggles undertaken were not successful (for example, in Malaya, Kenya, and Angola) and where independence was granted it was not

TABLE V · 1

Principal Conflicts in Colonial (Including Mandated) Territories,
1918–1965

	Year	Conflict	Result
Interwar	1918–21	Rebellion in Ireland against British rule	Independence for Eire granted
	1919–21	Revolt by tribes of Northwest India against Britain	Inconclusive
	1920–21	Revolt in Iraq against British mandate	Mandate maintained, but new treaty leading to final independence
	1920–26	Revolt by Rif tribes of Morocco against France and Spain	Protectorates maintained
	1920–32	Revolt by Senussi in Libya against Italian rule	Colonial rule maintained
	1925–26	Revolt in Syria against French mandate	Mandate restored

TABLE V · 1 (*Cont.*)

Year	Conflict	Result
1926–27	Revolt by Communists in Indonesia against Dutch rule	Colonial rule maintained
1929–34	Revolt by Atlas tribes in Morocco against French rule	Protectorate established
1930–31	Revolt by Communists and Nationalists in Indo-China against French rule	Colonial rule maintained
1936–39	Revolt of Arabs in Palestine against British policy	Mandate maintained
Postwar 1945–46	Rebellion in Syria and Lebanon against restoration of French rule	Independence attained
1945–49	Rebellion in Indonesia against restoration of Dutch rule	Independence attained
1945–46	Revolt of Communists in Philippines against US control	Revolt defeated, but Philippine independence granted
1946–54	Rebellion in Indo-China against French rule	Independence attained
1948–57	Revolt of Communists in Malaya against British rule	Revolt defeated, but Malayan independence granted
1952–56	Revolt by Mau-Mau ritualists against white domination	Revolt defeated, but Kenyan independence granted later
1954–59	Revolt of Greek Cypriots in Cyprus in favor of union with Greece	Independence granted, with Turkish rights preserved
1954–61	Rebellion in Algeria against French rule	Independence granted
1960–64	Rebellion in Angola against Portuguese rule	Colonial rule restored

[Sporadic riots and disturbances, as in Tunisia, Morocco, Malawi, and South Arabia, are not included.]

necessarily as a direct result of the conflict. In general, however, the movements that took place in the postwar period were better organized, better armed (often from outside the borders), and more generally supported than in the former period.

The next important difference between the two periods was in the attitudes of the outside world. After World War II, the forces of nationalism began to feel justified, not only by deep conviction, but by prevailing opinion throughout the world. New organs of opinion, in the UN, in the propaganda of hostile powers, in other new states, increased the self-confidence of independence movements. Even the faith of the colonial powers in their own prescriptive rights was weakened, if not yet wholly destroyed.

Finally, nationalist movements were not only more confident but more powerful. World War II transformed the situation. Some peoples (as in Malaya) had been supplied with arms by colonial powers to fight against their enemies. Some (as in Indonesia) had been supplied by other powers to fight against the West. Most could find some source, sometimes interested patrons, for the arms they needed. The colonial powers themselves, on the contrary, were weaker. They frequently had economic troubles. They often found it difficult to win support elsewhere, either moral or physical (the United States would permit no trade in arms, even to governing forces, in Indonesia and Indo-China). And this sense of increasing impotence sometimes increased their reluctance to make concessions.

There would seem to be certain factors that commonly characterized resort to violence. Of the postwar cases listed, the first five all occurred in territories that, for one reason or another, had acquired a considerable degree of independence during the war, and fighting was to resist the *restoration* of colonial rule. Of the other four, the Mau-Mau movement was abnormal in its association with primitive religious belief and ritual, and the revolution in Cyprus in being partly a communal conflict. Only the wars in Algeria and Angola, therefore, represent cases of a new and spontaneous outbreak of a violent struggle for independence by generally representative nationalist forces. Despite the common belief, this has not then in fact been the most common type of anticolonial conflict.

Motivations may be classified into four varieties. In some cases action was designed to win a promise of total independence or some intermediate objective from the colonial power (Algeria, Cyprus). Sometimes violence was partly designed to win concessions of a non-political nature, the release of a leader (Morocco, Malawi), the evacuation of a base (Tunisia), or the satisfaction of economic grievances (Philippines). Sometimes (as in Malaya and the Philippines) it resulted from attempts by a particular ideological faction to contest colonial rule and achieve leadership of the independence movement. Sometimes it has been designed largely to express an incoherent sense of dissatisfaction or unrest (Ghana, Kenya, Central Africa Federation, South Africa). And sometimes it has been partly intended to win attention and sympathy abroad, especially in the UN (Cyprus, Algeria). In some cases each motive may have been at work at different times. And in some more than one was at work at once.

One factor that has frequently precipitated violence, here as well as elsewhere, has been frustration. When colonial people have felt assured, as in Nigeria and the West Indies, of a steady progression toward independence, they would not normally consider it worth engaging in all the risks of prolonged hostilities against superior forces simply to speed that process a little. It was when they were faced with a blank wall of negation, when they saw no hope of progression unless this were wrested by brute force, that colonial wars tended to arise. It was when Ho Chi Minh, having acquired power within Indo-China before the French returned there, was told that his new government was to be deprived of all effective future influence, that he and his forces determined to resort to arms to assert their claims. And it was when the people of Cyprus were told that the demands they proclaimed could "never" be accorded, that organized rebellion broke out within a few months. It was when the nationalists of Algeria were informed that their country was "French" and could never, like their neighbors, aspire to an independent existence, that they felt forced to turn to war to seek some hope of progress toward their goal. And, finally, it was when the people of Nyasaland were given to believe that the Federation that they detested was permanent and indissoluble that they gave vent to their frustration in a series of violent disturbances. Where a movement for independence among a colonial people meets a sudden or a persistent frustration, clearly, the dangers of conflict breaking out in violent form are especially acute.

The colonial powers were often subject to another form of frustration. They were susceptible to the petulant vexation which arises from meeting an unexpectedly intractable impediment. In such a situation they might, like the Netherlands in Indonesia in 1947–48, suddenly vent their spleen in a spasm of rage against contumacious subjects. If their aspirations were frustrated by some upstart ruler of a once submissive state, they might suddenly explode in a fit of anger, like Britain against Makarios or France against Ben Bella. They were usually aging powers who, conscious of dwindling power, were determined to assert continuing greatness. Often their overseas possessions were virtually all that remained of former glories. And none were more determined to reassert vanished greatness than those (the majority) which had suffered temporary humiliation in the recent world struggle.

Another cause of conflict was that the colonial power might feel it must not yield in face of unlawful violence; any concession then became a sign of "weakness." The rebel forces on the other hand were convinced that force, and force alone, would wring the concessions they demand. When (as in Indo-China) one side secured supremacy in such a contest, an accommodation might eventually be reached. But when (as in Algeria) neither side could prevail, the struggle might continue almost interminably, each side too proud to consider the contacts which alone could precede an understanding.

Again, colonial disputes were apt to lead to violence because they often became inextricably entangled in the ideological contests of the time. The battles that the main antagonists dared not fight out face-to-face with all the perilous weapons at their disposal they could prosecute with far less hazard at arm's length in the enclosed arena of distant colonies. Nationalist movements could be encouraged, to undermine the position of the ruling power. Both ideological factions might support different nationalist movements within certain states. The tensions of the cold war were thus projected (in Malaya, in Indo-China, in the Philippines, and in Algeria) into the struggles for independence within those colonies.

Finally, conflict could arise not over the fact, but the speed or type of independence. Was the principle of one man-one vote universally applicable? Supposing power were handed over, but to forces generally considered unrepresentative? Where the peoples were of two or more nationalities, could the claims of minorities (the Turks in Cyprus, the Africans in Guiana, the Arabs in Zanzibar, or white settlers in Kenya and Rhodesia) restrict the right to independence? What were the basic human rights that could be demanded? Was the demand for intervention by international bodies in racial problems in South Africa equally applicable in the Soviet Union, the United States, or elsewhere?

There were, and still are, no mutually agreed answers to most of these questions. Recourse to armed force sometimes appeared to provide the only certain solutions.

International Law and Colonial Disputes

One factor aggravating colonial disputes has been the differing conception of legal "rights."

For long the contention of international law was that colonial conflicts were beyond the law itself. When the ruling houses of Europe finally secured unchallenged supremacy within their own states, they converted the feudal rights of overlordship into wider, almost unlimited, rights of "sovereignty." When they began to acquire new territories abroad, this umbrella of "sovereignty" was spread over remote portions of the globe. The settlements of trading companies were in time transformed into royal domains. New conquests were appropriated to the "crown" of the conquering power. And international law, devised in Europe by Europeans to regulate the relations of European states, asserted without hesitation that the territories such powers acquired at the four corners of the globe were all equally comprehended within the "sovereignty" which it postulated.

The consequences of this were three. On the one hand, any violation of the territory acquired became a violation of the sovereignty of the ruling power, and so a transgression of the international code. On the other, any act of violence or insubordination *within* the territories became an act of rebellion against the legal authority of the colonial power. Finally, no international authority could intervene over violence which took place wholly within the borders of the colonial empire concerned.

When, after World War I, the first international organization to preserve international security was established, it was accepted that the "sovereign rights" of colonial powers in the areas they had conquered could not be infringed by such an organization (though members undertook "to secure just treatment of the native inhabitants of territories under their control"). The territories they had acquired abroad were as immune from interference as those of the homeland. This was extended even to nations that had recently acquired independence: in 1925, after Egypt had been given full independence, the League declined to intervene in a dispute between Britain and Egypt on the grounds that this was not strictly an international affair. Since the dominant powers of that organization held here a common interest, they could in any case be expected to join with each other in resisting the pretensions of rebellious colonials. Before World War

II, armed nationalist movements on any scale within the colonies
were still rare. But if they had to do so, colonial powers could expect
to mobilize the bulk of opinion, at home and abroad, against attempts
at "rebellion," "sedition," or other challenges to legal authority. For
few then doubted whose were the rights.

After World War II, more than half the nations of the world were
ex-colonies. Everywhere colonialism was discredited. Governments and
public opinion alike increasingly attributed overriding rights now, not
to governments seeking to maintain their authority in distant regions,
but to the peoples demanding "freedom," "self-determination," even
"sovereignty" itself. Despite this change in attitude, within the newly
founded UN, the principle of nonintervention in colonial territories
remained established. Colonial powers again played a dominant part
in formulating the principles on which the organization was built. And
some important noncolonial nations had their own reasons for resisting
claims to overriding powers by an international body. There was thus
no longer any international consensus as to where rights lay.

The provisions by which nonintervention was embodied in the
Charter, like many in that document, were by no means unambiguous.
The chief reservation was contained in Article 2(7) which declared
that "nothing contained in the present Charter shall authorize the
United Nations to intervene in matters which are essentially within
the domestic jurisdiction of any state, or shall require the Members
to submit such matters to settlement under the present Charter. . . ."
Nothing in the Charter provided any guide as to the meaning of
the word "intervene" in this context. Some respected international
lawyers contended that there was nothing in the provision to prevent
discussion of matters within domestic jurisdictions. Others claimed
there was nothing to prevent even the passage of resolutions on them,
as long as these did not provide for "dictatorial interference," the
usual criterion of "intervention" under international law. The colonial
powers maintained that the clause prevented even discussion of such
questions and that it was for this specific purpose that it was inserted.

The matter was complicated by the apparent conflict between this
and other Articles of the Charter. The clause itself included the
reservation: "This principle shall not prejudice the application of
enforcement measures under Chapter VII," — that is, action undertaken under the authority of the Security Council in order to meet
"threats to the peace, breaches of the peace and acts of aggression"
(though some argued that colonial disputes could not represent a

"threat" to the peace since no international conflict was involved). Under Article 34, the Security Council was given powers to investigate "any dispute, or any situation which might lead to international friction or give rise to a dispute." Finally, under Article 73, all members of the UN undertook to carry out certain clearly defined objects, including "to develop self-government" in their administration of non-self-governing territories," while under Article 10 the General Assembly had the right to "discuss . . . any matters within the scope of the present Charter." These Articles alone could be held to provide a basis for the discussion of many colonial problems at the UN. The force of this contention depended on whether Article 2(7) is interpreted to override Article 73, or Article 73 to override Article 2(7). Such points have remained until today bitterly disputed.

International law was, however, implicated in another way: in the acknowledged responsibilities of contemporary international organs for human rights. The legitimacy of international concern over such rights is upheld in the Charter of the UN itself. This declares in its very first Article that body's interest "in promoting and encouraging respect for human rights." The Economic and Social Council possesses a Commission on Human Rights, with subcommissions. Numerous resolutions on the subject have been adopted by the Assembly. Other expressions of international concern exist in the form of regional conventions. The same concern was put into effect by the Nuremberg Trials when new principles of international law in this field were established.

In an increasingly interrelated and politically conscious international community, such rights inevitably included basic political, as well as basic social, rights. International concern over political rights in colonial and semicolonial states was expressed in the UN Charter. Under Article 73 all members "which have or assume responsibilities for the administration of territories whose peoples have not yet obtained a full measure of self-government" accepted the obligation "to develop self-government, to take due account of the political aspirations of the peoples, and to assist them in the progressive development of their free political institutions. . . ." This obligation, entered into by every member of the UN, might be applied as well to the internal colonies of Southern Africa as to the classical colonies, ruled by European states, in other parts of the world. It is an obligation, however, that has been consistently denied by the government of South Africa, and indeed by some other governments as well.

International Organizations and Colonial Disputes

Partly for these reasons there has been no uniformity in the response of the UN to situations of this kind. Article 2(7) was quoted on innumerable occasions as a bar to discussion. But such objections, as time went on, were more and more often overruled. Increasingly, the four main colonial powers, Britain, France, Belgium, and Portugal, found themselves alone, with South Africa, in resisting the inscription of such items on the UN agenda.

Success in quoting the Article depended partly on the nature of the issue. Over Cyprus, which was clearly a communal even more than a colonial problem, Britain could rouse some sympathy, successfully resisting discussion for some years. Over the policy of apartheid, the South African Government could expect none. In the case of the classic colonial issues, where colonial peoples were seeking forcible liberation from white rulers, including that of South Africa, it usually came to be held that such disputes represented at the least "threats" to the peace; and so were "international" in character and liable to discussion. Colonial powers could even then continue to declare that all such resolutions were violations of the Charter and without effect (as France did consistently). Or they could argue that the interference of an outside body, especially where ideological factors were injected, could only exacerbate the existing situation (as Britain did in the cases of Cyprus and Rhodesia at first).

The fact that international intervention thus remained possible but uncertain sometimes served to increase the likelihood of violence. Colonial peoples possessed an incentive to resort to violence to call attention to their plight. Both in Cyprus and in Algeria an outburst of armed clashes frequently occurred during the period immediately preceding the opening of the UN Assembly in September. On occasion, such an outbreak helped to procure UN intervention where no great interest had previously been taken (as over Angola in 1961). Sometimes the international outcry aroused by these disorders might force some modification in the policies of the government concerned: the world's reaction to the disturbances in South Africa at the beginning of 1960 forced even the South African Government to receive Mr. Hammarskjöld in that country, so for the first time acknowledging the legitimacy of international concern.

In practice, discussion of such matters became more and more a

matter of course. Apart from discussion and resolutions in the General
Assembly and the Security Council (from about 1961 resolutions on
colonial issues, which had previously been introduced in the General
Assembly, began to be increasingly often — as in the cases of Angola,
the Congo, Rhodesia, and South Africa — ventilated in the Council),
the UN has developed a series of other procedures for the discussion
of colonial questions. All matters affecting Trust Territories could
always be raised in the Trusteeship Council and, if necessary, brought
from there to the Assembly. But new devices were introduced for
discussing colonial territories proper. The provision in Article 73e
about the transmission of information on non-self-governing territories was used to justify the establishment in 1947 of a Committee
on Information from Non-Self-Governing Territories, which came to
be increasingly used as the instrument for pressure to hasten the
process of decolonization. More and more often the danger of "threats
to the peace" was used to justify Assembly discussion. Even economic
bodies, such as ECOSOC and the ILO, could bring their weight to
bear.

   In December, 1960, a resolution was passed in the General Assembly
containing a Declaration on the Granting of Independence to Colonial
Countries and Peoples, demanding that in all Trust and non-self-
governing territories "immediate steps should be taken" to transfer
all powers to the peoples of these territories. The following year
the Assembly established a special committee to study the application
of the Declaration and make recommendations on its fulfillment. This
committee (the Committee of 17, now 24) became a constant watchdog
of the Assembly on the process of decolonization. Its resolutions and
recommendations on such subjects became often more radical and
militant in tone than those of the Assembly and Security Council
themselves in discussing colonial problems. Its subcommittees examined
particular territories in detail.

   To assess the success of these various procedures and bodies is
more difficult. It is easy to show that independence was granted to
many colonial territories subsequent to discussion in UN bodies. It
is less easy to show this was cause and effect. Most of the colonial
powers were committed to bringing their colonial territories to independence eventually in any case. United Nations pressures may have
somewhat speeded the process. But colonial powers were probably
more influenced by a general change in world opinion, including that
in their own countries, of which UN resolutions were only one ex-

pression. Where the power concerned totally refused to comply (like Portugal and South Africa), UN action had far less success whatever the methods used (though it would be a mistake to conclude it was totally without influence).

It seems likely that the more publicized the action — an Assembly resolution rather than committee reports — the greater the response. The more specific the resolutions passed — for the reprieve of a particular political prisoner rather than the release of prisoners in general, for the abandonment of a particular provision rather than of a constitution as a whole, for a new constitution for a particular territory rather than "immediate independence for all colonies" — the more successful they have been. Calls to certain governments not to carry out a particular execution were sometimes successful whereas more general recommendations have often evoked little response. In specific cases the response that occurs is more unmistakable and exposed to the glare of publicity. In general, UN bodies have provided a focus for the expression of opinions and attitudes commonly shared throughout the greater part of the world. These might be defied, but they could rarely be totally ignored.

The effectiveness of international action in countering full-scale war of this type is also not easy to assess. Because of the dominance of colonial powers, and of existing conceptions of sovereignty, none of the interwar colonial conflicts was brought for consideration by the League. Even after 1945 the major conflicts of this type, in Indo-China, Malaya, the Philippines, and Kenya, were never considered in the UN. The cases of Syria and Lebanon in 1946 and Cyprus and Algeria were discussed, but the UN played no significant role in determining the outcome. There were many discussions on Angola in 1962 to 1963, but again these had little consequence, given the noncooperation of the colonial power. Only over Indonesia in 1947–48, where a good offices committee was sent and successfully brought both sides into contact, and over South Arabia in 1966–67, where a UN mission was set up to help ensure the fulfilment of UN resolutions and the establishment of a broad-based government, did the organization play any significant role. In both cases, UN influence was somewhat marginal. In the first case, the Netherlands decided to withdraw mainly on military and economic grounds. In the second, Britain had already announced its decision to withdraw before the mission was set up and the final outcome was little affected by any action of the mission. Nevertheless both cases indicate the type of role which the UN may play in such conflicts: that of go-between, conciliator, or mediator between two sides who might otherwise have no contacts, and the focus in exerting the pressures of world opinion. In some cases it might also play a part in supervising the transition to majority rule and ensuring fair elections in the immediate post-independence period (as in South Arabia, or in multiracial societies such as Fiji and the white-dominated countries of Southern Africa).

As the major colonial countries have passed to independence, new and more complex problems emerge concerning dependent territories. In these, the UN may play a different role. By the mid-1960's, most of the remaining areas still under colonial rule were very small territories, often islands or groups of islands, with small resources and populations ranging from 88 (Pitcairn Islands) to 100,000 or so. Such areas can scarcely hope to maintain a truly independent existence and often have no wish to do so. The situation is especially difficult where (as in Gibraltar or the Falkland Islands) the population does not want integration with the obvious neighbor. In all these cases, the UN may play a part, perhaps by encouraging association short of full independence, either with independent neighbors or with the metropolitan power, or even with the UN itself. In either case, it can help provide the economic assistance which can alone afford a meaningful independence.

The colonial situation is so rapidly drawing to its close that it is tempting to believe that the dangers of further violence in such cases are now diminished. Within some years this may be so. Meanwhile, however, it is precisely the most intractable problems which remain.

Conclusions

Colonies, therefore, external and internal, clearly represent one of the most common causes of conflict in the modern world. What are the principles and procedures that would be required to ensure a more effective resolution of colonial situations?

The first conclusion this examination suggests is that any constitutional system by which one race exerts effective power over larger populations of another enjoying inferior political or other rights, or over peoples in distant regions not adjacent to the home country, is likely to lead to conflict and violence in a short time. History has already proved this fact in the violence that has resulted. And such situations must, therefore, inevitably become subjects of international concern.

The present international community is distinguished in a fundamental way from any that has gone before in being far more closely
interrelated. Political developments, ideas, and aspirations in one part
of the world quickly exert an infectious effect on territories elsewhere.
International political parties and personal contacts promote direct
communication of political ideas from one region to another. International organizations transmit influences from other lands to any
area that comes under their attention. Though a century ago political
parties and doctrines in one country had little effect on any other
continent, today political theories and practices almost immediately
become world wide in their influence. Thus anticolonial feelings in
some countries, and the fame of anticolonial successes, must automatically affect the political situation in every other country of the
world.

But not only are internal populations influenced by those outside.
Those outside are influenced by those within. Policies and principles
of government that are totally out of keeping with accepted international norms may represent a standing invitation to violence, from
without the frontiers. This is true in a limited sense even where the
peoples concerned are all of a single race and the matter is more
fully "domestic": a new Hitler would invite external intervention. It is far
more true where they are of separate races. And it is above all and inevitably true where the peoples in question are related in race to those in
neighboring territories. For these neighbors will inevitably be incited by
the denial of rights to their kinsmen nearby.

Arguments which justify the attempt to keep large populations in a
position of inferiority on the grounds that they are of "lower capacities,"
or "not yet ready for self-government" or on any of the other grounds
traditionally put forward, are no longer relevant, even if they were
true. For the capacity to sustain those policies depends on international *beliefs* about the legitimate rights and opportunities of the
peoples ruled, not on those of their rulers. Here almost more than
in any other situation the generally expected structure of relationships,
within as well as between states, is crucial in its effect on the international order. The norm of majority rule is so generally accepted that
only this can overcome the danger of violence arising sooner or later.

The next principle that arises over colonial problems concerns the
basis of international intervention. In such cases intervention should
be based on the need to protect fundamental human rights (for
which the legitimacy of international concern is widely recognized)

rather than to force the acceptance of particular constitutional arrangements (which may open the way to unlimited international interference) or to meet imaginary "threats to the peace." This basis may make it easier to secure consensus concerning the right and wisdom of international action. It is accepted today that human rights include political rights. It can be shown that these are denied in colonial or semicolonial systems. Article 73 alone could be said to provide legal justification for intervention on these grounds. Intervention over human rights, by directing attention to the discriminatory nature of the treatment of inhabitants of such territories, lays emphasis on those elements of policy that are least capable of justification. More important, because it does not seek to place more weight on the terms of the Charter than they were intended to bear, it does not, like claims of threats to the peace, threaten to overturn the entire structure on which the international order is based.

The third principle required is that the protection of human rights is a multilateral responsibility. Revulsion at the indignities imposed by colonial and semicolonial regimes naturally sometimes stimulates demands for unilateral intervention. But the acknowledged *international* responsibility for human rights cannot extend to individual governments. However intense the feelings that inspire such demands, their fulfillment would only serve to destroy the wider basis of international order. The fact that the issues involved may relate to deep moral convictions does not affect this situation. A large proportion of the issues on which wars are fought can be claimed to have a moral justification. The age-old attempt to legitimize "just wars" was one expression of this sentiment. But the creation of a new category of "just wars" of this type, as an exception to the general prohibition of private violence, can no more be accepted in this case than in others. In the international field, as in national states, a condition of order is that the responsibility for remedying injustice takes only public, and not private, forms.[1]

[1] To accept that armed action against governments pursuing racial discrimination fell within some special category could indeed create precedents whose ultimate effect was unlimited. The same arguments used to justify unilateral intervention against regimes today denounced as "violating fundamental human rights," as "racialists," or "dictatorships," could be used tomorrow to justify similar intervention against many of these same states that had previously employed them. The principles involved in unilateral intervention of this kind cannot be distinguished in any categorical way from those that arise in any other case of threatened military action, official or unofficial, by one country to overturn a government in another whose policies it disapproves. If India is justified in the use of armed force to lib-

But the prohibition of action by individual governments in such cases does not necessarily exclude similar action undertaken by the UN itself, or under its direction. Here the principles involved are wholly different. Direct action to this end does, it is true, represent "intervention" (in the sense of "dictatorial interference" understood by international lawyers) and could thus be claimed a breach of the UN Charter. Yet it is arguable that this principle is overridden by the Charter provisions concerning human rights or that such an expansion of the Charter terms has already taken place. The interpretations placed on the Charter must certainly evolve as international society itself evolves. And existing international concern for human rights already provides the basis for extensive authority in this field.

The reason international authority requires caution in the use of forcible international intervention in situations of this type relates not to the words of the Charter but to the realities underlying it. Even if armed action was formally justified on the grounds of violation of fundamental human rights and of the Charter, such action might be claimed as a precedent for more general use of international armed force to coerce member states into compliance on anything claimed as a matter of human rights, or even other internal questions. Though eventually intervention for this purpose may come about, it is certain that at present it would remain unacceptable to very many members, including some of the most powerful. This is one of those initiatives, therefore, which, though possibly technically justifiable under the Charter, by arousing resistance, or total withdrawal among some members, might hinder rather than promote the process of international integration.

But there exist *procedures*, short of armed force, open to international organizations to influence the policies of member states in this field. A whole range of these is available. Even the repeated passing of resolutions on such matters can have some influence. It may help to educate authorities about the true nature of their own predicament. It may contribute to a readjustment of the expectations of such powers, not only on the legitimacy, and inevitability, of international concern, but on what policies it may be possible to sustain at home as well. The degree of political change that has occurred over the past twenty years, not only in the classical colonial situations, but

---

erate Goa from Portugal, or Zambia to liberate Zimbabwe, China would be equally justified in using armed force to liberate the Tibetan-speaking people of Northeast India from India, or the Chinese minorities throughout Southeast Asia.

even in the internal colonies of Southern Africa, is itself some evidence of the influence outside pressure may exert. These changes are probably more the effect of the influence of international opinion expressed partly in international organizations than of violent actions within the frontiers, which colonial governments have regarded as a question of honor to resist.

Pressure may be exerted on the colonial or semicolonial power also, as in the past, by requests for information; for reports by international officials; or for visits by specially appointed commissions. Committees may be set up of such authoritative character that their reports, whether statements of fact or recommendations of policy, may exert some influence. A universal breaking off of diplomatic relations may take place. Finally, economic or other sanctions may be exerted: a remedy that has already been internationally applied in Rhodesia. The withdrawal of all aid, or all imports, or all financial cooperation, if fully applied, could be a powerful ultimate sanction.

Such measures can be successful only if they are of a type that all, or most, members will be ready to cooperate in. Measures of enforcement that are inadequately supported weaken, rather than strengthen, international authority. Equally important, the demands presented must be of a type not too remote from what the member concerned may be ready to concede. This is a recognition of the elementary fact that, in all bargaining, demands must not be disproportionate to the inducements available. But it is a recognition also of the inescapable fact that political change, if not brought about by violent means, can come about only by a relatively gradual series of stages.

The true process that is at work all the time is an adjustment of mentality. For this reason demands are more likely to succeed if formulated so as not to appear as a *threat* to the community affected (which may only stimulate a reaction of hardening and rejection), but as an *encouragement* toward forms of evolution which may appear an escape from existing difficulties. Attempts to encourage and promote whatever elements in the situation already favor political evolution, and to exert leverage on this basis, seem to be more effective than direct confrontations aimed at a total reversal of all previous policies. Where, for example, policies directed to permitting an element of autonomy in certain areas or of certain types are already being pursued (as in the Bantustans of South Africa), efforts to insure that this is a real and effective and economically viable form of independ-

ence are likely to be more productive than those directed at a total
surrender of political power.

TABLE V · 2

Colonies: Available International Principles and Procedures

Principles	Procedures
Self-government within separate territorial units acknowledged.	Resolutions and other pressure in international organizations.
Nondiscrimination in political and all other rights. Basic human rights to be internationally protected.	Appointment of committees of inquiry or mediation.
Unilateral intervention for these purposes prohibited.	Visits by Secretary General or other personalities.
	Reference of basic human rights questions to Commission on Human Rights.
	Withdrawal of investment aid or other sanctions.

Most of the difficult situations of this nature remaining are in those
semicolonial areas where there are large minorities, usually Europeans,
who are not temporary administrators from overseas, but have deep
roots in the country. Often they have nowhere else to go if driven
out. They have thus something of the desperation of those driven
into a corner. Any stable solution must take some account of the
legitimate apprehensions of these minorities. Constitutional safeguards
to assure their future rights may help in achieving this purpose.
Assistance in emigration or resettlement can be given. Such safeguards are important in securing the purposes desired since, if international action is not equally firm in protecting the rights of whites
against blacks as of blacks against whites, whites may become yet
more fearful of relinquishing the rights they still hold.

In time, the problems of traditional colonialism, even the more
stubborn dilemmas of internal colonialism, may have ceased to exist.
New conflicts, less obvious methods of control by the strong over
the weak, new forms of economic exploitation of the poor by the rich
may replace them. Conflicts between privileged and underprivileged
areas are inherent in any international society where glaring differences
of wealth or status continue to exist. And it is arguable that some of
the resentments and frictions inherited from the colonial era will not

be eliminated until a more just international economic order, as well as political order, is created. Meanwhile, in the era of dying colonialism, it is necessary that outside opinion should seek those remedies and inducements which may provide the satisfaction of legitimate aspirations and the hope of political evolution, rather than the means of satisfying the greedy appetites of moral indignation or imperial pride.

CHAPTER SIX

Civil Wars

Civil Wars in International Relations

Even if all direct assaults, all disputes over boundaries, and all conflicts over authority imposed on peoples of foreign race were eliminated, however, conflicts might still arise over national interventions in internal disputes. Indeed in recent times the provision of assistance, in men, materials, or money, to those involved in civil conflicts elsewhere has become perhaps the commonest of all types of international military activity.

National intervention in civil wars has been known for several centuries. Its modern lineage might be traced back to the repeated participation of national forces in the religious and civil disputes of other states during the sixteenth and seventeenth centuries. For a time, after the community of nation states and the rules governing their intercourse had become more firmly established, this type of activity became less common. But in the nineteenth century it revived. And in the ideologically minded twentieth century, it has become a commonplace.

Sometimes intervention of this kind is designed to *maintain* the existing system of government against revolution. This was seen in the intervention of Britain, Prussia, and other nations against the revolutionary forces in France. It was manifested in the efforts of the rulers of the Holy Alliance to intervene in other states to overcome revolution there (as in Spain and Naples). It was practiced in the interventions of Prussia and Austria in the other states of Germany, and of Austria in Italy, in 1848. And joint intervention by combined forces of great powers took place to overcome the Taiping and Boxer rebellions in China.

But sometimes intervention takes place to help *overthrow* other governments. Britain, opposing the attempt of the Holy Alliance to stabilize the political status quo, gave active support to the revolutionary colonies of South America. She gave at least moral support to Greece, Belgium, and other states engaged in breaking away from their constitutional rulers. And during the American Civil War, she adopted policies which, though nominally uncommitted, represented assistance to the Confederate cause. France gave support for the Italian *risorgimento* in 1859–60. The United States in her interventions in Central and South America sometimes assisted revolutionary forces there. All these were equally an infringement of the generally accepted code governing such movements.

After World War I such forms of intervention became more common. Civil wars in the period 1915–1965 are outlined in the following table. As this shows, external intervention has throughout the period been common and has become increasingly so. In the interwar period, Western intervention in the Russian civil war, Romanian intervention in Hungary, that of the United States and Mexico in Nicaragua took more or less overt forms. Sometimes it was more discreet. The Nationalist revolution in China was secretly aided for a time by the Soviet Union. The Franco government in Spain was established partly through the armed assistance of outside governments.

The increase was natural, since by this time the world had become a single interrelated international political community. International political parties, such as the Communist and National Socialist parties, were at work in many countries of the world simultaneously. The shrinking of distance meant that, strategically, economically, or otherwise, governments had an increasingly close interest in political events in neighboring territories. As a result, any civil conflict, in whatever part of the world it might occur, might become part of a wider battle. Ideological expansion increasingly became a universal aim. And as the more blatant forms of aggression became more dangerous, and more costly in international good will, assistance to rebels within the state became more than ever an attractive instrument of national policy. Conversely, to their opponents the obstruction of these aims was essential to their own interests. Outside powers were no longer prepared, as their predecessors often were, to leave the outcome of civil struggles to native gods of war.

After World War II, intervention became even more widespread. Insurgent forces in Greece, Malaya, and Indo-China received help from one side of the Iron Curtain. Rebel forces in Iran, Indonesia, and Cuba acquired it from the other. Revolutionary forces in Laos received it from both sides at different times. Later, with many new independent states, new ideological factions emerged, receiving support from new

Table VI · 1

Civil Wars (Excluding Minority Conflicts), 1915–1965

Year	Country	Result	Intervention
1910–20	Mexico	Government overthrown (four times)	For government
1917–20	Soviet Union	Government overthrown	For government
1918–19	Hungary	Government overthrown	Against government
1918–19, 24–30	China	Government overthrown	Marginal
1919	India (Moplah communal movement)	Government maintained	None
1924–25	Arabia	Government overthrown	None
1925–27	Nicaragua	New government	For government
1927–36	China	Government maintained	Marginal
1928–30	Saudi Arabia	Government maintained	None
1928–29	Afghanistan	New government	None
1930	Brazil	Government overthrown	None
1936–39	Spain	Government overthrown	For and against government
1945–49	Greece	Government maintained	For and against government
1946–50, 1966	Philippines	Government maintained	For government
1946–	Colombia	Government maintained	None
1946–58	China	Government overthrown	Marginal
1947	Paraguay	Government maintained	None
1948–	Burma	Government maintained	None
1948–50	India	Government maintained	None
1953–59, 1961	Cuba	Government overthrown	Against new government
1955	South Vietnam	Government maintained	None
1957–60	Malaya	Government maintained	For government
1957–59	Muscat and Oman	Government maintained	For and against government
1958	Lebanon	New government	For and against government
1958–59, 1965	Indonesia	Government maintained	Marginal
1958–	Cameroun	Government maintained	Marginal

TABLE VI · 1 (*Cont.*)

Year	Country	Result	Intervention
1959–	Laos	New government	For and against government
1959–	South Vietnam	Regime maintained	For and against government
1960–65	Congo	Regime maintained	For and against government
1962–	Yemen	Government maintained	For and against government
1965	Dominican Republic	New government	Against rebels
1965–	Venezuela	Government maintained	None

[Civil disturbances and small-scale bandit or guerilla activity (as in Peru, Guatemala, or Thailand until 1966) are not included in this table.]

patrons. Rebels in the Yemen received help from Egypt; those in Venezuela from Cuba. Militant republican pan-Arabism fought conservative monarchist pan-Islam in the Middle East; revolutionary English-speaking pan-Africanism fought evolutionary French-speaking *négritude* in Africa; radical proletarian Castroism fought conservative militarism or gradualist middle-class social democracy in Latin America. Antigovernment forces all over the world learned to look for assistance to one or other of the various ideological groupings. On the other hand, governments and parties identified themselves, as never before, with the success of governments and parties of related views elsewhere. The political complexion of neighboring states became, because of the development of communications, more important than ever from a military point of view. The most powerful governments especially (the Soviet Union in East Europe, the United States in Central America, China among some of her border states) demanded dominant influence over the types of government existing in immediately neighboring territories.

Table VI.1 provides certain evidence about this type of conflict. Civil war is almost twice as common in the postwar as in the interwar period. Outside intervention is much more frequent than before. In the former period the result was more often that the government was overthrown, especially when there was outside intervention. In the later cases governments were more often maintained; and again this was specially so where outside intervention took place. Although, therefore, between the wars intervention was especially stimulated by the desire to promote change, afterward it was promoted by the desire to prevent it. In only two of the eighteen post-1945 cases did rebel forces succeed in overthrowing the government and establishing their own (China and Cuba):

in both of these there was little effective intervention in the fighting it-self and the previous regime was widely discredited both within and outside the country concerned.

Certain characteristics of these conflicts over the last twenty years are worth noting. They may be divided between those which concerned the total political system that should prevail in each country, and those which concerned the particular government that should exert power within an accepted system. Clearly all civil wars are in a sense ideological, in that they all concern the political complexion of the governing authority. But sometimes (Colombia, Muscat, Lebanon, and the Congo) the re-sult would probably not exert an overwhelming effect on the political structure as a whole. In others (Greece, China, Malaya, Laos, Yemen, and Vietnam) the outcome could be decisive in establishing a totally different system. Of the eighteen political civil wars in this period, about nine were wholly or partly undertaken by communist parties committed to the total overthrow of the existing system.

Second, it is noteworthy that most civil wars occurred where there was some genuine reason to doubt the representative character of the gov-ernment established in the region. This was either because there had been no free elections at all in the country in question (China, Indonesia, Muscat, Hungary, and Cuba); because there were grounds for suspecting the elections had been rigged, or certain parties had been banned (Greece, Cameroun, Laos, and Vietnam); or because there had been some radical change of policy by the government since the election (Lebanon, Congo). The main exceptions are the insurrections, mainly communist-led, in the newly independent areas of the Philippines, Ma-laya, Burma, and India. Even here the insurrectionary forces claimed, and perhaps genuinely believed themselves, to be more representative than the "bourgeois" forces in control of the governments concerned; and in general, once successive elections had shown the implausibility of this claim, that type of revolution tended to decline.

Third, whether such conflicts become bitter and protracted seems to depend, not so much on whether the war falls into one or the other of these categories, but on how far the two sides become associated with, or actively assisted by, outside powers. Where this occurs (as in at least twelve of the eighteen cases not involving minorities listed here), it sometimes makes it possible for one or the other of the factions involved to maintain its position far longer, and for the conflict to become far more intense, than would otherwise be possible. The wars in Spain, Greece, Yemen, and Vietnam were greatly magnified by this factor.

Fourth, it seems that there is considerable evidence that civil conflicts in the modern world occur especially in less developed countries of low standard of living and without stable political institutions. This is true to some extent even of those within Europe (Spain, Greece). It is even more true of those outside (China, Colombia, Laos, Lebanon, Congo, Vietnam). They have been almost unknown in the last century among those with high standards of living and developed institutions (northwest Europe and North America). Also, it seems that recently established radical governments founded through revolution (the Soviet Union between the wars, China, Cuba, Egypt since), especially when surrounded by hostile neighbors, are most active in fomenting civil war elsewhere.

It is thus important to try to determine which factors distinguish the cases in which outside intervention has occurred. First, as one would expect, outside intervention is far more common in areas that are geographically close to any of the great powers (as in Guatemala, Cuba, the Dominican Republic, Hungary, Laos, and Vietnam). It has occurred in areas which, if not immediately adjacent, are considered strategically important to some powers (Greece, Malaya, Yemen, and Lebanon). It has been rare in cases remote from all the principal powers (Cameroun and the South American republics) or where the country was already uncommitted (India, Burma). Outside assistance has varied from the supply of arms (various), military advice (Philippines, Laos, Malaya), military leadership (Muscat), naval support (Formosa and the Offshore Islands), air support (Laos), dispatch of volunteers (Indonesia, Congo), dispatch of troops (Lebanon, Dominican Republic), training and support of exiles (Cuba) to full-scale intervention (Vietnam on both sides). In general, intervention has been much more massive when it took place on behalf of an existing government (Malaya, Greece, Lebanon, Vietnam), than against an established government. The exceptions to this rule are the cases where a hostile regime has emerged or may emerge on the borders of a powerful state (Guatemala, Cuba, Dominican Republic, Hungary).

Finally, the evidence suggests that where one outside power or alliance becomes involved in a dispute of this kind, another almost invariably becomes so in due course. Among the cases here listed are a considerable number in which both sides have received assistance from elsewhere; and there are five or six in which neither side has done so. But, except perhaps for the civil wars in China (and even here assistance on the Nationalist side was not massive or decisive) and Malaya, there have been few in which one side, but not the other, has received substantial assistance from elsewhere.

The provision of assistance by outside powers in civil wars has thus become the typical form of war in the present era, characteristic of the age of ideological, rather than national, imperialism. As concern over political developments in other states becomes greater and overt aggression more discredited, it may become even more common. A situation could come about in which the old-fashioned national wars entirely ceased, but in which a universal civil war was conducted between multinational political creeds within unchanging national frontiers. Yet activity of this type is one over which international norms of conduct are, more than in almost any other case, uncertain or disputed.

Coups d'état

The attempt to secure power for a favored ideology within another state is not always sought through full-scale civil war. Sometimes more limited measures may be attempted.

Political power in most nations customarily rested with ruling elite or monarch. Physical power, in the shape of armed force, was normally loyal to this authority. Thus in the last resort its choices could usually be enforced.

In most present-day societies the allegiance of armed forces to the ruling power is less secure. Especially where, as in many states, there is no longer a traditional ruling family but only a group of ruling politicians, often ineffective, sometimes unrepresentative, the loyalty of the armed forces to the regime becomes increasingly tenuous. In such circumstances soldiers sometimes feel that they alone can rescue the nation from inefficiency, corruption, decadence, or dependence. Even where they do not believe they themselves can more effectively rule, they consider that they can more effectively *choose* the rulers. In some societies attempts by the armed forces to exert ultimate authority have become so common as to be habitual. In Japan, ancient and recent, in Latin America during the first fifty years of this century, and parts of the Middle East today, the coup d'état became institutionalized as a normal form of political change. Even in Europe such cultural traditions remain important; they allow, for example, the military in France to attempt, even in recent years, an influence on political affairs which would be unthinkable on the other side of the Channel. The more common military intervention becomes, the more easily it may be resorted to on subsequent occasions.

The forces involved in such attempts vary. The army is the service most commonly involved. In some cases the armed forces themselves may be divided into different groups, conservative and radical (prewar Japan or contemporary Turkey). In some cases there may be differences between the different services (modern Argentina and Brazil). Or there may be divisions between youthful elements, which become associated with revolutionary forces, and more senior officers, who use their influence in support of the status quo (Ethiopia in 1960).

Coups d'état, like support for civil wars, have become today an ever more tempting form of international activity. Usually the hidden hand behind such measures can, if required, remain concealed. Few would like to say with certainty how large a part foreign activity played in the successful coup in Czechoslovakia in 1948; in the rise to power of Mossadegh in Persia in 1951; in his subsequent overthrow in 1953; in the displacement of Lumumba in the Congo in 1960; or the successful reestablishment of a Lumumbist regime in another part of the country in subsequent months. So long as the previous regime can be claimed as nonrepresentative — which is rarely difficult — the exported coup d'état may even be justified to the world without. And since, in the Middle East, in Asia, and in Latin America, many armed coups have resulted in the establishment of governments more effective, whether or not more representative, than those which preceded them, outside Europe and North America the coup is not always regarded as a discreditable method of achieving political change.

Table VI.2 contains a list of the principal coups d'état carried out between January, 1960, and December, 1966 (comparisons covering earlier periods would be misleading because of the lack of independent states in many areas). The list does not include cases in which existing presidents or prime ministers took over full powers or coups which were defeated at the outset. Nor does it include gradual transfers of power over a considerable period (as in Indonesia, 1965–66).

A few general conclusions can be drawn from this list.

First, from a purely geographical point of view the most striking feature is the total absence of coups in Europe, excluding Turkey in this period (though many took place there in the interwar years, and there were European coups, in Czechoslovakia, Hungary, and France, between 1945 and 1960).[1] Among the other regions Africa (14) rivals Latin

---

[1] There has now (1967) also been a military coup in Greece.

TABLE VI · 2

Principal Coups d'état, January, 1960–December, 1966

Africa (excluding Arab countries)	Military or civilian	Ideological direction
Congo, September 14, 1960: Colonel Mobutu, the army commander, declares army is assuming power after President Kasavubu has dismissed Mr. Lumumba, who refuses to resign. On February 12, 1961, Lumumba is reported murdered. Throughout successive changes of government President Kasavubu remains in office until November 25, 1965; he is deposed by Mobutu, who assumes the presidency.	M M	Against politicians Neutral
Ethiopia, December 13, 1960: During the absence of Emperor Haile Selassie in South America, elements of the imperial guard and police, led by General Newaye, carry out a coup which collapses on the Emperor's return three days later.	MC	For democracy (unsuccessful)
Togo, January 13, 1963: President Sylvanus Olympio assassinated during army coup, and in May Mr. Nicholas Grunitsky becomes President.	M	For democracy
Dahomey, October 28, 1963: Colonel Soglo, army chief of staff, deposes President Hubert Maga and takes power himself pending new elections. These are held the following year when Mr. Apithy is elected. On November 29, 1965, Soglo forces the resignations of President Apithy and the Prime Minister, Mr. Ahomadegbe. Mr. Congacou, president of the national assembly, is installed as president of the country. On December 22, Soglo again takes power when politicians fail to agree on the composition of a government.	M M M	For democracy Neutral Against politicians
Zanzibar, January 12, 1964: Shaike Karume drives sultan into exile in Britain and becomes president. African parties break Arab hegemony and country later unites with Tanganyika to become Tanzania.	C	Racial leftward
Gabon, February 18, 1964: M. Jean Aubame, Opposition leader, heads a revolt which is supported by a group of young officers. President Mba is arrested, but the revolt is suppressed by French troops the following day.	MC	For democracy (unsuccessful)

TABLE VI · 2 (*Cont.*)

Africa	Military or civilian	Ideological direction
Central African Republic, January 1, 1966: President Dacko is driven from office by an army coup led by Colonel Bokassa.	M	? Rightward, anti-Chinese
Upper Volta, January 4, 1966: Colonel Lamizana, chief of staff, deposes President Yameogo and installs a military government.	M	For order
Nigeria, January 15, 1966: A group of young army officers kidnaps the federal Prime Minister, Sir Abubakar Tafawa Balewa, and kills two regional premiers; Sir Abubakar is later found murdered. On January 16 the remainder of the Nigerian cabinet calls on Major General Aguivi Ironsi, the army commander, to take over administration. *July 29, 1966:* General Ironsi overthrown by military coup of northern officers under Colonel Gowon.	M M	Against politicians for eastern region Against centralization for northern region
Ghana, February 24, 1966: President Nkrumah overthrown by military coup led by Major General Joseph A. Ankrah.	M	For democracy
Burundi, November 28, 1966: King and his government overthrown by military coup.	MC	Factional
Middle East		
Turkey, May 27, 1960: Army overthrows government of Adnan Menderes, who is arrested and subsequently tried and hanged. General Gursel becomes president.	M	Leftward
Syria, September 28, 1961: Coup ends union with Egypt (United Arab Republic) in force since February, 1958. Government of independent Syria headed by Dr. Mamoun Kuzbari. *March 28, 1962:* Army takes over power. President Kudsi resigns. Assembly dissolved. April 13: President Kudsi reinstated. *March 8, 1963:* Military coup. National Council of Revolution set up, including Baathists, Nasserists, and nationalists. *February 23, 1966:* Military coup led by left-wing Baathists. Dr. Atassi becomes head of state and Dr. Zeayen, prime minister.	MC M M M	Rightward Leftward Leftward Leftward
Yemen, September 27, 1962: Iman Badr, who had succeeded his father a week	M	For democracy, leftward

TABLE VI · 2 (*Cont.*)

Middle East	Military or civilian	Ideological direction

before, ousted by army coup in Sana. At first reported killed, the Imam subsequently reappears and heads royalist resistance against republican regime led by Colonel Abdullah al Sallal.

Iraq, February 8, 1963:   M   For democracy
General Kassim overthrown and killed by army and air force contingents under Colonel Abdul Salam Arif, who became president with a Baath government. November 1963: After quarrels inside the Baath party, President Arif assumes full powers and establishes a new revolutionary command.

Sudan, October 30, 1964:   C   For democracy
After student demonstrations and a general strike, military rule, which had been in force since November, 1958, replaced by transitional civilian government headed by Ser al-Khatim Khalifa.

Algeria, June 19, 1965:   M   Rightward
President Ben Bella (who had been in power since independence in 1962) overthrown and arrested. Coup led by Colonel Houari Boumedienne, chief of the armed forces, who becomes prime minister.

Central and South America

El Salvador, October 26, 1960:   MC   Leftward
President Jose Maria Lemus, a strong anticommunist, deposed by a mixed civilian and military junta under Colonel Miguel Castillo, who promises a return to constitutionality. On *January 25, 1961*, this junta is over-   M   Rightward
thrown by a new junta under Colonel Alonso Castillo Navarete, who promises to stop leftist trend and return to "authentic democracy."

Ecuador, November 7, 1961:   M   Leftward, for
President Jose Velasco Ibarra resigns under strong   democracy
pressure from army, which first installs an interim president but then gives way to air force pressure and accepts Dr. Carlos Arosemena, a leftist, as president. *July 11,*   M   Rightward, against
1963: President Arosemena deposed by military coup.   civilians
Junta established. *March 29, 1966:* Junta overthrown   MC   Leftward, for
by high command of armed forces. Civilian rule restored.   democracy

TABLE VI · 2 *(Cont.)*

Central and South America	Military or civilian	Ideological direction
Dominican Republic, January 16, 1962: Dr. Balaguer, who continued as President after the assassination of General Trujillo, resigns following military coup. On *January 18*, the military regime collapses and Dr. Rafael Bonnelly is installed as President. On *September 25, 1963*, Dr. Juan Bosch, who had been elected the previous year, is deposed by the army, which suspends the constitution. This regime lasts until *April 25, 1965*, when the leader of the ruling triumvirate, Señor Donald Reid Cabral, is deposed by a group of army officers. They try to reinstate Señor Bosch. Fighting leads to United States intervention and eventually to a temporary government under Dr. Hector Garcia Godoy, sworn in on September 3, 1965.	M C M MC	Rightward (unsuccessful) For democracy Rightward Leftward
Argentina, March 29, 1962: President Frondizi deposed by armed services; replaced by Dr. Jose Maria Guido. *June 28, 1966:* Dr. Guido deposed by armed forces under General Ongania.	M M	Rightward Neutral or rightward
Peru, July 18, 1962: Armed forces depose President Prado and form junta under General Ricardo Perez Godoy.	M	Rightward
Guatemala, March 31, 1963: Army seizes power "to defend Guatemala from the threat of communism." President Ydigoras Fuentes replaced by Colonel Enrique Peralta Azurdia.	M	Rightward
Honduras, October 3, 1963: Army takes over, sends President Villeda Morales into exile, and sets up military government under Colonel Osvaldo Lopez Arellano.	M	Rightward
Brazil, April 2, 1964: President Goulart deposed by armed forces, which install General Castelo Branco.	M	Rightward
Bolivia, November 3, 1964: Armed forces overthrow President Paz Estenssoro, and install military junta under General Barrientos Ortuno.	M	Against politicians
Far East		
Laos, August 9, 1960: Captain Kong Le occupies Vientiane and forces resignation of government of Tiao Somsanith. Prince	M	Leftward

TABLE VI · 2 (*Cont.*)

Far East	Military or civilian	Ideological direction
Souvanna Phouma later sworn in. *April 19, 1964,* Prince Souvanna Phouma deposed in military coup but restored on April 23.	M	Rightward (unsuccessful)
South Korea, May 18, 1961: Government of Dr. John Chang overthrown by military coup. Power assumed by Lieutenant General Chang	M	Rightward
Do Yung, army chief of staff. On *July 3,* he is arrested and effective power is assumed by Major General Pak Chung Hi.	M	Neutral
Burma, March 2, 1962: General Ne Win, chief of staff, overthrows government of U Nu and forms new government under revolutionary council.	M	Against politicians
South Vietnam, November 1, 1963: Army seizes control. President Ngo Dinh Diem and	M	Against politicians
his brother killed. *January 30, 1964:* General Nguyen Khanh assumes power in coup against General Duong	M	Neutral
Van Minh. *August 16:* General Khanh becomes President but resigns on August 25. Two days later becomes	M	Neutral
Prime Minister under General Minh. *November 4, 1964:* New civilian government under Tran Van Huong.	C	Neutral
December 20: Group of officers dissolves High National Council. After several more crises, effective power as-	M	Neutral
sumed by Air Vice-Marshal Nguyen Cao Ky in *June, 1965.*	M	Neutral

America (16) as the seat of the most numerous coups. The Far East (11) is not far behind, though the coups are mainly concentrated in three countries, and more than half the nations there are completely stable. All these overtake the Middle East (9) which, however, probably still has the highest number per country.

Second, concerning the instigators of coups, of these coups only two were undertaken mainly by civilians (Zanzibar possibly and Sudan certainly). As between the services, the army has been responsible, mainly or entirely, for about three-quarters of the rest. The others were mainly joint service operations. In three cases (Ecuador, Brazil, and the Dominican Republic) there was friction between services. In almost no case has a military coup taken place without the complicity of at least a part of the army. And in only one (Sudan) has the coup been almost entirely civilian.

Third, so far as the political purpose of the coups is concerned, they have not been, as one might expect, overwhelmingly rightward rather than leftward, except in Latin America. In the Middle East they were more often leftward or for the restoration of democratic rule. A great many coups have no clear ideological purpose. In Africa, they were often directed against politicians, political corruption, or political dissension in general. In a number of cases, on the other hand, they were for the *restoration* or establishment of democratic rule after a period of dictatorship or army rule (as in Togo, Gabon, Dahomey, Ethiopia, Sudan, Nigeria, and Ghana). In the Far East, too, they were sometimes against politicians in general or, as in Vietnam, represented squabbles between military factions, and only the two in Laos (left, right) and the first in South Korea (right) can be regarded as having primarily an ideological aim.

Fourth, it is noticeable that, with the exception of India, the developing countries that have remained free from coups d'état have been those which were economically most successful: Mexico and Chile in Latin America, Ivory Coast, Kenya, and Zambia in Africa, Malaysia and the Philippines in Asia. It is less clear which of these is cause and which effect.

The scale and loss of life vary from the coup in Zanzibar, in which probably several hundreds lost their lives and thousands were wounded, through a number in which casualties should be numbered in tens, to those in which there was no loss of life at all.

Clearly a means of overthrowing a government that is swift and sure, that can present the world with a *fait accompli* scarcely to be reversed, may often seem an even more attractive course than support for civil war. It is less expensive, both in military strength and in prestige. Often the occupation of a few key points, the radio station, the police headquarters, the principal airfields, and other communication centers, may be all that is needed to wrest political control. But the widespread adoption of the practice of selecting governments by armed *Putsch* would clearly threaten the international order. Particularly when this is indulged in competitively by rival factions, led or encouraged from outside the state concerned, such a custom may merely become the instrument of external aggression. And when those factions represent the main ideologies of the age, the dangers are multiplied. The successful accomplishment of each new coup may be denounced as unrepresentative by others so that a further coup may be attempted to reverse the first. The succession of such attempts which occurred in Syria between

1948 and 1953, and in Laos between 1959 and 1964, indicates the type of activity that may result.

Such conflicts have been traditionally regarded, even more than civil wars, as beyond international authority. Let us next, therefore, consider the attitude of international law on these questions.

International Law and Civil Conflicts

Under international law, as generally recognized today, where a civil war has broken out and any substantial part of a nation's territory is occupied by insurgent forces, other states possess not only the right, but the duty, to recognize the "belligerency" of those forces. Once the status of "belligerency" has been so acknowledged, the recognizing state comes under an obligation either to become a party to the war or to adopt a position of strict neutrality. If neutrality is undertaken, no assistance should be given even to the legal government, since this would constitute an illegal intervention and a violation of neutrality.[2]

In consequence, the recognition of belligerency of insurgents is, in practice, a calculated act of hostility toward the existing government. On the one hand it acknowledges the status of the rebel forces, who become an established authority in the eyes of the recognizing government; on the other, it prevents any form of assistance from being afforded, whether by the government or its nationals, to the government seeking to defend itself. Thus Britain, in according the status of "belligerency" to the Confederate forces in the American civil war, delivered a deliberate affront to the Federal Government. By refusing to grant General Franco's forces that status during the Spanish civil war, she withheld from his regime what would have been elsewhere taken as a mark of favor (though by granting him rights of "insurgency," and by "nonintervention," she granted him almost equivalent privileges).

The duty to accord the status of belligerency to insurgent forces under international law is so hedged around with conditions — the occupation

---

[2] See Oppenheim-Lauterpacht, *International Law* (London, 1955), II, pp. 249–50 and I, pp. 140–41. Some legal authorities recognize as legitimate assistance to a government to suppress an "insurrection." But this is generally regarded as unsettled. For a full discussion of the problem, see I. L. Brownlie, *International Law and the Use of Force by States* (Oxford, 1963), pp. 321–327; R. A. Falk, "The International Law of Internal War," in J. N. Rosenau (ed.), *International Aspects of Civil Strife* (Princeton, 1964); H. Wehberg, *Civil War and International Law* (London, 1938).

of a substantial part of the national territories, adherence to the rules of war, and the practical necessity of such a recognition — that it has become in effect, despite international law, a purely discretionary matter. In practice, at least since World War I, though civil war has abounded, the "duty" has scarcely ever been performed. The desire to avoid giving offense to a government that may yet prove victorious, the natural instinct to sit on the fence, perhaps even some fellow feeling between legal governments against revolutionary forces have served to prevent such action. In this, as in so much else, the theory of international law has been overtaken by current international practice.

When no recognition of belligerency is made, the rebel forces may be regarded as "insurgents" or "revolutionaries." Here, it is generally accepted, there exists no restriction on the degree of assistance which a foreign government or its nationals may afford to the legal government. Aid to the rebel forces, on the other hand, remains an offense if the situation is one of "revolution." Where it is one of "insurgency," there are no clear obligations and a number of interpretations have been put forward.[3]

But these rules too have not been widely followed in modern international practice. In practice there has been little attempt to distinguish between "belligerency," "insurgency," and "revolution." As we have already seen, even a century ago intervention in favor of rebels was widespread — indeed almost as common as that in favor of governments. With the shrinking of the globe and the increase of ideological fervor, such action has become commoner than ever over recent years. While each nation and alliance would indignantly denounce intervention by other states in such situations, most have been ready to undertake intervention in circumstances favorable to themselves (see Table VI.1 on pp. 142–143) and text on pp. 141–142.

Conversely, the principle that assistance to the legal government was unexceptionable where no belligerency was recognized itself began to be questioned. In certain circumstances any intervention is regarded as mischievous. Soviet assistance to the republican government in Spain was thought by many as reprehensible as German and Italian assistance to the rebels. British help to the Greek Government in 1944–45 was de-

---

[3] H. Lauterpacht, *Recognition in International Law* (Cambridge, 1947), p. 270; R. A. Falk, *op. cit.*, pp. 199–202. A set of rules concerning the rights and duties of foreign states in cases of insurgency was adopted by the Institute of International Law in 1900. A convention on the Duties and Rights of States in the Event of Civil Strife was signed in Havana on February 20, 1928. Neither of these sets of rules has been widely observed or even quoted.

nounced by some almost as much as Communist help to the rebels later. United States and British military assistance to the legal governments of Lebanon and Jordan in 1958 was widely regarded as a provocative action. Soviet assistance to what she and others regarded as the legal government of the Belgian Congo at the end of 1960 was equally considered a violation of current codes of international conduct.

Thus opinion on the legality of assistance toward the respective contenders in a civil war would be confused enough, even if it was always certain who was legal government and who rebel. But a patron who wishes, in such a case, to keep on the right side of the law has only to contend that the side he is assisting is the only true legal authority. The Chinese Government, in sending assistance to rebel forces in Algeria, could claim they were assisting the government they had recognized as legal in that country. The Soviet Government in flying arms to one of the factions in Laos in 1960–61, could claim that they were assisting the authority which not only they, but some noncommunist states, acknowledged as the lawful government. The United States Government, in assisting the opposition camp, could declare equally resolutely that they were supporting an authority they recognized as legitimate.

Each side in such cases will denounce the other for "intervention." Assisters of the legal government may protest more self-righteously than the others. Threatened governments themselves may air accusations of outside assistance to revolutionary forces to mobilize support from ideological allies (like the charges of external intervention made by the Nationalists in China and by right-wing governments in Laos). But, conversely, aiders of the rebels may denounce the unrepresentative, despotic, or seditious nature of the established regime, so discrediting assistance to lawful authorities (as was United States aid to South Vietnam or Soviet assistance to Cuba).

New problems arise over the actions of individuals. Help to rebel forces may be provided, not by sympathetic governments, but by sympathetic private individuals. "Volunteers" may be offered to a neighboring state (as provided by China in the Korean war, and offered by China and the Soviet Union in other cases). Individual "sympathizers" may pilot aircraft or undertake other assignments (as in the Indonesian revolt of 1958). "Mercenaries" may assist a faction which is financially in a position to employ them (as occurred in the Congo). "Freedom fighters" may undertake to fight on behalf of suppressed peoples in foreign lands (as in Angola or South Africa). Here too international law is unclear.

Since there is no widespread consensus on the legitimacy of aid to either or both parties to such conflicts, in practice outsiders have normally continued to offer assistance in mutual competition. International opinion, possessing no principles by which it could discriminate between such activities, has been wholly incapable of exerting any effective restraint over them. And international organizations have been inhibited by the same difficulty.

International Organizations and Civil Conflicts

For, although there has been uncertainty about unilateral intervention in domestic conflicts, there have equally been doubts concerning the legitimacy of collective intervention through an international authority. The Holy Alliance, it is true, was not inhibited by such doubts. It did not hesitate to intervene to suppress revolutionaries (as in Naples and Spain in 1819–20). Russia and Prussia intervened after the revolutions of 1848. But there was sufficient disagreement on such issues for these to be regarded rather as cases of national intervention than that of an international organization as such. The Concert of Europe would consider domestic disturbances (the Naples revolution in 1820, the Greek war of independence in 1827, and other troubles in Turkey). But joint intervention (as at Navarino in 1827) was the exception rather than the rule.

The League of Nations, when it was founded, was more concerned with preserving "sovereignty." The prohibitions of outside intervention in civil matters, which international law had established, were preserved in the Covenant of the League. Under Article XV, the Council was to make no recommendation on any dispute found to be "solely within the domestic jurisdiction" of a member. The League, as a result, effectively averted its eyes from such civil wars, for example in China and Spain, as occurred during that period. International action relating to Spain, such as the formulation and enforcement of "nonintervention" policies, took place outside the ambit of the League. In the many other civil disputes of that era, in Austria, Romania, Turkey, Iran, Nicaragua, Haiti, and other Latin American states, the League took no action.

Similar reservations in the UN Charter inhibited international action over civil wars after World War II. The main one was that of Article 2(7), prohibiting UN action on matters "essentially within the domestic jurisdiction" of each state. There was, as a result, no consistency in UN responses on such issues. Actions taken in the civil wars occurring during that time are set out in Table VI.3. Especially in the early years the

TABLE VI · 3

UN Action Against Civil Wars, 1946–1966

Civil war	UN action
Greece, 1945–49	Establishment of UN Special Committee on the Balkans and inspection of northern frontier
Philippines, 1946–50	None
Colombia, 1946–	None
China, 1946–49	None
Burma, 1948–	None
India, 1948–50	None
Cuba, 1953–59, 1961	None
Malaya, 1957–60	None
Muscat, 1957–60	Special Representative of UN Secretary General sent to investigate and report
Lebanon, 1958	Dispatch of observation group to prevent infiltration and supervise withdrawal of foreign troops
Cameroun, 1958–	None
Indonesia, 1958–59, 1965	None
Laos, 1959	Dispatch of Secretary General's Representative
Vietnam, 1959–	None
Congo, 1960–65	Use of UN troops, already dispatched, to restore law and order and unitary government
Yemen, 1962–	Dispatch of observers to prevent outside intervention
Cyprus, 1964–	Dispatch of UN peace force to prevent civil war and restore order
Dominican Republic, 1965	Dispatch of Secretary General's Representative to observe and report
Venezuela, 1965–	None

UN rarely intervened in such situations. Civil conflicts in China, the Philippines, Burma, Malaya, Indonesia, Cameroun, Vietnam, and other countries were studiously ignored by that organization. In the few cases where approaches were made to the UN (as during the Chinese and Greek civil wars), these had to be based on allegations of interference from without. In one or two cases, even though an appeal was made on grounds of external intervention, the UN deliberately decided not to take up the matter (as when, after the Chinese civil war, China complained of United States interference in Formosa or, during the civil war in Muscat, a number of Arab states complained of intervention by Britain).

In practice this principle of no international intervention has not been followed with any consistency. The UN has been ready to claim if necessary that even a purely domestic conflict represented a threat to international peace and security. In Lebanon in 1958, the UN assumed authority for the restoration of peaceful conditions after a domestic conflict in that country, pleading the threat of international action as an excuse. In the Congo in 1960–65, the UN, though nominally called in to expel external forces, in effect asserted jurisdiction over an internal dispute and was obliged ultimately to wield armed force to resolve it. In Cyprus a UN peace force was dispatched. Yet in a large number of the cases in which no action has been taken, the evidence of external intervention has been almost as great as in those in which UN assistance was accepted. In Vietnam it was much greater.

The UN, therefore, has followed no consistent policy on the matter. Nor, equally, has it maintained a strict interpretation of the terms of the Charter. It has adopted different courses on different occasions, according to the pressures of political interest and the needs of the moment. In practice, as the table shows, as time has gone on, it has become readier to intervene in such conflicts, even if there was only a threat of outside action.

In certain cases, therefore, the UN has taken action and sometimes produced significant results. In assessing the success of the various procedures used, one comes up against the same difficulty as in previous cases. The fact that peace followed the use of a particular measure does not prove that it resulted from it. On the whole, however, it would probably be generally accepted that of the issues listed, UN action was most successful in Lebanon and Cyprus. In the first case, external intervention was prevented, and the civil war pacified, within two or three months. In the second, though the underlying causes of dispute were not affected, considerably more peaceful conditions were assured, through the use of a neutral umpire and a buffer force, and again outside attack was prevented. Even in the Congo, the object of preventing external involvement was largely achieved and the evacuation of Belgian troops successfully accomplished. The cessation of infiltration and guerilla activity succeeded the dispatch of observers to Greece and may have resulted from their presence. But observers cannot achieve much when intervention has already passed a certain pitch of intensity (as in Yemen). What the UN has not been able to do effectively in such cases is to pacify a civil disturbance that has reached the stage of large-scale civil war (the Congo, Vietnam, and other cases), as opposed to sporadic disturbances (Lebanon and Cyprus). This suggests that UN action is usually effective only if it can be taken at an early stage when it will be better able both to inhibit external involvement and to restrain the course of internal disturbances.

United Nations action has been even rarer on coups d'état, as one would expect. In the vast majority of the many coups d'état which have occurred in the last fifteen years, no attempt has even been made to bring the matter before the UN. Yet a closer examination reveals that, here too, no consistent policy has been followed. At the time of the coup in Czechoslovakia in 1948, a request by the representative of the previous government for an investigation of the events preceding and succeeding that coup was inscribed on the agenda of the Security Council by an overwhelming majority, despite the claim of the Soviet Union that the question was one of domestic jurisdiction. It is true the reason given for this decision was a complaint that an outside power had "directly and indirectly" participated in the coup. But this could have been shown as convincingly in many other cases. And when in 1954 a complaint was submitted by Thailand that Viet Minh forces in Laos and Cambodia were planning to overthrow the legal governments of these countries, this too was discussed by the Security Council though once again little evidence could be brought of the involvement of foreign forces.

On occasion, therefore, the UN has been prepared to discuss coups d'état as well as civil wars, though it has usually felt it necessary to claim evidence of the involvement of an outside power. In the modern world, however, most such attempts are in some sense international in their effects. Almost any coup is likely to be of some advantage to one side or the other in the cold war. And in almost every case some evidence of foreign involvement may be available to those who wish to claim this. In a unified international political community as today's, any attempt to bring about political change by violence may be international in its implications.

A coup may, too, cause as much loss of life as some of the lesser of today's wars. It would be difficult to estimate whether the attempted coup in Ethiopia in 1960, launched from within the capital, caused fewer or more deaths than the civil war in Laos which took place in the same year, or even than an international war such as that launched against Guatemala in 1954. More important, the coup may, if it is succeeded by a whole series of countercoups designed to secure control for a particular ideology, quickly develop into something on a far larger scale. The events in Laos in 1960–61, starting as a succession of "coups," quickly developed into full-scale civil war. And it is possible to envisage a situation in which ideological warfare habitually came to be waged with organized bands of armed agents, carefully confined on either side to nationals of the coveted state, operating simultaneously in half the capitals of the world. Here too, therefore, effective international procedures may be required.

Conclusions

Civil conflicts thus have become the commonest form of violence in the modern world community. Such a change from a system primarily of transfrontier to one of intrafrontier activity has transformed the possibility of making either a balance of power system (of nineteenth-century type), a collective security system (of the League of Nations type), or an international enforcement system (of UN type) effective. The balance of power, or deterrent, system cannot work effectively for these cases because the power available to any nation or alliance *within* a particular state, depending partly on political factors, cannot be accurately measured in advance, and cannot therefore be effectively balanced and deterred. A collective security system becomes unavailable because of the difficulty of defining the actions against which collective action is to be taken in sufficiently unmistakable form to insure a unanimous response. International enforcement action is made difficult because, where civil war breaks out or a coup d'état is initiated, there may be no clear breach of the peace available for international retaliation: even the most powerful enforcement agency will find it difficult to accomplish anything effective when there exists neither identifiable criminal nor identifiable crime.

The first conclusion is that if an effective order is to be established all such conflicts must be recognized as legitimate subjects of international concern. If, in the modern world, even international wars are increasingly fought out within the frontiers of a single state, it is perhaps illogical that it is precisely these types of conflicts that, in theory, remain outside the jurisdiction of the UN. Of the list of wars in the postwar world (see pp. 183–185), a very large proportion have been nominally domestic conflicts. Such wars have been not only numerous but bloody.

More lives have probably been lost in them than in any other types of war waged during the period. They are often infected with the fanaticism of the religious wars of an earlier age. And possibly the greatest dangers of large-scale war today are those deriving from domestic conflicts in sensitive strategic areas between the great blocs.

In other fields the UN has not hesitated to give consideration to matters which were essentially domestic. The activities of the Franco regime in Spain, disputes within the colonies, the racial policies of South Africa, human rights in East Europe — items on all these have been freely adopted and discussed. It is true that sometimes the pretext has been put forward that these represented a "threat to international peace and security" or were in other ways a matter of international concern. But this was equally true of most civil conflicts. Few civil disputes are without international implications. An attempt to distinguish clearly how far the civil wars in Lebanon and the Congo (which the UN discussed), and the wars in Burma, Malaya, Indonesia, Vietnam, and Laos (which they did not) had international implications would prove unrewarding. Most civil wars represent a "situation which might lead to international friction or give rise to a dispute" (and so would be eligible for discussion under Chapter VI of the Charter). Many are even a "threat to the peace" (eligible under Chapter VII).

United Nations reluctance to become involved in cases of civil war is perhaps partly related to the ineffectiveness, rather than the illegality, of international intervention. It is true that in certain cases — where large-scale hostilities are already in progress, for example — there is little that UN action can usually achieve. In other cases, ideological dissension within the UN itself may inhibit effective action. But UN resolutions were used in coping with large-scale hostilities in Indonesia, Algeria, Kashmir, and elsewhere, and they might serve some purpose in other areas. If UN intervention could help bring about a solution in Lebanon in 1958, it might do so in other cases of civil conflict. If UN action could achieve the restoration of central government control and the limiting of foreign influence in the Congo and Cyprus, it might serve similar purposes in Vietnam and other cases. The principle of international competence over civil wars, therefore, clearly needs universal application.

A second, and complementary, principle is required to establish the limits of *national* intervention in civil wars. Since the present law is so confused, there is an urgent need that some UN body, perhaps the International Law Commission, should seek to formulate a clear body of rules on this subject. Where full-scale war has broken out there might be some advantage in a reversion to something like the rule formerly adopted under international law where the belligerency of insurgents was acknowledged: the prohibition of all unilateral intervention from outside, whether on behalf of "legal authority" or of "insurgents." In practice the distinction between legal government and rebel is often not easy to sustain. And its perpetuation leads to those types of situation, frequent in recent years, where both ideological contenders continue to send aid to the factions they favor, each insisting that this alone represents the "legal government." Even when there is no serious dispute over which faction represents the legal government, a sudden intrusion of external forces on its behalf may only precipitate corresponding counteraction from another quarter. The dispatch of armed forces by the governments of the United States and Britain to the legal authorities in Lebanon and Jordan in 1958, or of Soviet assistance to Lumumba in 1960, represented no violation of the current international code. Yet few would now deny that these actions aggravated existing tensions in the area, as was implicitly acknowledged in their subsequent cessation at UN request a few months later. In such cases it has been generally recognized that failure to observe complete noninterference might have resulted in the extension of the cold war into new areas already troubled by dangers of their own.

This rule need not prevent military assistance for any government engaged in internal security operations against subversive forces. It is the *individual* determination by each outside government of the status of the civil war that at present often leads to conflict. The UN might itself determine whether the situation was one of "civil war" (formerly "belligerency"), in which all assistance to either side was prohibited, or of civil disturbance (formerly "revolution"), in which the national government, but not its opponents, might legitimately receive assistance.[4]

---

[4] R. A. Falk, *op. cit.* "We need . . . to discriminate between internal wars that it is safe to treat as domestic so as to proscribe participation by nations or supranational institutions, and those that it is not because the internal area of conflict is the scene of indirect aggression or because it represents a struggle for certain minimum domestic rights that the world as an emerging and limited community is coming to recognise as mandatory." This distinction differs from my own in that it suggests that conditions which would exclude national intervention would also exclude that of international organizations. For a criticism of the concept of "indirect aggression," see p. 86, above note 24. On the other hand the suggestion that internationalization is permissible when the struggle is for certain "minimum domestic rights" is similar to that proposed in Chapter Five, p. 135, though once again there is a difference in that Dr. Falk seems to make no distinction between national and international intervention in such circumstances.

The UN might wish to designate conflicts as in the former category (and so exclude all outside intervention) in all cases where there was genuine doubt as to the constitutional character of the government, and to its right, therefore, to have support against the forces that challenged it; or where two or more factions could each present plausible claims to represent the legal government. It might do so where there was an immediate danger of the injection of tensions derived from elsewhere (say the cold war in Europe) into disputes not immediately related (the national conflicts of Africa and Asia). Finally, it might make such a declaration where not only the constitutional, but the representative, character of the government was in question, so that the UN would not be placed in a position of giving implicit moral support to a government against forces representing genuine national or popular aspirations, at least unless that government was ready to submit to a test of its popular support at the polls. In these cases no external assistance would be permissible at all.

In other cases, aid to a recognized government against rebel forces might be permitted if international authority for this had been obtained. Once it is accepted that all civil wars may represent a "threat to international peace and security," there is no reason why threatened governments should not themselves bring to the attention of the UN attempts to use force to undermine their authority. And where that organization is satisfied that there are no good grounds to question the claims of the government, it may sometimes authorize the provision of assistance, even use its own powers, to overcome attempts at subversion by violence. Conversely, assistance to rebels would be prohibited. Particular kinds of assistance to rebel forces would need to be proscribed. The arming or training of revolutionaries in foreign countries (the Cuban emigres trained in the United States or the Viet Cong in North Vietnam); the establishment of émigré radio stations and other propaganda organizations preaching the overthrow of a recognized government (the Free Thai radio broadcasting from China, or Radio Free Europe from West Germany); the harboring of rebel governments on foreign territory (the rebel Malaysian authorities in China or the Brunei government once maintained in Indonesia) — all of these might need to be outlawed.[5]

International bodies would therefore sometimes need to determine

---

[5] Certain elementary rules of this type are included in the Charter of the Organization of African Unity. This includes among its principles: ". . . unreserved condemnation, in all its forms, of political assassination as well as of subversive activities on the part of neighbouring states or any other states."

what represented the legal government. This already takes place by implication in decisions as to which government should occupy the national seat within the UN. If membership in that organization were taken to involve an obligation to recognize other accredited governments by its members, the conflicts that at present sometimes break out over legitimacy would be reduced. It would then become all the more necessary to establish objective criteria for recognition (like effective control over the territory of the state), such as international lawyers traditionally laid down, but which have been rarely observed in recent years.[6]

Once the representative or legal character of the government had been internationally established, support, even moral support, for "revolution" against it would be recognized as an offense against the international order. Support for revolutions elsewhere is not confined to any single nation or group of nations today. The United States Government has practiced it in Cuba, the British Government in Egypt, and the Egyptian Government in other Middle Eastern countries, as have communist governments elsewhere. All denounce it in others and indulge in it themselves. Yet such a practice, which involves in effect a form of limited assault against foreign governments without the expense and risk of formally making war, can itself destroy the basis of international order. Propaganda glorifying revolution, and attempts to designate revolutionary wars as "just wars," therefore, violate a basic principle of international order. For the attempt to spread revolution elsewhere may be as much an attack against that order as deliberate aggression across international borders.[7]

The final principle required here is that governments should themselves undertake responsibility for the actions of the individuals over whom they exercise jurisdiction. International principles on propaganda and revolutionary activity would be of little value if they applied to government radio stations, but not to other such stations in that government's territory; to the action of government officials, but not to the party members associated with that government; to official military

---

[6] For arguments in favor of internationalizing recognition, see R. A. Falk, *op. cit.*, pp. 223–226.

[7] Oppenheim's *International Law* states (Vol. I, p. 293): "Subversive activities against foreign states . . . when emanating directly from the government itself or indirectly from organizations receiving from it financial or other assistance or closely associated with it by virtue of the constitution of the state concerned amount to a breach of international law. The principles of independence and nonintervention enjoin upon governments and state officials the duty of scrupulous abstention not only from active interference, but from criticism of foreign laws and institutions."

forces, but not to paramilitary organizations, such as the CIA, or to "volunteers," such as those sent to Korea. And international principles governing intervention, therefore, would need to be enforceable by governments against their own nationals everywhere.[8]

Again there are implications for national as well as international policies. If it is true, as we have seen, that the involvement of one external power frequently leads to the involvement of another on the opposite side, such powers will be particularly cautious about intervening. If great powers are particularly sensitive about the areas on their immediate borders, there should be special caution about activity in such areas. If, as we have seen, civil conflicts are especially likely to occur in economically undeveloped areas, and where the representative character of the government is in question, counteraction will require to be economic and political as much as military. And assistance in establishing efficient and honest administrations and police forces may be more important than assistance in the military field.

The main *procedure* required to implement these principles is that in appropriate cases international actions to resolve the basic conflict of authority by a plebiscite should be undertaken. For all disputes of this category arise where the authority of the existing government is, for whatever reason, called into question. Circumstances may arise (as in Lebanon in 1958) when rival interpretations of the constitutional position are put forward, or (Korea in 1960) when the legitimacy of elections is challenged, or (the Congo in 1960–61) when there are rival contentions concerning the legitimacy of a particular authority, or (Laos in 1960) when a series of coups and countercoups has taken place, leaving the country divided. In all such cases there is only one ultimate method of resolving the issue: to test the rival claims to authority by an appeal to the polls. Many problems of this sort might be overcome if the UN determined at an early stage to put the matter to the test through elections. For few today dare to challenge the validity of such an appeal. Indeed the verdict of the polls is the only universally accepted test of legitimacy, the only basis for an international consensus on such matters.

There are already precedents for such a course. Conflicts of sovereignty in the Saar were resolved by internationally supervised plebiscites in 1935 and 1955. The Soviet Union herself in 1949 proposed a settlement

---

[8] Even traditional international law recognizes this duty: "States are under a duty to prevent and suppress such subversive activity against foreign governments as . . . armed hostile expeditions or attempts to commit common crimes against life or property." Oppenheim, *op. cit.*, I, p. 292.

of the Greek civil war through the conduct of elections under international supervision. Internationally supervised elections were promised (though never undertaken) as part of the settlement of the civil war in Indo-China. The holding of elections provided the only final solution to the civil disturbances in Lebanon in 1958. A UN plebiscite in the British Cameroons served to resolve months of civil dissension there. And a similar course might have provided the only satisfactory means of resolving disputes between rival authorities in Laos, the Congo, and Vietnam.

The adoption of such a procedure could also serve to deter the intensification of similar disputes in the future. As we have seen, the civil wars that have occurred in the postwar period have been almost without exception in countries where there was, for whatever reason, some reason to doubt the representative character of the existing government. Were international procedures available for establishing representative forms of government, such disputes might become less common. A government that felt confident of its authority should have no reason to resist a demand for the holding of impartially controlled elections. These need not always take the form of the multiparty contests favored in the West: the same object might be secured by some type of referendum, by which, for example, such regimes as those now established in Pakistan, Egypt, Iraq, and Burma, could demonstrate that they commanded widespread support.

Because of the necessity of recognizing the principle of popular sovereignty in cases of disputed authority, no system designed to preserve permanently established "spheres of influence," rigid lines of demarcation between particular ideological or political camps, or the "containment" of particular areas, can be long successful. Such efforts are doomed — not merely because they seek to maintain a rigid status quo in an essentially dynamic universe; but because they seek to subject the fortunes of one people and nation to the political or strategic conveniences of others. They are likely, therefore, in the long run only to provoke rather than prevent further conflict both within and without. What can legitimately be done, especially in view of the special sensitivity of great powers to the areas in their immediate vicinity, is to encourage small nations in such regions to preserve a policy of restraint in relation to their neighbors, and to refrain from recruiting them for hostile military alliances. Even this will not solve the difficult problems that arise in areas where natural spheres of influence converge. Here, only neutralization may provide a solution.

Procedures somewhat similar to these are applicable in cases of coups d'état. Where a constitutional and representative government was overthrown by an armed coup, the UN might refuse to recognize the credentials of the new government, unless it either reverted to the established constitution or agreed to a confirmation of its authority by UN-supervised elections. Failing such agreement, the new authority might be excluded from representation in the UN itself and in all the specialized agencies, and so lose the benefit of their aid and assistance. Members themselves could be called on to withhold both recognition and aid on the same terms. Something like this principle has already been applied on occasion by the United States over coups in Latin America, but has proved impossible to sustain over any length of time failing its application on an international scale.

Other procedures are available for other purposes. International bodies may seek *mediation* by appointing some mutually respected personality to suggest a compromise between the two factions (used in Cyprus in 1964). They may seek *insulation* of the conflict, by use of a commission to observe hostilities and prevent foreign assistance (used in Indo-China in 1954 and in Yemen in 1963). They may seek the *expulsion* of foreign elements already present (attempted in the Congo). They may seek *verification* through observers to report on the situation on the spot and advise (used for civil disturbances in Jordan and Lebanon in 1958). They may seek *separation* of conflicting forces, while negotiations

TABLE VI · 4

Civil War: Available UN Principles and Procedures

Principles	Procedures
No assistance to revolutionary government from outside the state.	Resolutions embargoing assistance to one or both sides.
No assistance to government forces without sanction of international authority.	Establishment of machinery, by observers and other means, for enforcing this.
No recognition of revolutionary government without international recognition.	Institution of procedures for conciliation or mediation.
Responsibility of governments for intervention by their nationals.	Conduct of plebiscites or elections under international auspices.

are conducted (something like this was achieved in Kashmir). Finally, they may attempt to bring up the dispute for *discussion*, in UN bodies, or, where suitable, in the International Court.

Intervention in civil conflicts elsewhere is a form of activity at present governed even less than most by any agreed principles. It is just because no understanding exists (as well as because they represent the most favorable investment for international activity with the most limited liability) that interventions of this type have become so attractive and so widespread. As in other cases, only agreed principles and procedures may reduce their dangers.

Bibliography

Eckstein, H. (ed.), *Internal War, Problems and Approaches*, New York, 1964.

Modelski, G., *The International Relations of Internal War*, Princeton, 1961.

Northrop, F. S. C. (ed), *Ideological Differences and World Order*, New York, 1953.

Rosenau, J. N. (ed.), *International Aspects of Civil Strife*, Princeton, 1964.

Wehberg, H., *Civil War and International Law*, London, 1938.

CHAPTER SEVEN

Arms Control

The Balance of Power and Collective Security

If these are the principal forms of armed conflict within the modern international system, what are the means of regulating them that have mainly been attempted?

The most direct has been the attempt to arrive at conventions, formal or informal, concerning the level, type, and disposition of armaments so as to reduce their dangers to a minimum. This is analogous to the situation in a crime-ridden city, if the citizens said to one another: let us undertake to hold, dispose, and display the arms we have in such a way as to minimize the danger and the threat they may present to each other.

Attempts have been made to adjust and regulate man's capacity for war from early times. Arms control is exhibited in primitive form in all attempts by victorious armies to cripple the capacity of the defeated power to resume hostile activities. It has been practiced in the destruction of the opponent's arms or the razing of his fortified places, in the restriction of weapons-making capacity, even in the policing of an occupying army. Its deficiency in that form as a means of assuring stability is that the balance arrived at by such methods is likely to be acceptable to only one party. Nor will that party usually possess the means to assure this balance for any length of time.

During the eighteenth and nineteenth centuries in Europe, a somewhat more sophisticated approach to the problem of the disposition of power in the international community became current. The system of the balance of power which then emerged, though today frequently condemned, in fact possessed many of the features of modern systems of arms control. First, it recognized the principle that there existed a *mutual* interest in a balance of power. It was for this reason that writers on international law at the time regarded attempts to disturb that balance as violations of the law, so entitling others to forcible retaliation. Secondly, it recognized that a balance might be sustained by *unilateral* moves to establish it, or to redress it should it be disturbed. It was indeed assumed that it was only through a series of unilateral acts by different powers that equilibrium was ever likely to be achieved.

To describe this, at least in its early form, as a balance of power "system" is to do it too much honor. For there was little attempt at systematic and explicit formulation of the balance required. In practice the balance that arose was to a large extent the end-product of competitive attempts by individual members to further their own power and counter that of others, rather than a common endeavor by the whole to keep the parts in equilibrium. For most, it was the balance available to one's own country or side that counted, not the overall balance. Because the balance was conceived in subjective terms, almost anything could be denounced as a threat to it. And the excuse that an opponent's actions had "disturbed the balance of power" served on countless occasions, from the British declaration of war in 1756, through Pitt's condemnation of the French revolutionaries, to Hitler's occupation of the Rhineland, as a convenient justification for whatever armed counteraction was demanded at the time.[1]

From 1815 on, there was something more nearly approaching a system. There did emerge now, as we saw in Chapter One, a conception of a *common* interest in the stability of the system, in the "European order," or the "European system," over and above the individual interests of each member in its own relative power. And, even though little attempt to establish an agreed *military* balance was made, an attempt to formulate the political basis of equlibrium was undertaken at innumerable congresses between 1815 and 1914. In 1814, Britain, Austria, Prussia, and Russia signed a treaty for the establishment of a "System of real and permanent Balance of Power in Europe." The Treaty of Vienna was designed to define the system. Without such a political consensus no system could be durable.

During the next century many vital aspects of the system — the neutralization of Switzerland, Belgium, and Luxembourg, the international-

---

[1] For accounts of the balance of power system at work, see F. V. Gulick, *Europe's Classical Balance of Power* (Cornell, 1955); Arthur Hassell, *The Balance of Power, 1715–1789* (New York, 1914); A. J. P. Taylor, *The Struggle for Mastery in Europe* (Oxford, 1954). For analysis, see I. Claude, *Power and International Relations* (New York, 1962); R. N. Haas, "The Balance of Power: Prescription, Concept or Propaganda," *World Politics* (July, 1953).

ization of the Rhine and the Danube, the conditions of independence of Greece, Serbia, Romania, Bulgaria, and other countries, the reunification of Norway and Sweden, and the reunification and division of the Low Countries, the regimes in the Congo, Tangier, and Shanghai — these and many other questions were settled, not by unilateral action of the powers most concerned, but by the deliberations of international congresses, and laid down in formal treaties. Probably more important questions were settled through peaceful discussion among the principal powers in this period than at any other time before or since.

But although some elements of a consensus in the international order were attained in this way, in many areas it was lacking. There were always elements at the margins of the system — in new continents, such as Asia and Africa, in new situations, such as the dissolution of the Austrian and Turkish Empires, on which disagreements could break out. Although satisfied powers, such as Britain, might remain at peace, the rising powers, such as Germany and Russia, always found features of the order they could challenge. Because no serious effort at a military balance was attempted until the end of the century, such challenges were not normally met until victory had already been won in single combat. Only from 1878 to 1914 was some stability in Europe achieved and then partly by transferring the contests overseas. By then something like a *military* balance was attempted, not through agreement but through alliances in various combinations. But this balancing of power did not prevent war being launched, somewhat against the odds (by two great powers against three great and several small) in 1914.

It is sometimes said that the balance of power system cannot work without a balancer, one power that by remaining detached from the system can throw its weight in the scales on one side or the other to maintain equilibrium, as Britain is alleged to have done in the nineteenth century. But the evidence that Britain, or any other power, has ever pursued such a policy consistently is slender. To be performed effectively the role requires an inconsistency and an ideological indifference, such as few powers find easy to achieve. If Britain had been performing such a role consistently she would have shifted alliances rapidly according to the fortunes of war. At least from 1870, and even earlier, she would have joined forces with those opposing Germany. In fact even at the turn of the century, because of traditional hostility to Russia and France, she was contemplating alliance with Germany. By splendid isolation, Britain secured a measure of peace for herself during this time, as isolation often will. But she did not do so for the continent, as is sometimes suggested. Moreover, there is no means of ensuring that there will only be one balancing power. Balancing by two or more may be contradictory and disturbing: it was the unpredictable effect of the balancing powers in the interwar period — Italy, Poland, Romania, and the Soviet Union — which did so much to destroy stability then.

Next, it is important to stress that, even if these difficulties are overcome and an effective balance is in fact maintained, it may not serve to deter war. Whatever the value of the system for preventing undue dominance by one or a few states (and even this was small), the system was never, even in its heyday, a system tending toward the maintenance of peace. It is doubtful if it was even conceived as such (it was designed to minimize the power of others, not to preserve the peace). Certainly war was no less common during that period.

For the main defect of the system is that there is no evidence that the readiness of powers, or alliances, to go to war is closely related to the power balance on either side. Even when the system was in operation, and the powers of Europe were neatly arrayed in rival camps in 1742, this did not prevent the two sides from going to war in the War of Austrian Succession. Nor, at the close of that war, and after the quadrille by which the alliances were subsequently remade in precise balance, were they deterred from once more resorting to arms within eight years in the Seven Years' War. In 1914 the rival powers of Europe could scarcely have been more exactly balanced; yet the central powers were not deterred from war in consequence. However conscientiously the rules of balance are kept, therefore, peace may not be secured. Sometimes what may be required is not a balance but a preponderance of power against the main threat to the peace. Even this may not be enough: Napoleon and Hitler defied impossible odds in launching wars.

This analysis suggests certain conclusions. First, any military balance must be accompanied, if it is to be successful, by a political consensus covering the basis of the international order. Second, the balance must be flexible, and not too closely conditioned by ideology, to take account of changes in alliance — itself difficult to achieve; and even so it may be difficult to take account of all the possible combinations and permutations. Third, it is necessary for balancing powers to be limited to one, or always to act together, if they are to be effective in assuring equilibrium. Fourth, sometimes it is not a balance of power that is required, but a preponderance of power against the main potential threat.

These conditions probably remain true. Equilibrium is certainly desirable. It may marginally deter war. But there is little evidence that *alone* it will secure peace.

The conception of a mutual and *acknowledged* duty to preserve a balance in the classical balance of power period represented the first emergence of some sense of community interest as well as of national interest in the way in which power was employed.

During the first years of this century, these concepts came to be largely abandoned. Complementary power policies were replaced by competitive ones. At the Hague Conferences the attempt to seek a balance by unilateral moves or tacit understandings was replaced by an attempt to achieve binding and specific agreements on levels of arms. The object of disarmament for a time largely obscured that of arms control.

From the end of World War I a new type of balance began to be envisaged. It came to be recognized that only an overwhelming superiority of power was likely to be sufficient to deter a nation determined on a course of aggression. This could only be achieved through a flexible system under which all would unite, irrespective of alliances and loyalties, against any aggressor which might appear. This was the system known as *collective security*. It might be compared to a plan within the crime-infested city by which all citizens agreed to join in giving chase to any among their members who should be caught undertaking an act of violence.

It cannot be said that in the interwar period this system was manifestly successful. In the first place, it was not always so easy as the theory presupposed to establish beyond dispute who was the aggressor in any case of conflict. In theory, this was to be resolved by declaring any power who refused to agree to a peaceful arbitration of the dispute to be the aggressor, against whom armed force would be mobilized. In practice, over the major incidents of the period, the Corfu incident, Greek-Bulgarian border disputes, Manchuria, and even Ethiopia, it was always possible to find doubts or ambiguities in the situation, which justified a refusal to take part in retaliatory action. It often seemed wiser in this situation to conciliate, to send a commission of inquiry, or to call a meeting of the League Council, than to undertake at a moment's notice all the expensive, dangerous, and provocative procedures of mobilization and armed counterattack.

The second great difficulty was that even if the culprit could be identified, the outbreak of conflict at the far side of the world rarely seemed of such immediate concern, or direct interest, to governments that they were prepared to undertake the type of action the system presupposed. Since justifications for inaction were always available, they were always utilized. *Regional* agreements for this purpose might sometimes be successful (at a later date the Organization of American States became a more genuine collective security organization) because here the national interest in defending the peace is greater. But a system calling for world action on these lines was almost certainly doomed to failure.

After World War II collective security was sought by giving the Security Council, in which the great powers predominated, the right to reach a "decision" which would bind all members to take part in a common action against an aggressor, and so remove the danger of hesitant responses. But since that power in practice was almost never invoked, the difficulty of securing common action on an impartial basis against an aggressor remained as great as ever. Even where a strong recommendation was made, as in the Korean War, only a small proportion of the membership, already joined by a common ideological interest, felt ready to respond.

There are in fact a number of characteristics of national behavior that inhibit the effectiveness of either a balance of power or a collective security system. First, there is evidence that the behavior and alliances of nations tend to be dominated by one particular national relationship at any one time. Thus Britain's relationship to Russia dictated her relations with other powers in the late nineteenth century, while her relationship with Germany transformed all other relations, including that with Russia, in the early years of the present century; France's relations with Germany before and between the wars determined all her other foreign policies; Pakistan's relations with India and the United States' with China recently have conditioned most other friendships and alliances. The effect of this is that it is usually virtually impossible to organize either an exact balance of power, or a preponderance of power against a potential aggressor, because each state is far more powerfully and immediately concerned by relations with immediate antagonists. Traditional alliances and friendships dictate policy far more firmly than abstract commitments can do. Finally, it is hard to rely on the effective participation of distant nations with only marginal interests. In practice nations find safety mainly in the balance they themselves, with one or two close allies, can effect.

Second, the establishment of either a balance or a preponderance of power is inhibited by ideological sympathies. Britain was for long deterred from making common cause with Russia in the late nineteenth century on these grounds, despite a number of common interests. France and Britain failed to join with the Soviet Union in establishing an effective system of deterrence against Germany during the thirties on the same grounds. And in the postwar world alliances have even more clearly been conditioned by considerations of ideology, rather than of balance or deterrence.

Third, national behavior suggests that deterrent policies, whether by an equality or superiority of power, as in the balance of power and collective security systems, are in any case unlikely to succeed unless accompanied by some attempts to rectify underlying grievances. Warlike tendencies among nations, at least in the modern world, usually reflect genuine dissatisfactions and resentments. The attempt to meet these by a purely military confrontation is unlikely to contain them effectively for very long. Both balance of power and collective security systems may encourage nations to give too much weight to power factors at the expense of the psychological factors that are ultimately more important. Conversely, attempts at conciliation without a sufficient measure of deterrence as an ultimate support are equally likely to be unsuccessful. While French policy to Germany in the twenties, with its inevitable stimulation of German nationalism, reveals the folly of deterrence without conciliation, British and French policy in the thirties, after German nationalism had already been aroused, demonstrates the complementary folly of conciliation without a sufficient weight of deterrence to back it up. Deterrence and conciliation are each useless without the other to support them.

Modern Forms of Arms Control

So the system of alliances, known as the "balance of power" system, had failed. The establishment of a collective security system had been found impracticable. As a result, after World War II, there was an increasing interest in the possibilities of controlling the distribution of power, without its abandonment, in such a way as to minimize the dangers of conflict.

At first the only arms control attempted was on a unilateral basis. Unilateral arms control was attempted in the restrictions placed on Germany's freedom to rearm after World War I. But in this case effective control was totally absent. Germany was quickly able to reach agreement with another power enabling her to start her military recovery. Even the victorious powers soon began to be conscious of the political liabilities of imposing a resented and ineffective inspection. And the nation on which restrictions were placed was eventually in a position to challenge the whole of the rest of the continent to battle. After World War II even more sweeping restrictions were proposed. The total disarmament of Germany and Japan and the partial disarmament of Italy were proclaimed. This time it was the powers to the west which, finding the restrictions no longer in their interest, assisted in their violation. And in all three cases the provisions were, within a few years, deliberately overturned and those penalized assisted toward rearmament.

Thus arms control on a unilateral basis has not, in recent experience, proved highly successful. But its history serves to demonstrate certain conditions which need to be fulfilled by any successful plan for arms control. No system of imposed restrictions (such as that imposed on Germany after World War II) could ever be effective, unless secured by an agency which had powers of inspection and enforcement adequate to maintain it against the power whose capacity was restricted, a condition not easily fulfilled. No set of limitations (such as those imposed on her after World War II) could be long successful unless subsequently impartially maintained without regard to sectional or national interests. Most important of all, no system will be enduring which does not provide for an equilibrium accepted by all principal powers, including those defeated themselves, as a just and stable one. The effect of these conditions is that normally the balance required cannot be imposed by some powers on others. It is of the essence that the balance is *voluntarily* accepted. Unless this is so it could be as quickly and as arbitrarily overturned as disarmament measures themselves.

Only during the last few years have methods of achieving a jointly agreed equilibrium comparable to those of earlier times once more been discussed. Because of the difficulty encountered in negotiating formal agreements, voluntary measures have been recognized as an effective alternative for assuring balance. Arms control then takes the form of a cumulative series of self-denying ordinances by two, or a number of powers, designed to secure balance at a constant or declining, instead of a rising, level of expenditure or firepower.

Such measures are best analyzed according to the functions they may perform; and in order of likelihood of mutual acceptability.

One object of arms control measures may be to secure *stability*. Both sides may be able to contribute to reducing dangers by the disposition of the armaments they hold, without consultation with the other. This may lessen the appearance of a threat and the dangers of misunderstanding in crisis moments. Such policies may be undertaken in the choice of weapons systems; by refraining from sudden military dispositions likely to arouse apprehension; by avoiding provocative means of procuring intelligence; by the adoption of "fail-safe," and other foolproof command procedures for nuclear striking forces; by the choice of invulnerable systems, such as missile submarines, to minimize the likelihood of preemptive attack; by care to avoid unnecessary secrecy, ambiguity, or uncertainty; even by the exchange of certain intelligence information on a voluntary basis.

One important class of stabilization measure is that which provides for the renunciation, explicit or tacit, of a certain *type* of weapon or warfare: for example, chemical or bacteriological weapons, or the orbiting of weapons in space. Another is that designed to prevent the access of *new* nations to a particular type of weapon: such as the nuclear test ban or a nonproliferation agreement. The latter type, however, depends on the haves being able to evince, or to compel, the cooperation of the have-nots, a condition not easy to fulfill. It is more likely to prove possible to secure their renunciation in particular *areas*: as in atom-free zones, where the sacrifice is at least equal for all neighbors. Restraints on *trade* in arms to particular regions or countries, for example, the Middle East, are another kind of stabilizing agreement.

Still another type of stabilizing measure is the adoption of restraints in the whole conception of strategy. This may come through the abandonment of the assumption of total war and an acceptance that wars may be of limited aim (as accepted even in the relatively large-scale Korea and Vietnam wars). Strategies may be adopted that concentrate attack on military rather than civilian targets (nowadays called counterforce doctrines), so reducing the likelihood that either side will initiate strikes against cities; in recent years the United States, but not the Soviet Union, has advocated such policies. After war has begun, strictly limited war aims can be publicized and demands for "unconditional surrender," which may prolong conflict unnecessarily, may be avoided. Finally, effective procedures for crisis management and flexible war plans may be adopted, so avoiding the danger that a crisis may be allowed to build up to unmanageable proportions (as government decisions, mobilizations, and inflexible war plans caused to happen in 1914).

Second, arms control measures may improve *communication*. They may serve, both at times of crisis and between, to inform potential adversaries of the capabilities or intentions of each power. This objective has long been recognized. When Alexander I of Russia made his proposals for disarmament in the early nineteenth century, the British Government suggested in turn that each state should explain to "allied and neighboring states the extent and nature" of its own armaments "as a means of dispelling alarm, and of rendering moderate establishments mutually convenient." At the Hague Conference of 1907, the British Government declared that they were ready to exchange with any other power their naval estimates and proposed program of construction, in the hope that this might lead to a mutual interchange of information. And one of the objects of traditional diplomacy, not always fulfilled, was to reassure interested powers concerning the intentions of governments. Some modern arms control measures perform a similar function. Communication in time of crisis may be facilitated by such measures as "hot lines" providing the assurance of contact between major capitals. Day-to-day communication may be provided by secret correspondence, such as that initiated between the Soviet Union and the United States in recent years; by the exchange of intelligence information, as has sometimes been suggested; or perhaps most important, by facilities for quick communication between military commanders in the field.

Some arms control measures may be designed to bring about *disengagement*. These are intended to create an area from which the forces of two or more nations are withdrawn altogether, in order to avoid frontline confrontation between them. Of this type were agreements in earlier times for the recognition of buffer states (such as Afghanistan between Russia and India, Tibet between China and India, and elsewhere). Modern agreements of this type are those suggested for the withdrawal of all forces, or of nuclear forces, or of some forces, from Central Europe and other areas. Nuclear-free zones, or agreements to thin out forces or arms may also be regarded as agreements designed to bring about particular forms of disengagement.

Another object of arms control measures is to secure *equilibrium*. Measures of this kind are agreements, whether formal or tacit, to restrain expenditure on arms (for example, the level of arms budgets) or the type of weapon or program introduced (renunciations of the anti-missile missile, gas, and germs, or of civil defense); to balance forces in particular areas (by limiting or excluding nuclear weapons in Central Europe); or to keep levels of particular arms (strategic missiles) or of manpower (total enlisted forces) roughly in balance. Here many of the important moves can be unilateral measures of defense policy, on levels of arms and other matters, rather than explicit agreements.

To establish a balance effectively, it is essential that the equilibrium achieved must be variable, by mutual consent, to take account of shifts in the balance of forces and other unexpected developments. Thus if an agreement were to be reached and, at a subsequent stage, an important power were to shift its ideological allegiance, or another were to adopt total unilateral disarmament, the advantaged side might (as in a formal disarmament agreement) be required to make voluntary concessions to sustain the balance. To preserve something like a balance, moves may need to be made by comparatively small steps. Reductions as well as increases in arms may need to be restrained in the interests of equilibrium. The interwar and immediate postwar period demonstrated sufficiently the risks involved in excessive unilateral moves for reduction.

Any system creating effective equilibrium today would have to be far more complex than those which have mainly been conceived or discussed over the past twenty years. For it is quite clear that the bipolar relationship that has dominated military relationships during that period no longer has any relevance to the effective distribution of forces in the world today. Effective power is likely, within the foreseeable future, to be increasingly centered within a number of regional and continental groupings, not of equal military strength, but politically increasingly cohesive and independent of each other. There will be many smaller powers that do not fit exactly into any of these. The situation may then revert to something more like the old-fashioned balance of power system — and so be far more complex and unstable — than the bipolar system of recent years. A bipolar balance of arms would need to be replaced increasingly by a multiple balance. We shall see in Chapter Eight some of the difficulties of achieving this.

To provide an assured balance, the establishment of physical facilities for *verification* of the potentialities and intentions of other parties is required. Thus other arms control measures may provide firsthand witness to one side concerning the activities and intentions of the other. The accrediting of service attaches in embassies may be regarded as an early example of this type of arms control measure. For it was designed to secure reliable, rather than sensational, testimony to the establishment and dispositions of neighboring powers. Recent measures for the same purpose are the so-called "measures against surprise attack," which have been at various times discussed since World War II. The establishment of control posts at communications centers, airfields, railway stations, and highways might make it impossible for one side to prepare the means of launching a sudden large-scale conventional offensive without warning. The institution of some form of aerial reconnaissance in designated areas, on frontiers, or farther afield, could provide similar reassurance. Finally, a more comprehensive system of control, inspection of strategic delivery vehicles and other measures, may be instituted.

TABLE VII · 1

Arms Control Measures: by Function

Function	Individual measures
Stabilization	Improvements in command structure or communication system, unilateral or agreed; renunciation of destabilizing weapons systems; nonproliferation agreements; unilateral arms restraints or reductions.
Confidence building	Declarations concerning intentions; agreements concerning production of inessential weapons (e.g., of fissionable materials); disposition of forces in nonprovocative fashion; mutual observation agreements.
Communication	Communication links between heads of government or capitals; arrangements for communication between commanders in the field; agreements to communicate military movements; improved diplomatic consultations, summit conferences, etc.
Verification	Exchanges of service attachés; mutual air inspection; agreements for control posts or mobile terms; inspection in particular areas and for particular weapons; arrangements for comprehensive inspection with unhindered access.
Equilibrium	Unilateral reductions in particular weapons to create balance; agreements to balance levels in particular arms (e.g., strategic missiles or long-range bombers); attempts to balance forces in particular areas (e.g., Central Europe or the Middle East); attempts to balance defense budgets.
Disengagement	Agreements to reduce force levels in particular areas; agreements to ban particular arms in particular areas; agreements for frontier demilitarization and control.

The combination of some or all of such measures,[2] it has been thought, could reduce the uncertainties of the existing military confrontation.

[2] For detailed discussion of a number of arms control measures of this sort, see D. G. Brennan (ed.), *Arms Control and Disarmament* (London, 1961); Evan Luard (ed.), *First Steps to Disarmament* (London, 1965).

They could bring about an increase in confidence, from which more am-
bitious steps might result later. Finally, if successful, they might even,
by reducing the purely military tensions between the principal powers
and blocs, go some way toward reducing the political barriers.

Contemporary Conflict

An approach of this sort appears at first sight more relevant to the real
problems of the modern world than some of those often considered. If
full-scale disarmament is beyond attainment, surely some limited measures of control, designed to make less probable the type of attack all
wish to avoid, might at least have some chance of success.

In a sense, it is true, such proposals have more prospect of succeeding
than total disarmament. The possibility of reaching agreement is here
probably rather greater. And the one or two small agreements of this
type actually accomplished, however limited in scope, show that in fact
agreements in this field are not unattainable. The doubt is not so much
how to reach agreement (though this remains difficult enough), but
what agreement may achieve. For the fact is that, even supposing all
problems and differences were overcome, and a system covering all the
proposals mentioned here were successfully instituted and consistently
maintained, it must remain questionable how far this would materially
reduce most of the dangers which confront the world today.

One kind of empirical evidence available in assessing such measures is
the kind of agreements actually reached in the past. A list of arms control agreements concluded since 1945 appears on p. 221. From this, one
or two conclusions emerge. The agreements reached have been those
improving stability rather than equilibrium or the other functional purposes considered. None had more than a marginal effect on the power
available to the parties concerned. They have either been mainly directed
at restricting the power of other nations (like the test ban) or have
related to armed power in any case not yet enjoyed (for example, in
space or the Antarctic). There is no clear evidence that any of them has
restricted a form of power that any nations actively wished to develop
for themselves. They (and corresponding unilateral measures) may have
contributed to maintaining stability, to reassurance against a development of power by the other side, or to the avoidance of *unintended*
dangers. It cannot be said that they have significantly affected the power
already available to states if conflict nonetheless arose. For the inescap-

able fact is that, whenever nations enjoy a significant advantage, they will not normally forgo this in the interests of equilibrium or stability.

A more important type of evidence available is the types of wars which in fact occur within the contemporary world and the effect such measures would have on them. Table VII.2 is a list of the principal conflicts, greater or lesser, which have taken place since the end of World War II:

TABLE VII · 2

Principal Wars, 1945–1965

Wars of aggression

(Wars resulting from a direct assault against the territory of one state by the forces of another.)

Korea, 1950–53	Egypt, 1956	
Guatemala, 1954	Hungary, 1956	Goa, 1961

Frontier conflicts

(Armed actions designed to further boundary claims, including those prosecuted by nongovernment forces.)

Eire–N. Ireland, 1945–60	Iraq–Kuwait, 1962
Arab States–Israel, 1949, 56, 67	Morocco–Algeria, 1962
Afghanistan–Pakistan, 1950–62	Somalia–Kenya, 1963–
Saudi Arabia–Abu Dhabi, Muscat, 1952–	Chile–Argentina, 1965
Cambodia–Thailand, 1953–	Somalia (including Somaliland)–Ethi-
China–India, 1954–62	opia, sporadic, esp. 1964
China–Burma, 1956–60	Yemen–Aden, sporadic
Egypt–Sudan, 1958	

Frontier claims

(Disputes over borders which did not involve armed action.)

Spain–Gibraltar	South Vietnam–Cambodia
Greece–Albania	Guatemala, Mexico–British Honduras
Germany–Poland	Morocco, Mauretania–Rio de Oro,
Morocco–Mauretania	Spanish Sahara
Niger–Dahomey	Argentina–Falkland Islands
Syria–Turkey	Venezuela–British Guiana
Jordan–UAR	Ecuador–Peru
Persia–Bahrein	Iran–Iraq
Philippines–Malaysia	Sahara, various
Japan–USSR	Antarctica, various
China–Nepal	and others

TABLE VII · 2 (*Cont.*)

New frontiers

(Armed action arising directly over the creation of new frontiers or states.)

Pakistan–Kashmir, 1947–49, 1965
India–Hyderabad, 1947
Arab States–Israel, 1948–49, 56, 67

Indonesia–Netherlands, 1961–62
Indonesia–Malaysia, 1963–

Colonial wars

(Wars in colonial territories where the colonial, or ex-colonial, power has been engaged in hostilities against indigenous forces, whether or not representative.)

Indonesia, 1945–49
Syria and Lebanon, 1945–46
Philippines, 1945–46
Indo-China, 1946–54
Malaya, 1948–57

Kenya (Mau-Mau), 1952–56
Cyprus, 1954–59
Algeria, 1954–61
Angola, 1960–64

(In addition there have been serious disturbances, sometimes involving heavy casualties, in a number of other colonies or semi-colonial countries, including Madagascar, Formosa, Tunisia, Morocco, the Belgian Congo, the Central African Federation, the Portuguese African Territories, British Guiana, Aden, and South Africa.)

Civil wars (political)

Colombia, 1946–58
Paraguay, 1947
Cuba, 1953–59, 1961
Muscat and Oman, 1957–59

Lebanon, 1958
Congo, 1960–65
Yemen, 1962
Dominican Republic, 1965

Civil wars (minorities)

Burma (Karens and others), 1948–54
Burma (Chinese Nationalists), 1950–
China (Tibet), 1951–
Iraq (Kurds), 1961–66

Sudan (Southern Sudanese), 1963–
Ruanda (Tutsis), 1963
India (Nagas and Mizos), sporadic

(In addition there have been a number of international disputes not involving casualties concerning minorities.)

Austria–Italy
Yugoslavia–Greece
Albania–Yugoslavia
Pakistan–India

India–Ceylon
India, Pakistan–South Africa
China–Indonesia
China–Siam, etc.

Civil wars (ideological)

(Wars in which a widely recognized government has been in conflict with elements declaring communist or anticommunist sympathies.)

TABLE VII · 2 (*Cont.*)

Greece, 1945–49	Malaya, 1957–60
Philippines, 1946–50	Indonesia, 1958–59, 1965
China (including some offshore	Cameroun, 1958–62
islands), 1946–58	Laos, 1959, 1960–
Burma, 1948–	South Vietnam, 1959–
India, 1948–50	Venezuela, 1965–

(In addition there have been sporadic actions against ideologically inspired guerillas or bandits [as in Peru, Guatemala, Thailand, and others] not amounting to full-scale civil war. There have also been large numbers of coups d'état, sometimes inspired or supported from without, designed to bring about the establishment of governments of a particular ideological persuasion.)

(There are also four nations at present divided on an ideological basis: Germany, China, Korea, Vietnam.)

This list does not purport to be comprehensive. It does not include civil disturbances, even where these have led to violence and casualties, unless they have taken the proportions of organized and enduring conflicts. It does not include riots against the governments of East Germany, Poland, and other countries; communal and linguistic disturbances, in India and other nations; or political conflicts leading to fighting in Hong Kong, Korea, Aden, Panama, and elsewhere, even when these have led to fairly heavy casualties.

Conflicts in the individual categories listed here have been analyzed in greater detail above. Four points may be immediately noted about this list. First, it is an extremely long one: the illusion that we live in a relatively peaceful world is largely ethnocentric, based on the fact that fairly peaceful conditions have prevailed in Europe and North America. The number of separate armed conflicts that have taken place during this time is probably as large as during any comparable period in history. It is true that a fair number of the conflicts were small in scale and involved few casualties. On the other hand, others — the Chinese civil war, the India–Pakistan conflict, the wars in Korea, Indo-China, Algeria, Indonesia, and Vietnam — have been on a very extensive scale, and the number of casualties altogether has run into several millions.

Second, nevertheless, none of the wars has been on the scale of an all-out world conflict. Almost all have been launched by single states, not alliances or groups. None has involved the use of nuclear weapons. Even the largest in intensity, such as those in Korea and Vietnam, have been deliberately limited, both geographically and in armaments. And most have been confined to restricted and defined objectives. There have been virtually no formal declarations of war throughout the period.

Third, the two major powers of the world have at no time been involved in direct hostilities with each other, even on a limited scale. Less still has either at any time launched, or appeared likely to launch, an overt act of aggression against the territory of the other. Insofar as either has become involved against the other, it has been by proxy only. No armed action at all has been launched directly against a nuclear power.

Finally, perhaps most significant of all, the great majority, indeed nearly all, of the wars appearing on this list have taken place within the frontiers of a single state.

The example of the past twenty years is no guarantee of the pattern of the next twenty. It is not impossible that there might be a reversion to the total wars of former years. The erosion of the nuclear deterrent, the rise of new nations imbued with the same passions and appetites as their predecessors, and facing less powerful sanctions to deter direct assaults, could yet bring a reversion to those practices. But, in considering this possibility, it is necessary to examine the underlying reasons for the new pattern here revealed.

The character and purpose of armed conflict has, in the years since World War II, undergone a radical change. First, aggression, in the classical sense of the word, is today an almost extinct form of international activity. Even among the few cases listed as direct aggression in Table VII.2, none took the crude form of an assault by one state against another with the object of total war, unconditional surrender, or large-scale annexation of foreign territory. Yet only thirty years ago such a phenomenon was a fairly common one. In the interwar period it was practiced successively against Manchuria, Abyssinia, China, Czechoslovakia, Albania, Poland, Finland, and the Baltic States. Both in Europe and Asia such an assault was the occasion for the last, perhaps the most murderous, blood bath which mankind has yet indulged in. Since 1945 this once virulent form of international delinquency has been virtually unknown. In the list here given only the attacks against South Korea and Goa are even slightly comparable. And both of these, being acts of national reunification, are not analogous to most of the interwar cases.[3]

Second, activity of that type is now irrelevant to the sort of struggle in which the world is absorbed. Increasingly today the world has become the arena for conflicts between disputing ideologies and political creeds,

[3] For a more detailed analysis of the external wars of the last century, see above, pp. 61–71.

rather than between states themselves. This is as true of the disputes emerging in the new continents of Asia, Africa, and Latin America, as in the better known cold war of the Atlantic World. It is true that often superficially ideological disputes only conceal the rivalries of states themselves. But conversely interstate disputes are today frequently genuinely expressed in a political form. The desire is increasingly for indirect, rather than direct domination: to achieve control by sympathetic governments from within rather than by direct administration from without.

Thus, third, means too are today quite different. The objective in the present world is not to paint new colors across the atlas, but to win friends and influence people; not to secure submissive populations in specific areas, but friendly governments and peoples all over the world; to gain, not territories, but human hearts. What governments seek above all is allegiance. And since allegiance is unlikely to be won by sprinkling hydrogen bombs on foreign populations, or even by hurling massed divisions of tanks and guns against them, the use of such crude weapons is not normally an attractive instrument of policy. The fact, already noted, that most wars, of all categories, in this list have been intrafrontier, rather than transfrontier, derives directly from this recognition.

This does not mean that dominion is never coveted, sometimes even beyond allegiance. Where important strategic interests are thought to be involved, for example, that may be the object. In such situations nations may still sometimes take steps to acquire effective control of an area, regardless of the effect on the minds of those within the territory concerned, or on international opinion as a whole (like the Soviet Union in Eastern Europe, the United States in the Caribbean, China in Korea). It may sometimes be thought that once the political kingdom has been assured, all else will eventually follow. But even in these cases the object has not been to wave the national flag across new territories. All that is necessary, for the ends of ideology, is to secure control by politically congenial native governments.

For this purpose, contemporary international practice provides countless methods, far less cumbersome, perilous, and politically expensive than direct assault. Aid may be given to a revolutionary movement, support provided for one side or the other in a civil war, agitation instigated or sedition preached, or a coup d'état attempted. Innumerable means may be found of securing the victory of a favored faction without committing any breach of the accepted code of international morality. These may be as attractive to the newly emerging creeds of the new continents as to the older ideologies of Eurasia. And a large proportion of the wars appearing in our list are of this type: externally supported efforts to overturn existing governments rather than full-scale attempts at subjugation from without.

The use of such methods may not only be as efficacious as more old-fashioned measures: it may transform the legal and moral position. If the Soviet Union had sought to win control of Czechoslovakia, or the United States of Guatemala, by overt acts of aggression against those states, their enemies might have been enabled to mobilize world opinion, invoke international intervention, even take unilateral or collective countermeasures, to resist the aggressor. But if an identical object can be achieved by means of a coup d'état or a civil war, or other political measures, without overt intervention, then it is the counteraction itself which may become, by current codes, an illegal and mischievous intervention in the internal affairs of others.

In these circumstances what power today will risk the danger of an all-out assault, even large-scale conventional war, let alone a suicidal, nuclear conflict, by undertaking direct and manifest aggression from without the borders of a desired territory, when it may achieve similar objects by action, immune from moral obloquy, undertaken, with little expense and less danger, within the frontiers of that state?

Limitations of Arms Control Today

What indication does this evidence provide of the practicability of effective arms control agreements? If these are today the profitable and normal means of achieving national and ideological interests, how far can arms control measures limit that type of activity?

Before considering the positive role arms control agreements play,[4] it is necessary to recognize some of their weaknesses in countering the instabilities common in the contemporary world.

Examination of the list of recent armed actions suggests that most of the measures of arms control generally proposed could have exerted little influence on them. The establishment of control posts at Soviet and United States airfields and other communication centers could not, for example, have prevented either side from flying arms to Laos, when both claimed to be supporting the legitimate government of that country. The institution of aerial inspection in Europe, even over the whole

4 See below, pp. 193 ff.

of the Soviet Union and the United States, could not have prevented the United States from sending troops to Lebanon, nor the Soviet Union from supplying arms to the United Arab Republic when the Middle East was the center of conflict, nor both powers from providing support for rival forces in Vietnam or for rival factions in Cuba today. The establishment of inspection teams to supervise manpower or weapons levels, even if such a system could be devised, could not have prevented the use of those troops or guns that remained to assist revolutionary forces in colonial countries (as in Algeria or Angola) or to assert frontier claims (as against India and Malaysia). The establishment of a neutral zone in Europe could not have prevented simultaneous assistance for opposing sides in civil wars in Greece and China, in Yemen and Indo-China; nor would it have influenced support for revolutions and counter-revolutions, or for opposing factions in innumerable civil conflicts all over the world today; still less the initial outbreak of those conflicts in the countries concerned.

Arms control arrangements are frequently designed to avoid the risk of misunderstandings and miscalculations. But it remains to be shown that, even under the conditions of modern armaments systems, misunderstandings and miscalculations are ever themselves the cause of war. In virtually all the examples listed, as in the more important conflicts of earlier ages, the outbreak of hostilities has not been the effect of accident or miscalculation as normally understood. It has been deliberate and calculated. Conflicts have been the effect of conscious decisions that in certain circumstances the deployment of some measure of force was necessary to assure certain assumed national interests. No arrangements concerning systems of arms dispositions, or methods of communication, or even arms levels, even if relevant, could have served to influence their outbreak, given that initial decision. For in these circumstances they would have been abandoned as quickly as they were begun.

Another of the dangers arms control measures are intended to overcome is that of ."surprise attack." This concern is perhaps, once more, the effect of an apprehension born of the experiences of an earlier generation. The swift and unexpected German assaults on Czechoslovakia and Poland in 1939, West Europe in 1940, and the Soviet Union in 1941, and the Japanese blitzkriegs against Pearl Harbor, Hong Kong, the Philippines, Malaya, and other parts of Asia have perhaps served to perpetuate the fear of sudden and unprovoked assaults against the external frontiers of a neighbor. Yet it seems unlikely that sudden massive onslaughts on the territories of neighbors are the real dangers of the present age.

Virtually none of the wars in the post-1945 list come within this class. The relative stability of frontiers, the generally acknowledged interest in the limitation of conflict, and the growth in the mobility of modern armies have transformed the situation.

Today, as we have seen, it is within frontiers rather than against them that most activity takes place. Measures to provide assurance about concentrations of troops, or to create demilitarized buffer zones, therefore, have little relevance to the dangers. When the Soviet Union and the United States began to dispatch arms to the Middle East and Laos, Hungary and Vietnam, no observation posts against surprise attack could have reported sudden and alarming massings of tanks and guns along the East-West borders. Nor could they have done so before the final explosion of open hostilities in the various colonial countries where this has occurred; nor before the eruption of civil war in Greece, China, Malaya, and elsewhere, let alone before civil wars where the outside powers are non-European, as in Yemen, Venezuela, and elsewhere.

Observers at airfields might *detect* such movements. But they could not prevent them. Even when, in extreme cases, large-scale mobilization of forces against other states takes place (as occurred, for example, over Berlin, Cuba, or the Sino-Indian border), it may be doubted whether the existence of observation posts in the area could exert any very effective influence on the situation. Sometimes troop concentrations are designed to be observed. In times of crisis the mutual desire to reduce apprehensions, effective in normal times, may be reversed — the desire may then be to increase fears, not reduce them (in the Cuba crisis both sides made dramatic shows of force to intimidate the other).

A third preoccupation of modern arms control measures is to overcome secrecy through communication or verification. This may sometimes have value. Communication in time of crisis may be important (as during the Cuba crisis), though this depends on what is communicated. If no concession is made, conflict may be postponed rather than averted. But there is no evidence that better communication could have prevented the confrontations in Korea, Suez, Laos, Vietnam, or others. Once again it is final intentions that count. Where, as often, conflict builds up gradually from small beginnings (as in Vietnam) or where the terms demanded are not mutually acceptable (as in the same case), measures of this sort are quite irrelevant.

In time of crisis, secrecy is not the usual condition of war preparations. The naval building races at the beginning of the century, the successive mobilizations in 1914, were not kept concealed from other powers. Threats against Czechoslovakia and Poland in 1938 and 1939 were uttered months before the final climax. When Britain and France began to concentrate force in preparation for an assault on Egypt, they made no secret of the fact; they publicly called up reserves and openly dispatched warships to the Mediterranean. When the Soviet Union determined to suppress the revolution in Hungary, she did not do so with tanks and troops whose existence had been kept concealed from all; she made use, before the world's attentive eyes, of troops whose existence had been known for years. An inspection agency that had revealed these facts would have told the public nothing it did not already know. Greater knowledge concerning the level or nature of armaments may possibly influence long-term intentions or decisions (though, as we have seen, even equilibrium has not deterred in the past). But it will not necessarily influence immediate decisions in crisis situations.

Fourth, for this reason, even the main object of arms control measures, to secure equilibrium, though of value in improving confidence, may have little effect in deterring the forms of international activity now mainly favored. For in engagements of this type the level of forces employed is so small in relation to total strengths that, even after an agreed balance had been achieved, armed action by a small part might still be freely undertaken (for the same reason unilateral policies of deterrence may be useless if the volume of deterrent power is disproportionate to the type of threat likely to be encountered: nuclear weapons may not deter guerilla forces). In such situations it is not the *level* of total arms which is the crucial factor, nor the *balance* between powers, but the *disposition* of those that are retained. Here, as elsewhere, therefore, ultimately it is not against the possession, or even the distribution of arms that effective action needs to be directed but against the way they are used.

Finally, it is at least open to doubt how far the achievement of this object would in fact prove effective, even in preventing that type of war apparently envisaged, and which today appears least probable, a full-scale conflict between the great powers. For, as we have seen, there is little evidence to support the belief that the existence of a balance of arms will alone serve to prevent the outbreak of war. Many examples show that assaults may sometimes be made even at a very heavy disadvantage in numbers in certain situations: where, for example, past successes have bred an undeserved confidence in destiny, or where a powerful sense of injustice has been aroused. Austria's ultimatum in 1914, when the balance could scarcely have been more exact, Germany's attack in June,

1941, adding the Soviet Union to her existing antagonists, Japan's adding the United States and Britain to China later that year, as well as infinite numbers of similar cases in the past, show that, though the assessment of opposing strength may be one factor affecting the likelihood of war, it is one that is only marginal in its influence. Rationalizations arguing the special qualities of native troops, or industrial capacity, or particular armaments, or the righteousness of the cause may convince goverments of countervailing advantages. Subjective calculations may create an assessment of superiority where outsiders would make contrary estimates. Thus, in the kind of situation in which a war might occur — in any great international crisis where emotions are powerfully aroused — considerations of balance may be only marginal in their effect.[5]

This is perhaps the most fundamental of all the weaknesses of arms control measures. In such situations all those measures of arms control, balanced defense policies, self-imposed restrictions, or mutual inspection, so carefully built up and maintained without difficulty in periods of little tension, are immediately thrown aside. In a situation where one side felt its own security threatened (for example, by an imagined or alleged breach of the agreement by the other side) or for other reasons favored a forcible response, it would itself abrogate all contracts, and seek to undertake just such mobilizations and concentrations as it regarded as necessary in the interests of self-defense. The fact that such measures were detected by international air inspection or control teams on the ground could not affect the realities of the situation. No inspection authority could prevent the train of events from continuing unless it were provided with armed strength comparable to that of the national forces involved, a goal that has not been suggested in this connection. The sudden and unforeseen mobilizations and countermobilizations that occurred in 1914, the deliberate and premeditated massing of German troops against Poland in 1939, might have been observed, reported, and condemned. But they could not thereby have been overcome.

Conclusions

What then is the role arms control agreements may play in preserving a more peaceful world?

[5] It is the assumption of the perfect rationality of states, inherent in much strategic writing of recent years, that is its greatest weakness (and is contradicted by much of the evidence of history quoted above). The evidence suggests that nations, like individuals (because their decisions are ultimately made by individuals), behave partly rationally and partly emotionally. While strategic writing could in theory

They are certainly not valueless. But the purposes they serve may be different from those usually claimed for them.

First, the very conception of arms control and discussion of such measures revives the concept of a *community* interest in stability and understanding, comparable to that once current in the idea of the "European system" in the nineteenth century. Even when no agreements are reached, discussion of such measures alone may bring governments to conceive their policy in terms of international stability and international balances, rather than national strength and national advantage. This process could be encouraged by the development of international bodies, official government committees or unofficial strategic institutes, to develop studies of *international policy* and international balances of strength to replace the purely national and alliance assessments normally undertaken today. Government policy decisions in the field of defense, and the recommendations of national ministries, are necessarily made purely in terms of national interests. There is need, here too, of international institutions that can approach such problems from an international viewpoint.

Second, the concept of arms control encourages recognition that significant measures of stabilization may be taken by individual governments even in default of formal agreements among them. We saw in Chapter One how often in past systems weaker nations have combined together against the most powerful (as against Spain in the sixteenth century, or against France in the late seventeenth century and in Napoleonic times). A somewhat similar process can be seen in the coalescence of the nations of West Europe against the Soviet Union in the fifties and some of those of Southeast Asia against China in the sixties. To some extent the nonaligned (Egypt, Pakistan, Iran, Indonesia) have been balancers between the great alliances. But to be effective, as we have seen, there is often need for explicit understandings on the basis of the status quo. This has been seen in the tacit recognition of geographical spheres of influence: the United States made no attempt to intervene over Hungary, and the Soviet Union was willing to withdraw from Cuba. But in the margins between spheres, Berlin, Korea, Vietnam, and the Middle East, no such consensus has existed. In many cases stability will depend on conscious efforts to achieve a modus vivendi even

---

make governments more rational, it cannot justify the assumption that other governments always behave rationally (they may not have read the writings). And even rationality can only be measured as it reflects an assumed national interest,
• which itself is a subjective assessment.

in these marginal areas, and on good communication, to facilitate such accommodations.

Understandings of this kind need not be overt. Where no explicit understanding is required, some of the difficulties that beset written agreements are overcome. The most important function of such arrangements is to capitalize and exploit whatever stability already is present by increasing mutual confidence. They may thus provide, in this field, those mutually respected *practices* which are one of the principal instruments of an effective social order.

Third, there seems to be some prospect, even without explicit agreements, for some informal understandings between states about the disposition of power. These might set a minimum distance for the stationing of missiles, heavy bombers, nuclear submarines, or other offensive weapons, from the borders of another state (some kind of understanding of this kind may have been reached as a result of the Cuba crisis of 1962, when the withdrawal of Soviet missiles from Cuba was followed within a few months by a corresponding withdrawal of United States missiles from Turkey). Other conventions might cover the distance from a frontier ground troops might be placed: there would be some advantage in an internationally accepted *practice* by which troops were never stationed less than, say, ten miles on either side of an international border. Eventually mutual self-denying ordinances of this kind might cover the development of particular weapons systems (such as the anti-missile missile); the use of particular areas for military purposes (such as the Arctic, space, the moon); the neutralization of certain areas (as achieved for Belgium and Luxembourg in the last century, for Austria, Finland, and Laos after 1945, and such as might be achieved for Indo-China, Yemen, Iran, and other sensitive areas today); the limitation of arms in certain areas (as in nuclear free zone agreements: these are much easier to arrive at than worldwide nonproliferation agreements, since the sacrifice is equal and mutual). Conceivably, such voluntary understandings could even cover such matters as the size of certain forces (such as strategic missiles), the proportion of national budgets spent on armaments, and other matters. Understandings concerning the principles of crisis management could be especially useful. For such conventions, too, the existence of some international body, whether a UN committee or an unofficial institute, to undertake research, to publicize existing levels, and to recommend suitable principles and criteria, could be of great value.

Another field in which informal understandings can be valuable is over military assistance. One effect of the widening economic gap between nations is a correspondingly growing technological and military gap. This widens between the greatest and the middle powers as much as between the developed as a whole and the developing. The result is that the most advanced military technology is increasingly confined to two or three superpowers, who thus have the means, through their assistance policies, to determine to a considerable extent the disposition of power among the second-class nations, while the first- and second-class together control the disposition of power among the smaller states. The development of some measure of understanding between the more advanced groups, especially in their aid programs for particularly tense regions, such as the Middle East and Southeast Asia today — balances, for example, between Israel and the Arab states, Cambodia and Thailand — might help to assure a more stable balance of arms and power in the world, and so lower marginally the risks of war. On the other hand, attempts by have-powers to prevent have-nots from imitating them (as in the test-ban or nonproliferation agreements) are never likely to succeed unless the haves are themselves prepared to make equivalent renunciations, and without effective control mechanisms even this may not always prove practicable.

Both these types of informal understandings may strengthen what understanding already exists by reducing purely military fears, and by delineating more clearly the thresholds whose crossing will bring serious danger of war. Whether they can be reached at all will depend on some measure of consensus in the first place. For it must be recognized that the contribution such measures, unaccompanied by other developments, could provide is necessarily limited. Though they may increase confidence, they cannot create it. The rudimentary measures of this type already introduced between the United States and the Soviet Union may be themselves only a reflection of the growing common interest as status quo superpowers, rather than an independent contribution to reducing tension between them. They give no indication whether similar agreements, covering new and rising powers which share no such common interest, may be attainable. Certainly no arms control agreement reached within the Euro-Atlantic world alone could today have any appreciable influence on the growth of new conflicts elsewhere. Effective agreements would need to cover above all those powers in Asia, Africa, and elsewhere most disposed to challenge the status quo — precisely those who have never been concerned in them so far.

Moreover, because such undertakings (like those for reductions of armaments) are likely to be overthrown and nullified at any moment when the existing confidence is undermined, their effects may be almost instantaneously eliminated once more. They may express a common *intention* to avoid war. But, as has been shown, if the intention of war is not present already, it is unlikely that war will occur in any case. It is where that intention is modified that the dangers begin. It is thus the intentions themselves, and the fears which create them, rather than temporary and specific arrangements reflecting them, that represent the crucial factor in the situation, and which require ultimately to be modified.

All this does not mean that attempts to achieve arms control are valueless and should be abandoned. But it remains doubtful whether any such system can alone do much to make the world a safer place to live in. It is not well equipped to meet those types of war which are today most common, and which will remain most probable. And it cannot influence underlying mentality or motivation in more serious crises.

The Widening Military Gap in Defense Budgets, 1957–1967

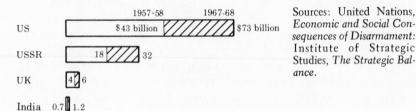

Sources: United Nations, *Economic and Social Consequences of Disarmament*: Institute of Strategic Studies, *The Strategic Balance*.

Bibliography

Brennan, D. G. (ed.), *Arms Control and Disarmament*, London, 1961.

Brodie, B., *Strategy in the Missile Age*, Princeton, 1959.

Bull, Hedley, *The Control of the Arms Race*, London, 1961.

Gulick, F. V., *Europe's Classical Balance of Power*, Ithaca, 1955.

Henkin, L., *Arms Control and Inspection in America*, New York, 1958.

——— (ed.), *Arms Control: Issues for the Public*, Englewood Cliffs, N.J., 1961.

Kahn, H., *On Escalation*, London, 1965.

Lefever, E. W. (ed.), *Arms and Arms Control*, New York, 1962.

Schelling, T. C., *The Strategy of Conflict*, Cambridge, Mass., 1960.

Schelling, T. C. and M. Halperin, *Strategy and Arms Control*, Cambridge, Mass., 1961.

Singer, J. D., *Deterrence, Arms Control and Disarmament*, Columbus, Ohio, 1962.

CHAPTER EIGHT

Disarmament

The Problem of Security

A more radical means for bringing about international order is to secure the total or substantial abandonment of armed power.

Here the method takes the simplest form conceivable. If the means of undertaking conflict are subtracted from the existing situation, it suggests, then conflict itself may be eliminated. Such a method might be compared with a proposal, in the crime-infested city, to bring about the abolition of violence through the abolition of firearms. It implies that it is not so much the criminals themselves that are dangerous as the instruments with which they may come into contact and which lead them to temptation.

There are obvious difficulties about applying such a principle, among nations as among men. First, the householder, confronted with the demand that he should renounce his army pistol, may feel reluctant to do this unless he is sure that no bandits will retain a superiority of power by other means. Next, however willing in principle to abandon his own arms, he will always wish for concrete assurance, through inspection or other means, that there remain no weapons concealed elsewhere which might be available to potential criminals. Finally, if he is to be asked to abandon his own existing forms of defense, he will demand to know what type of police force may be established to replace private armories, how it will be controlled, and the nature, powers, and weapons with which it will be equipped.

Each of these difficulties exists equally among nations. These too require assurance of equality in power; assurance against evasion; and assurance of a mutually acceptable public control to maintain justice in the absence of individual redress. These three conditions have not proved easy to secure. The effect of human history has been that the possession of arms often appears to nations the essential condition of survival. War has been always one of the normal forms of intercourse for the nation state. No nation has usually felt able, however peaceful its own intentions, to contract out of that contest. The capacity to kill, if not required for offense, might still be necessary for defense. Thus none could afford to be overtaken in a competition whose first prize was survival. Nor could any hope for a respite in the never-ending competition. For the arms race is one that has no winning post.

Could war then be abolished by the abolition of arms? Here, as elsewhere, only empirical study of observed facts can provide reliable evidence. The main type of evidence available in this field is that of the negotiations and agreements on the subject in the past. This may provide knowledge of the motives and preoccupations that mainly condition national actions in this field.

First, the negotiations. Though the idea of disarmaments has for hundreds of years been proposed by writers and philosophers, it was for long not seriously considered by governments. *Limited* groups of nations at times found sufficient trust to renounce war between themselves; but often only to enable them to make it more effectively against some other compelling threat. Some of the warring states of China, as we saw, reached understandings renouncing war; but as soon as one withdrew from the agreement the others were obliged to do the same. Certain of the Greek city-states agreed to settle disputes by periodic discussion or arbitration, but their aim was partly to be able to fight more effectively against invaders from outside the Greek peninsula. In modern times alliances and treaties of nonaggression have often had a similar purpose. One essential condition for the success of such arrangements is clearly, therefore, that membership should be universal.

Occasionally an *imposed* renunciation of war or armaments has been maintained for a time. Victorious powers have disarmed their victims. A single power has been able, from time to time, to establish such authority over a wide area that none have dared resort to war within it. The first Chin emperor in China, the Augustan emperors of Rome, were thus able to impose peace on areas hitherto rent with violence. But no empire has yet proved permanent. And no alliance has yet proved stable enough to maintain lasting supremacy. Another essential condition, therefore, is that arrangements should be voluntarily entered into if they are to be stable.

Proposals for abandoning armaments on a systematic and agreed basis were seriously considered only within the last century. There have been three main sets of negotiations. There were discussions in 1899 at the first Hague Conference. There were prolonged negotiations between 1926 and 1934, culminating in the Disarmament Conference of 1932–34. And from 1946 there have been continuous negotiations in many forums (see Table VIII.1). All this has not yet produced any significant degree of disarmament. Expenditure on arms over the past twenty years, both relatively and absolutely, has indeed probably been higher than ever before.

Such attempts have run into three main difficulties. The first is that deriving from national apprehensions for security.

Every government necessarily believes in safety first. All feel themselves under an obligation to their peoples to demand that any reduction of arms levels shall not endanger the security of their own nation. But the sad mathematics of international politics is such that the assessments by individual governments of their own national securities will not usually add up to a grand total representing international security.

For those assessments are inevitably conceived in subjective fashion. Because of the secrecy that necessarily surrounds arms levels, and the fears that become associated with them, subjective judgments may diverge widely from objective facts. The force levels that represent essential security for one may represent an intolerable threat for another. The unknowns involved are such that every nation demands a substantial margin of error. They require the *assurance*, rather than the hope, of safety. And this demand will often be seen by antagonists, according to their own subjective vision, as a demand for superiority, and provoke corresponding efforts to preserve their own safety.

This difficulty may be traced throughout the history of disarmament discussions. When, for the first time in 1816, the Russian Czar proposed to the other great powers "a simultaneous reduction of the armed forces of every kind," the Austrian government replied that, because of "the difficulty always of obtaining any true data from Russia," it would be impossible for other powers to take any steps to that end while they remained "uncertain of a reciprocity of confidence." [1] Again, when Germany, at the Hague Conference of 1899, refused to consider the proposals for disarmament put forward by Czar Nicholas II, Britain and other powers, though not themselves ill-disposed, felt unable to continue the discussions. When Britain and Germany became engaged in a naval race in the years before the First World War, neither side felt able to call a halt to its own program, even when this was explicitly requested, on the

[1] Sir J. Headlam-Morley, *Studies in Diplomacy* (London, 1930), pp. 254–258.

terms demanded by the other. Fears and suspicions were such that even an arms race appeared to provide greater security than mutual trust.

In the disarmament discussions which took place between the wars, the same problem arose. This was not because the desire for disarmament was not genuine. The revulsion created by the recent conflict was profound and universal. Most of the great powers sincerely wanted to prevent a return to the naval and military races of prewar days, and to reduce the existing burden of armaments. But they wanted this only on their own terms.

TABLE VIII · 1

Disarmament Discussions and Participants, 1899–1965

Disarmament discussions		*Participants*
1899	First Hague Conference	26 states: 21 from Europe plus US, China, Japan, Siam, and Mexico
1920	Permanent Advisory Commission of the League	Military experts of all leading services of the leading powers
1921	Temporary Mixed Commission	Military and other experts in personal capacity
1921	Washington Conference	US, Britain, France, Italy, and Japan
1926–30	Disarmament Conference Preparatory Commission	League plus US and Soviet Union
1927	Three-Power Naval Conference	US, Britain, and Japan
1930	London Naval Conference	US, Britain, and Japan
1932–34	Disarmament Conference	League plus US and Soviet Union
1946–50	Committee on Atomic Energy	Security Council plus Canada
1947–50	Committee on Conventional Armaments	Security Council plus Canada
1952–57	Disarmament Commission	Security Council plus Canada
1952–57	Disarmament Sub-committee	US, Soviet Union, Britain, France, and Canada
1957	Enlarged Commission	25 UN members
1958	Commission of all UN Members	All UN members
1958–63	Test-ban Negotiations	US, Britain, and Soviet Union
1958	Conference on Surprise Attack	Western and Communist
1959–60	Committee of Ten	5 Western, 5 Communist
1962–	Eighteen-Nation Disarmament Conference in Geneva	5 Western, 5 Communist, and 8 non-aligned

France was ready to preserve the power ratio established at the Versailles settlement because it kept Germany in perpetual inferiority to herself. Germany was not willing to preserve it, for the same reason. In the discussions in the late twenties Britain was ready to accept an agreed ratio of capital ships because her principal rivals, Japan and Germany, were thus forced into permanent inferiority. But she was unwilling, because of the long lines of communication the defense of her world-scattered empire demanded, to accept restrictions of other kinds. France and Italy were prepared to accept a limitation on the construction of capital ships, which had never played an important part in their naval strength. But they refused even to discuss a restriction of other naval vessels. The United States and Britain, as commercial powers dependent on a large volume of foreign trade, were anxious to abolish the submarine. Most of the land powers wished to retain it. France would agree to any limitation of naval forces which gave her superiority over Italy. Italy would accept any which did not.[2]

Agreement on the limitation of land forces proved equally elusive. Britain had for centuries relied exclusively on a standing army and wished trained reserves included in any assessment of war potential, whereas the conscript nations, such as France, resolutely demanded that limitations be confined to troops with the colors. Britain, preoccupied with the security of her empire as well as her homeland, demanded the right to preserve a relatively high absolute level of armaments though willing to see restrictions on such "offensive" weapons as aircraft, which tended to nullify the defensive value of British naval strength; but most of the other European powers wanted to retain aircraft and limit manpower. France, always dependent primarily on her vaunted army, wished to retain tanks and heavy guns; representatives of less well-equipped or less industrially advanced nations, such as Germany and the Soviet Union, wanted these restricted.

So divergent conceptions of security ensured divergent conceptions of acceptable agreements. The same problem frustrated discussions of disarmament after World War II.[3] Reciprocal security apprehensions at

[2] For a full account of the interwar disarmament negotiations, see J. Wheeler-Bennett, *The Disarmament Deadlock* (London, 1934), and *Security and Disarmament* (London, 1931); Joseph Nogee, *The Diplomacy of Disarmament* (New York, 1960).

[3] For a detailed account of the post-1945 disarmament negotiations, see B. G. Bechhoefer, *Post-War Negotiations for Arms Control* (Washington, 1961); Jean Klein, *L'Entreprise du Désarmement, 1945–1964* (Paris, 1964); Sir Michael Wright, *Disarm and Verify* (London, 1964); and Evan Luard, "The Background of the Negotiations to Date," in Evan Luard, ed., *First Steps to Disarmament* (London, 1965).

that time were reflected in the perpetually shifting emphasis in the plans of East and West for conventional or nuclear disarmament, according to their capabilities. During the early years, the Soviet Union, powerful in conventional weapons but without a nuclear capacity, felt her security demanded total prohibition of nuclear weapons; the United States, outgunned in conventional arms, regarded their retention as essential. During the late fifties, after the Soviet Union had developed a nuclear capacity but had had little time to accumulate stocks of fissionable material, she abandoned all previous demands for prohibition; the United States was ready to consider a cutoff that would limit Soviet production of material. The United States considered foreign bases essential to her security and that of her allies; the Soviet Union thought their abandonment vital to hers.

Even when one side changes its position, this may be accompanied by a corresponding move by the other in the opposite direction to meet new fears. In 1954, the Western powers were ready to accept manpower maxima for their armed forces of 1,500,000 for the Soviet Union, China, and the United States, and 650,000 for Britain and France; but the Soviet Union wanted larger forces. By the end of the decade the West demanded higher figures, and the Soviet Union wanted lower ones. During the late fifties, when the United States believed herself behind in missile technology, she resisted proposals, by France and others, for control of delivery systems. But in the mid-sixties, when she had a substantial superiority, she proposed a freeze of existing strategic missile levels; whereas the Soviet Union resisted it.

Similar subjective assessments condition the *political* aspects of defense policy. In the postwar era, for example, China regarded United States military assistance to Formosa as a threat to her security; the United States regarded its abandonment as a threat to Formosa's. The United States saw the dispatch of Communist arms to Guatemala and Cuba as a threat to the peace; those countries saw them as essential to the preservation of their independence. Any alliance, which may bring reassurance to one party, may seem threatening to another.

In fact the problem is not, of course, normally confined, as in these examples, to two complementary alliances. Even more complex is the problem of *multiple balances*. If the balancing of subjectively conceived security requirements is difficult enough when there are only two parties to the proceedings, it is infinitely more so when large numbers of individual states of disparate power and interests are involved. This can be seen in the infinitely varied positions on disarmament in the interwar period. Each individual power put forward proposals to suit its own particular apprehensions and ambitions. Thus, as we have seen, none matched another even remotely. And after a short period of polarized power in 1945-60, the same situation recurred once more from 1960 onward.

Any plan that is to be successful has normally to allay the fears of a number of individual nations and groups, of varying interests, capacities, and responsibilities. In the postwar world, it must reconcile the requirements of the two superpowers, anxious to prevent the growth of new nuclear powers, and to increase the capacity of their alliances for a purely conventional response; those of European nations, determined to acquire or maintain some nuclear capability and anxious, for strategic as well as economic reasons, to avoid dependence on conventional troops only; those of China, dependent because of technological backwardness on large land forces and reluctant to see any relaxation of international tensions; and all the varying demands and apprehensions of many other middle-sized and smaller powers — concerned far more with defense against each other than with the main alliance — which had been unrepresented virtually throughout the discussion yet could vitally disturb the balance. Yet this problem of determining the relative levels of individual types of armament for each nation or group, the difficulty that proved most troublesome in the interwar period, was scarcely seriously confronted after 1945.

One of the main difficulties is that, in such circumstances, as soon as one power demands certain conditions to match another, *third powers* may require countervailing concessions to match the second. Today, China may require to match the United States, or the Soviet Union, or both together. India may then require a new balance to match China. Pakistan may require concessions to match India; Afghanistan to match Pakistan; and so on. A nation that faces two potential adversaries may demand double the share that might otherwise be accorded. But each of its antagonists may require sufficient strength to match it single-handed. India may require to match China and Pakistan. But Pakistan may demand equality with India alone. The difficulties of matching individual nations are acute enough. When the various combinations and permutations, alliances and counteralliances are included as well, the complications in reaching equilibrium become almost endless.

Next, there are the problems that may be created by *new alliances*. For a solution designed to create equilibrium to be reliable, it must provide an equilibrium that is permanent. The switch of one nation from one alliance to another, or the desertion of others toward non-alignment, should require countervailing concessions from the side advantaged. These may not always be easy to procure. Moreover, once the disarmament process has begun, adjustments become more difficult. Although unilaterally determined defense policies may be adjusted to attain something like a balance, once a formal agreement has been entered into such adjustments may become more difficult to agree on. And as the level of armaments is reduced, the shift in the balance of power brought about by a change in alliance may become more crucial.

Finally, the effect of security apprehensions is enormously enhanced by the uncertainties that are inherent in any disarmament scheme. Some of the difficulties just described would be overcome by achieving total disarmament at one step. But the difficulties and imponderables involved in assessing the effect of a sudden alteration in existing arms balances, let alone their removal, are such that few nations will feel ready to exchange the comforting, if precarious, certainties of the present for the hazardous, and unknown, dangers of total disarmament. The change from a world mainly armed to one mainly disarmed is of such stupendous, almost unimaginable, type that many nations will feel reluctant to undertake the risks involved. They are likely, nearly always, to prefer the well-known security provided by armaments to the uncertain security provided by inspectors.

The evidence of these negotiations thus seems to confirm that security is still usually conceived mainly in terms of national military power. Since disarmament negotiations are conducted by representatives of the nation state or their alliances, it is the interests and purposes of the nation state, and the alliance, that remain inevitably the ultimate yardstick. While disarmament seems desirable to most powers, security appears essential to all. And the divergent perceptions of security prevent any consensus on levels of arms, which is essential if explicit agreements are to be reached. Thus the main practical problem is to devise objective criteria to determine the levels of arms held to replace the subjective assessments now normal.[4]

The Problem of Flexibility

The second of the difficulties revealed in the negotiations on disarmament is the special problem presented by changes in the structure of power.

[4] See below, pp. 223 ff.

A readiness to accept mutual cuts in armaments demands a willingness to accept the perpetuation of the existing power balance. Such a willingness is rarely present among all nations at once. Nations whose strength is rapidly increasing are often reluctant to see themselves deprived of the accretion of power and influence which a growth in armed strength may win for them. These catchers-up will regard any attempt at stabilization as a device by declining, or temporarily dominant, powers to retain their ascendancy. Nor is this necessarily evidence of aggressive intention. Even if peacefully inclined, nations will often demand, for negotiating or prestige purposes, armed forces commensurate with their historical power or status, as they themselves conceive these.

This difficulty may be seen throughout the history of disarmament negotiations. Thus when, in 1816, the Czar of Russia first proposed to other powers a mutual reduction of arms, Lord Castlereagh, conscious that Russia maintained the largest army in Europe and anxious to match this if necessary, demanded that each state should be able to determine the size of its armaments according to its own requirements.[5] When, in 1870, shortly before the outbreak of the Franco-Prussian War, the French Government suggested to the Prussians, through British intermediaries, that a reduction in armaments would be in the mutual interest of the two countries, the Prussian Government, now possessed of the capacity to equal and overcome the military might of France, was by no means disposed to view the proposal with favor. Again, when, in 1899, the Russian Czar proposed an understanding to stabilize the existing level of armed forces and military budgets, the German Government saw the suggestion as an attempt by Russia to preserve her own relative position in face of the rapidly growing might of her rivals, and refused to have any part in such an agreement. Finally, it was for the same reason that Germany, now catching up on Britain too, rejected British proposals for restraining the naval building race between 1906 and 1914 on the basis of a permanent British superiority. In such cases the clash of expectations is encountered in its most fundamental form. While for instance, in this last case, Germany could see no reason why, with a population larger than Britain's and as one of the leading powers of Europe, she should be condemned forever to an inferior naval strength to Britain's, Britain, conscious of German land power, and of her own defensive responsibilities overseas, was equally opposed to any adjustments in naval ratios. German military successes and growing power,

---

[5] Sir J. Headlam-Morley, *op. cit.*, p. 257.

which for Germany were the main justification for a better naval ratio, were for Britain the most powerful argument against it.

During the interwar period the same difficulty arose. Those powers that were temporarily satisfied with the new partition of the globe showed some willingness to stabilize arms levels. Those who were determined to challenge that settlement, or had deficiencies to redress, showed less enthusiasm. The United States and Britain were content, for a period, to accept limitations on the level of their navies, since they felt assured that in so doing they would retain superiority over the navy of Japan. Japan, on the other hand, though consenting for a time (in the Washington Agreements) to the ratios imposed, soon began to demand revision in her favor; later (in the London Treaty) she acquired for herself a more favorable proportion; and finally, determining to equal and outstrip her rivals, denounced the agreements altogether. Other, and lesser, naval powers, such as Italy, were equally reluctant to accept limitations which might frustrate their pretensions to great power status.[6]

But the conflicting attitudes of haves and have-nots were shown most clearly in the approaches of France and Germany. Throughout the protracted negotiations which took place between 1925 and 1934, the French Government exerted all their efforts to secure an agreement which might perpetuate the power ratio established at Versailles. They were determined that the Draft Convention, provisionally agreed on in 1930, should preserve the disabilities then placed on Germany. Germany, on the other hand, was resolved to acquire the right to equal military power with other nations. She refused to accept any agreement which might prevent this. She threatened withdrawal from the Disarmament Conference if her demands were not conceded. And she finally fulfilled this threat in order to achieve on a unilateral basis the rearmament measures other powers had refused to concede to her. Here again the catcher-up disrupted all hope of agreement.

The difficulty of the catchers-up presented itself in even more unmistakable form during the negotiations in the years after World War II. Then too, any power feeling itself inferior in one field resisted the imposition of controls in that sphere until it had made up the deficiency. Any that believed itself in a position of superiority, on the other hand, agreed readily to see stabilization imposed there.

At the end of the war the United States, possessing an effective mo-

---

[6] G. M. Gathorne-Hardy, A Short History of International Relations, 1918–1939 (London, 1950), pp. 191–192.

nopoly in the capacity to manufacture nuclear weapons, offered to place the production and possession of these under international authority and so to "eliminate the use of atomic energy for destructive purposes." This was taken as a gesture as generous as its refusal by the Soviet Union was obstructive and perverse. But its effect, whatever the motives behind it, would have been to place the Soviet Union in a position of permanent inferiority. For even if the United States had in fact destroyed her existing weapons, and the Soviet Union could have been satisfied of this, there was no means of destroying the capacity to resume manufacture in the case of world war or even in the case of a breakdown in the agreement. The United States would thus have held permanent technological superiority in case of emergency. The Soviet Union, therefore, as the catching-up power, proceeded to frustrate any attempt to reach agreement in this field. She demanded that control should come into operation only after all United States bombs had been destroyed, and concentrated on a call to "ban the bomb." Meanwhile she proceeded to redress her disadvantage by the acquisition of the atomic bomb in 1949, and of the hydrogen bomb in 1953. From this point her proposals for the prohibition of such weapons were abandoned. Instead she sought, by a ban on weapons tests, to prevent others from catching up in this field.

In the next period, the main catcher-up was Germany once more. The Soviet Union concentrated all her efforts on ensuring that Germany should remain disarmed as long as possible. Germany and her allies were correspondingly determined to resist this. And frequent Soviet proposals designed to limit Germany's military capacities were as frequently resisted by the West.

Over nuclear stockpiles and delivery systems the West was at an advantage. It thus sought to prevent the Soviet Union from catching up with it in these areas. In 1956 President Eisenhower proposed that the manufacture of weapons-grade atomic fuel should be subject to inspection, further production used only for peaceful purposes, and existing fuel gradually reconverted. A cutoff of nuclear production appeared in all Western disarmament plans. And later demands for a "freeze" in delivery systems would also have had the effect of preventing the Soviet Union from attaining parity in effective nuclear capacity.

In ability to procure intelligence about military dispositions and capabilities, the West was inferior. Here the Soviet Union could prevent the restoring of the balance by refusing to accept inspection in her borders. This would have nullified the advantage the essentially secret nature of her political system afforded her. To meet this, the United States introduced plans for "open skies" which would have done much to even the balance in this field. When the Soviet Union refused these, she attempted to put "open skies" techniques into effect on a unilateral basis. And though the United States was later in a position to acquire comparable knowledge through the use of reconnaissance satellites, the West has remained at a disadvantage in intelligence. Conversely the Soviet Union was at a disadvantage in consequence of the bases possessed by the West all around her borders. For long she sought to counter this by intensive propaganda. Her disarmament plans repeatedly called for dismantling bases as the first step in the program. And when she secured temporary superiority in the field of space research, she asserted that, without counterconcessions over United States foreign bases, she would not agree to the imposition of any controls over outer space, where she herself was better placed.

The refusal of a catching-up power to renounce its right to secure equality is not, however, a problem confined to the relations between the greatest powers. It arises in equally acute form over the demands of aspiring nations of the *second rank*, determined to obtain the means of clambering into the first. The intransigent attitudes of Italy and some other smaller powers in the interwar years, determined not to forego the chance to better their position, showed this difficulty.

It has been demonstrated again in postwar disarmament discussions. Britain, for example, resisted all proposals to renounce the right to test hydrogen weapons so long as she had not herself successfully tested a hydrogen bomb. Only after she had successfully completed her own tests in 1957 did she suddenly become converted to a ban on weapons tests. Afterward France and China similarly resisted a ban. And they would no doubt suffer a similar conversion only when they themselves had acquired the status they aspired to. The so-called nth-power problem is indeed only the modern formulation of the problem of the catcher-up. It is a difficulty which is by no means peculiar to nuclear weapons. It could well arise with equal force in the future in the case of nuclear submarines, strategic missiles, anti-missile missiles, supersonic bombers, guided weapons mechanisms, and any other item of military equipment possessing a high status value, for which a system of control is proposed. The haves may sometimes accept a partial limitation that preserves their relative superiority. The have-nots will usually resist it.

This evidence shows that any disarmament agreement comes up against the special difficulty of securing a balance, at each stage, that even rising powers will accept as a just one. In many ways the problem that was faced in the disarmament negotiations of the twenty years after World War II was less complex than those that can normally be expected on this point. Because at that moment power within the world was uniquely polarized, the problem was mainly that of achieving a simple one-for-one balance between two alliances. But in normal circumstances, each power, or each alliance, may confront a number of possible adversaries. And since always some among these are likely to believe they have ground to make up in particular fields before they can accept stabilization or reduction, the difficulty of finding a mutually acceptable moment for preserving the existing balance is not easy to overcome.

The problem of preserving an accepted and unchanging balance is accentuated by the fact of *technological change.* The result of this is that no equilibrium in armaments can ever be permanent in its effects. For it may at any moment be overturned by some advance in technology, undertaken perhaps for some totally different purpose. Thus, in recent years, developments in electronics, radar, rockets, aircraft, metallurgical and many other techniques, even if undertaken for purely peaceful purposes, could transform any balance of power a disarmament agreement had secured. This would create a new demand to catch up by those outpaced. Even industrial progress may upset the balance. The capacity to acquire armed strength is related to industrial power, technical skills, the structure of industry, and other factors. Even if a balance in weapons themselves were attained, even if all weapons were destroyed, no system of armaments control could bring about equilibrium in these. And the ambition of more backwar powers to catch up with those ahead might be as intense as ever.

The problem of the catchers-up may arise through the struggle to *maintain* supremacy between equals or through an attempt to *achieve* equality by those previously inferior. The fact that some of the weapons sought are never likely to be used is not in itself of fundamental importance. For, as some of these examples demonstrate, the right to catch up may be demanded as much from the desire for status as from that for defense. The transference of status symbols to other fields, scientific or cultural achievements, the exploration of space, the provision of economic aid, sports victories, and others, may do something to relieve the pressures within the military field. But though this process could have the effect of allowing the arms race itself to be run at a somewhat less strenuous pace, history shows little evidence that it could make nations, whether great or small, any more willing than at present to accept the perpetuation of a balance of power which they felt capable of adjusting in their own favor. The difficulty is, once again, that of securing objective definitions of the needs or rights of each power. Whether these relate to security or status, the difficulty of convincing powers in a position of inferiority of their validity is a formidable one.

The Problem of Control

There is a third problem whose solution is equally vital to the successful achievement of a disarmament agreement. This is that of the policeman: whatever agreement is reached requires some enforcement agency to control it. Differences here may concern either the *degree* of control that may be necessary or the *type* of control that is acceptable.

Metternich's apprehensions concerning the difficulty of obtaining assurance over the level of armaments maintained by other parties to a disarmament agreement have been echoed by the governments of subsequent generations. Sir Robert Peel, advocating a measure of disarmament in 1841, discounted the "romantic notion" that a nation, in undertaking disarmament, could rely with security on the "professions of its neighbours." At the Hague Conference in 1899, the British Government declared that the limitations and prohibitions on arms which had been suggested there would be valueless unless some organization could be called into existence which would secure their observance. But such suggestions were for long not seriously pursued.

During the interwar discussions on disarmament, France from the start declared the question of control to be crucial. Determined above all to achieve security against the rearmament of Germany, she maintained that no disarmament agreement could be effective without provision for enforcement by some international authority. Most other powers for long refused to consider this aspect of the problem seriously, regarding it as an unnecessary complication which would only make agreement harder. The United States and Britain, in particular, were opposed to international control. Only at the Disarmament Conference of 1932–33, did it begin to be accepted that some form of international supervision might be required. The British Draft Convention, which formed the basis of discussion during the last phase of that Conference, proposed the establishment of a Permanent Disarmament Commission with wide powers of inspection and control.

But there was little agreement on the form control should take.

Britain proposed the establishment of a special international body, resembling the postwar Security Council, to consider breaches of the peace, in which certain powers (naturally including Britain) would enjoy the right to veto. France, still obsessed with the desire to retain supremacy over Germany, demanded that the initial step should be the establishment of controls; only after this system of supervision had been tested would the necessary measures of disarmament be introduced. Germany herself met such suggestions, like the Soviet Union after the war, with demands for assurances that control would in fact be followed by disarmament.

After World War II the problem proved no easier than before. There was first, in general throughout the postwar discussions, a wide margin between the *degree* of control acceptable to the different powers, above all between the maximum acceptable to the Soviet Union on the one hand and the minimum demanded by the West on the other. This difference was reinforced by a difference of strategic interests. The secrecy advantage held by the Communist world meant that the United States had an intelligence interest in securing a high degree of inspection within the Soviet Union while the Soviet Union had a military, as well as a political, interest in resisting this.

These difficulties over the degree of control were compounded by even more complex difficulties over the *type* of authority which would be necessary. In the early years, when the United Nations was effectively controlled by a pro-Western majority, the West was ready to see any agreement controlled by a United Nations body. By 1960, however, when the composition of the United Nations had altered, the West began to demand a new "disarmament agency" or other enforcement body. This was perhaps designed to remove the danger of the Soviet veto to the system or to counteract Afro-Asian hegemony. The Soviet Union, on the other hand, would accept only a body in which she retained a controlling influence. In the immediate postwar years she resisted the creation of any kind of inspection organization. When forced to admit that some supervision of disarmament would be necessary, she demanded that ultimate authority must rest with the Security Council, where she retained the protection of her veto power.

There were similar differences over the *form* of controls. The Soviet Union, while accepting the establishment of control posts at communication centers, demanded that these should be confined to a few fixed locations and limited in number. The West wanted more posts, including a considerable number on Soviet territory. During the negotiations over the test ban there were differences over the *number, siting, powers,* and *composition* of the teams needed to control the tests, which were never resolved. There were for long differences over the *timing* of the institution of controls at the start of a disarmament agreement. Above all, though the Soviet Union repeatedly maintained that she would only accept verification of the numbers of weapons *destroyed* during the disarmament process, the West demanded inspection for those retained as well.

These difficulties once again reflected fundamental problems of any disarmament agreement. Of all the problems arising, that of the policeman is perhaps the most basic. A disarmament system necessarily requires some authority to enforce it. International suspicion is such that no nations today would accept on trust professions of disarmament by others. Yet an effective control body might exert such influence as some parties will be reluctant to accept. It is usually accepted that any disarmament agency that is to be successful — which would be able, that is, to impose its authority at a time of tension or mutual suspicion when the agreement might be abrogated — must dispose of a considerable degree of armed power, probably greater than any with which it might then be confronted. Yet it is unlikely that any nation will allow the establishment of an organ that might acquire the power to overcome national forces, unless it possessed itself some check over the way it might be used.[7] It was the recognition of this fear which made necessary the according of a veto to the permanent members of the postwar Security Council over international measures of enforcement. And it was the same demand that has conditioned the position of the Soviet Union and other powers that United Nations peace forces shall be subject to the Council. But if a disarmament agency was limited by a great power veto, it would be powerless to act in precisely those cases most dangerous to world peace. While, therefore, nations likely to control the force may be ready to accept its establishment, those likely to be outnumbered will be less enthusiastic.

The root of the problems that arise here lies in the existing structure of loyalties and suspicions. Governments and peoples alike have continued to see an alternative center of authority, of uncertain composition, powers, and attitudes, as a greater, rather than a lesser, threat to security, values, and cherished ways of life, than those it may replace. The fact that that authority might, in the last resort, be able to coerce lesser centers of power thus usually appears to them more inhibiting

[7] See below, pp. 253–256.

in relation to their own power than reassuring in relation to that of others. National authorities themselves are perhaps no more likely than previous centers of power to divest themselves, voluntarily and deliberately, of the supremacy they enjoy. And the only alternative means of establishing a single center of authority, world conquest, is one none has wished to see effected.

Types of Disarmament

These three difficulties are each inherent in any attempt to reach agreement on disarmament. There is another, not quite so fundamental, which has caused equally great obstacles. This concerns the type of disarmament to be reached.

In all ages the urge for disarmament is concentrated on those weapons which most arouse popular apprehensions. Yet such weapons are not always those which are most perilous. The most terrible weapons of previous generations are not usually those most dangerous to the present. The abortive attempts in the Middle Ages to regulate the use of the crossbow could not, even if successful, have proved fruitful in an age when the first firearms were being developed. The prohibition of the bombardment of towns from the sea, the poisoning of wells, the violation of flagbearers and heralds, and similar misdemeanors, contained in the Hague Conventions, could prove of little comfort in a war which, twenty years later, saw the introduction of dirigibles, tanks, submarines, merchant raiders, and other new instruments of war. The limitations on capital ships imposed between the wars could scarcely have deterred aggressive designs in an age when naval strength was being replaced and nullified by air power. The proscription of chemical and bacteriological warfare during the same years could never have served a very useful purpose in an age when experience had already demonstrated that such weapons were·too dangerous to use. The spirit of the Maginot Line pervaded even the field of disarmament. Once again, over the weapons that proved decisive in the war that was to follow, over the jet fighter, the saturation bomber, the magnetic mine, the torpedo, above all, the rocket and the nuclear warhead, controls or prohibitions were barely even considered. Some of these weapons were not invented. Few of the others were highly publicized.

This retardation process was even more clearly visible in the attempts to secure disarmament after World War II. Once again energies were concentrated on the weapons that had proved most terrible in the war just ended. Once again it was universally assumed that it was in this field that measures of control were most urgently required.

Because all were aware that nuclear weapons were the most powerful arms then known, it was now everywhere believed they were the most dangerous. Disarmament discussions in the United Nations were at first exclusively directed at nuclear weapons. And for long they remained the dominant concern of governments. The attitude of the public was perhaps even more unconsidered. The arrival of the bomb created a momentary disquiet. But few seriously questioned the decision to use it at all. There was at first no widespread political agitation against the continued development of such weapons. The surge of feeling about the danger of those weapons began to become powerful, in Britain and other countries, only in the late fifties and early sixties, precisely at the moment that the real danger such weapons represented had faded almost to the vanishing point. For by then the capacity to annihilate had become mutual.

Governments on either side knew, as a matter of certainty, that the launching of an attack with such arms must bring the danger, indeed the certainty, of instant retaliation in kind, a retaliation which would destroy all their major cities and a substantial proportion of their population (including, as never before with such certainty, those leaders who allowed nuclear war to occur). No defense system, not even anti-missile missiles, could be certain of destroying all incoming weapons. Even the use of tactical weapons, whatever their value as a more subtle and convincing deterrent, could quickly escalate to all-out hydrogen warfare. By the early sixties, both East and West began to re-equip their armies to enable them to respond effectively to conventional attacks with conventional weapons alone. And the probability that in such circumstances either side would be the first to employ nuclear weapons, with all the possible consequences, became increasingly remote.

But disarmament discussions remained concentrated on nuclear weapons. A number of beliefs encouraged an unrealistic conception of the dangers. Some claimed that the mere possession and accumulation of weapons in itself produced pressures for their use: a contention for which history provided little evidence. The examples of gas and germs, equally terrible weapons of mass destruction, had already showed that, in even the most desperate conflicts, the use of some weapons was avoided. More general was the fear that, even if no government consciously desired nuclear war, it might nonetheless come about, by accident or by miscalculation. Such fears were hardly more realistic than the belief that nuclear war might be waged by intention. The types of *accident* suggested were precisely those most carefully guarded against. Fail-safe procedures for aircraft, the double key system for weapons, electronic locks, checks, and counterchecks in the structure of command, all these made almost inconceivable an accidental or personal initiation of nuclear conflict. Still less was war itself likely to come about by accident. The occasion may sometimes be small. But the actual precipitation of hostilities occurs in modern times as a result of an act of policy — on one side or the other — a conscious decision, not by a general, but by a government or a group of leaders, faced with a particular situation or incident, to initiate war to further the interests of the nation. It is impossible to find any example of a war in the last century that can properly be said to have been accidental. War, in real life, does not "break out"; it is made — even if made reluctantly, and when made, the weapons to be used are carefully calculated.

Nuclear war by *miscalculation* is almost equally improbable. War of some sort by miscalculation is always a possibility. There have no doubt been wars in history resulting from some provocative action undertaken in the expectation, or at least the hope, that no retribution was to be expected. Such a risk remains today. Decisions for limited war may still be made. But *nuclear* war is a choice of policy no leader or group of leaders is likely, even in the maximum extremity, to believe to be worth the possible advantages to be gained. Against nuclear powers, the perils of escalation which any use of such weapons, even at the lowest level, would involve are so universally appreciated that the likelihood that any government would risk such an eventuality is remote. The invulnerable means of delivery now available ensure that no power can prevent a reply in kind which, in a few hours, might effectively destroy its existence as a nation. It is virtually certain, therefore, that were hostilities to break out between nuclear powers, the taboos against nuclear weapons would be maintained, as were those against gas and germs before, and as those against nuclear weapons have been over the last twenty years, even in the bitter interideological struggles in Korea and Vietnam, where the risk of retaliation did not seem high. And the widespread distribution of alliances today means that even against nonnuclear enemies none could be sure of immunity. Such self-denying ordinances are now dictated by the manifest self-interest of all.

But because of the common apprehensions, governments during the postwar years continued principally to negotiate, and publics chiefly to agitate, about precisely those weapons that had become increasingly obsolete. Long hours of negotiations and countless flights of ingenuity were diverted to attempts to devise a foolproof system for control over the manufacture and possession of nuclear weapons. Yet, either publicly or privately, virtually all powers admitted foolproof control to be unattainable. There is no inspection system even theoretically conceivable that could provide a cast-iron assurance against the retention of a few, or even substantial numbers, of nuclear weapons, each occupying only a few cubic meters, above ground or below, within the vast spaces of the Soviet Union and the United States. Some of the *means of delivery* could be controlled; but others, submarine missiles, civil aircraft, and more primitive devices, could not be certainly eliminated. And once it is admitted that there can be no effective means of controlling stocks and means of delivery, there no longer is any significant advantage to be gained by the prohibition or control of manufacture (which in itself would be almost equally difficult to verify). For, with the present size of nuclear weapon piles, the addition to these stocks of marginal numbers of the same type of weapon can have little effect on international security. And the development of new types of weapons, or the aspirations of other powers to nuclear capability, are more effectively checked (if they can be checked at all) by the control of tests than by any other form of supervision. The endless and highly publicized disputes on "controls" over nuclear weapons thus represented a search for a solution that it was physically impossible to secure.

Moreover, even if such a control were believed possible, it was open to serious question how far it was desirable. For if, as can scarcely be contested, nuclear weapons represent a deterrent force, their assumed destruction will make war not less, but more, probable. And international peace is certainly more secure when the deterrent is acknowledged and mutual than if it becomes possible for one power to achieve, or even to claim, a monopoly by stealth. For nuclear weapons are not a deterrent only against nuclear warfare. The fact that, despite the almost unceasing tension between East and West during the years after World War II, none of the numerous incidents that might have led to major war, if only with conventional weapons, in fact did so, was undoubtedly partly due to fear of the possibility, however remote, of nuclear warfare (though with nuclear equilibrium this fear may decline). Effective control over the possession and manufacture of nuclear weapons might, therefore, aggravate rather than decrease the effective perils the world faces. It might increase the danger of war by reducing its dangers.

Finally, the never-ending and only half-believed search for nuclear disarmament distracted the attention of the world from the possibility of controls in the conventional field. The fact that the wars which are fought in the modern age are in practice conducted with conventional armaments in itself indicates that it is in this sphere that the need for reductions, or equilibrium, is greatest. During the two decades after World War II there were few moments when there was not a conventional war, on a larger or lesser scale, in progress in one part of the world or another. The balance of power, for example, over Cuba or Hungary, was determined by available conventional, not nuclear, forces. Even if large-scale conventional war between major powers is not at present to be expected, there can be no assurance that, as the nuclear stalemate appears more secure, such a war will not become more probable. The risk then reappears that any power which calculates it has overwhelming superiority in conventional arms may be tempted to exploit that strength in the hope that, through fear of nuclear retaliation, it could secure its ends by the use of old-fashioned means alone.

Such a war could be little less calamitous than nuclear war itself. The missiles now widely available and the powerful conventional explosives that exist might well be such as to make most of the major cities of Britain, and perhaps of the United States and the Soviet Union, uninhabitable within days of the opening of a merely conventional war. Missile artillery with conventional warheads could wreak untold havoc on concentrations of troops and on occupied cities within their range. The napalm bomb, though used in Korea and Vietnam against forces unable to reply in kind, might be a less attractive weapon in the hands of an enemy. Still less is it possible to imagine what future developments may portend. Indeed it is possible that the most terrible weapons of future conflicts are no more known to the general public today than were jet engines, radar, rockets, and nuclear warheads before the last war. Among the many myths that surround the subject of disarmament none is more dangerous than the widespread identification of "conventional" warfare with war that is not too unsupportable.

Once again, therefore, negotiations became concentrated in one particular field. But if any control over armaments is to be achieved, it is perhaps most important today that it should be achieved in the field of tanks, aircraft, guns, and the other weapons most likely to be employed, rather than of those which have ceased to be a danger but remain some safeguard. Not only is this task more urgent, but, since the risk involved in a single evasion is less, its accomplishment might be more readily secured.

Analogous choices between weapons to be controlled will always be needed. For, as has been seen, the exclusive preoccupation with nuclear weapons over the past twenty years is only one particular example of the difficulty for all disarmament agreements of determining which are those weapons that most need to be controlled. It is certainly not always the most powerful — nuclear weapons today any more than gas or germs yesterday — for which controls are needed to affect the conflicts of the future.

The second problem arising here concerns the choice between total and complete disarmament in one step or disarmament by stages. Many have assumed that the object of negotiations must be the conclusion of a single agreement providing, in one leap, for the attainment of total disarmament covering all nations, all arms, and every species of military personnel that exists on earth. Not all negotiations have been of this type. Indeed it has been the attempts at more restricted agreements which alone have occasionally brought some success. The Washington and London naval agreements between the wars, the postwar negotiations on the demilitarization of the Antarctic and on a nuclear test ban, which started off with strictly defined and limited objectives, were almost the only discussions of the period which arrived at successful conclusions. For the most part, however, disarmament discussions have been undertaken on the assumption that the objective was an agreement that provided comprehensive disarmament in all fields. The negotiations at the Hague, though aimed at a reduction rather than the abolition of forces, were designed to achieve this in all fields simultaneously. The participants in the main disarmament discussions between the wars, though willing to discuss the possibilities within confined fields, retained the assumption that their ultimate goal must be a comprehensive agreement. After 1945 the concept that it might be possible to abolish all arms in one fell swoop became, in time, almost universal.

This assumption is a bold one. For if it is difficult to reach, among a large number of powers of different sizes, aspirations, and interests, a satisfactorily secured disarmament agreement in any one field, to achieve one that could abolish every type of weapon, nuclear and conventional, land and sea, offensive and defensive; that would provide in advance for the exact phasing of every subsequent step in the procedure; that at each such stage would assure an exact balance between all the major alliances and between each individual power; more, that would be viewed by every participating government as not placing it at a disadvantage at any point; and that was policed and enforced by an international authority acceptable to all — to achieve all this in a single agreement, formulated, by some prestidigitatious conjury of words, within the ambit of a single document, is a task that only wildly wishful thinking could believe attainable. It is a task that would be formidable enough if undertaken by mechanical brains assessing interests that could be mathematically ascertained. When undertaken by the apprehensive minds of merely human negotiators, anxiously nudged by suspicious soldiers and bewildered publics, it begins to appear only a dream, inviting but implausible. Such schemes involve a series of obligations and commitments so complex, uncertain, and delicately balanced that not even a single power, let alone all simultaneously, is likely to accept them without a much greater degree of mutual confidence than exists at present. Only one provision needs to be rejected by one power, one card removed from the castle, for the entire elaborately organized structure to come to nothing. The risk involved in embarking, irrevocably, on a journey of infinite peril, toward a goal which none can accurately foresee, is one which few powers will feel they can responsibly incur, unless on impossibly favorable terms.

There are indeed special difficulties about reaching agreement on extensive disarmament. For the lower the level of armaments left, the more difficult it will be to arrive at equilibrium. At such levels it requires only a relatively small violation, or a small amount of rearmament, or even a small miscalculation in the balance originally agreed, to place one power, or side, in a position of decisive advantage. Thus the nearer such a level is reached, the greater the apprehensions that each power, and each alliance, may feel about further reductions. The equilibrium already existing, however arbitrarily determined, will often appear to allow a larger margin of safety than levels approaching nearer to zero.

Indeed, even if effective disarmament agreements of this type could in fact be reached, they must still be only provisional, however comprehensive, unless there were agreement on more basic questions affecting interaction between states. For such disarmament agreements, while they may influence the existing level of armaments, cannot affect the capacity to *acquire* armaments when new crises or disagreements arise. Any agreement can be denounced at a stroke of the pen if a state of conflict between nations demands this. Even the total elimination of arms (which has never been proposed — even the most "comprehensive" plans now considered provide for the retention of internal security forces) could never provide absolute security, since no nation could be prevented, at a crisis of confidence, from once more resuming manufacture. Even while such an agreement remained in force, and was everywhere observed, therefore, each side might, so long as the possibility of breakdown remained, secretly devote its energies to developing the capacity to reacquire a war potential within the shortest possible time should a crisis occur. Only the renunciation of all industrial potential and all technological education could destroy the capacity to make modern war.

The fundamental fact behind this difficulty is that it is not the availability of armed force that causes the habit of resolving international disputes by force but the reverse. It is not weapons which create war. It is war that creates weapons. In negotiating disarmament agreements, as this record shows, nations have tended to disregard this simple but important truth.

Conclusions

The history of negotiations in these various fields thus reveals what have been the main obstacles to guaranteeing peace by abolishing arms.

Let us look next at the evidence of the agreements actually concluded. A list of those reached over the seventy years of negotiations on this subject appears in Table VIII.2. This represents another type of empirical evidence available in this field. Certain features may be immediately noted.

First, throughout this period the cases in which agreement has proved possible have in practice been those where negotiations took place for limited measures, covering a restricted type of armament, or a limited undertaking only. The negotiations for more comprehensive agreements, though perhaps more commonly undertaken, have been so far without effect. The limitations in the successful agreements have been of two kinds (the Antarctic and hot-line agreements are not strictly disarmament measures at all and are not here considered). Some have covered only a restricted range of armaments: only naval ships — and indeed only certain kinds of naval ships — in the Washington and London agreements of the interwar years (neither, for example, included submarines, carriers, or smaller vessels); only nuclear weapons in three of the postwar agreements (and even here only a very marginal limitation of the capacity to develop and deploy these weapons, rather than in the number possessed). In other cases, the number of nations participating has been restricted (only two to five in the case of the interwar naval agreements, the agreement on fissionable materials, and the hot-line agreement). And the number involved in negotiating them has sometimes been more limited still (only three nations effectively negotiated the Test-ban Agreement, though it has been ratified by many others). This has made agreement easier to reach.

TABLE VIII · 2

Disarmament and Arms Control Agreements, 1899–1964

Agreements

First Hague Conference	1899
(No agreement on disarmament but Hague Convention on law and customs of war and peaceful settlement of disputes adopted.)	
Washington Naval Agreement	1921
(limiting capital ships of US, Britain, France, Italy, and Japan).	
London Naval Agreements	1930
(limiting naval tonnage of US, Britain, and Japan).	
Demilitarization of Antarctic.	1959
Nuclear testing banned except underground.	1963
Communications link (US and USSR).	1963
Reductions in production of fissionable materials (US, USSR, and Britain).	1964
Treaty on peaceful use of outer space.	1967
Treaty on Latin American nuclear-free zone.	1967

Second, the agreements reached have tended to be those which stabilized existing balances, rather than brought about specific *reductions* of arms. The Washington and London agreements did not make necessary the scrapping of any vessels that would otherwise have been kept in service, but served rather to protect each power temporarily from the burden of a new race in the fields covered. The Antarctic Agreement demilitarized an area that was already demilitarized. The test ban, the fissionable materials, and the space orbiting argeements did not reduce the effective military capacity of any power from what they had already chosen to possess: they were designed to restrict the development of a similar capacity by other powers, or to restrict the development of the arms race into new fields. This does not mean that such agreements serve no useful purpose. Both in the interwar and post-war period, they may have significantly influenced some nations against *increasing* their capacity in a way they might otherwise have done. But it reflects the fact that it is much easier to persuade governments to agree to *restrict* their future capacities, than to *reduce* their existing power; and it is easier to agree to a restriction that is uniform for all than to arrive at explicit ratios of different levels for different nations.

Third, such agreements seem to have been mainly arrived at at times of relative détente between states. The interwar and postwar periods were characterized by alternating phases of détente and tension. In the interwar period, the Washington and London agreements (1921 and 1930) were both reached at times of relative calm (especially in the Far East) between the high tension periods immediately after the end of the war, in 1926–27, and after the opening of Japanese aggression in 1931. France and Italy were ready to take part in the relatively relaxed atmosphere of 1921, but not in the more competitive situation after 1930. Similarly, in the postwar world, it proved possible to reach agree-ment on Trieste and Austria in the fairly tranquil years of 1954–55 (the two Geneva Conferences), on the Antarctic in 1959 (Camp David), and on the test ban, the hot line, and others in 1963; whereas in the in-termediate, hot periods of 1947–52 (Eastern Europe and Korea), 1956–58 (Hungary and Berlin), 1960–62 (the U-2 and Cuba), and 1964–67 (Viet-nam) no progress was made. This tends to confirm that the general cli-mate of relations between states is more influential in determining the possibility of disarmament agreements than vice versa.

Finally, few of the agreements reached have been universally sub-scribed to. None, therefore, has managed to meet effectively the problem of the catchers-up. One or two, such as the prewar agreements, have lapsed because of violations by one or another power (this is a fate that could still befall the postwar test-ban agreement). The test-ban agree-ment omitted those most crucial to success. And the most stable seem to be those (such as the demilitarization of the Antarctic and the ban on orbiting weapons of mass destruction) that apply impartially to all.

It is also possible to examine the relationship between levels of arms and the incidence of war.

The evidence that the level of armaments is itself an important cause of tension and hostility between nations in modern times does not seem strong. For example, countries with high military expenditures, Russia at the end of the nineteenth century, France and Poland between the wars, South Korea, Turkey, and the Soviet Union today, are not those that have themselves mainly started wars. It can be shown that the level of arms expenditure of the United States and the Soviet Union rose fairly consistently between 1955 and 1965, yet most would accept that this period, as a whole, was marked by perpetually declining tension between these two powers. It can also be shown that the big increases that did occur, for example in 1960–61 and 1965, were the direct effect of immediate international crises, here over Berlin and Vietnam. The outbreak of most of the hostilities that occurred between the wars, and especially during the post-1945 period (see the list on pp. 183–185) does not seem to have been preceded by any increase in the arms budgets of the nations concerned. Finally, the experience of the thirties suggests that low arms levels as well as high may be a cause of war.

Taken together, these facts suggest that decisions on armaments are more often the effect, than the cause, of international tensions; and that decisions to make war are little affected by the *absolute* level of arms on both sides (though they may be by relative levels). It is true that both the first and second world wars were preceded by periods of intense rearmament, but this rearmament is more plausibly regarded as an effect, rather than a cause, of the tensions that anyway existed. It is by no means certain that, in the first case at least, rearmament would have led to war, but for the immediate incident which gave rise to it. And it might be as reasonable to argue that the two wars broke out *despite*, rather than because of, the arms races, whose effect is normally to increase equilibrium in available power.

The examination of these two types of evidence, negotiations and agreements, suggests certain conclusions for policy. First, because, as we have seen, subjective assessments of security often prevent agreement, an essential preliminary to an effective disarmament agreement may be devising some objective criteria for arms levels to replace the subjective assessments now necessary. If disarmament negotiations are ever to take a more constructive form than at present, therefore, it is perhaps toward the establishment of such criteria that they should above all be directed. These could act as some guide to unilateral armaments policies as well as to negotiated agreements.

Even here, considerable difficulties will arise (as was revealed when such criteria were discussed at length in the interwar negotiations). If, for example, a criterion based on population alone is chosen, others may claim (as then) that geographical factors give advantages to some powers over others. Some may assert, as Britain then claimed, that the nature of their overseas or other commitments demands that a special allowance be made. Others may demand a special allowance for length of frontier, or of coastline, or size and difficulty of terrain. Others again might insist that technological capacity is equally crucial in conditioning military powers, and that compensation must be made for deficiencies in this. And even if some generally acceptable criterion can be found, there arises the difficulty of relating so many warships allowed to a maritime power to the land divisions demanded by a land power, of relating regulars to reserves, and similar comparisons. Though a solution based on population is the simplest, there are serious difficulties over this, as may be seen if a situation is conceived in which China demanded four times the armed strength of the United States and three times that of the Soviet Union; India, four times that of Pakistan; the Arabs, ten times that of Israel, and so on. As this example shows, the levels dictated by any single criterion, or any mix between them, will not necessarily match what is needed from the point of view of balance between possible antagonists.

The next conclusion indicated is the need for the right institutions to establish these criteria. The divergent conceptions of equilibrium which we have examined arise above all through the fact that assessments and decisions relating to arms levels are taken entirely within a national framework. Again the need seems to be for the establishment of international institutions, whether intergovernmental committee or unofficial international strategic institute, to discuss the most suitable criteria for measuring and balancing armed strength. These are relevant even without disarmament. The publication of studies and recommendations by a body of this sort might act as some guide to national defense and military assistance policies and so promote equilibrium even if no public knowledge of levels of arms maintained were permitted. Even more important, they might serve to influence public opinion, and thereby encourage the conception of a common international interest in balance to replace that of a purely national interest in superiority.

Finally, the record shows the importance of communication in overcoming divergent conceptions of equilibrium. Without this, any move by one nation, even though designed to improve the balance, may bring a further move by another believing the first to have upset it. There may thus occur the cumulative and accelerating alternation characteristic of arms races. It is arguable that in the fifties the Soviet Union, through the secrecy of her policies, brought about a greater degree of rearmament by the West than was necessary and thereby damaged her own interests.

It is now known that estimates of Soviet conventional strength in the early fifties were inflated. Greater frankness about force levels, prior announcement of, or consultation over changes, may reduce the violence of these alternations, and so help in producing a more stable balance.

Even if all the problems here described were overcome and agreement reached, however, peace would not be secured. As we have seen, arms levels, even if reduced, can be quickly restored. Foolproof inspection is hard to arrange. Balances are hard to maintain indefinitely. Sources of friction may soon arise. There is in fact no clear evidence, nor obvious reason to suppose, that the danger of war has ever borne, or bears today, any close relationship to the volume of weapons possessed. There is certain historical evidence to support the opposite view (the fact that wars often break out when nations are poorly armed, as in the Napoleonic Wars, the Crimean War, the Balkan Wars, and others, or stay at peace when highly armed, as between 1948 and 1968). If the will to war itself is unchanged, arms will usually be found to wage it.

The attempt to secure peace through the abolition of arms suffers from the fundamental drawback that it is directed at symptoms rather than causes. The belief that since weapons alone make war possible, war can be abolished by the abolition of weapons is an illusion that is understandably attractive. All would like to believe that by striking off the limbs that offend them they might automatically reform their characters. But such experiments might only show that, where motivations remain unmodified, anatomical manipulation is unlikely to produce results.

This does not mean that negotiated agreements on disarmament have no contribution to make in establishing a more peaceful community, or can never be attained. The examination here made suggests that if negotiations were concentrated on specific agreements within limited fields, where the sacrifices of sovereignty and trials of confidence demanded could be readily assessed, some progress might be attained. It is through approaches of this type that the only effective disarmament agreements have been arrived at in the past. And it is likely to be through similar methods that they will be achieved in the future. By the progressive accumulation of agreements of this type, an appreciable influence on the total international environment might gradually be brought about. The most likely fields for these at present would seem the extension of demilitarization, from the Antarctic and outer space to the Arctic, the sea bed, and other areas; neutralization agreements, like that for Austria, in Indo-China and other delicate areas; new conventions to ban gas and chemical weapons such as napalm, and to bring up to date the laws of war; and possibly an agreement for the registration of arms sales and supplies. The best hope of progress in disarmament is probably not through formally negotiated agreements, but through unilateral measures. If individual powers can overcome subjective apprehensions sufficiently to initiate limited reductions in particular fields, they may sometimes evoke a response from antagonists, often themselves sharing a desire for lower levels. If each would, in turn, respond immediately and unhesitatingly to similar moves of other powers, a downward, rather than an upward, spiral may be set in motion. Even the controls to verify disarmament (such as the monitoring of tests) could sometimes be introduced on a unilateral basis.

Normally, however, the evidence we have examined suggests that levels of armaments are effects rather than causes, symptoms of developments in other spheres, rather than autonomous factors, the end product of frictions and fears rather than their creator. Only, therefore, when a more general harmony between expectations is achieved are underlying desires for high arms levels likely to be overcome. Only when desires to *use* weapons are significantly modified, it would appear, will desires to possess them be fundamentally influenced.

Bibliography

Barker, Charles A. (ed.), *Problems of World Disarmament*, Boston, 1963.

Bechhoefer, B. C., *Post-War Negotiations for Arms Control*, Washington, D.C., 1961.

Benoit, E. and K. Boulding, *Disarmament and the Economy*, New York, 1963.

Economist Intelligence Unit, *Economic Effects of Disarmament*, London, 1962.

Faber, H. W., *The Strategy of Disarmament*, London, 1962.

Luard, Evan (ed.), *First Steps to Disarmament*, London, 1965.

Melman, Seymour (ed.), *Disarmament: Its Politics and Economics*, Boston, 1962.

———, *Inspection for Disarmament*, New York, 1958.

National Lawyers' Guild, *Summary of Disarmament Documents, 1945–62*, San Francisco, 1963.

Nogee, Joseph L., *The Diplomacy of Disarmament*, South Bend, Ind., 1960.

Wheeler-Bennet, J., *The Disarmament Deadlock*, London, 1934.

———, *The Reduction of Armaments*, London, 1925.

Wright, Sir Michael, *Disarm and Verify*, London, 1964.

CHAPTER NINE

Authority

The Development of International Institutions

Since agreements to control armaments and agreements to abolish or reduce them have each proved unavailable, other methods of securing peace have been attempted. For hundreds of years there have been efforts to develop some kind of central authority able to maintain order among states.

The nation state has so far proved individualistic and lawless. War was already institutionalized as part of the behavior pattern of human societies when nations first came into existence. Conditioned by environment to engage in competitive struggle, they have normally been recalcitrant to all outside authority. The doctrine of "sovereignty" implied an unfettered freedom of action at home, a freedom liberally extended to relations with others of their kind. Because throughout most of history no nation was able to secure unchallenged supremacy among its fellows (as had been acquired within them), such behavior could no more be subdued than it could be discarded. The only recognized mechanism for regulating their relations was war itself.

The nation was elevated into a semipersonal entity, a revered abstraction, whose individual interests loomed so large as to obscure those of the community of nations as a whole. In the East, the authority of national rulers was sometimes believed sanctified by a mandate of Heaven. In Europe, monarchs equally often claimed a divine authority. When these began to lose their potency, new theories were devised to buttress, with an ideological foundation, the power of the prince, the absolute and perpetual might of the sovereign, or the unchallengeable authority of a state Leviathan. At the beginning of the nineteenth century still more elaborate justifications of the nation state were proclaimed, endowing such bodies with a transcendental or spiritual character, as of "God walking on the earth." Finally the slogans of nationalism first in Europe, later elsewhere, sealed the universal faith in the unrestricted authority of the nation.

Only slowly, with increasing contacts, did sovereign bodies more readily join in larger associations. In the Congress system in nineteenth century Europe, as we saw earlier, the major states began to discuss the affairs of the continent (and so, they believed, of the world) through periodic meetings between governments. This was an attempt to provide international authority through *ad hoc deliberation:* a conference was called at moments of major crisis.

The principal meetings are listed in Table IX.1. The system did something to provide the sense of a European community with its own conventions, institutions, and procedures. It reached joint decisions on many major questions, such as the neutralization of Belgium and Luxembourg, the division of the Low Countries, Egypt, the independence of Greece and Serbia, and many other matters. But the character of the system was in some ways that of a trade association for monarchs. It was used often to preserve their own common interests against the unruly, at home as well as abroad, rather than as an effective device for regulating international disputes. Since it depended on agreement, not majorities, when interests clashed completely it could perform no useful function. Where one power, as Britain did, refused to join in perpetuating the existing political order, while the rest wished still to do so, the system was unworkable. Again, where powers of rising strength, such as Russia and Germany, began to challenge the prerogatives of more anciently established powers, such as Turkey, Austria-Hungary, and France, agreement was impossible.

New forms of cooperation were developed for practical purposes. Even sovereign nations began to be ready in certain functional fields to yield some independence. They were ready, for example, soon after the middle of the nineteenth century, to join together in comprehensive international organizations to coordinate telegraph and postal services between them (the International Telegraphic Bureau in 1868 and the General Postal Union in 1874). In the years that followed they reached a series of cooperative agreements in the fields of copyright, customs procedures, trade marks and patents, telegraphic communications, railway coordination, systems of measurement, and other matters. (The main developments are set out in Table IX.2.) As a result, the habit of intergovernmental conferences, of correspondence and consultations between officials, became established more firmly.

TABLE IX·1

Chief Congresses and Conferences of the Nineteenth Century: Including Subjects Discussed

Congresses		Topics
Vienna/Paris	1814–15	Peace treaty, Quadruple Alliance
Aix-la-Chapelle	1818	France, Quadruple Alliance
Troppau	1820	Naples revolution
Laibach	1821	Naples revolution
Verona	1822	Italy, Spain, Eastern question
Paris	1856	Peace treaty
Berlin	1878	Eastern question

Conferences		
London	1830–32	Belgium
Rome	1831–32	Papal States
London	1838–39	Belgium
Vienna	1839	Eastern question
London	1840–41	Eastern question
London	1850–52	Schleswig-Holstein
Vienna	1853	Eastern question
Vienna	1855	Eastern question
Paris	1858	Principalities
Paris	1860–61	Syria
London	1864	Schleswig-Holstein
London	1867	Luxembourg
Paris	1869	Crete
London	1871	Black Sea
Constantinople	1876–77	Eastern question
Madrid	1880	Morocco
Berlin	1884–85	Africa

At the end of the century, governments began to attempt a more far-reaching regulation of their affairs. At the Hague Conference of 1899 they devised or developed procedures for mediation, arbitration, and inquiry to remedy disputes. They issued declarations of peaceful intent. They invented new regulations for the conduct of war. At the Second Hague Conference of 1907 they agreed to hold successive meetings of the same sort every eight years. So they began to advance from authority by ad hoc deliberations to that of an institutionalized machinery. But the next meeting had not even taken place before peace was shattered in World War I.

Only the shock of world slaughter on an unprecedented scale could stimulate the creation of a more permanent and far-reaching international organization. The horrors of that conflict induced a resolution, more deeply felt and widely shared than any held before, that at all costs no such disaster must be allowed to recur. So the League of Nations, "to promote international cooperation and to achieve international peace and security," was established. Apart from the United States and the Hejaz, every recognized state became a member of this at one time or another.

TABLE IX · 2

The Development of International Organizations, 1800–1965

Date	Political	Functional	Legal
1815	Congress system of periodic but ad hoc consultation between great powers established		[Numerous bilateral arbitration agreements]
1821		International Commission for the Elbe	
1831		International Commission for the Rhine	
1856		International Commission for the Danube with own flag and insignia	
1868		International Telegraphic Bureau (later ITU)	
1873			International Law Institute (non-governmental)
1874		General Postal Union (later U.P.U.)	
1875		International Bureau of Weights and Measures	
1881		International health offices set up at Havana and Vienna	
1885		Regulations for international telephone service agreed	
1890	International Union of American Republics		

TABLE IX · 2 (*Cont.*)

Date	Political	Functional	Legal
1899			Hague Conventions and declarations
1901		International Labor Office (nongovernmental) at Basel	Permanent Court of Arbitration
1902		First International Sugar Agreement	
1907		International Office of Public Health at Paris	Second Hague Conference: regular conferences agreed
1910	Pan-American Union		
1919	League of Nations	Organs of the League to deal with slavery, white slavery, drug traffic, communications, health, and financial assistance. I.L.O. established	Permanent International Court of Justice
1922		International Commission for Air Navigation	
1945	United Nations Arab League	Food and Agriculture Organization	International Court of Justice (within UN)
1946		UNESCO World Bank International Monetary Fund	International Law Commission (within UN)
1947		World Health Organization International Civil Aviation Organization	
1948	Organization of American States		
1950	Council of Europe	International Meteorological Organization	
1957		International Maritime Consultative Organization	
1959		International Atomic Energy Authority	
1963	Organization of African Unity		
1964		UN Conference on Trade and Development	

The main features of the system were an Assembly in which all members were represented, which met, usually once a year, in Geneva. This was authorized to deal with "any matter within the sphere of action of the League or affecting the peace of the world." The League Council, appointed by the Assembly, originally had eight members, including four permanent members representing the "principal Allied and Associated powers" (at first Britain, France, Italy, and Japan), but the membership was several times expanded. The Council was to meet "from time to time as occasion may require and at least once a year." In practice it came to meet every three months but could be called at any time in a situation of crisis, so far as existing communications allowed. This meant often not for several days. Most of the major crises and disputes of the period were considered in the Council and in the early years a few successes were achieved: over the Aaland Islands, the Albanian–Yugoslav incident, Memel, the Turkish-Iraqi border, the Greek–Bulgarian dispute, Corfu, and one or two others, settlements of a kind were reached. But unanimity was required (excluding the states against which action was contemplated) for each decision that might be reached, and this inevitably encouraged compromise. There was a Permanent Mandates Commission, composed of independent experts and not representatives of governments, which was advisory to the Council and was to supervise the exercise of responsibilities by the mandatory powers. Finally, the Permanent International Court of Justice was set up to hear legal disputes between nations, though at first this was only with their consent for each individual case.

Inevitably, the new organization was evolutionary rather than revolutionary in powers and functions. It thus only marginally altered the international environment. It was founded on the same concepts which had governed international relations in earlier generations. The Holy Alliance was preserved in the privileged position accorded to the "principal allied and associated powers" as permanent members of the League Council. The obverse concept of the "sovereign equality" of all nations, whatever their size and status, was maintained in the unanimity rule established in the Assembly. The processes of arbitration and judicial settlement earlier devised (see pp. 271 ff., below) were explicitly preserved in the procedures laid down for this purpose in the Covenant. Above all, the "sovereignty" which the diplomatic usage of nation states had insisted on through long centuries, remained largely unviolated. It was safeguarded by the rule of unanimity. And it was assured by the absence of any effective sanctions against transgressors.

This was a system of authority by *joint retaliation*. A true collective security system was envisaged. Members undertook individually to "preserve as against external aggression the territorial integrity and existing political independence" of other members by taking up arms against the aggressor. Economic sanctions too were proposed. But the will to apply them was lacking. The Council could make recommendations, but not decisions, on such matters. If the Council failed to reach unanimous agreement, members reserved "the right to take such action as they . . . consider necessary for the maintenance of right and justice"; which meant usually no action at all. Military help was to be accorded only on a voluntary basis; which meant it was never once accorded. If a member were to resort to war in disregard of the Covenant, other members undertook to sever commercial, financial, and personal intercourse with that state; and even here only once were measures of a mild character temporarily introduced.

The new system was in many ways an advance. The establishment of the principle of international action to counter aggression at least was valuable, even if the principle was inadequately applied. There was a genuine desire to banish war and restrain competitive nationalism. But there was insufficient realism about the deficiencies of the new mechanism. There were different conceptions of its purpose. To Wilson and his followers, it was a focus of international opinion that would be impossible to resist and could create a just world order. To France it was the framework for an alliance against Germany. To Britain it was a diplomatic device for facilitating contacts. But it was faced with an upsurge of inflamed nationalism among a few countries such as it would have been difficult for any international organization to contend with. And its difficulties were intensified in that it was called on to defend a settlement of the justice of which few members of the community were wholly convinced.

As time progressed, some efforts were made to remedy the more glaring inadequacies of the organization. Though "decisions" might require unanimity, "wishes" (*voeux*) came to be expressed by means of a simple majority. There was an attempt to provide for the compulsory arbitration of disputes (though this itself had to be voluntarily accepted and few nations did so). The smaller powers slowly began to be accorded a more effective share in the proceedings of the Council. But the basic principle remained unchanged: no decision was regarded as binding without universal consent. The organization was essentially a pact of nonaggression with unusually wide, though never universal, membership. Even United States membership could not, as is sometimes suggested, have made it more effective without a total change in the spirit that animated it.

The League might have proved an effective authority for preserving international law and order, with all its limitations, if it had been used with resolution. But resolution is just what was lacking. Revulsion at the recent slaughter was everywhere so intense that most persuaded themselves peace could be assured by merely wishing hard enough. The League appeared to some a magic amulet to ward off evils without the painful necessity for taking more strenuous measures. The war to end wars had already been fought. The unpleasant reality that peace might need to be imposed by the brute force of tanks and guns, rather than conjured by high-flown incantations, was too ugly to be looked in the face. In such circumstances those who were not too squeamish to invoke the brute force for their own private purposes inevitably had little reason to fear retaliation.

Thus, during the League's life, assaults were launched in turn against Manchuria, Ethiopia, China, Austria, Czechoslovakia, Albania, and Finland. Not once did any member of the League take up arms to "preserve as against external aggression the territorial integrity and existing political independence" of other members, as they had undertaken under Article X of the Covenant. Only once were the mild measures of "sanctions" provided for in Article XVI (against Italy) enforced and then they were abandoned within a few months, with the aggression totally unremedied. Successive aggressions by Japan in the Far East were met by a "Commission of Inquiry" and by a mildly deprecating resolution — in each case unaccompanied by action. And most of the nations of Western Europe passively watched their neighbors swallowed in turn until their own turn came for mastication.

The League performed some useful work in the social and economic field. New subsidiary organs emerged.[1] The International Labor Office did valuable work in establishing labor standards. The Transit and Communications Committee sought to coordinate transport. International social action on slavery, drugs, and prostitution was initiated. More important, the concept of a central organization responsible for peace all over the world now became established in the minds of statesmen and people everywhere. But for the most part, the League and all its resolutions never approached within measurable distance of the real world

[1] For a general history of the League, see F. P. Walters, A History of the League of Nations (London, 1952).

with which it was confronted. A new world was built of words alone. The speeches of statesmen treated of a mythical realm of "open, just, and honorable relations between nations" where "open covenants would be openly arrived at" and war would be forever "outlawed." Nations entered into a pact for the "renunciation of war." Governments subscribed to a "General Act for the Pacific Settlement of International Disputes." Individuals signed "peace pledges." All the words were no doubt genuinely meant. Only when confronted with the less elevating but more compelling power of tanks and bombs did the puzzled, well-meaning but irresolute statesmen of that age realize that words alone might not be enough.

The United Nations System

When preparations were begun for a new form of international authority, therefore, while war still raged, it was everywhere affirmed that the lessons from the last attempt would be well learned.

First, the new organization would be given effective power to enforce its decisions.

The new organization was without doubt better equipped than its predecessor. Decisions of the Security Council were now made binding on all. Membership of all the great powers, including the United States, strengthened the organization's authority. Votes on many matters could be taken by two-thirds or even, on less important questions, by simple majorities in the Assembly, or seven votes in the Council. This was to be a system of *compulsory enforcement* (only with immunity for some).

Sanctions were to be more powerful. Although the Covenant had left the provision of military assistance to the voluntary decisions of member states, the Charter provided that all members of the UN undertook "to make available to the Security Council . . . armed forces, assistance and facilities . . ." (Article 43), with which the Security Council was empowered to "take such action . . . as may be necessary to maintain or restore international peace and security" (Article 42). The Security Council was to take steps for the establishment of a permanent force to enforce its authority (Article 45). It could reach a decision on such a matter with only seven concurring votes (Article 27). And such a "decision" was binding on every member of the organization. For every member agreed "to accept and carry out the decisions of the Security Council. . . ." (Article 25.) The will of seven could now be binding on a hundred. This time the policeman was provided with a truncheon.

Second, the League's methods of conciliation and arbitration had proved ineffective. Thus new methods of resolving frictions which had not yet led to violence were devised, which might make unnecessary more drastic UN action. Chapter VI of the Charter, devoted to the "pacific settlement of disputes," provided for an elaborate series of measures for this purpose. These comprised settlement between the parties by "negotiation, inquiry, mediation, conciliation, arbitration, judicial settlement, resort to regional agencies or arrangements" (Article 33); "investigation" by the Council (Article 34); consideration by the Security Council or the Assembly (Article 35); the recommendation of "appropriate procedures or methods of adjustment" by the Security Council (Article 36 (1)); reference, in the case of legal disputes, to the International Court (Article 36 (3)); and a recommendation by the Security Council, when a dispute was thought likely to endanger international peace and security, of "such terms of settlement as it may consider appropriate" (Article 37). Only if all these measures failed, and a "threat to the peace, breach of the peace . . . [or] act of aggression" were to take place, would the Security Council begin to consider "measures . . . to maintain or restore international peace and security," including, in extreme cases, enforcement action.

Finally, the League, it was widely felt, had failed partly because it had taken too little account of existing international realities. The new organization was therefore designed to reflect, more accurately than its predecessor, some of the harsh facts of international life. It contained all the great powers. It acknowledged, in the provisions for a veto, the superior power of the mighty (this was understandable since the Charter, unlike the Covenant, was concocted by the mighty, being drafted even in its details by the United States, the Soviet Union, Britain, and China, and merely endorsed, with relatively unimportant amendments, by the assembled multitudes at San Francisco). It reserved exclusive power in the field of enforcement action to the Security Council. While in the League "any war or threat of war" was "a matter of concern to the whole League," in the UN members conferred on the Security Council primary responsibility for the maintenance of international peace and security. Enforcement action "under regional arrangements or by regional agencies" could only be taken with the authorization of the Security Council. Even the "inherent right of individual or collective self-defense" was conceded only until the Security Council has taken the measures "necessary to maintain international peace and security." But every such decision by the Security Council was subject to veto. As a result, though the great would be able to unite to secure enforcement action against lesser transgressors, they need never fear that such action could be directed against one of them.

Each of these three hopes — for greater effectiveness by enforcement, by conciliation and arbitration, and through a better understanding of the realities of international life — proved unfounded. In fact, the Security Council was provided with no more effective instrument to secure international order than its predecessor had wielded. In 1946–47 the Military Staffs Committee (consisting of military staffs of the five permanent members) discussed the form which members' contribution should take. The Committee was able to agree on certain principles governing the working of the force. But there was no agreement on other fundamental points. The Soviet Union, and other members, thought the force should be a smallish one (though even the Soviet Union thought the Council should have twelve divisions, six hundred bombers, and corresponding other arms at its disposal); whereas the United States wanted larger forces (including twenty ground divisions, three battleships, and fifteen cruisers). The Soviet Union thought that all the permanent members should contribute forces equal both in overall strength and in composition; the other members thought that contributions might be varied to take account of what each member was best equipped to contribute (this might have meant, for example, that the United States could, if required, contribute a nuclear striking force). The Soviet Union believed that the contingents should not in peacetime be located outside the member states which provided them and that no foreign bases need be used; most of the other powers believed the force could be held anywhere in the world and that military bases might be made over for this purpose. The Soviet Union demanded that if the forces were used, they should be withdrawn to their own territories within ninety days of the termination of the operation, unless the Security Council determined otherwise; the other powers wanted no such restriction made.[2]

The effect of the disagreement was that the Security Council never disposed of the armed forces with which it was intended to undertake enforcement action under Articles 42–44 of the Charter. The police-

[2] For more detailed accounts of these negotiations, see I. Claude, *Power and International Relations* (New York, 1962), p. 175; W. R. Frye, *A United Nations Peace Force* (London, 1957).

man's truncheon never came into existence. As a result the Security
Council has never once made, or considered making, a "decision" in
favor of joint enforcement action such as all members were pledged to
obey.[3] Some maintain that the UN is in consequence not enabled to
make such a decision. Even in the most extreme cases, such as the
Korean war and the Suez and Hungary attacks, the Council sought only
to make "recommendations" having no binding force, whereas the Assembly was in any case never empowered to make anything but "recommendations."

Next, the belief that the situations with which the UN would be
faced would take the form of orderly "disputes," progressing through
a consistent series of preordained stages until they reached the culminating point of a "threat to the peace, breach of the peace or act of aggression" was equally unfulfilled. This too was based on the experience of
an earlier age. A number of the dangerous situations which had arisen
between the wars had followed such a course of gradual evolution. The
quarrels between the Balkan States, the Manchurian and Chinese "incidents," the Paraguay–Bolivia war, Italian demands on Ethiopia, the disputes over German rearmament, even the Czechoslovakian disputes,
developed at a fairly leisurely rate, beginning often with smoldering
altercation, followed by a series of demands, threats and counterthreats,
mobilizations and countermobilizations, culminating perhaps in an ultimatum and, as a final resort, in war.

In the postwar world, all were quicker on the draw. When dissension
arose, violence, greater or lesser, usually followed almost immediately. If
it did not, it was not normally considered worth discussion by the Security Council. As a result most of the questions which were considered
in the Security Council, under whatever Article they might be raised,
had in fact already reached the stage of a "threat to the peace." The
series of procedures envisaged in Article 33 — running from negotiation
to judicial settlement — was scarcely ever passed through. In the early
years a few resolutions were passed recommending that the parties involved settle their dissensions by bilateral means. But in later years there
was scarcely any attempt to persuade members to exhaust these procedures before discussion at the UN was initiated. The effectiveness of the
organization came to depend entirely on the effectiveness of public
debate in the political organs.

Finally, the conviction that the UN would prove more effective be-

---

[3] It did make "decisions" in 1948 on Palestine, and in 1965 on Rhodesia, but neither
was for joint enforcement action.

cause its constitution reflected international realities proved equally mistaken. The veto, designed to achieve this, for long made the Charter not more workable, but less. It came to be used not only over matters of vital national interest but over every type of issue which arose, however little it affected the security of the permanent member concerned. It therefore often frustrated action in any direction. What the drafters had not realized was that in the postwar world the political battlefield would have become worldwide. Almost every issue that arose would be of some concern to world powers. Most "disputes" therefore would be not between two or three individual nation states, but between ideologies and alliances of global membership.

In the interwar era, private "disputes" between two isolated powers had been common. Altercations between Italy and Greece over Corfu, between Poland and Lithuania over Vilna, between Hungary and Rumania over Transylvania, between China and Japan over Manchuria, between Peru and Colombia over Leticia, between Italy and Ethiopia over Walwal, and many others took place. For disputes of this type the armed concert of great powers which the Charter purported to establish might possibly have proved effective. But the system was not equipped to meet the worldwide ideological struggles of the postwar age. The two principal powers of the world were themselves antagonists in the chief of these. Each was equipped with a veto. Each was determined that no action of the new organization should result in any diminution of power and influence for its own faction. There was scarcely a single issue which did not in some way affect the mutual relations between the two principal blocs. And when, later, new blocs and groupings emerged, almost as important in their influence as the earlier ones, they too often proved equally inhibiting to effective joint action. There were few items on which one party did not attempt to frustrate the proposals of another. There was, therefore, scarcely a single problem on which the great powers could together make common cause to keep the peace.

There was another way in which the Charter reflected the realities of a previous generation. The new organization was based on the principle that certain powers were to enjoy a privileged and protected position. They gained not only the protection afforded by the veto but a position of enduring influence by virtue of their permanent membership in the Security Council. But the powers that acquired these privileges were the mighty, not of the postwar, but of the prewar age. They did so (as the permanent members of the League Council, Britain,

France, Italy, and Japan, had done) by virtue of being important members of the victorious alliance in the recent conflict, rather than of any objective assessment of numbers, wealth, or power. The effect of this was that, throughout the first twenty years of the UN's history, two powers of the second rank, less populous and scarcely more powerful than half a dozen other member states — Britain and France — were permanent members. In addition, for two-thirds of that time, by accident the government controlling a small island with a population of only a few million — Formosa — was another. Among the rank and file of the membership, on the other hand, each member state enjoyed exactly equal voting and other rights, regardless of glaring disparities in numbers, power, and contributions. Far from reflecting international realities, therefore, the structure and composition of the UN was remote from the actualities of the postwar international scene. And the unbalanced distribution of power and authority was the source of increasing frictions and discontents.

Thus though the UN was better equipped, it was better equipped to meet the problems of another age. Some modifications of the original system began to be devised to meet each of the three main obstacles which had presented themselves.[4]

The fact that no forces were made available to the Security Council under Article 43 was not at first regarded with any great dismay. For the difficulties inherent in creating, equipping, and controlling an international armed force were now more widely understood. The failure of the negotiations in the Military Staffs Committee did not prevent the establishment of a Truce Commission, a Truce Supervisory Organization, and a mixed Armistice Commission, including several hundred men, in Palestine. But the outbreak of the Korean war made more than ever apparent the difficulties and misunderstandings that could be created by the lack of any ready-organized UN force. In 1950 the Uniting for Peace resolution was passed, adapting the system in important ways. It was proposed that members should hold armed contingents permanently ready for use as a UN unit at the request of the General Assembly. A "Peace Observation Commission," to "observe and report situations anywhere in the world likely to endanger international peace," was set up. And new powers were given to the Assembly to offset the difficulties caused by the use of the veto in the Security Council.

[4] For a general account of the birth and development of the UN, see I. Claude, *Swords into Ploughshares* (New York, 1964); H. Nicholas, *The United Nations as a Political Institution* (London, 1959).

The replies of member states to the request for forces revealed the reluctance of many to make troops available for UN purposes. Only four members made affirmative answers to the request. Their offers amounted to 5,000 troops, mainly from Thailand. Every other reply was vague or evasive. In the majority of cases the main concern of members was to reserve the right to decide in what circumstances their troops should be used. And when, a decade later, a few states agreed unilaterally to make available standby forces for peace-keeping purposes, these too reserved the right themselves to determine in what circumstances they were to be used. The UN was thus unable to procure a truncheon either in the form originally proposed or in this modified form because no member was yet ready to act unhesitatingly as a truncheon, no matter what the occasion for its use — perhaps too, because few were anxious to expose themselves to the truncheon's buffetings.[5]

Second, the UN began to find accommodations to meet the fact that the situations it faced did not always fit neatly into the succession of categories presupposed in the Charter. This was done mostly by disregarding the terms of the Charter. States were asked increasingly rarely to exhaust bilateral procedures. Almost identical situations have been considered at different times under different Articles and different Chapters. Even when situations have certainly reached the stage of "threats to the peace," the Security Council has invoked Chapter VI, relating to peaceful settlement, more readily than Chapter VII, which provides for mandatory action and which, like its predecessor, Article 10 of the Covenant, has not been effectively used. And the commonest solution of all, now indeed the rule, has been for the Security Council to base its action on no Article of the Charter at all. On a number of occasions it explicitly decided to delete reference to a particular Article. In practice, therefore, the organization continued largely to ignore the successive procedures for settlement so carefully laid down in the Charter.

Finally, because the veto turned out to exert such a paralyzing influence on its effectiveness, the UN began to grope for means to counteract it. As early as at San Francisco, many of the smaller powers had expressed their misgivings at the power which the sponsoring states provided for themselves by this mechanism. Already then the powers of the Assembly were somewhat strengthened (though the permanent members continued to insist that no procedures, even for peaceful settlement, should be initiated if any of them opposed them). Later, new

[5] The development of UN peace-keeping capacity is considered further on pp. 250–259, below.

means were devised for lessening the power of the veto. While in theory the Assembly was prevented, under Article 12, from considering matters under discussion in the Council, it began to be argued that it might consider "different aspects" of the same question, so that a permanent member could not frustrate discussion there. A number of issues (Greece, Palestine, and Korea) were brought directly to the Assembly. In 1947 an "Interim Committee" of the Assembly was created to consider urgent matters between its normal sessions. The convention grew up that abstentions in the Security Council did not constitute vetoes.[6] Finally, in 1950, the Uniting for Peace resolution established a new procedure by which any urgent matter affecting peace and security, on which the Council was unable to reach agreement, could be brought by two-thirds majority to an emergency session of the Assembly, which could consider appropriate collective action.

There can be little doubt that this procedure was, as the Soviet Government alleged, an illegal one. It violated two of the fundamental principles on which the Charter was based: that action to keep the peace was the responsibility of the Security Council (and so liable to veto); and that no fundamental amendment of this, or any other provision of the Charter, could be made except by the procedure outlined for that purpose in Chapter XVIII (also involving the consent of permanent members). But to admit that the procedure was illegal is not to accept that it was undesirable. Many of the most important actions of the UN (including those concerning Suez, Hungary, and the Congo) were only made possible by invoking the resolution. The Soviet Union herself has, on at least one occasion, consented to its use. Without it the UN might be incapable of discussing effectively precisely those crises which are most dangerous and difficult.

As a result of these developments the Assembly for a time took on some of the functions originally reserved to the Security Council. Many matters have been considered impartially by both. Although during the late forties the Security Council met something like 130 times a year, by the late fifties it met only 40 or 50 times; by the sixties, sometimes only about 30 times. And though the Assembly in theory was to meet only for two or three months in the autumn, its discussions increasingly often had to be extended by means of special sessions later in the year. The Assembly's growing membership, more than doubling, raised its

6 This was later supplemented by the tradition of obtaining a "consensus," formulated by the Chairman of the Council's discussions so obviating a vote and a possible veto.

importance. And between its sessions increasing authority was delegated to the Secretary General. Although the Assembly was unable to make the mandatory decisions which the Security Council was designed to make — but almost never has — in practice the Assembly's "recommendations," such as the call to China to desist from aggression in Korea, and the appeal to Britain and France at the time of Suez, came to be one of the UN's most important weapons, with a force it was politically very expensive to resist. One effect of this was that the permanent members become less and less, as the Charter had originally provided, above the law. Instead of an organization run by the mighty to insure law and order among the *hoi polloi*, it became, to some extent, an organization run by the *hoi polloi* to keep in order the mighty themselves.

In the early sixties, there was some attempt to restore authority to the Security Council. Its membership was increased from eleven to fifteen. Peace forces in the Congo and Cyprus were established now by the Council. Other permanent members, as well as the Soviet Union, sought to restore the Council's authority. But the new relationship could not be altogether reversed.

Thus the UN system became increasingly unlike what its founders conceived. The basis of authority became *institutionalized discussion*. Because it possessed no armed force to secure the peace as originally intended, the UN had to rely mainly on the power of resolutions and appeals rather than enforcement action. Because the situations it found itself confronted with were infinitely various and individual, it found it more expedient to deal with each on an ad hoc basis and without reference to the Charter, rather than by following a strict order of prescribed procedures. Because the top people of the world were unable to reach agreement among themselves, the small fry were obliged to undertake a far greater responsibility in finding the means of meeting critical situations than had ever been intended. Although in its early years the UN was above all a forum for wrangling among the two great ideological camps, as time progressed it became more and more a theater in which the uncommitted could call a plague on both their houses; where words once again had to substitute for deeds; where resolutions became more and more frequent, though not necessarily more frequently obeyed. The danger of this development was that on many issues the great powers came to act and negotiate quite independently of the UN. It had not yet learned the secret of authority without power.

Development of the United Nations System

Though there was little growth in effective international authority, as time went on the UN progressively increased its responsibilities. The scope of the organization's activities was always considerably wider than that of its predecessor. It had, for example, directly or indirectly, undertaken a number of functional activities in fields in which the League had never engaged. International organizations with responsibilities in new spheres were set up. Health, food, education, finance, banking, technical assistance, regional economic surveying, statistics — all these and others, previously the responsibility mainly of national agencies, now became the concern of international authorities. These bodies, and existing organizations in the fields of labor relations, drug traffic, civil aviation, and other matters, were brought into relationship with the new body through special agreements. The responsibilities of the League for mandated territories were extended by the Trusteeship Council of the UN. Members accepted new, and more sweeping, obligations in the field of human rights. And in the undertaking to obey unconditionally all "decisions" of the Security Council, members accepted a restriction of sovereignty more categorical than any that had been asked for by earlier organizations.

The authority of the UN, nevertheless, was limited in a number of ways. The chief of these was the restriction on its competence in matters affecting national sovereignty. The provision in Article 2(7) that "nothing contained in the present Charter shall authorize the United Nations to intervene in matters which are essentially within the domestic jurisdiction of any state" could be quoted, as we have seen, in many disputes by members wishing to resist international intervention. Members accepted at first the limited nature of the UN powers, especially in matters not affecting peace and security. They sought to conciliate antagonists rather than impose solutions. Resolutions on Indonesia, Kashmir, and South Africa's racial policies sought merely to bring about an amicable settlement between the parties.

But as time progressed, the organization became more and more confident in asserting its powers. A majority of the Security Council was ready to assert authority and recommend solutions — on the nationalization of oil in Iran, the administration of the Suez Canal in Egypt, free elections in Germany, and human rights in East Europe — all matters which had little to do with peace and security. More important, the functional bodies gradually extended their scope. In particular the development of various assistance programs began to give the UN potentialities in the economic field which neither its predecessor nor itself had previously possessed. *Executive functions* now supplemented multilateral discussion as the basis of authority.

Economic responsibilities were perpetually extended during the organization's history. Pressures for their development was one of the effects of the influx of newly independent states. The World Bank, which began on a modest scale principally in Europe, gradually extended its activities, especially after 1960, when it improved its terms for developing countries. The program of technical assistance of the UN proper was extended in 1949 in the Expanded Program of Technical Assistance, to which member states made annual pledges of gradually increasing size. Soon there began to be pressures from the less developed countries for a Special United Nations Fund for Economic Development. Though the wealthier nations rejected this, those pressures did lead to the establishment of the Special Fund, designed primarily to undertake preinvestment studies and assistance in developing countries. This was followed by the International Development Association, designed to give loans on especially favorable terms to developing countries to overcome the difficulties of repayment from which many were suffering. Later the Special Fund and the technical assistance program were merged in a single United Nations Development Program. The activities of the specialized agencies expanded over the years, and their total budgets doubled or trebled during their first twenty years of existence. Finally, the Trade and Development Conference, after a first session in Geneva in 1964, was established on a permanent basis with meetings every three years and a Trade and Development Board to undertake activities between meetings. Though these economic activities are not strictly the concern of this study, their development, the increase in the numbers working for international organizations, and the growth of budgets all contributed to an increasing consciousness all over the world, and especially in developing countries, of the benefits international organizations could procure.

A second development was the steady increase in the number of countries which were members of the UN. Total membership increased from 51 in 1946 to 121 in 1967, so that well over half were new members by the end of that period. More than two-thirds were developing countries from Asia, Africa, and Latin America. Such members were perhaps more acutely aware of the benefits an effective international authority could provide, both in assisting the poor and weak, and in restraining the overbearing and mighty. They were able to use their influence and voting strength in the Assembly to demand strong action on decolonization and the racial problems of Southern Africa (though they never voted as consistently as a bloc as has sometimes been suggested). Here too, the powers demanded by the organization became wider.

A third factor affecting the development of international authority during this period was the evolving role of the Secretary General and his staff. The first Secretary General, Mr. Trygve Lie, had been no less ready to make suggestions and express views than his better-known successor, Mr. Hammarskjöld. Mr. Lie's suggestions — for example, for the establishment of a UN guard, or for the recognition and admission of Communist China — were, however, not always well judged and were often not adopted. Moreover, his clearly defined position in favor of UN action in Korea and other matters finally forfeited him the support of the communist states and made his position almost untenable. The difference in his successor was not only his much greater caution on delicate political issues, but the greater awareness everywhere of the role which a Secretary General might play as an impartial umpire in sorting out difficult situations. In the cases of the United States airmen imprisoned in China, the Offshore Islands, Suez, the crisis in Lebanon and Jordan, and Laos, he revealed the valuable part quiet diplomacy could play. Finally, in the Congo operation he, like his predecessor, played a more active and committed role than the communist countries were prepared to accept, so that even before his death his position was becoming increasingly precarious. As a result, his successor, U Thant, adopted a considerably less active role and withdrew into something much more like the traditional anonymity of a permanent official. This may in part have been due to the difficult financial crisis in which the organization was involved during a large part of his tenure of office. Nevertheless, the Secretariat as a whole, like their opposite numbers in other organizations, have continued to demonstrate the part which "international men" can play, within the context of modern international relations, in strengthening, however marginally, the power of international authority.

Finally, during this period, there was an increasing development of regional organizations to provide a supplementary form of international authority at the periphery. The importance of these was twofold. On the one hand, there were certain functions, economic cooperation, development of communications, the protection of human rights and others, that are best organized at a regional level. On the other, for some purposes, including matters of peace and security if some degree of intervention is necessary, the influence wielded by immediate neighbors may be more acceptable to nations than a more distant authority. Some bodies of this kind had existed for years. The Concert of Europe, concerned primarily with European affairs, might be regarded as the first. The Organization of American States in its original form dates back to the 1880's. In its modern form it was established at Bogotá in 1948, in fulfillment of the Treaty of Rio, providing for mutual assistance and pacific settlement, signed in the previous year. The main organs are the Conference meeting every five years; the Council of Ambassadors, meeting as an executive committee; the Secretariat; and, in practice the most important, the Council of Foreign Ministers, which is called when required to deal with crisis situations. There are also occasional specialized conferences dealing with technical and other matters. The Arab League was founded in 1945, with a League Council in which each state is represented, meeting when required, a Secretary General, and a Secretariat in Cairo. It has established some effective organs in the economic field and set up a peace-keeping force in Kuwait in 1961. But its influence has been weakened because of sharp political differences among its members, which have been allowed to influence its proceedings. The Council of Europe, established in 1950, has avoided this difficulty by restricting entry to "democratic" states, and concentrating largely on technical committees and periodic assemblies of parliamentarians. On the other hand, the exclusion of many European states has inevitably reduced its scope of activity, and the main achievements are the establishment of the Commission and Court of Human Rights. Finally, the Organization of African Unity was founded in 1963 and includes virtually all African states except those that are white-governed. It has proved useful in solving, or at least appeasing, certain local disputes between members, but effective action here too has been limited by political differences. Perhaps the most successful regional organizations have been economic: the UN Economic Commissions, established for each continent except Australasia, mainly undertaking surveying and statistical work; and a number of common markets and free trade areas, notably in Europe.

But the most important development of authority during this period was the increasing reluctance of the UN to be deterred from action by pleas of violations of national sovereignty. Even in the early days, rationalizations could be found to justify the overriding of sovereignty if political passions were sufficiently engaged. In January 1946, a subcommittee appointed by the Security Council reported that the internal activities of the Spanish Government constituted a "potential" threat to international peace. In December of that year a resolution was passed by the Assembly suggesting that the Security Council should consider adequate measures to remedy the Spanish situation if a democratic Spanish government were not established within a reasonable time. Many members had doubts about such attempts. Even on colonial questions some hesitation was displayed. Attempts to pass resolutions on the colonial policies of France in Morocco and Tunisia, and of Britain in Cyprus, or on the dispute between Indonesia and the Netherlands over West Irian, and other matters at first failed to secure the necessary two-thirds majorities. But as time went on such incursions became more frequent and more habitual. Though in the early years the UN had only discussed the policies of the South African Government toward people of Indian and Pakistani ancestry as a "dispute" affecting the three nations, from 1952 it began to consider the racial policy of that government toward its own nationals in general terms. Colonial issues were more and more frequently introduced. In 1961 internal disorders in Angola were discussed in the Security Council by unanimous consent. In the same year the Security Council adopted a recommendation urging that the UN should "take immediately all appropriate measures . . . including the use of force, if necessary, in the last resort" to "prevent the occurrence of civil war in the Congo," regardless of its government's will. And on Rhodesia in 1965, the UN authorized the boarding of a tanker by British warships to enforce the oil embargo.

Discussion of the "legality" of this extension of authority is no longer relevant. It can be persuasively maintained that the current practice of the UN violates the text of Article 2(7).[7] If this was not designed to prevent the passing of recommendations, it was only a tautology, for there is nothing in the Charter (outside Chapter VII, which is anyway excluded by the Article) that could give rise to any other form of "intervention" in domestic affairs. But once the decision was made, on whatever pretext, to widen the area of authority, such arguments become unrewarding. The real effect of a recommendation cannot be unmade by quoting the letter of the Charter. Even the use of the veto, though it may prevent the passage of a resolution, will not diminish its

[7] See Chapter Five, pp. 128–129.

force. For this depends not on its legality, but on the strength of world opinion it can mobilize. In each individual situation a majority will usually be in favor of invoking international authority: while in 1956, Britain and the Soviet Union both denounced the attempts of the UN to intervene in matters in which they were interested parties, both insisted on the right of the UN to take action against the other.

But though the general trend was toward an extension of authority, there was no consistency about this. Governments might be ready to assert the UN's authority over other governments, even despite the precedents so created. They were less enthusiastic when its actions were directed toward their own state. The Indian Government, which was among the most insistent in asserting the competence of the UN to discuss many colonial problems and the internal policies of the South African Government, resolutely denied its jurisdiction over Hyderabad and Kashmir. Britain for long rejected UN competence in all colonial questions, yet voted for consideration of the coup d'état in Czechoslovakia, of the conditions for free elections in Germany, human rights in Hungary, and other matters. The Soviet Union has energetically championed the right of the UN to consider many colonial problems or the "aggressive acts of the United States" in relation to Formosa; but has stubbornly denied its competence over the blockade of Berlin, the Korean war, which she declared a "civil conflict," or the intervention of Soviet troops against the effective government in Hungary. New states often denied UN jurisdiction over their own affairs; yet passionately demanded international action on South Africa.

As a result, there was no more consistency in the decisions of the UN as a whole on such matters than there was in the voting of each individual delegation. Certain kinds of problems were discussed in some cases but not in others. Coups d'état, colonial affairs, racial policies, civil wars — all these matters have been raised when political circumstances favored it but not in other cases. More important, the action decided on has been varied. No objective principles have been found. This inconsistency has fatally weakened the UN's potential influence. For authority, to be effective, must be predictable.

The difficulties involved in strengthening international authority are apparent. The process can only take place as a result of the combined decisions of governments. Today many governments still have reason, on various grounds, to resist the encroachment of international bodies. Great powers resent the nagging self-righteousness of the small. Communist states fear that, so long as they are outnumbered, any significant extension of international authority may endanger their position. Colonial powers seek to retain their freedom of action unimpaired. Ex-colonial peoples sometimes see the exercise of UN authority as an attempt to reimpose colonialism in a new form. In the final resort these resistances can nearly always be successfully maintained. The UN is rarely in a position to impose its decisions by force. When vital security or other interests seem at stake, the nation state can still resist international intervention — as China did in 1950; as the Soviet Union was ready to do in 1956; as South Africa has so far been able to do. If international authority is to be strengthened effectively, the processes by which it is exercised need careful examination.

United Nations Armed Power

The most obvious method of remedying this situation would be to provide the UN with such a measure of armed force as would enable it to enforce compliance, irrespective of a state's willingness to cooperate. The authority of multilateral discussion and executive functions would be joined by that of coercive power.

For hundreds of years there have been plans for the type of international force which might be capable of imposing its authority on erring or unruly national states. The force envisaged under Articles 42-44 of the Charter was of such a nature (though it could not have been used against the will of the permanent members). A number of disarmament proposals have included provisions for a world enforcement authority with a measure of armed power. A number of writers have sketched plans, more or less elaborate, for a world in which international authority was imposed by such an agency. And the emergence of a number of peace forces in recent years has also encouraged the hope that this may be the simplest road to an effective international authority.

Even the League established two peace forces. One, composed of Colombian soldiers wearing League armbands, was used to administer an area in dispute between Colombia and Peru for a year under a League Commission; and another, composed of the forces of four states and financed by the League, was established to administer the plebiscite in the Saar in 1935 under the authority of the League. After World War II, when the negotiations for a Security Council force had broken down, Mr. Trygve Lie proposed in 1948 the establishment of a "small UN guard force" of 1,000–5,000 men, which might be used "in the conduct

of plebiscites" or "the administration of truce terms, or as a constabu-
lary under the Security Council or Trusteeship Council in cities like
Jerusalem or Trieste" — in other words for very much the same purposes peace forces were later used. Like the proposal made later under
the Uniting for Peace resolution, this concept of a permanent force

TABLE IX · 3

UN Peace Forces: Observers and Presences, 1946–1966

Date	Place	Unit	Authorized by
1946–54	Greek border	Commission of investigation (1946) followed by observers under UNSCOB and Peace Observation Commission	Security Council General Assembly
1948	Palestine	Mediator (1949) and UN Truce Supervision Organization	Security Council
1948	Kashmir	Observers under UN Commission (1948–50) and UN Representative (1950–)	Security Council
1948–49	Indonesia	UN Good Offices Committee, Commission and Observers	Security Council
1950	Korea	Forces contributed by 16 member states placed under UN command	Security Council
1956	Sinai	UN Emergency Force (UNEF)	General Assembly
1958	Lebanon	UN Observer Group in Lebanon (UNOGIL)	Security Council
1958	Jordan	Secretary General's Special Representative established	Secretary General
1959	Laos	Secretary General's Special Representative established	Secretary General
1960–65	Congo	UN Force in the Congo (UNOC)	General Assembly
1962–63	West Irian	UN Temporary Executive Authority and Security Force	Secretary General
1963–65	Yemen	UN Observer Group in the Yemen (UNYOM)	Security Council
1964	Cyprus	UN Force in Cyprus (UNFICYP)	Security Council

aroused considerable opposition and had to be dropped. A large UN
force was established and fought in Korea, but this was rather an alliance
of like-minded states fighting under the banner of the UN than a UN

force in the proper sense. Teams of observers were established in Greece (1946), Indonesia (1947), Kashmir (1948), Palestine (1948), and later in Lebanon (1958), and Yemen (1963). UN presences, single representatives of the Secretary General to observe, report, and conciliate, were established in Jordan in 1958 and in Laos in 1959. The first true UN force was the UN Emergency Force established after the Suez operation in 1956 (with troops from ten countries), which patrolled the border between Israel and Egypt till May, 1967. A second force was sent to the Congo in 1960, in the first place to secure the evacuation of Belgian troops but increasingly to maintain law and order and preserve unitary government within the country, and was for this reason involved in a considerable amount of fighting. A third force was sent to administer West Irian during the period between its evacuation by the Dutch and the assumption of authority by Indonesia (pending a theoretical ultimate self-determination). Finally, a fourth force was established in 1964 to take over from the British the task of restoring law and order after communal disturbances between Greeks and Cypriots in Cyprus.[8] These operations led to a severe financial and constitutional crisis within the UN. Most members assumed when the first forces were established that they would be paid for by the organization as a whole through contributions assessed in the normal way. The Soviet Union, France, and other countries, however, made clear their objections to paying for them in this way. The International Court of Justice, in an advisory opinion, ruled that such operations were for the normal purposes of the organization and that their costs could therefore be assessed in the normal way, although outside the regular budget. This ruling, which could not bind the organization, was endorsed by the Assembly by a considerable majority. For a time some powers threatened to apply Article 19, under which members in arrears with their contributions, including the peacekeeping costs under this interpretation, might have been deprived of their right to vote in the Assembly. One session was entirely missed in consequence, and finally the threat was dropped. A few nations made voluntary contributions to bridge the gap, but neither the financial crisis, nor the constitutional dilemma which created it, was resolved. And though the amount of money involved was comparatively small, the UN as a whole remained in deficit for a number of years in conse-

---

[8] For a full survey of League and UN peace forces until 1965, see D. W. Bowett, *UN Peace Forces* (London, 1964). For a shorter account, see Evan Luard, "UN Peace Forces" in Evan Luard (ed.), *The Evolution of International Organizations* (New York, 1966).

quence. It was thus inhibited from establishing any new force except on the basis that it should be paid for by the parties involved or by voluntary contributions. The West Irian and Cyprus forces had to be financed in this way, and the latter had to be renewed every few months by Security Council decision. On the other hand, a number of nations (the Scandinavian countries, Canada, the Netherlands, New Zealand, and others) unilaterally earmarked forces for use in UN operations if necessary. Others (Britain) made available logistic support. And there continued to be hopes that the development of UN armed power might be the means of establishing a more peaceful world over the years to come.

In practice, however, it has proved possible to mobilize UN forces, of limited dimensions and capabilities, only as voluntary contributions to meet particular situations on an ad hoc basis. This could normally only be achieved when the force was expected to do little actual fighting. The force could never be an effective instrument for "enforcement" purposes under Chapter VII of the Charter. It could usually be used only with the consent of the host country. It could be used only in ways that contributing nations approved, so that when its functions were extended, some might demand to withdraw their units (as certain African nations withdrew troops from the Congo) or demand special conditions and assurances (as happened over Cyprus). Sometimes the forces of particular nations might be refused (as Egypt refused to accept units from certain states in 1956). Such forces have represented something new and important in the international environment. But they can never be the powerful instrument of international authority which the UN's founders had envisaged.

Here, as in the field of disarmament, it is tempting to believe that the desired object, apparently in the interests of all, must be easily attainable. All would like to live in a world of law and order. And it is attractive to suppose that this could easily be achieved by the creation of an international force of sufficient power to keep the peace. But it is necessary to examine the difficulties to be faced in creating such a force.

The crucial point concerns how an international force is to be controlled. Most people today accept that, to create a more orderly world, the nation state must be ready to accept a diminution of its sovereignty. But the creation of an enforcement agency possessing military power superior to that of individual states would represent not the diminution of sovereignty, but its abandonment. The problem of the policeman arises here in its most elemental form. So long as some powers, or groups of powers, continue to harbor fears that the authority proposed might fall under the control of hostile groups, or a combination of such groups, and so be used in ways which could seriously endanger their interests, its establishment is always likely to be resisted. And so long as it is resisted in areas where effective power now lies, its creation will remain impossible.

It was just such resistances that were revealed in earlier negotiations. Many today might be prepared to accept the position held by the Soviet Union during 1946–47. This reflected the apprehensions that will always be felt by nations in a minority, fearing the use to which the force might be put. To meet those apprehensions, most today would be prepared to settle for a force of limited power, with contributions of equal strength from the great powers, with no permanent foreign bases, and with only limited powers of occupation after the conclusion of any enforcement action taken. But even if all these provisions were now accepted, it is unlikely that agreement would be reached on the establishment of a force with a power sufficient to overcome national forces. For the most basic of the problems, that of the control of the force, would remain.

Fears on this score could be reduced by a veto. Even in 1946–47, it was accepted that the force to be created would only be used within the terms of Chapter VII of the Charter, and that it would therefore be subject to the veto power of permanent members. Since that time, the establishment of the Uniting for Peace procedure and the creation of peace forces by the Assembly have destroyed this premise. No member could now be assured that any permanent force created would not, at some time in the future, be used against its own territory. The fundamental assumption of the founders of the UN, the immunity of the permanent members, has thus been challenged. The change has no doubt been, in most ways, an advance. It enabled the UN Assembly to take emergency action in Egypt against the wish of two of the permanent members and to establish the first peace-keeping force there. It made possible discussion of Hungary and Lebanon. It allowed the UN to continue its activities in the Congo when total deadlock had been reached in the Security Council. But its effect is that some major powers will be still more disinclined to establish forces that might come under the control of nations, or combinations of nations, inimical to their interests.

Demands that only the Security Council should authorize and control peace forces and proposals for a tripartite division of authority within the UN Secretariat are manifestations of this concern. But if accepted, the veto would fatally weaken any force. At any moment one power or another might halt its operations. The problem of "how many fingers on the trigger" is thus as stubborn in the case of effective UN action as it is in the case of defense alliances. Any system of control, to be acceptable, would have to assure various elements, whether individual powers or groups of powers, that enforcement action would never be taken without their consent. But any system which achieves this may merely ensure that, in the most perilous situations that could confront the world, where the essential interests of all groups are endangered, the international force is powerless. The UN is faced here with an insuperable dilemma. Either the forces it creates are so strong that important powers or groups will demand to exert a veto over their use or they must remain so weak that they can never effectively challenge those powers or groups.

Even if no veto were demanded, doubt might remain whether effective action in defense of members attacked, or threatened, could be mobilized. And so long as this remains the case, nations will demand the right themselves to retain the level of armed force necessary for their own defense. Analogies commonly made between the development of international authority and the development of a central authority within the state are misleading. Power within the state has normally been acquired by armed conquest by a single authority claiming unquestioned submission. Only if an individual nation were to achieve such undisputed domination over all others could a similar process come about within the community of nations. So long as this remains unattainable, or unacceptable, so long as the control of physical power within the world, therefore, remains diffused, an effective central authority can only be built up by the voluntary submissions of those who now exert it. This process may be encouraged by suitable means (as will be later argued). But it is one quite other, much slower, and more arduous than the forcible assertion of power by a single center of authority within the state.

Nor is the development of world hegemony by two, or several, of the most powerful nations over the rest, as is sometimes suggested, any more likely to prove an effective means of establishing supranational authority. This would raise even greater difficulties than the five-power hegemony established in the Security Council system. First, it presupposes an identity of view among the powers concerned over the various disputes that may arise all over the world. Such a consistent harmony of views is most unlikely. Every dispute in the modern age, even in remote parts of the world, may be of interest, direct or indirect, political or strategic, to the dominant powers. And the greater the concentration of power among two or three separate states, the more likely their interests are to diverge in these disputes. A common interest in security will not always be sufficient to induce an agreed viewpoint on every issue in every corner of the world. Though on some matters they may unite in the face of new challengers to their own power (like Britain and Russia against Germany sixty years ago, or the United States and Russia against China now), on other matters they may remain rivals rather than partners (as on the Middle East or Vietnam today).

More important, such a diarchy is not likely to remain long acceptable to other members of the world community. Even if no one among these emerges to challenge the ruling powers, together they will become increasingly resentful at the pretensions of the leaders. They may join in alliances, or continental groups, to withstand the rulers. We have seen how often this occurred in previous systems. It is, for example, scarcely conceivable that today the developing nations of Africa, Asia, and Latin America, let alone China, would long tolerate a situation in which their affairs and disputes were settled at the whim of the two great powers of the Euratlantic world. Within the international community, as much as within the national, order must, if it is to be stable and enduring, rest ultimately on consent rather than coercion.

The difficulty of securing the central control of armed force is the result of real human apprehensions that receive expression in demands of sovereignty and the claim to national forces. Only as fears about the motives of other states come to diminish, may national resistances become less insistent. To seek, without such a change, to impose a central power might be only to change the name of national wars to civil wars without affecting their real nature. The belief that the desire for mutual security may be the spur to nation states to renounce sovereignty is an illusion which ignores the psychology of nations in the modern world — a psychology conditioned by five thousand years of violent and unscrupulous intercourse. It is when the fear of other states becomes less, not more, compelling that the representatives of nation states may feel the confidence to allow the creation of international force more powerful than that they themselves control; and by then it may not be necessary. As with disarmament, the goal becomes attainable only when it is no longer required.

Within the near future, therefore, it is unlikely that the UN will have at its disposal force comparable to that at the disposal of nations. There may be a further development of lesser forces.[9] Though these cannot be used to challenge sovereignty, they may be used for certain other purposes: to patrol a threatened frontier (as the UN Emergency Force in Sinai has done); for policing a disputed territory or organizing a referendum (like the force in West Irian); for restoring law and order in areas where this had for some reason broken down (as was attempted in the Congo); to allay intercommunal friction (like the force in Cyprus). Sometimes unarmed observers may perform useful functions (as in Kashmir and Lebanon); and for these purposes the Peace Observation Commission, set up under the Uniting for Peace resolution, could be called on more often.

The emergency forces so far called into action by the UN have had to be mobilized, at very short notice, from among the national forces of member states. Forces could be far more quickly and efficiently mobilized if held ready for that purpose. The problems of logistics, lines of command, language, and coordination would have been tackled in advance. This, perhaps, is the next logical development of UN authority. Member states might be required, as a few have done (and as the Uniting for Peace resolution demanded), to earmark special contingents which could be made available at a moment's notice. The training and organization of these could be closely coordinated. Those responsible for organizing such operations would then know immediately what forces or equipment were available, of a suitable nationality, in geographically convenient locations, when they were required. And armed forces would come increasingly to be thought of as being international as much as national in purpose.

If such a system were to be introduced, there would be need for explicit understandings about the principles to be followed by the forces established. Some members would demand that their forces would be used only with their consent, that is, only on *occasions* which they approved. Others might require agreement on the *type* of use to which they would be put. So far, differing principles and procedures have been adopted. When the UN Emergency Force in Sinai was established, it was declared as a basic principle that the force could operate only with the consent of those nations on whose territory it functioned. In the Congo, though the force originally entered that country with the con-

---

[9] For studies of UN forces, see D. W. Bowett, *United Nations Forces* (London, 1964); G. Rosner, *The United Nations Emergency Force* (New York, 1963); W. R. Frye, *op. cit.*; A. L. Burns and N. Heathcote, *United Nations Forces from Sinai to the Congo* (Princeton, 1963).

sent of its government, it was maintained there afterward for some time against the wish of most of the different factions holding authority there, including that of the president whose legal status had been acknowledged by the UN. In Cyprus, equally, there were differences concerning how far the force set up was to act only in support of the recognized government and how far to keep the peace between that government and those opposing it.

Some of the principles laid down in theory, as that the UN would not "take the initiative," or would not "alter the political balance," have in practice proved almost impossible to fulfill. Ad hoc interpretations have been required. This may preserve flexibility, but it is *general* principles concerning the conduct and range of activity of such forces that are required if hostility to the idea is to be reduced. The according of superior force to international authority will not be conceded until individual nations have confidence that that power will not be abused. Law-abiding citizens within the state are ready sometimes to concede coercive force to the forces of law and order because they feel assured that these will not exert their power in a way so arbitrary as to endanger their essential interests. Only as a similar confidence begins to be established about the activities of international policemen will nations, too, cease to insist on the right of superior strength. They could be assured that peace forces would be deployed only in accordance with the principles laid down, and under the direction of an appropriately balanced UN body. "Peace-keeping" might be more clearly defined and distinguished from "enforcement." The immunity of the permanent members might be reaffirmed. And representation in the controlling body might be reserved to those members which took part in the financing of the operation (this would provide a powerful incentive for financial support).

In time the activities of these forces might exert increasing influence. The ratio of international forces to national within the international community could gradually increase. Nations might become ready to commit most, or even all, their forces for international purposes if it were provided that they could withdraw some or all of their contingents when they felt it necessary. The very existence of such forces would discourage the hope of achieving a settlement of scores in private and raise the credibility of some collective action: it is this credibility that, in the past, collective security systems have always found it most difficult to provide. If wisely used, the forces might come to enjoy a moral authority which would make their operations difficult to resist. To perform some useful functions, an international police force is no more obliged to wield a power superior to that of the nation state than, to be an effective law enforcing agency, a police constable in Britain needs to carry a revolver. In both cases they attain their ends mainly through the respect which they enjoy throughout the community at large.

International armed forces will remain, therefore, within the foreseeable future of only limited physical strength. But through the wise *use* of the limited power they possess they may acquire an authority out of all proportion to their numbers.

Authority Without Power

The fact that within the foreseeable future international authority is unlikely to dispose of overwhelming power does not mean that it cannot increase its influence by other means.[10]

There are many types of authority which command obedience even though they do not dispose of forcible sanctions to require it. The father of a family may win the obedience of all its members though he never raises his hand against any. Teachers may win unfailing submission though they never wield a cane and are powerless before the combined forces of their pupils. Political authorities too may win obedience without superiority of power. The elders of a tribe, an African chief, a divine monarch, the early kings of Europe, the conventional authority accorded in the British Heptarchy and the Warring States of China to a particular state as preeminent, the authority of the Federal Government of the United States and Switzerland in early days, these are all examples of authority exerted without power. To say that authorities win obedience because they enjoy respect is only tautological. What we wish to know is why they enjoy respect.

One reason why they may enjoy respect is because of *conditioning*. The force of teaching and example, and perhaps innate drives toward imitation and conformity, may be sufficient to ensure that we *wish* to respond to the authorities to which we are subjected. The son who obeys his father obeys not so much his father as the society which instructs him to obey a father.

In the international field the conditioning of national attitudes takes place through two processes. First, there is the education of individ-

[10] For a comparison of the nature of authority in the national and international fields, see Appendix III, pp. 329–331.

uals. If this is such as may inculcate respect for international authorities, it is likely that the individuals concerned may subsequently, in positions of command within nations, feel a continuing respect for, and desire to obey, international authority. Conversely, individuals taught in youth to idealize national independence and to despise international organizations are unlikely to show respect for this authority at a later stage. Thus the manner of education *within* individual states may be important in influencing the character of the international community as a whole.

But an equally important source of conditioning is that which takes place within the international environment itself. The example of other states; the respect for international authority expressed within international organizations, and in national behavior generally; the influence of press, public opinion, and political comment, abroad as well as at home, may all affect the degree to which states feel disposed to conform. All contribute to the background against which decisions are reached. Each time a state responds to a call of international authority will increase the tendency of other states to do so; each example of defiance may encourage others in defiance. These create the *reinforcements* that influence responses on subsequent occasions.[11] Finally, as among individuals, *habituation* to particular behavior patterns, once the required responses have begun to be inculcated, may further encourage conformity.

International bodies may themselves undertake activity designed to affect conditioning and so transform the structure of loyalties. Steps may be taken to improve information about the world organization. Governments or organizations may encourage the flow of books, films, and other material or promote visits to the organization's headquarters or other agencies, comparable to action undertaken by individual governments for public relations purposes. They may encourage publicity directed at newspaper editors, Members of Parliament, and other opinion leaders. Above all they may encourage appropriate education of schoolchildren and members of the ordinary public. Apparently trivial matters of ceremonial and display can be influential. International authority would be strengthened by the flying of the UN flag in all member states on UN day, so recalling to the man in the street the universal membership of the world organization. Ceremonial surrounding the UN's important occasions or functionaries, comparable to that which

---

[11] See Chapter Two, p. 44, above.

surrounds state functions and dignitaries, may elevate its importance in the public mind. Television coverage and films of UN meetings, shown on screens all over the world, could do much to promote the sense of a common central authority. Through such small initiatives, eventually, the structure of loyalties is slowly modified. Authority becomes legitimized, so that its influence is increasingly unrelated to power. The conception of a joint interest in a common order, comparable to that in the "European system" in the nineteenth century, comes to displace that of individual national interests.

Respect for authority may develop from another source. A body of elders or a parliament of delegates may be obeyed because they speak on behalf of a wider public. Authority without power may be respected because it is felt to be *representative*. It will then come to appear self-imposed, voluntarily accepted rather than externally enforced. The demands it makes are internalized so that submission seems by consent rather than by coercion.

International authority, too, is more likely to win submission without power if it is seen to be representative. This would mean, first, that it must be fully comprehensive in its membership (as today it is not). It would mean also that its principal executive authority, the Security Council, should be more representative than today of the main political forces of the modern world. Permanent membership would then be related to existing population and importance rather than to historical accident. Probably only four nations are today of a size worthy of this status: China, India, the Soviet Union, and the United States. But the UN is unlikely to seem representative in any true sense as long as the inhabitants of Nicaragua receive a representation about four hundred times greater than the people of India, or as long as the two hundred million people of the United States possess one vote while the two hundred million people of the rest of the continent possess twenty. As the Soviet Union has three effective votes, so might all powers with more than 100 million population; whereas those of 30 to 100 million might have two. The rule of the "sovereign equality" of nation states was a convenient diplomatic courtesy in an age when all knew that polite fiction was belied by brute power. But in an age when it is hoped that ballots may come to replace bullets as a means of settling the world's problems, it has become more important that the distribution of votes correspond to the realities of numbers rather than the accidents of frontiers. Certainly unless it does, UN resolutions may seem of less importance to UN members and be more readily defied.

Besides conditioning to increase respect, and representative bodies to increase consent, international authority has a third, more important instrument to increase its influence among individual states.

Within societies, as we saw earlier, rules are often the ultimate rulers. Such rules preexisted a *coercive* authority in most communities. Central authorities themselves are usually conditioned by the laws and customs already widely acknowledged. They may be able to enforce their power only insofar as they respect these. The king's judges and sheriffs in medieval England were able to exert authority without power because the authority of the customary rules they applied was acknowledged even where the authority of the king himself was resisted. Conversely, where rules are totally unacceptable to general opinion, no authority on earth may be able to enforce them. The fact that a superiority of armed force is not available to international authority need not therefore make it powerless.

It is true that the rules imposed among individuals, whether children or adults, may, if all other forms of socialization fail, be imposed by force as the ultimate resort. Yet it remains to be proved, in either case, that force is the essential condition of winning obedience. A great deal of evidence suggests, on the contrary, that where, for one reason or another, the normal methods of socialization have failed, correction through coercion may be less effective than ever. The record of parental upbringing by force alone, or of penal systems that attempt coercive methods, certainly provides no evidence of their efficacy. The instruments that most effectively bring about compliance, it can be shown, are not physical chastisement or compulsion, but the bestowal or withdrawal of praise or blame. But the desire for respect, admiration, love, and good name is today almost as clearly marked among nations as among individuals. And the sanction these rewards bestow may furnish the most effective means of socialization in this case, too.

The infringement of accepted norms may be made politically expensive among nations as it is socially expensive among individuals. The increasing convergence on certain principles within international organizations[12] demonstrates the beginnings of such a development. The political costs of nonconformity (as paid by South Africa over apartheid, or by the Soviet Union over Hungary) already exercise some deterrent power. More detailed principles of conduct would require constant reiteration. Perpetual repetition in international political bodies

[12] See Appendix II, pp. 329 ff.

is more effective in instilling them deeply into public consciousness than the occasional and disputed judgments of international law courts. Rules that become sufficiently internalized cease finally to appear hostile and externally imposed. Individual members in this way may be forced to be free — not by a mystical or supernatural general will, but by the conditioning imposed by social pressures, which converts passive obligation into active will.

Some of the particular principles a peaceful international community would require have been suggested earlier, and others are considered later.[13] Such principles come to have significance for members of the community in which they operate partly through the rational faculty of universalizing general rules from particular cases. This increase in rationality takes place within the international field as in other communities. Here, too, members may become increasingly aware, even if only subconsciously, that certain principles of interaction are the condition of peaceful coexistence. Behavior that had been considered unregulated is gradually classified and graded under principles that cover more and more detailed aspects of conduct. Broad categories that may once have been adequate ("aggression," "sovereignty," and "territorial integrity") become defined and subdivided in more meaningful ways. And principles whose purpose and interrelationship are clearly understood gradually exert a more powerful influence on the community's members. Conditioning and rationality thus mutually reinforce each other.

As we saw in earlier chapters, authority without power may also be strengthened by *procedures*. Some of these, too, have already been described. Such procedures are one form of practices, ad hoc arrangements for dealing with specific situations and disputes. These, as we have seen, are among the basic norms conditioning individual responses within a social environment.

International procedures may serve to alter the conventional exchange of national move and countermove at an ever higher tension by interjecting a *pause* within the sequence of escalation. This may allow stresses to relax, and less emotional attitudes to be brought to bear, and finally to encourage a downward spiral in place of the continuous escalation. The effect is to create a substitute chain of events, in prearranged form, which may slow down the rate of reaction, lower temperature and tension, and provide the mechanism for evolving a mutually acceptable solution.

[13] See Chapter Ten, pp. 289–292.

A number of procedures for dealing with disputes have been developed since the early days of international organizations. Such procedures are as susceptible to empirical examination as the situations that have made them necessary. Such an analysis is attempted in Appendix IV.

This analysis suggests that calls on the parties to negotiate have rarely produced much result unless some external stimulus to concessions is provided. Public discussion in the General Assembly, though it may prove useful as a mobilization of opinion and as an outlet of emotion in place of more violent action, can sometimes be an intensifying factor, especially when negotiations are at a delicate stage and the need is to avoid public postures. The large-scale commissions of inquiry (as employed over Manchuria and at first over Palestine) seem to be less effective for the purposes of conciliation than a smaller body or single mediator. A single mediator has proved most effective where his soundings have been entirely confidential and without prior commitment, and free from detailed supervision by UN bodies (West Irian, Thailand–Cambodia). Recommendations to resort to the International Court are possible only when both parties are willing (Colombia–Peru) or obliged (Guatemala–Liechtenstein) to accept them, and have rarely brought a resolution of important political issues (Gibraltar). Observers on the spot, though they can provide information and act as a restraining influence in some circumstances (Greece, Israel, Kashmir), unless entrusted with mediatory functions will probably not appreciably influence underlying problems (Yemen, Indo-China). Finally, regional organizations, whose influence with governments may be more powerful than that of the UN as a whole, appear in certain situations to be more effective as peacemakers than the UN itself (Morocco–Algeria, Kuwait).[14]

Another procedure, scarcely used so far, which could be useful is of a more long-term type. We have seen in earlier chapters that one of the difficulties of the UN in dealing with many conflicts is that, despite the Charter provisions enabling it to examine "disputes" before conflicts arise, in practice it examines them usually only after war has already broken out, when they are most difficult to deal with. Machinery for "peaceful settlement," as we shall see in the next chapter, cannot do much to help in this situation unless members choose to make use of it. On the other

[14] It is, of course, a mistake to judge such procedures only by their capacity to bring about a "solution" to a dispute. For many disputes can never have a "solution": the only settlement acceptable to one party will be unacceptable to another. Conciliation is thus a better test than resolution of disputes. International organizations may encourage the use of concessive means even when they cannot influence ultimate ends.

hand, if the Secretariat were to undertake long-term factual studies of many of the major international disputes that exist — e.g., frontier disputes and claims, civil conflicts, minority disputes, and disputes over waterways or natural resources — when the quarrel became acute, or whenever the UN decided to take it up, the essential facts would be readily available. Even in preparing such reports, the Secretariat might be in a position to undertake some conciliation behind the scenes. The reports themselves could stimulate the appointment of a mediator or some alternative procedure. At present, surprisingly, the UN rarely calls for such reports unless the Secretary-General himself takes the initiative. Yet these could provide the essential "fact-finding" without establishing a special body for the purpose — a proposal that has aroused much controversy.[15]

New procedures could be developed. Regular summit meetings of top world statesmen may be organized to improve communication. Parliamentarians might be brought into greater contact. Meetings between officials, less politically committed, may be organized to establish understanding. Greater use of regional organizations could be made. International organizations certainly need to experiment with new forms of procedures, and to study and compare them systematically, if their authority is to be extended further.

The third main instrument available to an authority without power is that provided by *precedents*. Here the value of the procedure derives not from its proved efficacy as a means of conciliation, but from the very fact that it is established as a traditional pattern of response. Where a procedure becomes established as the normal and habitual means of action in a given situation, it comes to influence the expectations and behavior of the principal protagonists. Just as workers in labor disputes become mentally prepared for the procedures established and hallowed by time, so the nation that has become involved in a dispute may become mentally prepared for the procedures of reconciliation laid down by an international organization. Substitutes for the traditional responses to signals — mobilization, threats, ultimata, and the like — may be instilled. Expectations are channeled into new directions. The first reaction may become not to reach for a gun, but to reach for an accommodation.

A procedure can only become a precedent of this sort if it is employed with considerable consistency and regularity. Perhaps the only proce-

---

[15] For the past three or four years, the UN has been discussing proposals for the establishment of a "fact-finding" body. But these have always ended in deadlock because of differences over the duties and powers of such a body.

dure used by international authority in that way so far is that of resort to the Security Council. The expectation of this response probably serves already to influence the reactions of nations at time of crisis. Even here, however, the fact that many disputes, including some of the most important, are never submitted to that body considerably weakens the influence the procedure might otherwise exercise. Only when that procedure is invariably applied or other precedents are equally deeply instilled will they become effective influences on reactions in time of crisis.

The procedures and precedents examined so far are mainly those concerned with conciliation and pacification before conflict has become intense. Where armed conflict has already arisen, other techniques may be required. Even if overwhelming coercive power is lacking, more limited forms may sometimes be mobilized. Where the main need is a restraining influence or objective information, a truce commission or observers may prove useful (as employed by the League over Manchuria and by the UN over Palestine and the Yemen). A representative of the Secretary General may act as a contact or mediator between the two sides (as in the Congo and Cyprus). A buffer zone between two contestants may be established (as employed on the Israel-Egypt border).

Other means, not involving armed force, may be used. The failure of economic sanctions during the interwar period should not encourage the conclusion that such methods can never be effective, for at that time the sanctions excluded important suppliers and the most vital commodities. In 1950 the UN established, under the Uniting for Peace resolution, a Collective Measures Committee to study and report on methods, including economic and financial measures, which might be used to maintain and strengthen international peace and security. Under its organization some economic sanctions were imposed during the Korean War. And similar measures have had some success since, against Rhodesia.

Such measures require a considerable time to take effect. Their success is vitally dependent on the assurance that all or nearly all member states will apply them. And their immediate result is sometimes to encourage defiance rather than compliance. They are mainly useful, therefore, in situations of deadlock where the object is to induce a government to vacate a position already held or to abandon a policy already initiated. The economic sanction most immediate in effect may be the withholding of oil supplies or other essential materials from those who are without them. For some countries an effective sanction would be the threat to withhold all economic assistance and investment from without. Economic sanctions are certainly a form of international pressure which might be useful in some circumstances. A corollary to this might be that the initiation of unilateral economic embargoes by individual states or alliances, without the sanction of international authority, such as have recently been common, should be proscribed.[16]

In the immediate future, perhaps, the increase of UN authority, in the absence of power, will depend mainly on the willingness of governments to support and acknowledge that authority with consistency, even in cases not clearly to their interest. Most governments have been sometimes ready to call in its aid against other governments. But they have often been less willing to acknowledge its resolutions when these were not advantageous to themselves. The text of the Charter is so full of ambiguities and inconsistencies that in almost every situation it is possible to find a text to justify defiance. In this, as in other fields, the actions of governments will be primarily conditioned by the trend of their own national opinion as a whole. In many cases it is the sanction of that opinion that will alone secure compliance, for no other overwhelming sanction exists to coerce them.

The strengthening of international authority is unlikely to be achieved by a stroke of the pen, through the adoption of some of the ingenious paper schemes that have sometimes been advocated, or by some dramatic revision of the Charter. It is more likely to come about by a slow but steady accretion of influence and authority, the gradual expansion of its activities in new fields, the growing increase in respect for its decisions among governments and individuals. Those who champion drastic methods sometimes justify them with the contention that it is dangerous to seek to leap a chasm in short steps. Yet it may be equally rash to try to clear a river at a single leap. By making careful and calculated use of the steppingstones that lead across, it may be possible to build up an authority that it will be increasingly difficult for even the unwilling to resist.

Bibliography

Bailey, S., *The General Assembly of the U.N.*, London, 1960.
———, *The U.N. Secretariat*, New York, 1962.

[16] For a full survey of the economic and financial measures which might be used by the UN as a means of exerting its authority, see the First Report of the Collective Measures Committee, established by the General Assembly in 1950, Supplement No. 13 (A/1891) to the official records of the Sixth Session.

Bloomfield, L. P. (ed.), *International Military Forces*, Boston, 1964.

Bowett, D. W., *United Nations Forces*, London, 1964.

Claude, I., *Swords into Ploughshares* (3rd ed.), New York, 1964.

Deutsch, K. W., *Political Community at the International Level*, Princeton, 1954.

Goodrich, L. N. and A. P. Simons, *The United Nations and the Maintenance of International Peace and Security*, Washington, 1955.

Hovet, T., *Bloc Politics in the U.N.*, Cambridge, Mass., 1960.

Luard, Evan (ed.), *The Evolution of International Organizations*, London, 1966.

Mangone, G. J., *A Short History of International Organizations*, New York, 1954.

Nicholas, H., *The United Nations as a Political Institution*, London, 1959.

Reuter, P., *International Institutions*, London, 1958.

Rosner, G., *The United Nations Emergency Force*, New York, 1963.

Russell, R. B., *History of the U.N. Charter*, Washington, D.C., 1958.

Walters, L. P., *A Short History of the League of Nations*, London, 1952.

CHAPTER TEN

Law

The Development of International Law

Another means of securing peace is through the development of a legal system by which nations may be constrained to keep the peace. Any authority needs to apply a system of rules. The attempt to create these in the international field has mainly sought to reproduce a legal system analogous to that applied in national states to individuals.

When communities began to come into frequent contact with each other, attempts to secure order and security among them took this form. Some of the city-states of Greece began to develop rules to govern relations between them. Conventions concerning declarations of war, the inviolability of heralds, the sanctity of holy refuges, and other matters emerged. In India, long before the period of a centralized empire, rules of international conduct were regarded as an integral part of the general "duty" which was to guide all human activity. They included rights of sovereignty and jurisdiction, the forms of diplomatic usage, and the conventions surrounding the conclusion of treaties and alliances. In China, while there remained a multiplicity of warring states among her own people, certain moral injunctions relating to the relations of states were expounded, though, as we saw, not always regarded. The Romans, for whom a written law was the essential fabric of social life at home, enacted an international law, a "law of the peoples," defining the conduct of relations with foreign peoples in explicit form. Elaborate rules concerning matters of peace and war were evolved. A complex code of maritime law was drawn up.

In medieval Europe, the growth of a large number of independent nation states, having close, and often hostile, relations made the definition of conventions governing their intercourse appear more necessary than ever. Rules of maritime and trading law began to be codified. From the middle of the fourteenth century a number of writers began to suggest regulations covering the conduct of war and other aspects of international relations. An accepted code governing the dispatch and treatment of diplomatic envoys began to be evolved. Utopian schemes for some sort of international confederation were even put forward with a permanent court of arbitration, or a central assembly, to maintain perpetual peace.

Meanwhile there developed an increasing respect for the sanctity of legal procedures within the state. In some states the law courts asserted and attained an authority independent of the sovereign power and enforced laws derived, not from the written statutes of king and parliament, but from the ancient customs of their peoples. There was a widespread belief, inherited from classical times, in the preeminence of another law, more fundamental still, a natural law rooted in the immutable principles of reason. This respect for law was inevitably once again extended to cover the field of international conduct, where the unreason and the disorder of human relationships were most evident of all. During the sixteenth century and especially in the first half of the seventeenth century, when international conflict reached a level of barbarity perhaps never equaled, some legal writers began to devise a code of conduct for states which might restore to the community of nation states some semblance of order. This code, distinguishing as in ancient times between those wars that were "just" and those that were "unjust," was regarded by them as analogous to the systems of law established within states.

During the next two centuries this system of international law was developed by a number of writers. It was not suggested that all wars were illegal. But there was an attempt to distinguish those which were permissible from those which were not.[1] The belief that such rules were rooted in a law of nature, independent of the will of nations, receded. There were many who maintained the so-called positivist view that states were subject only to those laws and customs which they themselves explicitly acknowledged. It thus became easier than ever for sovereign states to justify themselves by the declaration that those wars which they fought were "just" and those of others, "unjust."

Since there existed no institutions to lay down the law, still less to apply it in individual cases, the new conceptions of international law

[1] See Chapter Three, pp. 72–78.

remained mostly theoretical. They were discussed mainly by academic lawyers and theologians. They certainly affected little the actual conduct of international relations. Many statesmen probably remained totally unaware of most of the rules laid down. Even among lawyers there was little agreement on the law's substantive principles. And many uses of armed force, as we have seen earlier, have remained permissible, under all interpretations, even until today. Only during the nineteenth century was there, gradually, a growth of treaties, bilateral and multilateral, whose provisions were recognized to possess the force of law for those who became parties to them. But they were respected because they were treaties, not because they were "international law." The comity of nations, to whom this "law" was thought to apply, was gradually extended outward from the center of Europe. By 1856 it included Turkey; by 1914 it covered most of the sovereign states of the earth.

The growth of international law was accompanied by the growth of international litigation. The practice of submitting some of those disputes which might otherwise have led to conflict to arbitration by some impartial body began to emerge. Such forms of settlement had been used by some of the city-states of Greece. Similar methods were adopted by the cantons of Switzerland. From the end of the eighteenth century Britain and the United States agreed to submit various differences between them to mixed arbitration commissions composed of nationals of the two states. During the nineteenth century in a number of cases foreign sovereigns were requested by two governments to adjudicate on a dispute. In 1873, an Institute for International Law was founded to formulate the rules for arbitration. By the end of the century the submission of disputes to such arbitration became increasingly common.[2]

An attempt was made to strengthen and to codify this procedure at the two Hague Conferences of 1899 and 1907. A "Convention for the Peaceful Settlement of International Disputes," providing for the use of mediation, conciliation, and arbitration to settle contentious issues, was signed. In the years before World War I more than a hundred bilateral and multilateral agreements providing for similar procedures were entered into. A permanent panel of arbitrators was established. Some began to hope that by these means law might be made to replace war as the normal means of resolving international disputes.

Yet it was taken for granted almost everywhere that in practice only

---

[2] See J. H. Ralston, *International Arbitration from Athens to Locarno* (Stanford, 1929). There are said to have been 217 arbitral or other judicial awards among nations between 1794 and 1897.

certain essentially unimportant types of dispute would prove suitable for arbitration. International law still recognized the right to secure redress by force as an ultimate resort. An international legal tribunal attributed superior rights to certain powers that had sought to assert financial claims against Venezuela by armed force. The Hague Conventions of 1899 and 1907 recognized arbitration as the most effective and equitable means of settling only "questions of a legal nature, and especially . . . the interpretation or application of international conventions." Many of the rules devised were directed, not to the *prevention* of warlike conflicts, but to making them somewhat less barbarous when they occurred. For even the smallest matters there was no provision for compulsory arbitration. And many states specifically excluded from the scope of bilateral agreements questions that affected "the vital interests, the independence, or the honor" of the two states. For questions of honor, they continued to maintain, like duelists, could be determined only by brute force.

Law in Place of War

The belief that violence was the only ultimate sanction where vital national interests were at stake was encouraged by the fact that there was no international authority to enforce the law or to provide alternative redress. The horrors of World War I stimulated some attempt to remedy this situation.

It began to be recognized that, since the arbitration procedures previously instituted specifically excluded precisely those types of dispute most likely to lead to conflict, they would require amplification. The organization then established was intended to provide for the peaceful settlement even of those issues not suitable for legal adjudication. Under Article XV of the Covenant of the League, members agreed to submit to the Council "any dispute likely to lead to a rupture, which is not submitted to arbitration or to judicial settlement."

Yet the emphasis remained on legal forms of settlement. These legal procedures were strengthened and elaborated. Under Article XIII members agreed to submit those disputes "which they recognized to be suitable" to judicial settlement or to arbitration. "Judicial settlement" was to be secured by recourse to a newly established Permanent Court of International Justice. The judgments of this court were to be binding on the parties. But recourse was to be voluntary, except when, later, some states voluntarily accepted automatic jurisdiction on legal questions. The types of dispute declared to be generally suitable for this procedure were disputes on the interpretation of a treaty, on a question of international law, on alleged breaches of an international obligation, and on the reparation to be made for these. "Arbitration," which could be supplied by any arbitrators agreed on between the parties, was encouraged by the conclusion of many new agreements, bilateral and multilateral, for such a procedure and by the conclusion of a "general treaty for the pacific settlement of international disputes."

The provisions for judicial settlement were severely hedged about. Though the older reservations concerning "national honor, independence, or vital interests" were no longer publicly flaunted, alternative reservations were now inserted in their place. It was generally accepted that legal procedures were unsuitable for "political" disputes. Compulsory jurisdiction was specifically restricted to "legal" questions. Only about half the members of the League agreed to accept the compulsory jurisdiction of the Court, with numerous reservations and for varying periods of time. In practice the exemption of "political" disputes from those regarded as justiciable could be used to claim the exclusion of almost any dispute desired. In the very first case in which the Optional Clause, providing for compulsory arbitration, was cited, it was contended that the restriction to "legal" disputes automatically meant that all "important" issues must be excluded. Even within the limited field remaining, the jurisdiction of the Court was frequently contested by one party or another; sometimes its decisions were not respected; occasionally "national" judges expressed dissenting opinions favorable to the case of their own nations.

The reservations in disputes suitable for "arbitration" were not quite so rigid. But their effect was identical. The general belief that "important" disputes were not suitable for arbitration any more than for legal settlement meant that the procedure was never likely to be used as a substitute for war, since any issue which might be the subject of war was, inevitably, important. At the same time a whole series of other reservations, relating to "matters of domestic jurisdiction," conflicts with the terms of constitutions or national legislation, the interests of third parties, territorial integrity, disputes belonging to the past, and others, were used by governments wishing to refuse a resort to arbitration. The permanent Court of Arbitration, though it still exists, was only once used to settle a dispute since 1932. Arbitration by other procedures has become increasingly rare. In a number of cases, an arbitration award was not accepted. In others, submission to arbitration was refused altogether.

For those "political disputes" not submitted to these processes, alternative procedures had to be found. Even these were legal in form. In the League international dissensions continued to be treated as if they were civil lawsuits. The parties were to submit statements of their cases in writing with relevant facts and papers. The Council was to endeavor to effect a settlement (like a court), publishing a statement setting out the facts (like a *procès-verbal*) and the terms of settlement arrived at (like a judgment). The tribunal had to reach unanimous agreement on their verdict (like a jury). But if this could not be achieved, members were allowed (unlike private litigants) "to take such action as they shall consider necessary for the maintenance of right and justice." Sovereignty still asserted the claim in the last resort to judge individually where "right and justice" lay. Might was still the final arbiter of right.

But it soon began to be evident that neither the strictly legal nor the new political procedures were alone sufficient. Only a limited number of issues fell into the category described as "suitable" for legal settlements. "Political" issues did not always prove susceptible to settlement by the method laid down in the Covenant. Important states were not members of the League. Thus where other methods had failed, an intermediate procedure, called "conciliation," began to be evolved. Arrangements of this sort were included in the Locarno agreements, the General Convention for Inter-American Conciliation, the General Act for the Pacific Settlement of International Disputes, and various other undertakings. The procedure involved investigation of the facts and the recommendation of a settlement by impartial assessors. In some agreements "conciliation" was made obligatory for nonlegal disputes. But the parties were not obliged to accept either the report or the recommendation. In practice the procedure was rarely used, and when it was used, it was usually ineffective. Indeed it was perhaps never likely that it would be used, for those who were unwilling to accept a settlement by existing remedies were usually those who were unlikely to be "conciliated" by any other.

It is possible that the formulation of these various procedures did something to encourage the slow development of the concept that nations should no longer make themselves — at least no longer declare themselves — a law unto themselves. International law, if not obeyed, at least began to be quoted. There was a reversion to the concept that that law was not limited by the positive submissions of individual nation states but enjoyed a more independent authority. Some began to assert that international law was a complete system, which, even when no precedents existed, could find, on the basis of general principles, a legal answer to every dispute.

But the content of the law which the court applied was essentially a rigid and unchanging one. Its sources were explicitly confined to international conventions and treaties; international custom, when this provided evidence of a general practice accepted as law; the "general principles of law accepted by civilized nations"; and judicial decisions and the teachings of international lawyers insofar as these served as evidence of existing law.[3] The judges of the International Court specifically declared, and its Statute confirmed, that it was not open to them to settle any dispute on the basis of equity, as opposed to received law, unless both parties specifically requested them to do so. There existed no legislature to amend or revoke the existing sources of the law. In such circumstances the law must inevitably function mainly as an instrument for preserving the prerogatives of the haves. It could never be used as an agency for adjustments to satisfy the aspirations of the have-nots. Because it recognized the sanctity of all existing treaties and obligations, it inevitably served to perpetuate the status quo.

There were more fundamental reasons why the new procedures were incapable of providing a magic recipe for "peaceful change," for allaying international frictions without recourse to the barbarities of war. These rested in the realities of contemporary national psychology. War was not always so dangerous that, judged purely on considerations of national self-interest, it must unquestionably be excluded as an act of policy. It was not always so profitless that its attractions could be dismissed as the great illusion. And whatever nations asserted in the abstract, in concrete situations few were ready to allow matters of the most vital interest to be left to the uncertain and frustrating procedures of litigation, rather than resolved, in the final resort, through a contest of national wills by the time-honored expedients. War was so firmly institutionalized in the behavior of nation states that, even though none consciously wished for it, situations still arose where it seemed the only honorable, the only favorable, the only natural outcome. Basic expectations were in this respect unmodified. So long as there existed tensions, grievances, and unsatisfied aspirations, for which armed conflict seemed the normal means of resolution, war must inevitably, when the appropriate stimulus occurred, erupt again. It was, in the nature of things,

[3] These were the sources of international law laid down in the Statute of the Permanent International Court of Justice.

the aggrieved, the resentful, the greedy, who were first disposed to revert to such procedures. But the state of mind that made such a course possible was, at bottom, shared by all.

Indeed all explicitly reserved the right of recourse to war in the final resort. It is true that many signed the Paris Pact "for the renunciation of war" (1929). But even in entering into this, all made reservations. Most arrogated to themselves the right to determine when war might be necessary in "self-defense." In some cases, "self-defense" was explicitly defined to include the defense of physical interests outside the borders of the home territory.[4]

The principles of international law themselves were not more influential than before. Perhaps greater lip-service was paid to them than in earlier ages. Some held that the Paris Pact for the first time made war itself illegal. But it is doubtful if statesmen were significantly influenced by it in their actions, at least over the most important questions. And even if they were, as we saw earlier (Chapter Three), there always remained justifications or exceptions, which provided loopholes in case of necessity.

Not only were few nations prepared finally to renounce the right to resort to war in certain circumstances. There were no effective sanctions to compel them to do so. If only one powerful state refused to make use of the new procedures, they were effectively destroyed. If only one nation made manifest its determination to prosecute its aims by other means, then all had to be prepared to do the same. Many talked of "conciliation"; but none suggested what should be done when a nation (such as Japan over Manchuria, or Italy over Ethiopia) refused to be conciliated. Law becomes effective not when it it pronounced, but when it is obeyed. And law could not be substituted for war without the means of law enforcement.

The attempt to create a simple analogy between international and municipal law was a misleading one. The bold, bad barons of Britain and other European countries were made subject to the king's courts, not because the king's law declared that they should be so, but because the king's law was able ultimately to exert more power than those who sought to resist it. The parties to civil disputes today are normally con-

---

[4] Britain made a reservation aimed at ensuring freedom of action in relation to the defense of the British Empire. The United States made a reservation designed to ensure that United States action to protect any part of the Western hemisphere should be covered by the phrase "self-defense." Both demanded the right to determine themselves what represented "self-defense."

tent to accept recourse to the courts because they have been conditioned to prefer public legality to private justice. For international disputes no such conditioning had taken effect. Nor did there exist any superior force which might deter independent action. And there still existed alternative means of redress, long sanctified by tradition, more satisfying, and, to the powerful, more effective.

Many of the basic sources of conflict could in any case scarcely have been solved by any legal means. Their roots were not juridical but psychological. The resentment of Germany at the disabilities imposed on her at Versailles, the acquisitive urges of Japan, Italian dreams of imperial grandeur, the security anxieties of the capitalist-encircled Soviet Union, stresses and strains of this sort — the true origins of the conflicts to come — were not susceptible to settlement by the type of glorified civil lawsuit which international lawyers dreamed could solve the problems of the world. Governments, if not lawyers, showed some consciousness of this in their assertion that "political" disputes could not be solved by judicial settlement or arbitration. What they did not provide was any effective "political" means of resolving such disputes.

The sanctions exerted by opinion were little more effective than those of authority. For opinion was no more adjusted than governments themselves to a world in which force had been abolished. Few wanted war. But there were few who, when it came to the point, would not follow their governments if these chose to lead them in that direction. There were fewer still who had sufficient confidence in the efficacy of the new legal procedures to be sure that, in every situation, law alone could provide the world with effective security.

International Law After 1945

World War II showed how precarious was the hope that law could be made to abolish war. When, after that struggle, a new effort to build a more peaceful world was attempted, the implications of this lesson began to make themselves felt. It now became clear that indeed, as some international lawyers had always asserted, no firm dividing line between "legal" and "political" disputes was possible. But the true conclusion, it came to be realized, was not that of the lawyers — that all disputes should be submitted to legal decision. It was that, to provide the type of procedure appropriate to the existing stage of international relations, all disputes should be subjected to a political settlement.

Some such shift in balance was made more possible by the new institutional structure created. Although before the war the main emphasis of international procedures had been on arbitration and judicial settlement, after the war it was increasingly on the adjustments effected by the Security Council and the General Assembly. The "decisions" and "recommendations" of these political arms of the UN now acquired a force almost as binding as those of judicial bodies. "Important" questions could now be as subject to international solutions as "legal" questions. The League concept of international bodies as law enforcement agencies for charging criminals was replaced by the concept of public meetings for discussing matters of public concern within the political bodies of the new organization.

There had been some interchange between legal and political procedures even between the wars. But the prime emphasis then had been on the legal processes. Under Article XV of the Covenant it was laid down that only those disputes which were not submitted to "arbitration or judicial settlement" under Article XIII should be submitted to the Council of the League. A number of disputes were submitted first to arbitration. Only if this failed were they forwarded for discussion by the Council. In some cases the Council itself decided that a dispute already raised before it should be submitted to arbitration. And if a matter was sent for discussion in the League after judicial proceedings had begun, it was assumed that, should the political discussions achieve nothing, the matter would revert to decision by the Court. But where it was accepted that a dispute was "political" and so "non-justiciable," the usual conclusion was not that the matter must therefore be settled by the League instead of by the Court. It was that these were matters on which the rights of unrestricted national sovereignty had been explicitly reserved.

In the postwar world, the effect of the essentially political character of disputes was quite different. The various procedures for judicial settlement, arbitration, or conciliation set out in Articles XII–XV of the Covenant of the League and in the Protocol on the "pacific settlement of international disputes," though preserved and even elaborated in the UN Charter, were bundled into a single sentence of Article 33. They represented merely the preliminaries, the formalities that would have to be passed through before a matter became fit for discussion in the UN. Once this had been done, it became the subject of "investigation," "recommendation," or, in the case of a breach of the peace, "decision," by the Security Council. Under the Covenant, the League had the right to discuss such disputes only if they were submitted by one of the parties or in the extreme case where they had led to "war or the threat of war." Under the Charter, the Security Council could, at its own discretion and "at any stage of the dispute," recommend "appropriate procedures or methods of adjustment"; or, once the situation became more acute, "such terms of settlement as it may consider appropriate." The potential scope and opportunity of international political discussion were thus now enormously increased.

In practice, as has been seen, the preliminaries came to be increasingly ignored. During the early years of the UN there were a number of cases in which it was contended that the opportunities for bilateral negotiation had not been exhausted (the Corfu Channel case [1946], the Egyptian question [1947], the Tunisian question [1952], and Trieste [1953]). In a very small number of cases the Security Council declined altogether to consider a question for this reason (the Iranian question [1946], and the Syrian and Lebanese question [1946]). In a number of others it passed a substantive recommendation calling for further efforts to reach a settlement between the parties. India's complaints about South Africa's racial policies were at first met by a request for negotiations between the parties. The items concerning Tunisian and Moroccan demands for independence were similarly disposed of. In other cases the recommendations were for a procedure of mediation or conciliation such as Article 33 proposed. A form of mediation was attempted over Kashmir. A good-offices committee performed a similar function in the dispute between the Netherlands and Indonesia. A UN mediator was appointed to help secure an armistice in the Arab-Israeli war.

But from the mid-fifties the Security Council was usually ready to make its own recommendations on any such matter as soon as it was brought to its attention. Many of those disputes which in the interwar period would have been regarded as suitable for determination by arbitration or judicial settlement — for example, concerning aircraft incidents, the treatment of minorities, the observance of treaty obligations — in the postwar world were normally discussed in UN political bodies. And those "non-justiciable" disputes, which between the wars had either not been discussed at all or only quite inconclusively within the League, came to be considered by the UN on a more regular basis and with a rather more effective determination.

Thus the political rather than the legal procedures began to be the main focus of attention, and so, where dispute arose, to appear as the obvious recourse. Conversely, the legal procedures declined in effectiveness and importance. While in the interwar years the Permanent International Court of Justice heard about sixty cases, including some of considerable political importance, in the twenty years after World War II the International Court delivered judgments on less than a score of cases, mostly of quite small importance. In a number of others the Court was obliged to conclude that it lacked jurisdiction owing to the refusal of one of the parties to accept jurisdiction, or for other reasons. In one of the very few important cases, the judgment delivered was deliberately flouted (Corfu Channel). And in another the judgment, however justified according to the strict letter of the law, was considered by many governments as out of harmony with current world opinion (South West Africa).

The fact that disputes were increasingly settled in a political rather than a legal forum transformed the type of settlement arrived at. One result was that they were likely to be mainly settled on political rather than legal principles. This brings gains as well as losses. As has been seen the disputes determined by the International Court or by arbitration could be settled only through the rigid application of accepted international law. Consideration *ex aequo et bono* (on grounds of equity) was only possible when specifically requested by the parties. In the postwar world, disputes settled within the Security Council or the Assembly were determined at least partly on the basis of political expediency. With all its disadvantages this may allow an element of flexibility which legal judgments sometimes lack. It may bring liberation from the terms of treaty texts or precedents. It may allow a consideration of common weal as well as of "respective rights," of the changing needs of a changing society as well as of formal obligations. In theory at least, it makes possible decisions on grounds of equity alone.

The shift in emphasis indeed was little remarked. The attempt to apply and develop the traditional international law continued to be pursued. New law even continued to be made. The Charter itself provided a new source of law. The War Crimes trials created new categories of international offense, including "crimes against peace," the "planning, preparation, initiation or waging of a war of aggression, or a war in violation of international treaties, agreements or assurances . . . ," genocide, and other offenses. The trials finally established the disputed principle that individuals, as well as states, could be the subjects of international law. The International Law Commission, set up by the General Assembly to carry out its function of "encouraging the progressive development of international law and its modification," formulated a draft declaration on the rights and duties of states, a draft code of offenses against the peace and security of mankind, and draft conventions on statelessness and on diplomatic intercourse and immunities.

A convention on Genocide was adopted by the Assembly (1948). A Declaration on the Legal Principles Governing Outer Space was proclaimed by the Assembly (1963). Covenants on Human Rights were prepared (1966). Some contended that decisions by UN bodies themselves could create new law.[5] In general, public documents, the Charter, international conventions, and judgments of the International Court counted for more than before in relation to bilateral and other limited treaties.

Such developments, however, it must be accepted, have had no great practical effect. The Nuremberg principles have never been applied, and scarcely quoted, in subsequent cases. The draft Conventions have not concerned contentious subjects, and only three have been converted to formal international Conventions.[6] Attempts to arrive at an agreed definition of aggression were without success. A UN conference on the law of the sea reached agreement on four draft conventions dealing with various relatively noncontroversial matters, but could not reach agreement on the most fundamental point at issue, the breadth of territorial waters. An ad hoc UN committee considered the law of space but reached no agreement on the important points. As in other ages, international law was better in providing a *modus vivendi* on relatively uncontroversial points than a means of resolving the issues which most aroused conflict.

In fact attempts to preserve peace through the development of a legal system were even less likely to prove successful in the postwar world than before. For over most of those types of behavior which then had become most commonly adopted — the dissemination of inflammatory propaganda, the harboring and encouragement of revolutionary elements by foreign powers, the engineering of coups d'état through nationals of the state concerned, the waging of civil war by proxy — international law, new or old, had nothing at all to say. They had never been treated by the traditional system. No principles had been evolved to cover them. On almost all the major issues of the post-1945 world — the nationalization of the Iranian oil and the Suez Canal and the responses to

---

[5] See R. Higgins, *The Development of International Law by the Political Organs of the United Nations* (London, 1963).
[6] On the relatively uncontroversial matters of the Reduction of Statelessness (1961), Diplomatic Relations (1961), and Consular Relations (1963).

it, the Cuban crisis, the Berlin blockade and the Berlin wall, Tibet, Formosa and the offshore islands, Chinese representation at the UN, freedom of navigation through the Tiran Straits — international law was silent or ambiguous, and international lawyers, if they pronounced at all, showed themselves hopelessly divided. International law, like other legal systems, could only successfully enforce principles which international opinion, lay or expert, in some degree accepted. And on many of these matters both law and opinion were undecided.

Legal procedures might play a role even if law remained undeveloped. It is sometimes suggested that international organizations have tended to concentrate too much on means of pacifying disputes after they have already reached the stage of conflict, and not enough on resolving the underlying issues that have led to conflict. It is said that by making a greater use of certain semilegal procedures they might more successfully tackle the fundamental issues in disputes.[7] Among the procedures that have been recommended are bilateral agreements for inquiry, conciliation, or adjudication of disputes; the greater use of advisory opinions by the International Court of Justice or other bodies; the appointment of a mediator or conciliator; and greater use of the permanent Court of Arbitration, perhaps brought into relation with the UN, or of the UN Panel of Inquiry and Conciliation, set up in 1949 and never used. There may well be scope for greater use of some of these procedures. There is certainly need for more extensive research into the efficacy of each. But it is doubtful how far legal procedures of this sort can really resolve the type of international issue that in fact sometimes leads to war. Though there are certain types of dispute which can sometimes be solved by legal means, these are not the kinds which would have led to war. Certain issues, over frontiers, interpretations of treaties, or other matters, are already submitted to arbitration of one kind or another. But it seems most unlikely that the issues which, over the last fifty years, have been the principal cause of conflict or war — Manchuria, Ethiopia, Austria, Czechoslovakia, Poland, Berlin, the Offshore Islands, Formosa, Suez, Hungary, Goa, Cuba, the Arab-Israel and Kashmir disputes — could have been "solved" by such procedures, nor would there have been agreement, not even among lawyers, on what principles should have been applied to them. For nearly always in such cases it is over underlying principles that conflict arises: traditional sovereignty or a new one, self-determination or prescriptive authority. Though one party usually favors

---

[7] See, for example, the report of the David Davies Memorial Institute, London, on *The Peaceful Settlement of International Disputes*, London, 1966.

the status quo and the letter of the law, another seeks to change the status quo and overturn the letter of the law. Legal procedures may resolve lesser disputes or find compromises where both sides are ready in the final resort to compromise; but not those conflicts that arouse the deepest passions. Many of the most dangerous situations cannot even be classified as "disputes," for which, given the right procedure, the appropriate "solution" can be found. For some situations there are no solutions at all; the attempt to find one may itself provoke further dispute, and the only peaceful answer is to learn to live with them.[8]

Thus the principles of international law remain subject to dispute on the matters of most vital importance. It remains bounded by the formulations of a limited number of international conventions and acknowledged customs. Even where it is clear, it is not always obeyed. And because there exists no procedure for legislation, there seems little possibility of establishing a purely legal system more capable of flexibility, more tolerant of change, or more closely related to existing patterns of national conduct.

The United Nations Charter

Probably the most important source of international law today is the Charter of the United Nations. This has replaced or reformulated a number of traditional doctrines. It does so especially in its prohibition of the "threat or use of force." It defines a number of procedures to which all members are bound. It establishes new obligations in the field of human rights.

But there are many difficulties of interpretation. As international lawyers have often pointed out, the Charter is frequently ambiguous; it is sometimes inconsistent; and it is often remote from current practice and opinion. On one or two crucial points, the texts in different languages do not coincide. There is no established means of determining, beyond possibility of future dispute, which interpretations are correct; or, when two articles appear to be in conflict, which has the over-

---

[8] In fact there has been no shortage of machinery for peaceful settlement for those who wish to use it. Besides the Permanent Court of Arbitration, almost totally unused for 35 years, the UN set up in 1949 a Panel for Enquiry and Conciliation, which, like the Panel of Field Observers set up at the same time, has never been used at all. Regional machinery, such as the OAU's Commission of Mediation, Conciliation and Arbitration, have been equally little used.

riding force. Yet the procedure for amendment is so cumbersome as to be impossible for most purposes.

Some of the inconsistencies are fundamental to the UN's purposes. Article 2(1) declares that "the organization is based on the principle of the sovereign equality of all its Members," yet the binding nature of the decisions of the Security Council, and the very composition of that body, contradict this aspiration. Article 2(7) says that nothing in the Charter "shall authorize the United Nations to intervene in matters which are essentially within the domestic jurisdiction of any state," yet Articles 10, 62, and 73 challenge this provision. The division of powers between the Security Council and the Assembly, laid down in Articles 10, 11(2), and 12, is capable of almost any interpretation that may be placed upon it, and has indeed received it. Article 53(1) specifically prohibits enforcement action under regional arrangements without the authorization of the Security Council, whereas Article 51 affirms the right of "individual or collective self-defense" which might, under certain interpretations, allow virtually any action to be taken by them in time of emergency. There is no attempt to define many of the most essential terms used in the Charter, such as "intervene," "dispute," "international peace and security," "situations which might lead to international friction or give rise to dispute," "breach of the peace," "party to a dispute," "regional arrangement," and many others. As a result there has been widespread disagreement about the proper interpretation of some of the Charter's provisions.

Nor are there means of securing an authoritative ruling on such points. Under Article 96, the General Assembly or the Security Council may "request the International Court of Justice to give an advisory opinion on any legal questions." Such advisory opinions were given on the dispute which arose over the admission of new members, on compensation for dismissed international civil servants, on the question of payment for emergency forces, and other matters. But advisory opinions cannot be binding. And there is nothing in the Charter specifically recognizing the competence of the Court to interpret it. Nor is there any procedure, as in the League, by which the Assembly or any other body can determine all future interpretations of a given Article. On the instructions of the Assembly, the Secretariat has compiled an elaborate analysis of the practice of the UN in interpreting its Charter. But the analysis does not, and could not, purport to lay down any case law that binds future UN decisions.

Some means of establishing authoritative interpretations is essential to securing an effective international order. Advisory opinions of the International Court on contentious points, even though they might be challengeable, might prevent purely arbitrary interpretations of individual members and groups. Such opinions would need to be based, like judicial opinions in other spheres, on the current needs of the international community, as much as on a concern for the "intentions of the drafters." If adjusted, like the interpretations of the Constitution by the Supreme Court of the United States, to the developing needs of the community, opinions of this sort might serve as an important means of securing some liberation from rigid subservience to the Charter's terms.

Alternatively, the Assembly itself might undertake to establish authoritative interpretations of the most glaring anomalies and inconsistencies. Once again, in the absence of specific authority in the Charter (the right of the Assembly to interpret was explicitly rejected at the founding conference), these interpretations could not be binding. But they might, like the adoption of new procedures already undertaken, in effect prove difficult to challenge. At least they could help to make the UN more consistent and impartial in its responses.

The dangers of the existing situation are not that the UN may sometimes override the existing terms of its Charter. All legal systems are able to survive only through those gradual extensions and adjustments by which the letter of the law is accommodated to the spirit, outdated theory reconciled with current practice. What is dangerous is that there should be no means of establishing a single and authoritative interpretation, however remote this may be from the intentions of those who drafted the document, to establish a norm for existing practice. Where interpretations become entirely arbitrary, to be changed and challenged at will, the document ceases to be able to perform the function for which it was designed. UN action will cease to be effective because it will cease to be predictable. A Charter which is neither interpreted, amended, or regarded becomes a dead letter.

A more satisfactory means of resolving the ambiguities of the present Charter in the long run is not by interpretation but by revision. Under the terms of the Charter, amendments, although they only need the approval of two-thirds of UN members, require the assent of all permanent members. A proposal to call a review conference was, as the Charter provides, placed on the agenda of the Tenth Session of the General Assembly in 1955. That Assembly decided that such a conference should be held at "an appropriate time" and set up a committee to keep the matter under review. The Soviet Union and Poland, however, stated immediately that their delegations would not take part in the work of the committee or in any action aimed at reviewing the Charter. Since that time nothing more has been done. The decision to hold such a conference is not open to veto. But so long as one of the permanent members remains likely to veto a revision, and others are only luke-warm, it is unlikely that any significant steps will be taken in this direction.

There are a number of changes which might be introduced when the opportunity occurs. The provisions concerning the Secretariat and some other organs of the UN might be amended. It is unlikely that a tripartite division of authority between political groupings, such as has been suggested, could provide an effective executive arm for the UN. If it is found necessary to place restraints on the office of the Secretary General, this is better achieved by a careful definition of the tasks with which he is entrusted. It would be possible to keep him under closer scrutiny by the Security Council, at least in his control of peace-keeping operations. And it is essential to balance the composition of the Secretariat as a whole.

The powers of the Assembly, especially in relation to peace forces, could be reaffirmed or redefined, either in resolutions or in amendments to the Charter: perhaps in a whole new Chapter between VI and VII. Some of these problems were considered by the Committee on Peace-keeping established in February, 1965. Though this was not finally able to reach agreement, many of the important issues were clarified, especially in the guidelines suggested by the Secretary General and the President of the Assembly. If the Assembly's powers were strengthened, the immunity originally accorded to the permanent members might have to be reinforced: for example, by a firm assurance that UN forces created by the Assembly would not be used against the territory of one of them, and by satisfactory arrangements for control of the forces. This would merely reflect existing realities, as the orginial veto power was intended to do. But to give the Assembly powers in this field would ensure that the veto could not be used to frustrate any action of this sort. So long as the Assembly was able to pass recommendations when the Security Council had failed to do so, it might not matter if these were not binding on all members. Compulsory financial assessments could be reserved for "decisions" of the Security Council under Article 25.

Many other, smaller modifications could be made to reconcile some of the ambiguities and inconsistencies of the Charter. "Intervene" in Article 2(7) could be defined. The relative power of the UN and regional security organizations could be more clearly laid down. The Charter was formulated at a time when the real problems of the postwar world had not yet been revealed. As a result, like some other written documents, it is better fitted to cope with imaginary situations than with real ones. To adapt the UN to the situations actually experienced in the postwar world, rather than those derived from memories of an earlier age, some modifications are now required. Within the foreseeable future, wholesale revision is likely to give rise to almost insuperable difficulties. But for this reason there should be at least some procedure for establishing definitive interpretations of the existing Charter. These could provide the basis for a changing order. For whatever the rules of international law adopted, the most important thing is that they should be capable of expanding and developing to meet new needs.

Conclusions

What then is the role which international law can play within the existing community of nations?

International law was formulated mainly by continental lawyers. From them it acquired the Roman and positivist legal attitudes which, though formally renounced, still largely dictate its form. The attempt to establish an international legal system on this basis demonstrates the misleading effect of trying to create direct analogies between municipal and international law. In an advanced society, where powerful agencies for enforcement exist, effective order may be achieved by the strict application of a code of carefully framed, contractual obligations, written or acknowledged. But in a more rudimentary form of community, a more rudimentary form of law may prove more appropriate.

The international community today has none of the characteristics of an advanced society. It has no central authority wielding superior powers. It has no common cultural, legal, or political framework. And it has no means of making new law to match new conceptions of equity. It is thus most doubtful whether in it a complex and rigidly defined code such as international lawyers have sometimes sought to devise could any more prove to be an effective instrument of social order than a similar system could among a savage tribe. Certainly if, as has sometimes been asserted, a condition of law is its enforceable character, there has never been, is not now, and within the foreseeable future cannot be, an international law in the proper sense of that word.

For a more rudimentary form of organization, without the means of enforcement, the customary law built up from below, as in primitive societies, or the common and case law of the Anglo-Saxon system, provide better analogies. The fact that international law recognizes international custom as one of the many sources of international law does not serve to transform it into such a system. For under international law custom is only accepted as a source of law where it can be shown as evidence of a "general practice accepted as law." "Usage," which in a common law system might be sufficient to provide the basis of law, in international law is expressly disregarded. As a result, adjustment to the changing nature of international society and opinion is especially difficult. Of the three devices that have been recognized as the means for bringing about such adjustments, none has, in the international field, proved satisfactory. Legislation is impossible because no legislature exists. Equity is excluded, since international law does not recognize equity as a source of law. And legal fictions are ruled out by the scrupulous concern of international lawyers for the intention of the drafters, rather than, as is possible in the common law system, for the needs of society. Deprived of the necessary instruments for adjustment, international law has become subject to a retardation which robs it of effective influence.

The change from a legal to a political framework for resolving disputes might, in a community without the means of enforcement, have represented an advance. The transfer of responsibility for formulating rules of international conduct to the ad hoc decisions of UN political bodies could have remedied the defects of traditional international law. Gradually these decisions could build up a body of customary rules and conventions more appropriate to the existing level of international organization than the precise provisions of a comprehensive legal code. Political bodies, so empowered, might find it easier than legal tribunals to apply the legal fictions — or the political expedients — which can make the rules more flexible and more responsive to current international realities.

Lawyers, especially international lawyers, frequently assume there is only one kind of norm: legal norms. In fact the difference between the various types of norm available is essential to an understanding of any social structure, and of the international community in particular. The development of the communal practices, conventions, and morality discussed earlier can only take place if it becomes a conscious concern of political bodies, seeking to examine the norms of conduct necessary to maintain a viable international order. So far not only international law but international organizations have failed, as we have seen, to provide many of the principles required to cover contemporary types of conflict. But only the development, and consistent application, of an appropriate code of international conduct, covering the types of behavior currently favored by nations, is likely to prove a guarantee of social order. The behavior of nations is conditioned by that process, as is that of individuals. Their conduct, equally, may be determined by expectations and conventions as well as interests and desires. Principles of behavior, and procedures of adjustment, may secure the means of taming the aggressive and antisocial instincts of nations as they have of men themselves.

If an effective body of customary rules is to be built up, certain conditions must be fulfilled. First, a far greater consistency than hitherto would be necessary in the decisions and remedies applied by international agencies. Even unwritten law, though it may be flexible enough to adjust itself to a changing society, must be consistent enough to avoid appearing arbitrary. If it seems entirely capricious, it cannot effectively influence behavior. Law must provide the basis for a stable as well as a developing society. Alternations between application of the rules and failure to apply them, among nations as among children, become merely bewildering. Past exceptions will be remembered and quoted, providing a perpetual opportunity for challenge or evasion. The direct association of specific classes of conduct with specific results is totally destroyed. If the strict application of legal procedures carries with it the danger of rigid uniformity, there is an even graver danger that the actions of a primarily political organization may err in the opposite direction.

Second, rules will only be made into effective rulers if it is recognized that an entirely new code is today necessary, more appropriate to the world we live in than that built up over the past two hundred years. This would need to cover those types of action and situation most prevalent in the modern age, on which the accepted body of international law is entirely silent. To counter, and to deter, those forms of behavior most favored in an age of interideological struggle, a new and more detailed rulebook may be required. There are a number of particular principles, in addition to those related to particular types of conflict outlined in earlier chapters, which a contemporary code might need to incorporate.

The first and most elementary arises from the frequency of restricted acts of force, short of outright aggression. The permissibility of these is preserved in the theory, as well as the practice, of international relations. The most recent edition of the best-known British authority on international law (Oppenheim, 1955) holds that "in the absence of a central authority for the enforcement of the law of nations, states have on occasion to take the law into their own hands. Self-help, and intervention on the part of other states which sympathize with the wronged one, are the means by which the rules of the laws of nations can be, and actually are enforced."[9] This principle has been put into practice by governments on a fair number of occasions within the last twenty years, even apart from the more serious cases of aggression. India's decision to bring about the forcible accession of Hyderabad, large-scale acts of retaliation by Israel against towns in Gaza and Syria, British retaliatory raids on Yemen, French action in bombing Tunisian villages and storming Bizerta and boarding foreign merchant ships, Soviet intervention against Poland, United States shows of force in the Mediterranean and Caribbean are all examples, over and above those of outright aggression, of armed action by one state against another without international authority nor even any preliminary attempt to secure redress through international action. The first need perhaps is for UN bodies to seek more consistently to discuss every violation of the obligation under Article 2(4) for members to refrain "in their international relations from the . . . *use of force*" unless wielded in furtherance of a UN resolution. If such a principle is to be established, UN delegations, or the Secretariat (under Article 99), may need to be more consistent than formerly in ensuring that all actions of this type, as well as more serious breaches, are brought to the attention of the UN, and so made subject to the deterrent power of its censure.

It may be almost as important, second, to seek to enforce the Charter's injunction against "the *threat of force*." These threats are common and may serve, almost as much as the actual exercise of force, to increase international tension and promote the danger of more serious conflict. British shows of force against Persia and Egypt, Soviet threats of retaliation with nuclear rockets, mobilizations and countermobilizations over Berlin — such moves, even if intended only as warnings, might, with only a little miscalculation, trigger off conflict on a far larger scale. So far the UN has virtually never sought to enforce the prohibition of the "threat of force" which its Charter contains.

A third principle arises from the close involvement of great powers in conflicts all over the world. This creates a need to isolate each con-

[9] L. Oppenheim, *International Law* (London, 1955), I, 14.

flict that arises from outside influence, and so to insulate it as far as possible from the passions of the ideological and great power conflicts of other areas. The crises in Lebanon and Jordan in 1958 were partly solved by the removal of foreign military forces from the area. At the time of the war in the Belgian Congo in 1960, it was everywhere accepted that an essential object was to keep the struggle free of cold war rivalries. In the Middle East an embargo, or balancing, of foreign military assistance to the region, once discounted, is still urgently required to secure equilibrium today. In other areas where the policy was not followed, as in Laos and Cuba, conflict often proved bitter and protracted. If in such situations the UN were consistently to demand *nonintervention*: to stop the provision of military assistance from outside the borders; to outlaw the dispatch of arms from outside; to forbid the harboring of revolutionary organizations; above all, to proscribe the provision of active military assistance across the frontiers, it might be possible at least to restrict the area and the scale of those types of hostilities most favored in the modern world. And in some cases long-term neutralization, as achieved in Switzerland, Belgium, and Luxembourg in the nineteenth century, and in Austria, Antarctica, and Laos since 1945, may be valuable.

The fourth principle of international action is required to meet the fact that in contemporary conflicts, even where national intervention is condemned, that of individuals may be condoned. The dispatch of "volunteers" from China to Korea and the threat of similar action by the Soviet Union in the Middle East, the participation of United States nationals in uprisings in Indonesia and Cuba, the use of South African, Belgian, Rhodesian, and other mercenaries in the civil war in the Congo — all these examples demonstrate how international military activity may be concealed under the subterfuge of personal initiative. This requires the principle that governments take *responsibility for the acts of their own nationals*. Only if individual nations are ready to use all the means at their disposal to prevent these activities will it be possible to overcome the risks of international wars being fought out by squads of foreign legionaries masquerading in other uniforms. The action of the British Government in threatening to withdraw the passports of British nationals taking part in the civil war in the Congo is an example of the type of action which can be taken by governments to meet such situations.[10]

[10] There already exists in international law a duty to prevent domestic territory from being used as a base for hostile activities overseas. For a discussion of the existing

Finally, the principle already suggested in the case of civil wars may need to be more generally applied. This is to seek, where the situation requires it, to resolve a struggle for authority by consulting popular feelings. For not only civil wars, but most colonial disputes, frontier issues, even some cases of direct aggression, are at bottom disputes over where authority within defined areas should lie. If these are no longer to be determined by contests of strength, new and generally acceptable procedures for that purpose are required in their place. Internationally supervised elections, a procedure almost universally accepted, alone meet these conditions.

These, and others indicated earlier, are only a few of the principles which may become the condition of peaceful coexistence in a community of independent and competitive states. Eventually the type of customary law here described might be codified in more detailed and explicit form.[11] Just as generalized and empty injunctions to individuals ("be good") can have little influence on conduct without detailed rules to implement them, so generalized principles for nations ("be peace-loving," "do not commit aggression") have little meaning without the detailed rules to provide content. Certain principles could be enacted in the form of resolutions in the General Assembly. General resolutions, unanimously adopted, such as those forbidding genocide or the placing of nuclear weapons in outer space, already provide examples of embryonic international legislation of this type. Even though these are not at present formally binding on members, they may, where the majority is sufficient, be

---

law, see M. R. Garcia-Moro, *International Responsibility for Hostile Acts by Private Persons against Foreign States* (The Hague, 1962); H. Lauterpacht, "Revolutionary Activities by Private Persons against Foreign States," *American Journal of International Law*, 1928, pp. 105–130.

[11] Over the last few years, the formulation of some basic principles governing relations between states has been discussed in a Special Committee on Principles of International Law Concerning Friendly Relations and Cooperation Among States of the UN. The seven principles they were asked to discuss were the prohibition of the use of force; the peaceful settlement of international disputes; the duty not to intervene in matters within the domestic jurisdiction of any state; the duty of states to cooperate with one another in accordance with the Charter; the principles of equal rights and self-determination of peoples; the sovereign equality of states; and the principle that states shall fulfill in good faith the obligations assumed by them in accordance with the Charter. The Committee was able, in 1966, to report widely acceptable principles on peaceful settlement and sovereign equality, and some progress on three of the others. The Committee was reconstituted and has been asked by the Assembly to submit a full report, which "will constitute a landmark in the progressive development of codification of these principles." By some such process as this it might be possible eventually to develop the type of code of international conduct that has been suggested here.

difficult to defy with impunity. Where a sufficient degree of agreement existed, it might even prove possible to codify them in formal Conventions. At present such Conventions are binding only on those states which themselves ratify them. But as the international system develops, it might finally become possible for the Assembly to declare that, where the majority, or the number of ratifications, is sufficient, they will be regarded as equally binding on all.

The formulation of an accepted body of doctrine of this type could have effect only if widely publicized. Already the international community has become an increasingly autonomous organism, having its own interests and purposes independent of the interests and purposes of individual states. As publics too become conscious of their interest as members of the wider society, sovereign authorities become more effectively inhibited in their freedom of action. By that process the law of nations ceases to be a law between states. It becomes a law above them.

Bibliography

Brierly, J. L., *The Law of Nations*, Oxford, 1955.

Brownlie, I., *International Law and the Use of Force*, Oxford, 1963.

Corbett, P., *Law and Society in the Relations of States*, London, 1951.

Falk, R. A., *Law, Morality and War in the Contemporary World*, New York, 1963.

Higgins, R., *The Development of International Law through the Political Organs of the U.N.*, London, 1963.

Jenks, C. W., *The Common Law of Mankind*, London, 1958.

Jessup, P. C., *A Modern Law of Nations*, New York, 1948.

Kaplan, M. A., and M. O. Katzenbach, *The Political Foundations of International Law*, New York, 1961.

CHAPTER ELEVEN

Opinion

Opinion as a Social Force

Neither authority nor law is ever entirely independent of opinion. Authority must embody, as a minimum, the opinion of those who exert it: whether a single autocrat, an unrepresentative oligarchy, a small, educated elite, an officer caste, the bourgeoisie, the urban proletariat, or an entire electorate. But it must take at least some account of other opinion. If it outrages the prejudices, the aspirations, the livelihood of the masses, it may find, however overwhelming its own power, that government becomes impossible. It must thus always to some extent conciliate the most vital interests and aspirations of those it governs.[1]

Law too, though it may be partly independent of authority, cannot be altogether independent of prevailing opinion. It cannot entirely ignore inherited traditions and deeply rooted suppositions. Law needs to be applied as well as invented. In primitive societies where customs are enforced by communal bodies, or in more advanced societies where the common law asserts supremacy over royal power, the application of the law usually asserts widely held views and values regardless of the will of ruling monarch or minority. And even in societies in which written law has become the basis of social order,

[1] Cf. David Hume, *Essays*, Vol. I, Essay vii: "As force is always on the side of the governed, the governors have nothing to support them but opinion. It is therefore on opinion alone that government is maintained." Compare also, A. V. Lindsey, *The Modern Democratic State* (London, 1943), p. 94: "The rules which can be enforced in any society depend largely on how far they represent what people are prepared to do. For the State's compulsion . . . can only help to make all men do always what most men are prepared usually to do."

294

the interpretation and developments of such laws has usually reflected the movements of opinion within society as a whole.[2]

But the influence opinion exerts is not usually direct. Authority, so long as its exactions have not been such as to make existence intolerable, has at most times enjoyed a wide degree of independence in its everyday application. Law, so long as it was not altogether incompatible with the traditions or vital interests of the people, has sometimes been remote in its particular demands from the views of the masses. Each might need to be acceptable to certain sections of the population: priests or nobility, army or gentry. But they have usually been sufficiently powerful and self-assured to be independent of the bulk of opinion, which is generally inarticulate or submissive. The main impact of opinion on the acts of governments is thus not through any immediate sanctions it is able to exert. Opinion commands influence because those in authority have usually been, to a greater or lesser degree, subject to the same stream of thought and sentiment which dominates society as a whole. This stream may have derived from a ruling class, from a dominant religion, or a leading school of thinkers. But the values, sentiments, and morality which it makes current among educated sections of the population have been absorbed, willy-nilly, by those who govern. And certainly, to command respect or to win renown, they have been obliged to take some account of the valuations prevalent in the society they ruled.

Opinion, however, may also have influence in areas where neither law nor authority seek to impose themselves. Opinion may be especially crucial in formulating new attitudes, for example, on matters falling on the fringes between previously accepted morality and legal obligation, between sin and crime. Only when these concepts are formally crystallized will they be reflected in the mobilization of new demands, or the relinquishment of old, by authority and law. For the nature of law and authority is essentially sluggish and inflexible. Public opinion is the transmission belt by which these unyielding entities are made to reflect the movements at work within essentially dynamic societies.

Opinion in modern societies is more broadly based than in any previous time. It is more articulate, and it has become more powerful in its impact on the behavior of governments. The spread of education, the rapid social mobility of modern societies, the increasing power

---

[2] Cf. A. V. Dicey, *Law and Opinion in England* (London, 1940), pp. 9–16.

of labor movements, the broadening of the franchise — all these have the effect that the mass of the public has begun, as never before, to influence and even, in a limited sense, to create opinion as well as to receive it. Conversely, the development of representative institutions and widespread lip service to the ideal of democracy have made governments more responsive than before to the direct promptings of opinion. With improved methods of gathering news, the spread of new media of communications, and the growth of political consciousness, the mass of opinion has become better informed and more vocal. On the one hand, therefore, the stream of opinion dominant within society is on more equal terms with and more independent of those in authority than in earlier times. On the other, the decisions of governments reflect more than ever before sentiments and attitudes that are fairly widespread within society.

The role of opinion within the society of nations is especially vital. Because in that society authority and law are both fragmentary, opinion sometimes has to deputize for both. Because there exists there no legislature capable of defining in unambiguous terms rules of conduct which all acknowledge as binding, norms of behavior can only be established, as in other rudimentary societies, by the pressure of opinion within it. Because there exists no coercive authority capable of assuring compliance with its wishes, the only effective sanctions are those which are wielded by international opinion as a whole.[3]

The actions of governments at home are already to some extent conditioned by prevailing domestic opinion. While governments may enjoy considerable independence over some matters, on the most vital decisions of policy they are likely to be at least influenced, consciously or unconsciously, by the attitudes generally held within their society. In the foreign policy field this influence is more marginal but nonetheless significant. For the expectations which, as has been seen, are especially powerful influences on national responses to international events are generally the expectations of opinion as a whole: nationalistic or appeasing, bellicose or pacific. And governments usually share these.

But, even in one nation, opinion is at present not consistent. It is certainly not clear. Above all, it is not always conciliatory. Opinion in different nations is more manifestly conflicting. Thus though the views

---

[3] Cf. Lord McNair, "International Law in Practice," in the *Grotius Society Transactions* for 1946: "It is only by the development of world public opinion directed towards an extension of the realm of law in international relations that the sphere of uncontrolled State discretion, which at present often leads to legal anarchy, can be curtailed."

and actions of governments in the international field may be influenced by opinion, this does not mean, as was once supposed, that they will thereby become peaceful. By obeying opinion, as at present constituted, they would be less peaceful than ever.

Home Opinion and Foreign Policy

What is the kind of influence *home* opinion exerts on governments? Here too some empirical evidence may be obtained, though it is not easy to assess, from public opinion polls and surveys, or from studies of individual issues and decisions.[4]

The home opinion that exerts itself within this field, as in other matters, is not homogeneous. It is composed of a number of different strands of varying breadth and of varying influence. In different types of society the various strands will be of different degrees of importance. Within a single society, the different strands may express varying, even diametrically opposed, viewpoints. Some strands are partisan and emotional, others are informed and detached. The views expressed in the speeches of delegations at New York will not necessarily resemble those expressed in popular newspapers at home. Those expressed in a university common room will bear little affinity to those expressed in the public bar. All together, nevertheless, represent an organic, interrelated whole. Each is to some extent influenced by the movements of the others. All will reflect in different ways the situation in which the nation is placed and the trends to which all are subject. The same general shifts of attitude, the same external events, the same new concepts, slogans, and catchwords enter into the thinking of everybody simultaneously.[5] Though governments are not usually *deflected* by public opinion, they may *reflect* the same movements manifested there.

[4] For studies of the role of opinion in influencing foreign policies, see B. C. Cohen, *The Influence of Non-Governmental Groups on Foreign Policy Making* (Boston, 1959); J. Frankel, *The Making of Foreign Policy* (Oxford, 1963), pp. 70–83; R. C. Snyder, *et al.*, *Foreign Policy Decision-making* (New York, 1962); the Brookings Institution, *The Formulation and Administration of U.S. Foreign Policy* (Washington, D.C., 1960); B. C. Cohen, *The Press and Foreign Policy* (Princeton, 1963); L. Markel (ed.), *Public Opinion and Foreign Policy* (New York, 1949); G. A. Almond, *The American People and Foreign Policy* (New York, 1950); J. Rosenau, *Public Opinion and Foreign Policy* (New York, 1961).

[5] For an analysis of the degree of consensus normally existing on foreign policy, see G. A. Almond, *op. cit.*, pp. 117–120, 158 ff.

It is possible to point to some cases in which home opinion has been of major importance in influencing changes, or even reversals, of a government's foreign policy. One of the best-known cases of this kind is the repudiation of the Hoare-Laval Pact and the resignation of Sir Samuel Hoare as a result of the outburst of indignation in Britain that followed publication of news of the Pact in 1935. In other cases the influence of views known to be widespread among the public may have less dramatic, but more lasting, influence. It is known, for example, that Stanley Baldwin was profoundly influenced in the policies he pursued toward Germany by his knowledge of British opinion expressed in the Fulham by-election and the peace pledge. Similarly, in the hard line it adopted toward China during the early 1950's the United States administration was considerably influenced by knowledge of the strong anti-Chinese sentiments prevalent within the United States press and opinion generally at this period. In many cases opinion cannot guide policy in any direction because it is itself divided between diametrically opposed viewpoints. This was to a great extent true, for example, of British opinion over Russia in the twenties and Germany in the thirties, or over German rearmament and the Suez operation in the 1950's. Sometimes a widespread public reaction against a particular individual may bring about his dismissal and so, indirectly, a change of policy: the downfall of Josef Strauss, the former Defense Minister in Germany, and the consequent decline of the policies he advocated might be regarded as an example of this kind of development. Finally, the degree of influence public opinion can exert will be strictly conditioned by the type of government in power and the degree of its sensitivity to popular opinion: Soviet or Chinese policy can be almost indifferent to public opinion; French foreign policy under General de Gaulle has been little influenced by the powerful expressions of opinion in favor of European institutions, and against the *force de frappe*, in the press and elections in France.

There are many and obvious difficulties in seeking to examine empirically the impact of opinion on government policies in any field. Where a change of policy follows a change in public attitudes, there can be no certainty that the two are causally related. Changes in opinion generally may be *accompanied* by corresponding changes in the opinions and attitudes of decision makers, rather than the cause of such changes. One recent study of six United States Government decisions, including three in the field of foreign affairs, concludes that public opinion does seem to influence public policy on most issues.

It suggests that "public opinion seldom acts positively to promote a new policy, but it often acts negatively to demonstrate its dissatisfaction with existing policies."[6] First, it sets limits to the government's initial decisions and policy making by making clear what the public will stand, and, second, officials will generally be reluctant to maintain existing policies in the face of widespread popular disapproval. The study also notes "the marked tendency of the public to fall in line to support a policy or decision once it has become a *fait accompli*." This is a conclusion that has general application, as can be seen by reference to almost any declaration of war or support for military expenditures (though it is less true of developments that can be fairly easily reversed, such as the Hoare-Laval Pact). Public support for the decision of the United States Government in favor of the Bay of Pigs operation in 1961, even after it had failed, is known through opinion testing (a corresponding finding was made in relation to British public opinion after the Suez operation).

The study also notes that during the earlier stages of the Castro regime in Cuba, opinion "had very little, if any, effect" on United States policy toward Cuba, "partly because of its lack of certainty and unity." This confirms the obvious fact that governments have little reason to be influenced by public opinion if this opinion, as revealed, for example, by newspaper editorials or parliamentary speeches, is hesitant or divided. But the study also suggests that during the early part of 1960 "the mounting hostility of the American people towards the Castro regime seems to have had an influence on policy"; this suggests that a strong wave of popular emotion, especially hostile emotion, is the most likely type of opinion to influence policy in a positive direction (British attitudes to Russia in the late nineteenth century or interwar period, French toward Germany in the twenties, and United States attitudes to China after 1949 are examples). There is another important conclusion, that "in almost all the cases reviewed, the government itself, the President or some government department was often able to influence public opinion considerably, through information, propaganda, and official actions," though public opinion was also influenced by other factors such as "significant events, private interest group propaganda, and the content of the mass media." Thus not only does public opinion influence policy, but policy influences opinion.

[6] H. L. Childs, *Public Opinion* (Princeton, 1964). For a study of the effect of public opinion on Congress, see Markel, ed., *op. cit.*, pp. 85–96.

The effect of home opinion on the policies of governments is therefore not normally simple or direct. There is a mutual interaction. No public is altogether immune from the promptings of leadership. No government is entirely independent of those movements of opinion which make themselves felt within society. The relationship varies widely in different types of societies. In particular, there will be great variations in the type of opinion that is influential. The distinguishing factor will lie, first, in the accessibility to the public of the channels — newspaper articles, broadcasts, speeches — through which opinion may make itself felt on governments; and, second, in the diversity of such channels.

Both these elements are important. *Accessibility* is important since it may determine how deep-sprung is that opinion which can exert influence. In many societies, though genuinely free and democratic, only a very small section of the population in practice ever possesses the opportunity to express its views on matters of public interest. The mass of the public, because it is not in the habit of formulating and expressing opinions on such matters, will tend to accept those views which it reads or hears. It is inclined to consider that affairs of state are best left to those who understand them.[7] It tends to feel it is in any case unable to influence most of the important decisions that are made.[8] Only a very small class of opinion makers — journalists, commentators, politicians, and other professional publicists — normally have the opportunity to make their views known and are thus in the habit of formulating and expressing original opinions on the most important issues of the day. They will usually manufacture the views, the slogans, and attitudes current among society as a whole. The accessibility of correspondence columns, political platforms, and other alternative means of exerting influence thus determines the character of the opinion that receives widespread expression. The type of constitutional system — the existence of a specialized foreign affairs committee, the frequency of debates, the liability of ministers to questions — will also condition the influence opinion can exert and the type which exerts it. So will the educational system, particularly the universities: if academic pronouncements or student movements and demonstrations are powerful (as in Latin America or Indonesia in recent years), they may influence foreign policy more than M.P.'s.

[7] See L. Markel, ed., *op. cit.*, pp. 9–11, 49.
[8] G. A. Almond, *op. cit.*, pp. 83–84.

Similarly a *diversity* of channels is important because this determines how widely spread is the opinion represented, how far it reflects the varying attitudes of disparate interests and groups. Different sections of the population have differing opportunities for making their own interests or views felt. In Britain today, for example, the trades unions are frequently accepted as a fifth estate, with privileged access to the government, able to make frequent public statements. As a result, the views of this section of the population exert a far greater influence than those of housewives, among others, who have no effective channel for expressing their views as a group. In Japan a fairly high proportion of the newspapers, and an even larger proportion of university teachers, are radical or left-wing: this may affect not only the volume of opinion expressed in favor of particular causes, but the opinion current within the public as a whole. In Britain a substantial proportion of the House of Commons are company directors, followed by a considerable number of lawyers, which may mean that the interests and views of these classes, on foreign policy as on other matters, receive more publicity there than those of any other. The fact that in the United States the representatives of the Atomic Energy Commission feel free to give high-powered publicity to their views on certain disarmament problems whereas the State Department, whose views do not always coincide, feels inhibited from using such means may not only give a false picture of the state of American opinion, but may actually influence that opinion in a way it would not be likely to follow if it were told both sides of the case. The fact that in Britain during the thirties lobbies and newspaper interests favorable to Germany were more influential with governments than those favorable to France or Russia may have influenced British policy in that period.

These two factors, the depth and breadth of the opinion that is publicly expressed, seem to be more important in determining if it makes itself felt on governments than how far such governments are "democratic." A system of periodic elections provides only one act of limited choice within several years. Because it is concerned with the entire performance of a government in a wide range of activities over a long period of time, such a choice can never give any indication of views on particular actions or attitudes, nor even on a specific field of affairs. Except at the moment of that choice the mass of opinion in "democratic" societies is never consulted about the actions taken in its name. Since under most modern democratic systems the most important division of powers has been destroyed, and the majority of the peoples' representatives in parliament linked, by close bonds of loyalty and hope of advancement, to the executive, their own influence on government actions is strictly limited. Insofar as governments are influenced by that type of opinion, it is only at their own discretion. On some matters they may pay heed. On many others they will consider it "responsible" to ignore public views. On others they may hope, by "news management" or other methods, to be able to mold the opinion that is generally held.

Indeed it is likely that on a large number of individual foreign policy issues many democratic governments are totally ignorant of the opinion of the mass of society. During elections the entire sphere of foreign affairs will play only an insignificant role. The population as a whole are usually without either the channels or the incentives for the expression of their own views. Correspondence columns in newspapers could only serve to formulate a representative sample of opinion if the letters published were scrupulously chosen as the most representative of those received, rather than as the most original, challenging, well-written, or closest to the views of the editor. Even so they would represent the views only of that section of the population which writes such letters: perhaps the most vocal, enterprising, or self-seeking. Only public opinion polls or regular referenda provide the means by which opinion as a whole, rather than the opinions of specialized opinion makers, could be assessed.

A government may of course be influenced by opinion-making organs, however narrowly based, if it feels these may influence a large section of opinion against it. Thus the most important factor affecting the influence of opinion on governments is the degree of government control over the organs through which it makes itself felt, by which opinion may be guided. (These two forms of control are not identical: it is possible for a strict censorship of individual expressions of opinion to be enforced, even though no attempt is made to mold opinion by other means; or, conversely, for powerful political propaganda to be diffused by a ministry of national guidance or similar organs, even while opposition views are allowed free expression.)

It is the extent of these controls, rather than any difference in formal constitutions or in the popular support which governments enjoy, which provides the essential difference between democratic and totalitarian states. A plebiscite in communist nations today, for example, might show as great a degree of public support for the existing authorities in those countries as a plebiscite in democratic states. It might show that the foreign policies those authorities followed found as wide a measure of favor as those pursued by democratic governments. The real difference is that, while in democracies the actions of governments, even between elections, are necessarily to some extent molded by opinion, in totalitarian states opinion may be to a considerable degree molded by governments. Where opinion can be manufactured, governments come to be largely immune from its influence. Probably even in such states the influence of widespread opinion is more powerful than is generally acknowledged elsewhere. At the very least, the opinion dominant among the party activists and officials exerts some influence on governments.

But the gravest deficiency of opinion as an influence on foreign policy is the lack of specific content in its demands. Even if it is influential with governments, and even if it were mainly peace-loving — neither of which are always the case — it might provide no clear instruction for governments to follow. As we saw in Chapter Ten, the injunction "be peace-loving" gives no specific guide for action; and this will be more than ever so if it is accompanied by the instructions "protect national honor," "avoid appeasement," "defend national security," "defend vital interests," "assist friends," "resist potential aggressors," and others. However passionately it desired peace, opinion could only guide governments if it knew for certain how peace was to be procured. And at present in most countries it has as many different recipes for this as there are holders of opinions. Without clearly conceived and agreed principles of international conduct, whose observance it could consistently demand, it is powerless to influence governments effectively.

Foreign Opinion and Foreign Policy

But opinion at home is no longer the only force which exerts itself on the actions of governments. We need next, therefore, to consider the influence of the *foreign* opinion exerted on governments.

Until recent times, opinion abroad had no appreciable effect of any sort on the policies of governments. For most governments were both ignorant of, and indifferent to, the opinion of peoples outside their own lands. Because foreigners were remote peoples of strange customs and outlandish tongues, their good will was not highly valued.

Because their newspaper articles and statesmen's speeches were little quoted, their attitudes were scarcely known. The opinions influencing the actions of different governments thus consisted of a series of isolated national blocs, each independent of the other. While each could exercise a limited influence on the conduct of its own government, each government — and each opinion — was largely cut off from the influence of opinion abroad.

The isolation which formerly divided these separate blocs of national opinion has today been partly destroyed. Improved means of communication make governments far better aware of reactions elsewhere. More intensive diplomatic contacts and membership in international organizations make them far more concerned over foreign opinion. To satisfy opinion at home at the expense of alienating opinion abroad becomes less and less acceptable in a world of ideological competition. To acquire for their nation the social standing all seek, governments try to make their actions appear roughly in conformity with the standards generally accepted.[9] Because foreign opinion is nearly always one factor that is taken into account, it may sometimes serve to restrain the more extreme response. When fear, jealousy, insecurity, pride, frustration, and ambition become aroused, nations, like individuals, cannot judge their own situation, or determine their own actions, on an objective or rational basis. Pretexts which would appear pitiably flimsy when pleaded by others sometimes appear overwhelmingly convincing for themselves.[10] Foreign opinion may serve in these circumstances as a disinterested judge, a form of social conscience, more consistent, because less volatile, than the temperamental promptings of opinion at home. The social pressures which international opinion exerts on the behavior of nations thus might perform a function comparable to those exerted on the behavior of individuals within societies. A wider consciousness of *external* assessments of the collective role of the nation will modify the way that role appears for each individual within it. And the divergent visions and viewpoints of wholly isolated national states may be modified by the adoption of social judgments derived from the community as a whole.

International opinion itself, however, is by no means a homogeneous entity. It may vary, not only from nation to nation, but according

---

[9] For discussion of the influence of foreign opinion on the policies of governments, see J. Frankel, *op. cit.*, L. Markel (ed.), *op. cit.*, pp. 143–213; J. W. Burton, *International Relations* (Cambridge, 1965), pp. 108–112, 116–118, 152–160.

[10] See the justifications quoted on pp. 308–309 below.

to allegiance, to continental grouping, or to stage of economic development. Nongovernmental opinion may be different from that expressed by governments. The foreign opinion that is nearest at hand may exert quite different pressure from that further afield. Certain sections of it — that of great powers or key neutrals or allies — may count for more than that which is for some reason discounted. Different governments are influenced by different sections of international opinion. Toward incidents concerning small isolated powers, international opinion may take up a uniform attitude. But toward those affecting the main alliances, it may exert partisan and conflicting pressures.

For in the modern world there are new subjective influences perhaps more dangerous than those of national drives and desires. The more ancient forms of national assertion today are increasingly replaced and sublimated in the more respectable, though no less virulent, loyalties and appetites of ideology. Even these may reflect personal psychology. The schizoid-paranoid tendencies which, on a communal level, were formerly expressed in the religious partition of the globe between forces of demons and of angels, of darkness and of light, or of infidels and believers, are often today reflected in a political partition between those who, ideologically, are damned and those who are saved. The persecution complex, which, at the communal level, once found expression in fears of the devil and his machinations, is today revealed in apprehensions of the evil conspiracies of opposing political groups, whether communists, capitalists, or neocolonialists. Within the blocs united by such faiths, opinion may become almost as remote from others as that within each nation once did. Their members may be convinced that any action may be justified if it furthers the interests of the cause: if it promotes the "defeat of reactionary counterrevolutionary forces," the "containment of communism," or the "struggle for national liberation." Such groups are not always bound by ideological ties. The links may take the form of loyalty to regional groupings or of the class solidarity of the nationally underprivileged. If the interests of such groups are sufficiently cohesive and compulsive, their members may be as ready to find justifications for acts of collective self-assertion or self-preservation as are some of the adherents of ideological alliances. Expectations become synchronized *within* each group; but more at variance than ever *between* them.

Here too, therefore, only external opinion will modify the partial judgments of each individual group. Sociological study has long confirmed that in-groups, when isolated, serve by mutual influence to reinforce and strengthen the prejudices of each member. Outside judgments — the uncommitted and nonaligned — can serve as a parameter. Those nations which are not ideologically committed will sometimes pass objective judgment on the behavior of those which are. Those peoples which are geographically remote can sometimes provide an impartial assessment of the actions of distant nations, or groups of nations, embroiled in altercation. These judgments are influential only if they are widely known and so can be accurately anticipated in advance. Where governments are ignorant of the likely response, or able to mislead themselves, international standards are easily swept aside by partisan emotions.

Among such groups and among nations alike, it is those who are closest in touch with foreign opinion who are most likely to be conciliatory in approach,[11] and so to favor concessive policies. Foreign offices are normally more so than defense ministries. Greater knowledge gives a clearer idea of the resistances to be overcome as well as the interests to be recognized.[12] Opinion makers, political leaders, editorial writers, news commentators, and others, if they have this knowledge, sometimes help in guiding the public to greater awareness of the interests of others and so to more balanced and purposeful attitudes and behavior. Outside the state, international authority may equally assist in moderating the delicate and volatile temperament of nations by increasing knowledge of external reactions.

Probably the body of foreign opinion which most immediately influences governments is that expressed in the UN. There is considerable evidence that governments attach some importance to avoiding resolutions of condemnation there. The fact that General Assembly debates are likely to degenerate into popularity contests or exercises in mutual denigration is thus not always to be deplored. For it is precisely by these means that the behavior of governments is subjected to the standards of external opinion as a whole.

[11] Cf. J. Frankel, *op. cit.*, pp. 72–73; L. Markel (ed.), *op. cit.*, pp. 57–59.
[12] For a more detailed analysis of this process, see Appendix I.

Opinion in International Society

How far then do these two factors, home and foreign opinion, working separately on individual governments, serve to strengthen or weaken the basis of international order?

Public opinion at home has certainly not in the past normally been an influence in favor of pacific policies. It was often not consulted on such issues. But, if it was, it was likely to be more, not less, bellicose than governments: more disposed toward coercive rather than concessive attitudes. Popular reactions in France to the Ems telegram, in Britain to the Boer War, in Italy to Fiume and Corfu, in Germany to the humiliations of Versailles were incentives to warlike, not peaceful, decisions. The social conditioning which the competitive nature of the international system had brought about in all nations usually ensured that the mass of opinion would react pugnaciously to situations of humiliation or threat and favorably to decisions in favor of war. The cult of the nation, of national glory and national conquest, the symbols, flags, anthems, emblems, and uniforms, that surrounded this, the systematic veneration of the monarch, the national history and the national name, the glorification of battle and of death for the motherland — all these helped to ensure an enthusiastic response to decisions likely to involve untold death and suffering. Just as in primitive societies decisions to make war, even when initially undertaken by a war leader or group of elders, might be received by all with acclamation, so in the nation state a similar enthusiasm for warlike policies could frequently be counted on — as in the examples just quoted. Indeed, throughout the whole history of nations, there is scarcely a single example of a decision in favor of war that has been rejected, or even criticized, by the majority of public opinion at home. Though occasionally a war that has been inefficiently conducted (Russia in 1917), or long protracted (the United States in 1967), has aroused discontent, this has not applied to its original initiation. The Boer War, the Suez operation, the Indo-China and Vietnam Wars, are examples of wars that have been strongly disapproved by considerable sections of the population, but these have always been minorities consisting mainly of intellectuals. Thus, whether or not opinion was influential, it could not influence governments in favor of peaceful policies because opinion itself was not normally pacific. The conditioned reflexes of patriotism, the communal morality of the nation state, served to justify policies and decisions, joint activities and individual deeds, which purely personal morality would have found unbearably repugnant.

Over recent years this distorting lens of patriotism may have begun, in some areas at least, to lose some of its potency. Only fifty years ago the public assertion by national leaders of military ambitions or expansionist policies was commonplace. Thinkers seriously declared that only the selective influence of war could preserve the human race from degeneration. Throughout the first forty years of this century, Japanese statesmen, generals, and writers openly asserted the aggressive ambitions of their nation against its neighbors. During the thirties the ruler of the Italian people, in repudiating the disarmament conference then in progress, declared that he did not believe in the possibility or the advantages of perpetual peace and eulogized the ennobling influence of war. German statesmen in the same period made speeches glorifying war and imploring German motherhood to intensify their productive efforts to provide the material for future German armies. Elsewhere declarations were made which, though more restrained in language, were little less inflammatory in effect.

Such statements are uncommon today. Current conventions are almost unanimous that "peace" is desirable. All unite in denouncing "war." The difficulty is in knowing what those terms denote. Statesmen and their publics are no doubt sincere in their distaste for "war" as a general principle. But general principles permit exceptions in particular cases. Such exceptions tend to concern the particular wars undertaken by one's own nation. These are in the interests of peace or to prevent war. Or they are not wars at all, but "peace-keeping operations," "security actions," "liberation struggles," or "freedom-fighting." Abstract condemnations of the concept "war" will rarely influence attitudes and decisions when war appears necessary; any more than abstract disapproval of "ill temper" affects the temper when it is aroused.

Thus the change, though certainly significant, is not so profound as it at first appears. Even today governments still hold in particular cases that the use of armed force is justifiable. There are numerous examples over the last few years of such justifications. Statesmen have been ready to support such action to protect vital interests of security: as when the President of the United States declared in 1961 that "if the nations of this hemisphere should fail to meet their commitments against outside Communist penetration then . . . this government would not hesitate in meeting its primary obligations which are to the security of our own nation." They have justified it to overcome colonialist or otherwise unrepresentative forces: as when the leaders of communist parties from all over the world declared in 1960 that "all the socialist countries . . . recognise their duty to render the fullest moral and material assistance to the peoples fighting to free themselves from imperialist and colonial tyranny." Or to ensure respect for international obligations and preserve national interests: as when the British Prime Minister asserted in 1956 that nothing in the Charter abrogated a government's right "to take such steps as are essential to protect the lives of their citizens and vital international rights." Or to remedy the injustices of imperialism: as when the Indian Prime Minister claimed in 1961 that Portugal's refusal to negotiate had made the use of force over Goa "the choice . . . of a lesser evil." In the modern world the concept of the "just war" may thus be merely replaced by the concept of a justifiable use of armed force. And the national self-righteousness of earlier years has often only been replaced by an ideological self-righteousness that is almost as aggressive.

Opinion has never seriously contested such claims. Often, as we have seen, the situation is genuinely ambiguous. It may be believed that armed action has already been assisted or engineered by another party. There may be doubt whether a conflict is purely domestic or partly international. There may be differences over what measure of outside support for the respective contestants in a civil dispute is acceptable. In such circumstances opinion, even though perhaps more peace-loving, more informed, and more influential than ever before, exerts no effective influence. For it is itself uncertain.

Within this category of ambiguous conflicts especially, therefore, distorting lenses continue to dictate judgments. Where no clear principles are recognized, assessments tend to be swayed by ideological or national predilections. Home and foreign opinion now come to diverge. Activities that seem legitimate when conducted by friends appear unpardonable when undertaken by enemies. Many in the United States will condemn assistance to a guerrilla movement in Indo-China, but commend it in Cuba. Many in China think traditional rights of sovereignty outweigh the current balance of loyalties in Formosa, whereas in other colonial territories the reverse is asserted. Many in Britain upheld the refusal of a colonial government to negotiate with rebels under threat of force in Cyprus but condemned it as reactionary and unrealistic in Algeria or Angola. Many in India proclaimed self-determination for Goa but deny it for Kashmir. Such examples could be indefinitely multiplied. There exist no clearly enough established principles to help maintain consistent standards. Opinion, both within nations and between them, is without the objective standards for pronouncing on national behavior.

Conclusions

The hope, once widespread, that opinion could, alone and in itself, be the guardian of peace is based on a misapprehension. Its failure, in the era when most was hoped from it, sufficiently proved that opinion is powerless unless guided and focused by an effective code of action. The *desire* for peace is no influence for peace at all. Principles are powerless without opinion to enforce them. But opinion is equally helpless without the detailed and explicit principles that are its only weapons.

To be effective, such principles need to be widely disseminated. Only explicit formulation and deliberate publicizing in international resolutions, in understandings among governments, and in the education of publics could insure that the code was influential. Only when it becomes deeply instilled in this way, is it likely to be sufficiently deeply internalized to be influential in times of crisis and emotion. The creation of *new* principles and norms is especially dependent on the positive influence of international bodies. Rules that only *reflected* opinion would be not only incoherent and divided, but might well be never-changing.

Only when principles are thus established and understood, is opinion, at home and abroad, an effective influence. The ineffectiveness of the existing system of international law does not derive mainly from the character of the order it enforces, nor from the lack of coercive power to enforce it, but from the fact that it is divorced from the final sanction of opinion. Even if it possessed forceful sanctions, it would remain dependent, like other legal systems, on its acceptability to opinion as a whole. Without sanctions it is more than ever so.

But international law is largely unknown. And even where they know it themselves, governments have no difficulty in disregarding it when they find it inconvenient or in finding rationalizations to plead its inapplicability, precisely because they know it has as little influence on the thinking of their publics as it has on their own. Scarcely even conscious of its content, publics cannot demand its respect. What ultimately influences governments is not what they believe the law to be, but what they believe the opinion they value demands of them. By its remoteness from general opinion, international law, however revered by lawyers, has failed to acquire the only attribute which, in default of sanctions, might give it potency.

One of the main characteristics of opinion as a sanction is its virtually inescapable character. Among individuals, some may be ready to defy physical and other sanctions, but few can remain totally indifferent to the force of general public disapproval. Among nations too, some may deny or defy the authority of an international court, or the force of a General Assembly resolution; but they cannot escape, and will rarely totally ignore, for long, the pressures of world opinion as a whole if this is exerted with sufficient consistency and power. But the condition of this influence, in both spheres, is that a single set of standards, with common norms, is influential for all.

Bibliography

Almond, G. A., *The American People and Foreign Policy*, New York, 1950.

Beloff, Max, *Foreign Policy and the Democratic Process*, Baltimore, 1955.

Brookings Institution, *The Formulation and Administration of U.S. Foreign Policy*, Washington, 1960.

Buck, P. W. (ed.), *The Control of Foreign Relations in Modern Nations*, New York, 1957.

Childs, H. L., *Public Opinion*, Princeton, 1964.

Cohen, B. C., *The Influence of Non-Governmental Groups on Foreign Policy Making*, Boston, 1959.

———, *The Press and Foreign Policy*, Princeton, 1963.

Elder, R. E., *The Policy Machine*, Syracuse, 1960.

Markel, L. (ed.), *Public Opinion and Foreign Policy*, New York, 1949.

Padover, S. K., *U.S. Foreign Policy and Public Opinion*, New York, 1958.

Rosenau, J. N., *National Leadership and Foreign Policy*, Princeton, 1963.

CHAPTER TWELVE

Peace

It is not the purpose of this study to lay down the international law. New codes of international behavior can be formulated only through the collective procedures available for that purpose within international organizations. All that can be shown here is that new norms of conduct are required: that the laws of Grotius can no more cater for the types of international crime now favored than the statutes of Charles I's day could provide against the delinquencies favored in twentieth-century society. New taboos must be related to the forms of social intercourse which prevail. They must consider the way nations do, as well as the way they should, behave. If attempts to create a more peaceful system of international interaction are to be successful, therefore, the same techniques may need to be applied to the study of the behavior of nations as are applied to that of individuals. There is no branch of sociology so important to mankind as the study of the psychology and social habits of nations, and none that has been so neglected. Yet without some such empirical approach, it is likely that many of the efforts made to pacify the self-destructive urges of nations will fail in their purpose.

There is no field in which the attractions of a nonempirical approach are so compelling. Mankind's deepest aspirations — for security, love, for life itself — provide in advance Utopian pictures of that type of society which we all aspire to, and which we should like to believe, with sufficient good will, could easily be brought into being: a world in which nations live together in unchanging harmony, in which all weapons of destruction were abolished, or in which a secure and unchanging equilibrium was assured. But the fact that a condition is desirable does not prove that it is attainable. And the drawback of such imaginative exercises is that they tend to omit from the picture the obstacles that lie in front of the goal. Practical schemes must consider means as well as ends, map out the route as well as the goal. The most successful routes in this case are likely to be discovered only through careful examination of the way nations in practice behave. A science of international relations may be able to contribute by analyzing the nature of current national conduct, and so of an international order consistent with the observed behavior of states.

The attempt to achieve a more peaceful world by the laborious and uncertain method of reforming the behavior and procedures of nations may seem, by comparison with the destruction of arms or the establishment of a world government, at once unexciting and over-ambitious. But it may be a task more relevant to modern needs. Within the foreseeable future no disarmament or arms control agreement is likely to reduce the total available destructive power even to the level of twenty or thirty years ago, much less to a level below that necessary to wage the limited conflicts of the present age. Nor are attempts to establish a world authority with overwhelming power likely of attainment. Because, as has already been seen, warlike conduct is culturally conditioned — a product of the society within which nations move — it is changes in that environment that will be ultimately effective in regulating this conduct. There seems little reason to doubt that nations are as susceptible to the normative influences of the society they dwell in as individuals within theirs. By these means a community may be established in which violation of the established norms may appear as eccentric an aberration as deeds of violence within the state.

The function of a mutually recognized code of this kind is to *harmonize* expectations in such a way that clashes of expectations and the violence that results no longer occur. The development of a consensus concerning the external relationships of states is not dependent, as is sometimes suggested, on a corresponding consensus on the principles of government within them. The consensus required concerns only limited principles of international interaction which do not presuppose identity of values in other spheres. Nor does it necessarily demand any close sense of community between states. Indeed there would appear to be no near relationship between a sense of community and a capacity for peaceful coexistence. The fact that a large proportion of the wars of recent years have been civil wars within communities of relatively homogeneous culture and stock itself indicates that a sense of community is no guarantee against disorder. Conversely, other states and areas have remained relatively peaceful without any large measure of cultural uniformity.

Whether or not any sense of community between nations exists, a consensus on the principles of interaction between states will be necessary if peace is to be sustained. Although this consensus is required between governments in the first place, it can be sustained only if understood by the public opinions which influence governments.

Sometimes, it may be contended, armed conflict is the effect of dissensions concerning basic conceptions of justice and order, which no system of conventional arrangements could influence. Here even the premise is not certain. Conceptions of justice and order (like conceptions of jealousy, honor, or pride) may themselves be socially derived. The establishment and inculcation of common expectations concerning the basis of international relationships may influence that sense of justice, as other expectations do. Moreover a system of order between states does not necessarily imply that peace is valued above justice. It recognizes only the need for more impartial agencies of justice than armed might.

It is true that the effectiveness of such a system presupposes placing the belief in international order at a fairly high level among the total hierarchy of values. Without this, dissension, even on matters not related to interaction between states, might become the cause of international conflict. For however sentiments of justice concerning *national* rights may be harmonized, it is improbable that a corresponding harmony of conceptions concerning *individual* rights or internal political systems will quickly come about. This would involve an extension of the area of consensus, and a standardization of values within the world community, that few would welcome. For this reason the ancient principle that the internal order of states is not normally subject to forcible intervention from without remains a vital one, even within an integrated and perpetually interacting community of nations. Although elementary human rights must be everywhere protected, above all the right of each individual to choose his own political system, the principles that govern other elements of personal interaction may long continue to diverge. To this extent the reconciliation of international order with a diversity of values demands the *retention*, not the abandonment, of sovereignty.

It is precisely to safeguard diversity that principles of order are required. The tolerance of dissident values required here is not different in kind from that required within states, however unified and highly organized. Coexistence, between states as within them, is dependent on a high level of mutual toleration.

Intolerance cannot be abolished by decree. It springs perhaps more than any other human quality from the deepest springs of personality. But self-knowledge may reduce its effects. It is those who have lived exclusively within a narrow environment who tend to assume most automatically the absolute superiority of their own system and the values acquired within it. Greater knowledge may both modify those views and increase awareness of the relativity of all such opinions. If the Hobbesian solution of value conflicts — setting up a conventional authority to determine them for all — is today unacceptable or impossible, the corollary is to accept the *fact* of diversity; and so renounce the luxury of applying individual standards to other men and other societies. The object then becomes not to smooth away differences, but to live with them. Not compromise, but tolerance.

It is indeed an overinflamed sense of justice that has above all destroyed the basis of tolerance in the past and been responsible for a large proportion of the violence that has defiled man's history. Its moderation demands, as a first step, recognition that all conceptions of justice are by definition subjective. The sympathetic imagination, which is at the root of all moral sentiments, is here extended not merely to the *situation* of others, but to their conceptions of justice as well. The true justice is then the recognition of others' sense of justice. The ultimate justice becomes a balancing of justices.

There are signs that even now a slightly more pacific international society may be emerging. Already the most heinous international crimes may be less prevalent. If this has come about, it is perhaps no great credit to man. It is fear, not love, which has brought him to reason.

But if fear has outlawed big wars, it may, too, outlaw small ones. For governments today fear opinion as well as bombs. If not coerced by it, they can at least be influenced. Properly equipped, opinion could wield sanctions as powerful in their way as those of arms. It may establish a commonly expected structure of relationships to become, here too, the foundation of a harmonious order. So eventually a society may be created in which arms themselves become, like revolvers for the law-abiding citizen, a cumbersome and costly superfluity.

General Conclusions

Below are set out the main empirical conclusions of this study having a bearing on the theory of international relations.

1. During the present century, there has been a marked decline in wars by the forces of one state against the acknowledged territory of another: from about twenty-two in twenty-five years a century ago to sixteen, fifteen, and nine in each succeeding period (pp. 62–64).

2. Where external wars have occurred it has been increasingly for coercive or for irredentist, rather than territorial, motives, and they have often been limited in form (pp. 65, 68). Whether this results from will or necessity, it probably represents, or has brought about, a genuine shift in the fundamental motivations of states.

3. On the other hand, a large and increasing number of conflicts in the modern world are domestic in origin, being either the effect of movements of subject peoples for independence, or civil wars (Chapters Six, pp. 142–146, and Seven, pp. 183–185). A number of these involve some external intervention. This too probably reflects a basic change of motivation among states, from desire to win direct physical control over particular territories to desire to win indirect political control.

4. The great majority of wars have involved single nations on either side (pp. 67, 185). With one or two exceptions, they have also almost all been started by a single government rather than by a group or an alliance (*ibid.*).

5. Most wars seem, especially since 1945, to arise out of specific incidents and disputes, rather than to be the effect of deliberate policies of aggrandizement or aggression by governments (pp. 65–66). External wars are more often undertaken to restore a status quo previously disturbed (Guatemala, Hungary, Suez, Cuba [1961, 1962], Kashmir

316

[1965]) than to change it (Korea, Goa). Even the latter are felt to re-establish the lost national unity (pp. 68–69).

6. A number of the wars of the modern period have arisen from the security apprehensions of great powers concerning the areas immediately adjacent to their borders (pp. 69–71).

7. There have, however, also been a considerable and increasing number of limited conflicts concerning frontiers, a number that has tended to increase rather than decrease (pp. 96, 100–102). Nations seem more inclined to make war over issues of this kind, however small the intrinsic value of the territory, than over issues of trade, tariffs, or investment that are far more important to their basic interests (pp. 41, 99).

8. Nations do not appear to be decisively influenced by considerations of the power balance in reaching decisions to go to war. Wars have often been undertaken against overwhelmingly superior forces, or when the balance was very evenly matched (p. 173).

9. Perhaps for this reason, balance of power systems, insofar as they have been pursued at all, have not been successful in procuring peace (pp. 173–175). In fact the number of external wars when this system was at its height (1750–1914) was probably higher than in any other period before or since.

10. There is little evidence that the political complexion of the government in power significantly affects its likelihood to resort to war (p. 66).

11. There is little evidence that economic factors are a significant influence in causing war (pp. 65–66). Poverty does not seem to be in itself a cause of war, except possibly of internal war: external wars have been started as often by highly developed as by less developed countries. But new states may be rather more subject to war (pp. 57–58). Frontier conflicts, as might be expected, occur frequently among new states (pp. 95, 99).

12. The countries most active in fomenting civil war elsewhere have been recently established radical governments founded through revolution, especially when surrounded by hostile neighbors, such as the Soviet Union between the wars, China, Egypt, Cuba since (p. 145).

13. But large-scale intervention in civil wars occurs more frequently to defend governments than to overturn them, and this object has in most cases been achieved (p. 143).

14. No nation has initiated a war against a nuclear power (p. 186).

15. Nations have still not proved capable of reaching agreements for mutually acceptable balances of arms (Chapter Eight). Nations that are rising in power are especially reluctant to contemplate agreements of this kind (pp. 204–210).

16. The agreements so far reached on disarmament and arms control have provided for only marginal restrictions in power, and never any actual reduction, usually among a few powers only (pp. 221–222). They have been reached primarily at periods of low political tension (pp. 222–223).

17. A balance of power has rarely been pursued for its own sake. Normally each state seeks the maximum possible power for itself (pp. 171–174).

18. A collective security system has never yet been effectively put into practice (pp. 174–176).

19. Conflict is especially common in ambiguous situations where sovereignty is obscure (pp. 66–67) or the international rulebook is unclear (passim, pp. 76–78, 127–130, 154–157, etc.).

Although some of the implications of these conclusions have been noted in the text, it may be worth bringing them together here.

Balance of power. Because nations are not decisively influenced by considerations of balance in crisis situations and because it is very difficult to construct a credible balance that holds for all powers, all alliances, and all situations, a balance of power system, even if it were made a self-conscious and consistent policy of states, is unlikely to be effective in securing peace. This is especially so in the modern world, where so many wars are at least partly internal. For here the balance of *effective* power may be quite different from the *external* power in theory available. In particular it is difficult for accurate anticipation of the balance to take place, and it is this anticipation that is decisive in making the system work. The balance between a guerilla force and sophisticated weapons may be especially difficult to calculate.

Deterrence. Some of the same considerations apply to deterrence. While deterrent power and deterrent policies may inhibit the use of the most powerful weapons available where the possession of these is mutual, they will not necessarily affect the use of lesser degrees of power, where the response cannot be certainly anticipated. Deterrence is particularly difficult to bring to bear in cases of internal war, where it may be hoped that all outside powers will remain uninvolved, and where the level of activity may be on a totally different scale from that of the main deterrents wielded. Deterrence may therefore require to be exerted at several different levels.

Bipolar system. Theoretically if the world were divided, or largely divided, into two cohesive blocs, each equipped with roughly comparable power, and each resolved to make use of that power in any case of conflict, there would be a considerable chance of maintaining peace through the mutual desire to avoid all-out global conflict. In practice, it will very rarely be possible to create blocs so cohesive that a united response by all members to any incident, however small, in whatever part of the world, will appear credible to the other bloc. Nor can individual acts by particular members be prevented (Suez, Korea, Offshore Islands, Cuba). Nor, usually, will the world be universally mobilized into blocs of this kind: though, for a period from 1950 to the early sixties the majority of the more developed countries of the world were so involved, even this did not serve to prevent minor conflicts occurring, and there always remained large areas on the periphery, within the Afro-Asian world, which were not included. Especially when new great powers emerge, such as China today, the effectiveness of such a system must decline.

Collective security. The possibility of a collective security system is fatally weakened by the fact that such a system so far has never been effectively operated. The system depends to a crucial degree on the credibility of the collective response of all the international community against the alleged "aggressor." Nations contemplating conflict may in most cases be fairly confident that such a response will not prove possible to organize. In addition they may be able to rely on ambiguity concerning the action, or over which nation is the aggressor.

Collective enforcement. Many of the same difficulties surround this system, which is that nominally established in the UN Charter. Here too, whatever the words of the Charter, it may prove difficult to mobilize a powerful joint response in answer to the Security Council's call, and here too it may prove difficult to identify the aggressor effectively. Once again the lack of success in the past weakens deterrence. National interest is often too marginal to ensure response.

It is unlikely that the international system at any one time can ever be satisfactorily classified under any simple heading of this type. The current system has elements of all of these systems. It is perhaps best described as a community of independent units, with a high degree of intercommunication and subject to many common influences, but possessing no overwhelmingly powerful central authority.

Conclusions. The fact that within this community wars so often occur as a result of the specific decisions of governments concerning specific incidents suggests that one of the most important means of securing a more peaceful community must be through effective machinery for the management of crisis situations to limit conflict. The fact that these incidents often concern the internal situation in particular states suggests that the principle of securing the insulation of internal political situations from outside intervention is an important one. The fact that nations, especially large nations, so often react violently to situations in countries on their borders that seem to imperil their security suggests a need both for the international community and individual states to show special concern to avoid provocations of this kind. The fact that conflict so often occurs in ambiguous situations for which the present international rulebook makes no provision suggests the need for a more accurately defined body of community rules and conventions to guide national responses in such situations. Only this could provide the kind of equilibrium which is finally required in international relations, the equilibrium of expectation.

Appendix I

Conflicts of Motives Among States

The goals pursued by states may be divided into two categories. Action designed to increase certain values for an individual state may bring about a corresponding increase in that value for other states. For example, activity designed to increase equilibrium, or international trade, or peace, for one state will automatically produce a similar increment in these for others (at least some others). Among individuals such values as love, social intercourse, and friendship have the same effect. Others, on the other hand, are opposite in effect. For these, attempts by one state, or person, to maximize the value for itself, will automatically reduce the corresponding value for others. An attempt by any state to increase its *relative* status, influence, popularity, or power, must, by definition, bring a corresponding reduction in the same value for some or all other states. Among individuals the desires for prominence, power, or wealth normally compete with those of others. Here the values are *subtractive* rather than *additive*.

Clearly, both nations and individuals possess numbers of values, some of which fall into either category. It is likely, therefore, that all or most will be in some degree, or in some matters, cooperative and in some competitive. And the relative degree to which this is so will depend, for men and for nations alike, on the *mix*, or hierarchy, of the values and interests they pursue. No system of analysis that assumes the nature of nations to be "essentially" one or the other is likely to prove satisfactory among nations any more than among individuals.

The fact that in a particular sphere men, or nations, have interests in common does not of course prove that they perceive this; or that they acquire either desires or forms of activity appropriate to the interest concerned. The fact that a value hierarchy or a system of interaction is *predominantly* competitive may serve to condition the way a nation or individual seeks to realize values in the majority of contexts, whether or not this is the most appropriate. The existence of a predominantly competitive form of interaction between states may cause them to seek to maximize wealth by competitive means (such as tariff protection, or autonomous investment) when they might in fact maximize that value more effectively by cooperative measures (such as expanded international trade or external invest-ment). This fact accounts for many policies of states in the period of maximum nationalism between 1815 and 1945.

But interaction between states will be affected not only by the values and objectives which they hold, or perceive, but by the *means* they adopt to secure these. Two basic types of means are available in any human situation in which individuals or groups, having varying or conflicting views or interests, come into interaction. In all such situations the individual or group, irrespective of the nature of its goals and values, may seek (whether consciously or unconsciously) to assure its own goals and values without modification, so that to the maximum degree attainable all concessions necessary for adjustment are made by the other parties; this may be called an essentially *coercive* attitude or policy. In this case the objective may be pursued either by physical force; by manipulation, that is, by seeking through direct but nonforcible action on antagonists to bring them to submission; by intrigue, that is, by action directed to third parties designed to secure the submission of the second party; or by persuasion, that is, by seeking to bring about a voluntary but total concession by the other party. Or the course adopted may be one in which it is recog-nized from the start that to bring about an acceptable interaction the subject must himself be ready to make modifications in his basic goals; that is, an essentially *concessive* policy or approach. In this case the objective may be sought either through bargaining, which recog-nizes that a modification of initial demands may be required; through unilateral concessions, made in the hope of counterconcessions from the other side; or through accommodation, tacit understandings, and compromises by which each party obtains as much as it thinks reason-able compared with the demands of others.

Most individuals and groups will adopt positions somewhere between these two extremes. But there will be sharp differences over how far coercive or concessive attitudes are adopted in particular subjects or fields. Whether a predominantly coercive or concessive policy is adopted by individuals may depend on many factors. It will depend on basic personality traits, deriving from innate and early acquired characters; on the culture within which the particular confrontation takes place, encouraging a basically competitive or cooperative approach (in most developed societies internal political procedures are such as to encourage a recognition that interest groups and individuals will rarely attain their original demands unmodified, whereas in the international field, at least until recently, the reverse has applied); on knowledge of the other party's will or demands, which may serve not only to induce *realism*, better understanding of the difficulties of securing one's own objectives, but *recognition* of the rights and aspirations of others, so that there will be greater readiness to concede; on the image of the other party, that is, whether he is conceived as wholly hostile, so that there is a pre-existing disposition to conflict, or as morally antipathetic, in which case there may be felt a moral as well as personal duty to resist his demands, irrespective of content; finally, on the fields of activity concerned, which may be conceived as competitive or cooperative (so that groups may be ready to adopt a concessive approach in matters connected with social relations, but not in those associated with economic affairs; or to accept international cooperation in the field of trade but to resist it in the field of immigration). The way in which ends are conceived is the crucial point. Sometimes even a total failure to achieve the desired ends will be regarded as preferable to modifying even slightly ends themselves conceived as "good."

Governments, like individuals, clearly adopt sometimes coercive, and sometimes concessive, attitudes and policies for achieving their ends. Which of the two predominates will depend, here too, on the field of action concerned, the personality traits of leaders or nations, and, above all, on the general culture within which governments operate. It varies also over time, with perhaps a slow increase of concessive over coercive attitudes. This trend results mainly from an increase in knowledge and awareness (the third factor mentioned above) brought about by the development of communications. Those who have no full awareness of others and their rights (like the psychopath, or the ultranationalist state) will adopt coercive behavior. Awareness brings, among nations as among individuals, both greater realism concerning the difficulties and costs of coercive action, and greater recognition of the rights and desires of other states. In general, governments will be more affected by these developments than their populations; and for this reason will normally also be more conscious than they of the value of concessive rather than coercive policies. Only where populations achieve the same knowledge of the desires of other states and the necessary means of reconciling values and desires as their governments, therefore, are they equally favorable towards concessive behavior.

Appendix II

United Nations Procedures for Crisis Situations and Their Functions

At the immediate outbreak of conflict, the most commonly used procedure is immediate *discussion*. The Secretary General has the right to draw the UN's attention to matters likely to lead to dispute and any members, as well as those involved, may raise them. The effect is that each combatant is made subject to international influences. At the immediate outbreak of an incident, international discussion is especially valuable since it may sometimes be easier to bring about some modification of attitudes at this time than later, when positions have hardened and concessions become more difficult. At present, however, a very large proportion of the cases of violence that occur never reach the UN at all. Of the list of postwar cases on pp. 183–185, less than half have even been considered in the UN. Even of the wars of direct aggression, one, that against Guatemala, was never substantively discussed because of pleas that it should be considered by regional bodies alone. That against Goa received only perfunctory discussion, owing to the widespread reluctance of many members to condemn that action. Comparable actions, such as that of China against India's borders, intense hostilities in Laos, the war in Vietnam, and incidents in Berlin, have never been considered. The UN often behaves as though only an aggrieved party has the right to bring a dispute before it. In fact the Charter is explicit that any member may bring any dispute or "any situation which might lead to international friction or give rise to a dispute" to the attention of either the Security Council or the General Assembly.

Next, there are procedures to bring about *communication* between the parties themselves. Even in public form, that is within an open UN meeting, this may be useful in bringing parties together and making them subject to international pressures. The need for the participants in the Suez adventure to explain themselves publicly in this way may have contributed to the early Israeli agreement to cease fire and the subsequent British decision to withdraw, which without such contacts might not have taken place. The recommendation by UN bodies of specific interim solutions may modify wholly self-formulated objectives. Continued communication between the disputing governments, which international bodies may facilitate, provides opportunities for bargaining, and for modification of original positions and objectives. These have rarely been easily available in previous ages once conflict had started.

Next, action can be taken by the Secretary General or his officials to promote *conciliation*. The negotiations undertaken under the Secretary General's auspices over the Berlin blockade and the Suez Canal, and the contacts he facilitated between Chinese and Western officials at the beginning of the Korean War are examples of the types of informal action which, though not wholly successful in these cases, could often promote a settlement. Mediators appointed for Palestine, Kashmir, and Cyprus have had varying success. The confidential nature of such exchanges and the noncommitted position of UN officials may play a vital part in bringing forward compromise positions that are morally difficult to resist.

The next need which often arises is for exact, on-the-spot information about a situation. Such forms of *verification* may be undertaken by the dispatch of observers or a fact-finding mission. Though it may not always be feasible after the event to discover exactly how an incident took place, in certain cases it may be possible (as in Korea) to anticipate trouble by sending a commission to the spot. Other information may be vital: to know the nationality of the forces involved (as in Katanga, Guatemala, or Indo-China), whether they come from outside the borders or within (as in Greece, South Vietnam, or Malaysia), from where their arms are obtained (as in Laos, Yemen, or the Congo).

For investigations of more long-term and general nature a commission of *inquiry* may be sent. This may consider not only immediate military but underlying political factors. It may assess the general attitude of the population (as in the Borneo territories of Malaysia in 1963); it may consider particular technical or economic problems (as used in the currency regulations applied in Berlin in 1948); it may supervise the general enforcement of law and order in the area (as used in the Indo-China territories in 1954); finally, it may make more sweeping inquiries and recommendations on political matters in dispute (as in Korea from 1946–50).

In other cases the important need is for *stabilization* of a position already agreed to in principle. Here the dispatch of a more permanent force of observers (as in Lebanon in 1958) or a UN presence (as in Jordan in 1958 and in Laos in 1959) may exercise a restraining influence. In the most extreme situations of this kind, though probably rarely where fighting is to be expected or already taking place, a UN peace force may be dispatched as a stabilizing influence (as in the Congo, Cyprus, and West Irian).

Finally, in certain cases, it may be possible to secure the agreement of both parties to *adjudication* of the issues in dispute by some mutually acceptable procedure. Especially, but not only, in cases where the point at issue is primarily legal, international bodies may suggest the submission of the dispute to arbitration, that is, to decision by some mutually acceptable third party (as Argentina and Chile did in submitting their frontier dispute to arbitration by the British queen, that is, to a legal commission appointed by her). Or they may recommend a judgment by the International Court of Justice (as was done in the case of the border dispute between Thailand and Cambodia).

For a comparison of the *effectiveness* of various international procedures, see Appendix IV.

Appendix III

The Special Nature of International Authority

Certain special features distinguish the authority asserted in the international field from that elsewhere.

First, there is the *diffuseness* of decision making in the international community. An authority that is to be effective must have speedy and reliable procedures for reaching decisions in time of crisis. Within national governments, the vital decisions and initiatives in a large number of fields are reached by intimate bodies, of limited numbers — cabinet or council of ministers — meeting at frequent intervals and in private. Even if final decisions are nominally that of a larger body — the national legislature or electorate — in practice the function of these is increasingly that of discussing and confirming, but not reversing, decisions already reached by the executive body. The executive itself, however, is under a standing obligation to explain and defend its decisions outside, not only to legislature, but to press and public beyond. This remains true, at least to some extent, even where nondemocratic forms of government are practiced. Because in practice decisions are almost never reversed, the two processes of *decision* and *discussion* become increasingly separate and distinct: decision first, discussion afterward.

In consequence, there rapidly emerges within the decision-making group a sense of close solidarity against those before whom they must justify themselves, a solidarity which may soon become greater than that which binds them to members of their own party within the legislature or elsewhere. The division between cabinet and chamber becomes bigger than that dividing the parties. Where there is a coalition of divergent groups, or committees composed of different parties, as in local government, the loyalty that binds the group together will often displace that to individual parties. This improves the efficiency of decision making but further differentiates the procedures of decision and discussion.

In the international field, these two processes are undertaken by the same bodies. And the two are combined (in Security Council or General Assembly discussions) in a single process. That process, moreover, takes place, not in private as in a cabinet, committee, or civil service, but in public. This means it is far more difficult for those involved to abandon a posture of partisan antagonism for the sake of a common front (as members of a local government committee of different parties often do); or to abandon committed positions for the sake of a decision (as conflicting ministers in a cabinet may be ready to do).

Second, the corresponding need for joint *justification* by decision makers before a common public never arises, since the original decision has been undertaken in public and has become inextricably fused with the process of discussion. The effect is that it becomes extremely difficult to build up any close sense of solidarity, or identity, within the decision-making group. The divisions *within* the decision-making bodies, such as the Security Council or General Assembly, are far more important than the division *between* the decision-making group and the decision-discussing groups.[1] The situation is only comparable to that which would arise within national states if the important decisions there were reached not by some executive body or cabinet, meeting in private, but through public argument and discussion in the national legislature by individual members without party attachments.

At present almost the only international bodies which enjoy something of the exclusive and intimate character that executive bodies elsewhere possess are those composed only of officials (such as the Administrative Committee on Co-ordination). If the Security Council, or other bodies, were able to hold some meetings in private, it might be easier to reach effective decisions without the inhibiting effect which public knowledge of the positions taken by individuals may exert, and to establish some of the sense of solidarity before an external

---

[1] Perhaps the only exception to this was at San Francisco, where there emerged a genuine solidarity within and conflict between permanent and nonpermanent members respectively. It is significant that the permanent members there sometimes met privately.

public that other executives acquire. At the same time, both the members themselves and the outside public might acquire a greater consciousness of the public, international interest overriding individual national interests, comparable to the sense of the public interest over-riding sectional interests commonly conceived in national decision-making bodies. (Discussions in the corridors, though better than nothing, cannot be a true substitute, since they are carried on by small groups and are spasmodic.)[2] In such a framework the world would come to approach problems increasingly from an international rather than a national stand-point.

A third special characteristic of international authority is that, be-cause the process of discussion and deciding is public, the pressures leading those involved toward conformity with majority views are more powerful. Because of the political cost of expressing views which arouse widespread hostility, attitudes become subject to a process of continuous *convergence*. This affects decision as well as discussion. That process can be clearly traced even in the relatively short history of UN bodies during the last twenty years. On many important ques-tions of political doctrine or constitutional interpretation, such as colonialism, apartheid, domestic jurisdiction, human rights, and repre-sentation in UN bodies, there has been a perpetual shift in publicly expressed views toward the norm upheld by the majority. Britain, which for long strenuously maintained that discussion of apartheid or colonial problems represented a violation of the Charter, by the early sixties had been induced to abandon this view. The Soviet Union, which for long resisted attempts to establish a UN peace-keeping capacity, began marginally to modify that attitude. The United States, which for long resisted moves to establish UN bodies wielding wide powers in the field of economic development, was convinced in time to abandon this position. This convergence is the automatic effect of the fact that today nations, like individuals, become increasingly more concerned over reputation than over power, desiring more to be in-ternationally liked than internationally feared. Within the unstratified and unstructured society of international organizations, conformity thus plays an even larger role than in other communities, where status may be acquired by a larger variety of means. Here all are, to greater or lesser degree, other-directed.

---

[2] The Security Council has now adopted the practice of regular, private lunches. Though not an adequate substitute for private meetings, these could be used for confidential discussions and to develop solidarity.

For this reason, authority in the international community differs radically from that in more authoritarian societies where there is a wider distance between decision makers and the rest. Although for more authoritarian leaderships the process of decision making itself may be easier, that of securing willing compliance may be much harder. Sociological study has confirmed the assumptions of political theorists that the greater the degree of interaction and, above all, of participation in the decision-making process, the more readily and effectively will decisions be obeyed.[3] Change within the total structure may be brought about more readily. Communication is improved. For an authority that is in any case without the means of forcible coercion, such procedures are especially important. The process of convergence here described may, in the absence of more fully developed decision-making procedures, assist in creating the sense of internalized, self-imposed norms than any social order ultimately requires.[4]

[3] Cf. J. Klein, *The Study of Groups* (London, 1956): Mutual discussion allows "culturally approved decisions to be taken by the members and is a much more effective agent of change than are policies handed down from above. . . . Increased interaction between the members brings about a closer unity of norms than would otherwise have been the case, and this makes possible the evolution of an informal system of control in which all members reinforce for one another the decisions they took together."

[4] For a fuller analysis of the differences between decision making in national states and international organizations, see Evan Luard (ed.), *The Evolution of International Organizations* (New York, 1966), Chapter I and Conclusions.

Appendix IV

The Main Types of International Procedures for
Settling Disputes, with a Comparison of Their Effectiveness

The following are the main types of procedure of peaceful settlement
used by the League and the UN.

1. Calls on the parties to negotiate among themselves. These were
made by the League of Nations over Ethiopia (1935), and by the
UN on the problem of Indian and Pakistani nationals in South Africa
(1946), Kashmir (1952), and West Irian (1955). They produced little
significant result in any case. If the situation is one requiring international action, all chances of settlement by negotiation will usually
already have been exhausted.

2. A special meeting of the General Assembly to consider the problem. This was employed by the League over the Bolivia–Paraguay
war (1934) and over Ethiopia (1935), and by the UN over Palestine
(1947–48), Suez (1956), Hungary (1956), Lebanon and Jordan (1958),
South West Africa (1967), and the Israel–Arab war (1967). Over
Suez and Lebanon and Jordan there was considerable effect. Over the
Israel–Arab war there was some, though the main influence was action
taken outside the UN. The other special assemblies achieved little.

3. When fighting has already broken out, calls for a cease-fire have
normally been made, usually by the Security Council. This occurred
over Indonesia (1947), Arab–Israel (1948–49) (a number of times),
over Hungary (1956), Suez (1956), India–Pakistan (1965), and the
Israel–Arab war (1967). Though the third of these had little effect,
in the last three cases they were formally accepted by the contestants,
were followed within two or three days by truces, and were certainly

significant factors in restoring peaceful conditions. Over Indonesia and Palestine, they had temporary effect. In general, therefore, their success has been surprisingly high, though this depends greatly on timing and the military situation at the time.

4. Commissions of inquiry or investigation. These were used by the League of Nations over the Albania–Yugoslavia case (1921), the Greco-Bulgarian dispute (1925), Manchuria (1931), and other cases. They were used by the UN on Korean unification (1947), Hungary (1957), and apartheid in South Africa (1962). On the whole, though some pressure may have been brought to bear, little effective change was brought about in these cases. Such commissions are very slow in operation. They have no effective sanctions. Sometimes they are intended as a substitute for action.

5. Commissions whose function is mediation or conciliation rather than enquiry. These were appointed by the League of Nations in the Aaland Islands dispute (1920), the Bolivia–Paraguay war (1933), and by the UN on Indonesia (1947), Palestine (1947), Korea (1951), Indians in South Africa (1952), Kashmir (1958), and the Congo (1960). Some success was achieved in Indonesia but little in the others. A body of this sort may find it more difficult to win the confidence of both sides and to secure complete secrecy than a single mediator (see 6 and 7 below).

6. The appointment of one or more mediators. A "mediatory group" of six states was appointed in the Bolivia–Paraguay war in 1934–35. Forms of UN mediation were applied in Palestine (1948), Kashmir (1950), and Cyprus (1964) after 1945. No success was obtained in the last two cases, but there was some in the first two. Even here this was only after the main result had been determined by armed force.

7. A representative of the Secretary General may be appointed for private and informal consultations. This was not used by the League. It was employed in the postwar period in the dispute between Thailand and Cambodia (1958), in West Irian (1962), Buraimi (1963), and Muscat (1965). There was substantial success in the first two cases. Even in the second two, open hostilities subsequently ceased. This must be regarded therefore as a relatively successful measure.

8. The dispatch of observers to the scene of hostilities. Observers were used by both the League and the UN in the Greek-Bulgarian border dispute, and by the UN in Lebanon in May, 1958, and in Yemen in 1963–64. There was some success in verifying disputed facts and (in the first three cases) in acting as a restraining influence.

9. A more permanent representative or "presence" may be established as an expression of concern and to exert a restraining influence. This was employed by the UN in Lebanon and Jordan in September, 1958, in Laos in 1951, and in Cyprus in 1964. There was some success in all these cases.

10. A visit by the Secretary General himself. This was not used by the League. It was employed, or attempted, by the UN over Hungary (1956), South Africa (1961), Bizerta (1961), and the Congo (1961). There was little direct effect in any case.

11. Confidential negotiations under the auspices of the Secretary General or President of the Assembly or Council. These were employed commonly by the League, and by the UN in the Berlin blockade (1949), Chinese intervention in Korea (1950), Kashmir (1950, 1957), and the nationalization of the Suez Canal (1956). Limited progress was made in the first and last cases.

12. A technical commission to examine certain facts influencing a dispute and to make recommendations. This was employed by the UN in the currency dispute in Berlin in 1948. The World Bank proved successful in resolving the Indus Waters dispute and in negotiating compensation terms for the nationalization of the Suez Canal (1957). In both these cases there was considerable success for the limited purposes proposed.

13. A recommendation that the dispute be referred to the International Court of Justice. This was proposed by the League on Corfu (1923) and by the UN in the case of the Corfu Channel (1947). There was little effect in either case, even though in the second a judgment was obtained. It represents an additional pressure for recourse to the court, though this cannot be compelled unless compulsory jurisdiction has been accepted.

14. The question may be left to a regional organization. The League of Nations referred the Bolivia–Paraguay war first to a Pan-American Commission of Investigation and Conciliation and the UN left the Costa Rica–Nicaragua (1948, 1955), Guatamala (1954), Honduras–Nicaragua (1957), Kuwait (1961), Cuba (1961), Panama (1964), and Morocco–Algerian (1963) disputes to similar organizations. Over Guatemala, Cuba, and Panama these had little success, but there was some at least in all the others.

Assessments of the relative successes of these various methods must be largely arbitrary. It is impossible to tell with any certainty how far the conclusion of a settlement in any case has resulted from the nature of the dispute, the character of the disputants, the balance of power between them, external influences, or other factors, besides the nature of the procedure adopted. When a larger number of cases is available, and a more detailed examination is undertaken, the relative effectiveness of different types of procedure in moderating different types of conflict may be more easily assessed. But, even now, it may be possible to arrive at tentative conclusions.

Calls on the parties to negotiate have rarely produced much result unless some external stimulus to concessions has been provided.

The large-scale commissions of inquiry (as employed in Manchuria and at first in Palestine) have been less effective for the purposes of conciliation than a smaller body, or a single mediator.

Single mediators have proved most effective where their soundings have been entirely confidential, without prior commitment, and free from detailed supervision by UN bodies (as in Palestine). Representatives of the Secretary General have been especially successful.

Public discussion in the General Assembly, though it may prove useful as a mobilization of opinion, and as an outlet of emotion in place of more violent action, is sometimes an intensifying factor, especially when negotiations are at a delicate stage and the need is to avoid public postures: discussion of Cyprus at a delicate stage of negotiations in 1965 certainly hindered rather than helped a settlement. Impartial calls for a cease-fire, however, have had a high success rate.

Recommendations to resort to the International Court are possible only when both parties are willing or obliged to accept them. Even here these recommendations have rarely brought a resolution of important political issues.

Observers on the spot have served to provide information and a restraining influence in conditions of tension. They almost certainly provided a restraining influence on the Arab-Israel borders and in Kashmir. But unless entrusted with mediatory functions, they do not appreciably influence the underlying problems and violence may recur (as both these examples show).

Regional organizations, whose influence with governments may be more powerful than that of the UN as a whole, appear in certain situations to be more effective as peacemakers than the UN itself:

they provided some reconciliation over the Ecuador–Peru war in 1942, in the Algerian–Morocco war, in the Dominican Republic, and on the Somalia border disputes.

Permanent facilities, such as the Court of Arbitration, the UN Panel of Arbitration set up in 1947, and the Peace Observation Commission have remained almost unused. This may be because their availability has not been sufficiently publicized for them to be exploited by the UN political bodies. But it is more likely because ad hoc arrangements for each individual case have been found more suitable.

INDEX